P9-CQQ-190

The Contained Garden

Kenneth A. Beckett·David Carr·David Stevens

PENGUIN BOOKS

The Contained Garden
© Frances Lincoln Limited 1982

The Contained Garden was
conceived, edited and designed by
Frances Lincoln Limited,
Apollo Works, 5 Charlton Kings Road,
London NW5 2SB

Editor: Carole McGlynn
Art Editor: Sally Smallwood
Section editors: Lionel Bender,
Karen Hearn
Designer: Langley Iddins
Picture researcher: Janice Croot
Editorial Secretary: Gillian Bussell

Managing editor: Daphne Wood

All rights reserved

First published in 1983
by The Viking Press (A Studio Book)
40 West 23rd Street,
New York, N.Y. 10010

Published simultaneously in Canada by
Penguin Books Canada Limited

Reprinted in Penguin Books in 1987, 1988

ISBN 0 14 046.805 6

(CIP data available)

Printed in Yugoslavia
Set in England

Contents

Introduction 6

Choosing Containers 7

Looking after Plants and Containers 19

Designing with Plants and Containers 58

Plants for Containers 94

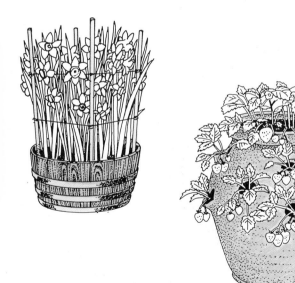

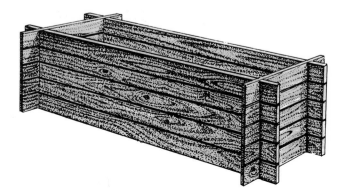

Each of the three main authors is a gardening professional in his own right. They all bring their particular expertise to the book, together with many years of practical experience of growing plants in containers and using them creatively.

*KENNETH A. BECKETT, who has written Plants for Containers, is a horticulturist. He trained at Wisley, the Royal Horticultural Society's garden, and has since worked at various botanic gardens, research stations, nurseries and public parks, in England and the United States. He was Technical Editor of *Gardener's Chronicle* for several years, and now acts as consultant for a number of leading book publishers. He has written hundreds of articles, especially for the RHS Journal, *The Garden*, and for *Greenhouse* magazine, and his books include *Amateur Greenhouse Gardening*, *Evergreens*, *Growing Hardy Perennials*, *Greenhouse Gardening* and *Love of Trees*, a dictionary of botany and an encyclopedia of gardening in serialized form.

DAVID CARR, author of the practical sections of the book, is a freelance gardening consultant. He studied horticulture and has worked in the commercial field and written extensively for the gardening press, both as a staff writer and a freelance journalist. His books, on a wide range of gardening topics, include *The Beginner's Guide to Good Gardening*, *Lawns*, *Propagation*, *Vegetables*, *The Gardener's Handbook* and *Gardening Step-by-step*.

DAVID STEVENS, who is responsible for the design aspect of the book, is a landscape architect in private practice. He studied in London and worked at Syon Park. He is consultant landscape designer for *Homes and Gardens* magazine, and has won five awards for gardens he has designed for them at the Chelsea Flower Show, including a Gold Medal in 1982. He has contributed to several gardening books and is the author of *Planning a Garden* and *Do-It-Yourself in the Garden*.

*The Fruit and Vegetables sections of Plants for Containers were written by BRIAN FURNER and edited by Kenneth Beckett. Brian Furner was a horticultural journalist and photographer who specialized in vegetables. He was a Fellow of the Linnean Society of London, a member of the Royal Horticultural Society and a member of the Soil Association. An exponent of organic methods, he co-edited *The Basic Book of Organic Gardening*. His published books include *The Kitchen Garden*, *Fresh Food from Small Gardens*, *Organic Vegetable Growing*, *Less Usual Vegetables*, *Food Crops from your Garden or Allotment*. Brian Furner sadly died in January 1982.

Introduction

Growing outdoor plants in pots offers great scope and versatility; it can bring you many of the pleasures of a garden even in a restricted space. However, container growing is not simply a matter of sticking garden plants in pots and expecting them to thrive. As the plants are grown in a limited amount of soil, with their roots confined, they have special requirements. Suitable species must be chosen initially, as some tolerate this restriction better than others and there are many dwarf and slow-growing varieties that are ideally suited to this form of cultivation. This book sets out to give you all the practical information needed to enable you to choose a wide range of plants and to grow them successfully, as well as providing ideas for planting and positioning containers imaginatively.

The first chapter, **Choosing Containers,** looks at the wide range of containers available, from pots, tubs and troughs to urns and hanging baskets. The merits and drawbacks of different materials are discussed and practical considerations such as durability and weight outlined, to help you select the right type of pot for your location. There are illustrated instructions on making your own window box and fitting containers securely, as well as suggestions for improvising plant containers from old or domestic receptacles.

The practical know-how needed in order to get the best out of your container garden is to be found in the second chapter, **Looking after Plants and Containers.** Advice is given on tools and equipment, choice of potting mix, preparing and planting up containers properly, watering and feeding the plants, staking, pruning and most forms of propagation. Common pests and diseases are shown in color photographs, to aid identification, with details of how to control and eradicate them.

The third chapter, **Designing with Plants and Containers,** explores ways of matching the plants with the pots and using them to good effect by grouping them in a creative and pleasing way. The fundamentals of plant design, involving color, texture and shape, are outlined and planting suggestions given for distinct shapes of containers. Different treatments are shown for a number of common outdoor locations or areas, including entrances, steps, windows, walls, balconies, roofs and terraces. Designs for single-species and mixed planting cover both seasonal change and permanent display.

Plants for Containers, the last chapter, highlights the most successful plants for containers. The groups range from conifers to alpines, and include climbers, roses and fruit and vegetables; each plant is illustrated and every entry gives detailed botanical and horticultural information. Tried and tested suggestions are given for different orientations – sunny, shady, sheltered or exposed – as well as a list of plants that need minimal time and effort. Finally, a calendar of work provides a quick, easy-reference guide to what to do when, season by season.

CHOOSING CONTAINERS

Containers are extremely versatile. They come in a wide variety of shapes and sizes and the choice of materials is large, so there will be something to suit every situation. A selection from the vast range of manufactured containers available is shown on pages 10–13. You can also construct your own and economically produce an individual container which is tailor-made to fit a particular space. Similarly, you should not ignore the unusual possibilities presented by old or secondhand receptacles, or domestic ones intended for a completely different use, which can often be both original and eye-catching. Some ideas for improvised and homemade containers are given on pages 14–18, with suggestions for fixing and installing them.

You need to bear in mind many practical considerations when making your selection, and it is equally important to suit the container to the planting in it and to the particular location. The overall style of a container should blend easily with the setting, be it formal or informal, contemporary or traditional; it will help if its color echoes that of materials or paintwork used outdoors. All pots have their own character, not just inherent in their shape but influenced also by their size, the material of which they are made, and the material's texture.

The size of your chosen containers will naturally depend partly on the space available – not only floor-standing space but also the precise length and width of a window sill, for example. It will also be governed by the plants you intend to grow in them: you will need deep pots to accommodate the roots of large shrubs or small trees intended as a permanent feature, whereas many annuals do not require much more than 15 cm/6 in depth of soil to grow satisfactorily.

The strength of a container should be related to its size – in general, the larger the container the greater strength needed – and the ability to withstand a few knocks is always essential. This does not necessarily mean that the weight has to increase with the pot's size; on the contrary, large containers should be of minimum weight when used on a roof terrace or a balcony, or if you intend to move them around from time to time. It is really only practical to use heavy containers in a permanent siting and at ground level; on the other hand, small pots should be sturdy enough not to get blown over when used outdoors. Large pots and window boxes will need to be planted *in situ* – they will be impossible to move around when filled.

The durability of a container, in other words the length of its useful life, depends to a large extent on the resistance of the material to the effects of weathering. Extremes of temperature cause the alternate expansion and contraction of containers and potting mixes and can weaken all but tough materials. If winter temperatures in your area fall very low, you might avoid using pots made of terracotta, for example, which is subject to cracking (unless you can bring them indoors or protect them during the coldest months). Resistance to rust, rot and corrosion is an essential quality in long-lived materials, but usually this can be assured by treating the natural material against such hazards.

Any container should be safe for plants as well as for people and pets; ideally, materials used should be inert and not react with fertilizers, moisture or chemicals. Maintenance needs to be borne in mind too – to reduce this, choose a stain-resistant material with a practical surface finish and texture. Smooth, hard glossy surfaces are easiest to clean, though rough textured finishes blend visually into an outdoor setting more easily.

You should also consider the porosity and insulation properties of different materials. Porous ones like unglazed terracotta act as a membrane losing moisture, and so potting mixes become cooler and drier than those in impervious receptacles. Insulation can be a significant factor in the survival of many container plants overwintered indoors.

Finally, cost will probably play a part in your choice of container. This element needs to be assessed along with the various practical and aesthetic considerations; the following comparative survey of different materials should help you to make a realistic choice to meet your own requirements.

The right material

In broad terms, containers can be divided into two categories: those made from natural materials and those made from synthetic, or man-made, substances. The distinction is blurred because synthetic materials often imitate a natural one, for example plastics made to look like lead, or concrete textured to resemble natural stone. Though it may seem preferable to avoid these facsimiles and to choose materials for what they are, the modern materials are often lighter, cheaper and longer-lasting than the natural ones they imitate.

Stone

The color or shade of natural stone will depend largely on the region from which it is quarried, and texture will vary according to the way it is fashioned; compare, for example, a rough-cut sandstone trough and a highly polished marble urn. Stone can add character to most settings, traditional or contemporary, if positioned sensitively. Its unobtrusive natural color usually looks best against a background of a single color or texture – painted stucco, warm brickwork or formal hedging are all suitable. The inherent weight of stone is often matched by a visual strength that can stabilize a composition, though of course its weight makes it unsuitable for anything other than a ground-level location. Another advantage is that it quickly acquires a patina of age, its surface providing a ready host for mosses and lichens, creating a weathered appearance. No maintenance is ever necessary, beyond the provision of a drainage hole if this does not already exist.

Being tough, and therefore difficult to quarry and to work, makes natural stone expensive and relatively scarce, though some of the cement-based reconstituted stone is an excellent imitation. Old stone sinks, sometimes on sale secondhand, are probably the most widely-used type of stone container today. The kind of stone may need to be considered before planting – you should avoid planting acid-loving subjects in a limestone container, for example.

Wood

Wood is an especially versatile material, blending easily with most settings. Rugged half barrels can be simply stained, to produce an informal receptacle for a wide range of plants; alternatively the same tub could be painted black and white for a more sophisticated setting. White Versailles tubs are undoubtedly formal and classical in appearance, whereas a window box can provide a positive link between landscape and any style of architecture through the chosen design, finish and color.

Being easy to cut and assemble, wood lends itself readily to home construction (see the instructions for making a window box on pp. 14–15); if you are making a wooden container, use one of the rot-resistant hardwoods, including oak, teak, meranti, mahogany and cedar. Sound wood is strong and durable but will need treating with a suitable preservative to seal the surface against boring insects. Avoid creosote, which is harmful to plants, giving off injurious fumes in warm weather.

Wood is also a good insulator, evening out extremes of temperature. It is of intermediate weight and often used for medium- and large-sized containers. It has been mainly superseded by lighter-weight, cheaper plastics in the manufacture of seed flats.

Metal

Metal containers are not commonly seen today because of the high cost of the traditional material, lead. The hazards of rust and corrosion and the dangers of metal toxicity to plants have also contributed to their decline, though it is possible to overcome these problems by treating containers with rust killer, through galvanizing (painting a special solution over ironwork) or the use of tar or rubber-based paints. Wire-framed hanging baskets, for example, are usually either galvanized or plastic-coated.

However, you may be lucky enough to have or to come across a large old metal container such as a trough, tank or boiler and, suitably treated, these can be of great decorative value – lead, copper and iron were either beaten or cast and there was a great range of ornamentation.

Terracotta

Materials such as terracotta or earthenware (made from clay) seem to fall halfway between the natural and synthetic finishes and can often usefully link the two. They have a warm, red-brown earthy appearance and can be simply formed or molded into intricate patterns to suit virtually any situation.

The unglazed pots are porous, which means that plant roots in them are cooler and dry out more rapidly than those in glazed or plastic pots due to evaporation of moisture on the outside surface. They also have a rough exterior finish, which quickly tends to become stained and green through algal growth; this enhances the natural appearance, but makes the pots more difficult to clean and disinfect before replanting with something else. Porous pots need to be soaked before potting to rehydrate them and to remove any chemical in their walls.

A glaze, often over a decorative surface, will subtly change a pot's character by introducing a pattern and polishing the surface. The glossy or matt finish is impervious to the passage of water and nutrients, so moisture loss and greening are not encountered, but it is essential to ensure the provision of drainage holes. Glazed pots are also easier to wash, disinfect and generally keep clean; naturally they are more expensive than the more functional, porous kind. The glaze can be damaged by frost.

Terracotta containers come in many shapes and sizes (see p. 10), from simple pots to square-sided decorative planters, urns and troughs. They are heavier than their plastic imitations and somewhat brittle. They do not stand much rough handling and are easily broken if dropped, knocked or carelessly stacked. They also shatter or crack readily during severe frost, due to the expansion of the potting mix. If possible they should be brought indoors during cold winters.

The simple, round terracotta pots are reasonably priced up to about 25 cm/10 in in diameter, after which the high cost of producing them by hand makes larger pots and more decorative containers fairly expensive. Their cost has favored the popularity of the much cheaper plastic equivalents, with their light-weight and non-porous qualities.

Plastics
This material has many advantages, and is particularly successful used in bold, fluid shapes, often hard to create in any other material. The range of modern geometric containers looks very fitting in a contemporary setting and, being suitable for indoor use also, can effectively blend indoors and out, for example on a balcony; the more sophisticated ones may incorporate a self-watering system.

This general heading covers a wide variety of materials used in the manufacture of plant containers; the different types vary considerably in strength and durability. Heavy-duty engineering plastics are used for prefabricated rigid containers which are strong, durable, fairly lightweight and obtainable in sizes suitable for small trees and large shrubs. It can be molded into various glazed or matt finishes and is consequently widely used in reproduction work. Tubs, troughs and planters may be made to resemble stone, pottery, metal and wood, along with many other forms of textured surface. These plastic containers are obtainable in bright colors as well as neutral shades. Being fairly light they are suitable for use on roof gardens and balconies where weight is an all-important consideration.

A variety of materials, including polythene, polypropylene and polystyrene, is also used to make a range of lightweight, reasonably durable rigid pots, hanging baskets, seed flats, troughs and drip trays. Though moderately strong, these plastics do become brittle in time, due to an internal chemical reaction as a result of strong sunlight, and are more easily broken as they age. These materials, obtainable usually in shades of terracotta, brown, green and buff as well as black and white, have a smooth, matt or glazed surface, making them easy to clean and disinfect before re-use. They are impervious to moisture and, as we have seen, plant roots tend consequently to be a degree or two warmer than those grown in porous earthenware. Less frequent watering is another advantage. Plastic hanging baskets are convenient as no moss is needed and they can be fitted with a built-in drip tray.

The introduction of thin, flexible plastic sheet, usually colored black or green, has led to the manufacture of a range of inexpensive containers to throw away after use. Examples include growing bags as well as small pots. The containers are strong enough for a season's use, lightweight, safe for most plants and non-porous. The problems of storage when not in use, and cleaning out and sterilizing before re-use, are avoided.

Concrete
The ability to cast a fluid material into a vast range of shapes and textured finishes opens up many possibilities. Concrete can successfully be used alone, molded into simple bowls and planters; alternatively, powdered stone, and possibly aggregate, can be mixed with cement to produce a reconstituted stone container at a fraction of the cost of carved stone. You can treat an old sink with a cement-based mixture to resemble weathered stone (see p. 19).

The transport and purchase price of precast concrete containers may still be fairly prohibitive initially, though concrete will not involve any maintenance costs. The great weight of concrete is another of its drawbacks, limiting its use to ground level. However, containers made of this material, especially when reinforced with internal wire or metal rods, have great strength and durability, making them very suitable for large, permanent plants or plant groupings. Concrete has considerable heat retention properties, buffering sudden changes in temperature, though it can be cold in winter.

You should allow concrete containers to weather in order to wash out any alkaline materials before planting.

Fiberglass
This modern, man-made material is increasingly used in molded prefabrications, being fairly strong and durable as well as light in weight. One of its main garden uses at present is as a liner for small pools, but it is also made into tubs and urns.

Fiberglass is reasonably priced and one great attraction is that tears can easily be repaired (a kit is available from builders' merchants). The main disadvantage is that grades currently available are inclined to be brittle. It is usually colored gray, brown or black and is safe for plants, and frost-proof.

Asbestos-cement
This man-made material was, until recently, popular for containers that are modern and functional in design. Its greatest advantage is that it is light in weight while being quite durable. However, the recent adverse reports on the safety of asbestos-cement building products has restricted its use in many countries for the manufacture of containers.

All shapes and sizes

Pots: plain and decorated
Terracotta or clay pots can be functional or highly decorative. Some of the styles may come glazed as well as unglazed, and many simple shapes are also available in lighter-weight plastics, with more drainage holes. 1 and 5-7. Traditional pots come in many sizes, from 7.5–45 cm/3–18 in diam. Standard pots are as deep as their diameter. 2. Matching saucers: sizes from 7.5–45 cm/3–18 in; may be glazed inside. 3. Straight-sided, shallow terracotta pot with handles, 30 cm/12 in diam. 4. Tall clay 'chimney pot', 25 cm/10 in diam., 60 cm/24 in high. 8. Clay 'half pots' are half the depth of their diameter; various sizes from 13–25 cm/5–10 in high. 9. Square plastic pot in sizes from 5–15 cm/2–6 in. 10. Clay planter with 'figurine' relief; 33 cm/13 in diam. 11. Bowl-shaped ridged terracotta pot, 25 cm/10 in diam. at top. 12. Heavy, handmade fluted clay planter; three sizes, 40–53 cm/16–21 in diam. 13. 'Basketweave' pot in reconstituted stone, 25 cm/10 in high. 14. Terracotta 'wine jar' 60 cm/24 in high. 15. Shallow 'geranium pot', 40 cm/16 in diam. at top. 16. Wide, fluted pot made in glazed ceramic, 38 cm/15 in high, 25 cm/10 in diam. at top. 17. Glazed earthenware 'Chinese storage jar', in several sizes from 35–55 cm/14–22 in high. 18. Decorated day planter, 22 cm/9 in diam. at top, 38 cm/15 in high. 19. Terracotta 'olive jar', for trailing species; 53 cm/21 in high. 20. Square fluted terracotta planter, in three sizes, 35–45 cm/14–18 in high and wide. 21. Vase-shaped clay pot, 53 cm/21 in high, 28 cm/11 in diam. at top. 22 Ridged bowl, reconstituted stone, 55 cm/22 in diam. at top, 45 cm/18 in high.

Hanging and wall-mounted containers

1. Wall-hung basket in plastic-covered wire. 2. Plastic pot with built-in drip tray, suspended by stiff plastic wires; various sizes, 20–30 cm/8–12 in high, 17–25 cm/7–10 in diam. at top. 3. Decorated terracotta wall trough, 45 cm/18 in diam. 4. 'Swallow's nest' wall pot in reconstituted stone, 43 cm/17 in high, 20 cm/8 in wide. 5. Plastic multi-holed hanging pot, 33 cm/13 in diam. 6. Plastic hanging basket on chains with clip-on drip tray, 22–38 cm/9–15 in diam., 13–22 cm/5–9 in deep. 7. Traditional wire hanging basket; various sizes, 22–38 cm/9–15 in diam. 8. Wooden barrel on chains, 30 cm/12 in high, 23 cm/9 in diam.

Troughs and window boxes

9. Alpine trough 26 cm/10½ in high, in reconstituted stone; two sizes – 109 × 66 cm/43 × 26 in or 81 × 55 cm/32 × 22 in. 10. Elm trough, 23 cm/9 in high, 19 cm/7½ in wide, in two lengths: 90 cm/36 in and 120 cm/48 in. 11. Fiberglass trough painted white, 75 × 20 × 25 cm/30 × 8 × 10 in. 12. Lightweight asbestos-cement trough, 106 × 30 × 15 cm/42 × 12 × 6 in. 13. Plastic window box with drip tray, 38–106 cm/15–42 in long, 15–20 cm/6–8 in wide. 14. Self-watering white P.V.C. window box, 20 cm/8 in high, 19 cm/7½ in wide at top; three lengths: 50–67 cm/20–27 in. 15. Slatted hardwood trough 127 cm/50 in long, 30 cm/12 in wide and high. 16. White P.V.C. trough comes in kit form, 100 × 33 × 35 cm/40 × 13 × 14 in. 17. Streamlined plastic trough comes with glossy finish: 162 × 30 × 40 cm/64 × 12 × 16 in. 18. Terracotta trough with decorative relief: 55 × 23 × 28 cm/22 × 9 × 11 in.

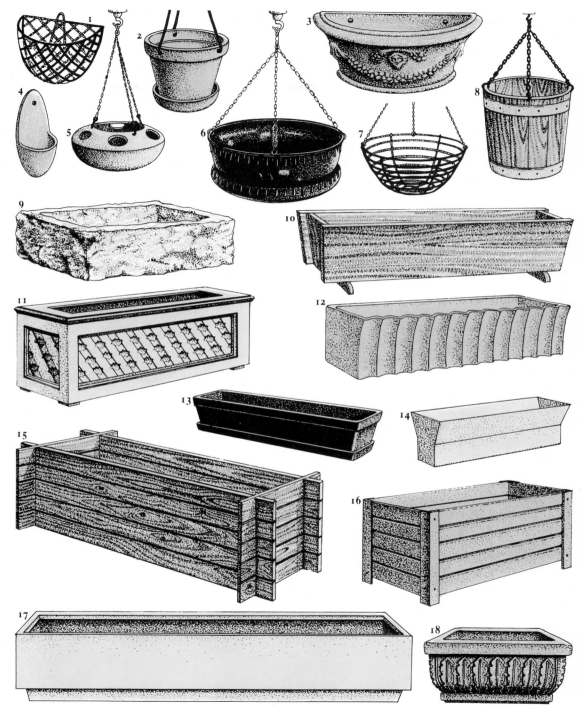

Urns, tubs and large planters

1. Small 'Regency' urn in reconstituted stone: 48cm/19in wide, 38cm/15in high. Matching pedestal 43cm/17in high.
2. Versailles vase in classical bell shape; reconstituted stone, 53cm/21in wide, 67cm/27in high.
3. Asbestos-cement combined urn and pedestal in two sizes: 91cm/36in high, 61cm/24in diam. or 61cm/24in high, 53cm/21in diam.
4. Asbestos-cement bowl on pedestal, 46cm/18in high and wide. 5. Terracotta 'Tuscan' urn, 60cm/24in high, 38cm/15in diam.
6. Plastic container for a corner; 60 × 60 × 38cm/24 × 24 × 15in.
7. Stained wooden half barrel; various sizes from 30–90cm/12–36in diam., 23–45cm/9–18in high. 8. Square wooden tub, 38cm/15in wide and high. 9. Terracotta bowl, 50cm/20in diam.; matching pedestal, 58cm/23in high. 10. White P.V.C. self-watering square tub comes in kit form, 50cm/20in wide, 48cm/19in high. 11. Square self-watering P.V.C. planter, 47cm/18½in wide and high. 12. Round plastic tub; several sizes, 38–55cm/15–22in diam., and various heights; casters available for larger models.
13. Wooden cask, 20cm/8in wide, 30cm/12in deep. 14. Cone-shaped planter in asbestos-cement with its own stand; 60 or 75cm/24 or 30in diam., 28 or 30cm/11 or 12in deep.
15. Wooden Versailles tub; also made in asbestos-cement, to imitate wood. Several sizes, 45–60cm/18–24in wide and deep. 16. Reconstituted-stone flower tub in three sizes, 45–75cm/18–30in diam., 23–40cm/9–16in deep. 17. Shallow dished concrete planter; two sizes – 75 or 120cm/30 or 48in wide, 17 or 25cm/7 or 10in deep.

1. Cone-shaped concrete planter: 100 cm/40 in diam., 25 cm/10 in high. 4. 'Romanesque' bowl-shaped planter, reconstituted stone; 81 cm/32 in diam., 33 cm/13 in high.

Interlocking containers

2. Square stacking concrete planters with aggregate finish; 75 cm/30 in wide, 27 cm/10½ in high.
3. Hexagonal P.V.C. containers in bright colors. Various sizes, up to 90 cm/36 in diam., 45 cm/18 in high.
5. Sectional containers in stone or concrete, 45 cm/18 in high, straight edge 38 cm/15 in. 6. Interlocking 'lattice' pots in glass-reinforced cement stack against a wall; each dimension 30 cm/12 in. 7. White plastic spiral planter, each tier 25 cm/10 in high, 38 cm/15 in diam. For alpines, herbs, annuals and perennials. 8. White plastic 'tower pot', each stacking unit 30 cm/12 in high. Potting mix is inside and planting in the pockets; good for strawberries. 9. Plastic modules can be used singly or interlocked; 45 cm/18 in cube.

Special-purpose containers

10. Plastic water-garden basket in many sizes for aquatics or as liner for long trough (see p. 26).
11. Plastic potato barrel comes as kit, 73 cm/29 in high, 60 cm/24 in diam., and in other sizes (see p. 31 for planting up). 12. Plastic strawberry barrel in kit form, with lid, 60 cm/24 in high, 38 cm/15 in diam. (see p. 30). 13. Terracotta strawberry pot; plant strawberries, alpines, bedding plants or bulbs in the pockets or cups; various sizes, up to 75 cm/30 in high. 14. Clay parsley pot with saucer 22–45 cm/ 9–18 in high; small herb plants or seeds are pushed through holes into moist potting mix. 15. Terracotta crocus pot: small bulbs are fitted into holes; height 25 cm/10 in.

Making your own containers

When there is such a wide range and choice of plant containers obtainable commercially, it may seem unnecessary, at first, to make your own, particularly as the manufactured articles are generally more than adequate. However, there are several good arguments for doing so. The first, and perhaps most forcible point is that you may be unable to find a container of the right size to fit a particular position, for example a wall recess, a narrow window sill, or patio area. The second is originality – making something different from the mass-produced pot, trough, tub or box. You may wish to construct a container of some novel or unusual shape, or possibly to make use of a familiar object such as a sink, suitably modified for plants. Third, you may be encouraged to set about making your own container simply because you have suitable lumber lying idle and are handy with tools. You will then have the satisfaction of constructing a low-cost, but none the less attractive, container. The familiar window box is but one example of the sort of build-it-yourself container that could be undertaken by most.

Making a window box

The details given opposite are for the construction of a simple box measuring 90 cm/36 in long, approximately 17 cm/7 in wide by 19 cm/7½ in deep.

You can adjust the length to suit your individual situation but it is unwise to exceed 120 cm/48 in because, when the box is filled with potting mix, the weight will be considerable. If your window is wider than this, it is usually more practical to use two short boxes as opposed to a single long one. If you design your own window box it is advisable to make it not less than 15 cm/6 in wide and 15 cm/6 in deep. The potting mix will dry out too quickly in anything smaller than this.

Requirements

LUMBER
4 pieces 19 × 6.5 × 2 cm (7½ × 2½ × ¾ in) end pieces A
5 pieces 15 × 4.5 × 2 cm (6 × 1¾ × ¾ in) cross-members B, central support F
4 pieces 90 × 6.5 × 2 cm (36 × 2½ × ¾ in) side-members C
2 pieces 87 × 4.5 × 2 cm (34½ × 1¾ × ¾ in) outer bottom rails D
2 pieces 87 × 3 × 2 cm (34½ × 1¼ × ¾ in) central bottom rails E
4 pieces 15 × 2.5 × 2 cm (6 × 1 × ¾ in) rounded beading G

Ideally, use seasoned hardwood such as oak, or, if available, redwood, both of which are long-lasting. Softwood lumber will soon rot. Be sure to select pieces of wood that are not split and are free from knots, signs of rotting and woodworm. You will save considerable work by buying lumber already planed and cut to length. (The sizes given above are for lumber prepared in this way: in planing a surface up to 6 mm/¼ in in thickness is lost.)

ADDITIONAL ITEMS
You will need an assortment of 30 mm/1¼ in and 40 mm/1½ in long galvanized or brass screws; 25 mm/1 in long brass brads or tacks; wood preservative; and varnish or paint. A drip tray is also desirable. The box described here is designed to take a standard 85 × 17 × 2.5 cm/34 × 7 × 1 in aluminum model.

TOOLS
Requirements for preparing the lumber, assembling the parts and giving the box a coat of preservative or paint are quite modest: coarse and fine sandpaper, the use of an electric two-speed drill, a 5 mm/³⁄₁₆ in diameter twist bit, a screwdriver, a joiner's hammer, a try square (an L-shaped piece of metal or wood with the arms set at exactly 90°), a ruler, and a paint brush. If you intend using secondhand lumber, you will also need a tenon saw and pliers.

Preparing the lumber

Check over the pieces of lumber: are they the correct length and are the ends square? This last point is most important, as otherwise the box may not only look unsatisfactory, but will be unsteady. You can test for squareness or, if you are using secondhand lumber, mark off the pieces of wood before sawing, by simply using the try square. With one arm of the tool firmly against the side of the lumber, the other arm will lie across the neighboring face, allowing you to mark off the right angle or square off.

Where necessary, cut lumber to the required shape and size. Smooth off saw cuts, corners and any rough edges, first with coarse sandpaper, then finishing off with fine. In the case of secondhand lumber, remove any nails or screws before cutting to size, and smooth with a plane or mechanical sander.

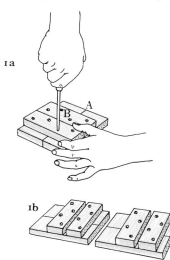

1a

1b

1 Making the end sections
On two end pieces (A), measure and mark off the positions of the cross-members (B) using the try square and ruler. The top cross-member should be 2 cm/¾ in below the rim, and the second member 6 cm/2¼ in from the bottom. Then take two cross-members and, in a zigzag pattern, drill and countersink four holes in each; fit with 30 mm/1¼ in screws to the end pieces (1a). Work on a level surface. Repeat the process with the remaining two end pieces and two cross-members (1b). Check that no screw heads are projecting.

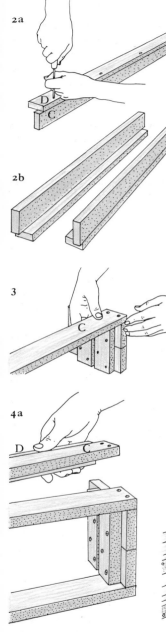

2a

2b

3

4a

D C

4b

5 Securing outer bottom rails
Place the box upside down. Drill and fit ends of outer bottom rails to the cross-members of end sections using 40 mm/1½ in screws.

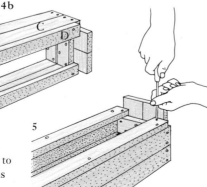

5

2 Making side+bottom rail units
Take one side-member (C), measure and mark off 2 cm/¾ in from each end on the narrow, 2 cm/¾ in thick bottom edge; this marks the position of the bottom rail. Drill and countersink four evenly spaced holes in the edge of one outer bottom rail (D) and fit to the side-member, flush with the outer face, using 40 mm/1½ in screws (**2a**). Repeat the process for the other side of the box. The made-up units, when arranged as in the finished box, should be mirror images (**2b**).

3 Fitting side-members to end sections
Take the two made-up end sections and two remaining side-members (C). At each end, on the face of side-members, drill two holes. Fit the side-members flush with the end sections and level with the top, using 30 mm/1¼ in screws.

4 Completing the sides
Take one of the side-members with outer bottom rail attached, drill two holes at each end, and fit hard up against the top side-member. Make sure the bottom rail is positioned with the projecting piece facing inward, and fit with 40 mm/1½ in screws (**4a**). Repeat with the other unit (**4b**).

6 Fitting the central bottom rails
Position the two central bottom rails (E) in the center space, leaving three drainage gaps each approximately 1 cm/½ in wide, drill and fit to the cross-members of end sections using 40 mm/1½ in screws.

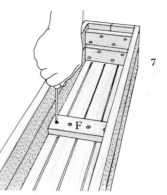

7

8 Securing the beading
Conceal the exposed screw holes on the sides of the box by covering with the pieces of rounded beading (G). Fix these in place with brass brads or tacks.

9 The finishing touches
Give your now-assembled window box the final inspection, making sure all screws are firmly in place. Sand off any rough edges, corners or surfaces, and wipe down with a clean cloth to remove remaining loose sawdust. Then paint the box, both inside and out, with non-poisonous wood preservative, staining the outside to the shade required. Finally, apply two coats of exterior grade polyurethane. Alternatively, paint the box in the traditional manner, using primer, undercoat and top paint. As an extra precaution to prevent soil staining the wood, cover the inside of joins between the sides and ends with builders' waterproof adhesive tape before planting up.

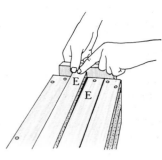

7 Fitting the central support
Turn the box the correct way up. Inside, on the bottom, measure and mark off the midpoint 43 cm/17 in from each end. Drill and fit the central support (F) to each of the rails using 30 mm/1¼ in screws: this is used to strengthen the box.

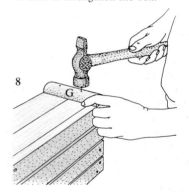

8

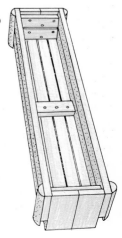

9

Installing and fitting

The installation of containers at ground level, on walls, window sills, and in roof gardens needs some forethought and attention to detail. It is necessary to consider not only the amount of sun, shade, and shelter at all times of the year, but also the overall design of the site, setting the container securely in position, drainage, and the protection of plant roots and containers from the excesses of wind, snow, frost, ice and water.

Ground-level container gardens

One of the first requirements for any container is a firm, level, well-drained base. In a garden, or if you are building from scratch a patio or similar area where you intend to position several large or heavy containers, it is a good idea to lay paving slabs on a 10–15 cm/4–6 in thick base of consolidated hardcore (rubble), overlaid with a 3 cm/1¼ in or more thick layer of gravel and a similar depth of sand. This composite base serves a number of purposes: it reduces ground settlement, improves drainage and diminishes frost heave or lifting. To help drainage, you can lay the paving slabs with a gentle slope, and angle them toward a gutter or drain to dispose of surface water. Avoid standing pots or containers directly on soil as this encourages the entry of worms and other pests. Using a base of loose gravel, covering drainage holes with fine zinc gauze, or even placing a plastic sheet beneath the containers, will give some protection.

You can place barrels on a firm, porous, gravel base, but they look best and are safest standing on a complete circle of bricks with a drip tray positioned centrally. Square planters can also be raised on bricks, this time on three sides only and with a removable drip tray set on the floor underneath. With troughs bearing drainage holes, raise the containers slightly on supports to allow a tray to be placed below, or stand the troughs in pebble-filled watertight trays. Small pots, liable to be blown over, are best stood in compact groups or plunged up to the rims in trays filled with peat, pulverized bark or sand.

Sinks, large troughs and concrete planters to be set permanently in a container garden usually look most effective when raised on a plinth. This can be constructed from stone, brick, or concrete blocks or similar building materials. For stability, plinths are normally best mounted on a 5–7.5 cm/2–3 in thick concrete base over clean hardcore, sand and gravel, as above. Bricks, stone and concrete blocks are safer and less liable to movement if cemented in position. Small quantities of cement, ready mixed with aggregate and needing only the addition of water before use, can be readily obtained, packed in handy bags, at most hardware stores. Check that the concrete has set completely before mounting the container on the plinth. (In warm weather concrete will set hard in a day but in the cold in about a week.) If the container is set near a walkway or in a place where it is likely to be knocked against, cement it to the plinth.

Roof gardens

Whenever plants are to be grown in containers on top of a building, two items of great importance are making sure the roof is waterproof, and keeping weight to a minimum. In setting up a roof garden, lay a waterproof membrane, usually composed of layers of tar and mineral felt, and cover this with a lightweight, tough, wearing course. Walkways and other areas can be surfaced with light composition or asbestos tiles to protect the membrane. In areas liable to sudden, heavy rain squalls, stand all containers on lightweight, slatted planks to ensure unimpeded movement of drainage water from the base of containers into gutters and drains. When installing large containers in roof gardens, place them over or near load-bearing walls, which can take the weight, and close to walls or panels for wind protection. (If necessary, use the services of a surveyor to determine your roof's load-bearing capacity.)

Supporting a window box

To support a box just under a window, use stout steel angle-brackets with the ends bent upward to hold the box in place. It is advisable to secure the box further by attaching hooks to the box ends and, using short lengths of metal chain or wire, connecting these to hooks screwed into plugs in the wall on either side of the window frame. Even if you are able to rest a window box squarely on a wide, flat window sill, still use the hooks and safety chains. For a window at ground level, you can place the box on a pedestal or plinth set on the ground beneath the window.

Supporting wall and hanging containers

The most common method of supporting these containers is to use steel brackets or wall-mounting hooks. (Wrought-iron brackets should be painted or otherwise treated against rust.) Make sure the supports are strong enough to carry the containers when filled with potting mix and plants. When choosing wall brackets for hanging baskets, bear in mind that the length of the arm must be greater than half the diameter of the basket to avoid plant spoilage through catching on the wall.

Fitting a bracket

Once you have decided on the height and position of the basket/window box/container, make allowances for supporting chains or wire and determine the exact spot for the bracket. Holding the bracket in the required position, check that it is vertical by means of a spirit level. With a pencil, mark off the exact positions of the fixing screws. Then, using a two-speed electric drill set at the slower speed and fitted with a suitably sized masonry drill, make holes of sufficient length and size to take wall plugs and fixing screws. Tap in wall plugs and make sure they are a good tight fit; then fit on a bracket using suitable screws.

Fitting a window box beneath a window

Unless you have a wide window ledge and either sash windows or casement windows that open inward, you will have to set a plant box under the window. Use a box that spans the width of the window frame. To secure the safety chains linked to hooks in either end of the box, drill holes in the masonry on the outside of the house 25 cm/ 10 in up from the window sill and about 10 cm/4 in either side of the window frame, insert wall plugs and screw in strong steel hooks.

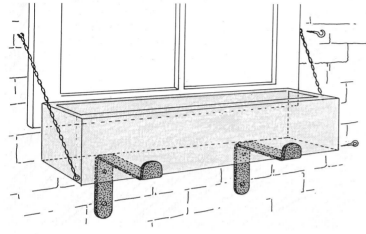

Setting a box on a window sill

If the window sill is not perfectly horizontal, fix wedge-shaped pieces of wood (suitably treated with preservative) beneath the box, making sure these are sufficiently thick and spaced well apart to accommodate a drip tray (not shown). On some older houses window sills have built-in iron guard rails. These are ideal to hold a window box firmly in place. If there is no guard rail round the edge of a sill, secure the container using hooks and chains, as shown above. Fill with low-growing plants.

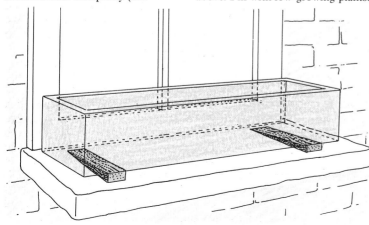

Wall supports for hanging baskets

These come in a range of sizes to suit different diameter baskets and in a variety of styles, for example a decorative, wrought-iron support (a), a swivel-arm unit (b), and a cane and raffia support (c) (suitable for lightweight baskets only).

Fitting overhead hooks

To suspend hanging baskets from a building overhang, use swivel hooks. These are usually fitted in place by means of a circular metal plate that is screwed to the underside of a stout beam. The center of the metal plate is threaded to take a hook that is simply screwed into the plate and through into the beam. Where you need to provide a means of raising and lowering the basket, for example to water the plants, this can be achieved by attaching a small pulley in place of the swivel hook. The pulley unit will require a guide for the rope, plus a stay to tie the cord securely. The guide, like the pulley mounting, should be firmly fitted to a beam by means of a metal plate secured with screws or bolts. Fit the stay to the wall using screws and wall plugs.

Overhead supports

Ordinary hooks screwed into a wooden beam invariably provide insufficient strength to support hanging containers since these are extremely heavy when planted up and well watered. Use instead special-purpose supports such as a stout swivel hook (a), which allows considerable freedom of movement, a hook with a self-locking pulley unit (b), or a heavy-duty, general-purpose workshop or garage hook with a plastic sleeve to prevent rusting (c). Before attaching a basket or pot, be sure that the hook is fitted firmly by tugging it gently.

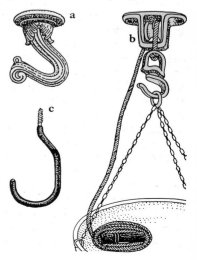

Using a trellis

If you are growing tall, erect or climbing plants in containers you must provide some sort of support for stems. A trellis is ideal for this. To set a trellis on a wall, fit it very firmly to a light wooden frame or posts nailed to plugs inserted in the wall. Alternatively, nail or screw the trellis directly into plugs in the wall through 2.5 cm/1 in cube wooden blocks. By mounting a trellis away from the wall in this way, air can circulate behind the plant stems. A wooden trough filled with climbing plants can form the basis of a screen. Fit a trellis inside the back of the container, which can then be used as a freestanding unit in any suitable site. Secure the trellis to the container; always use screws, not nails. Commercially available trellises usually come ready treated with wood preservative. If you are making your own trellis, treat the wood with a non-toxic preservative.

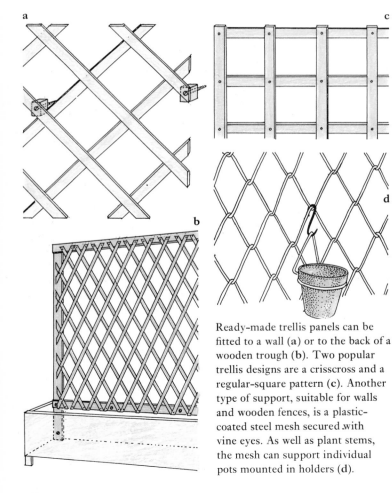

Ready-made trellis panels can be fitted to a wall (a) or to the back of a wooden trough (b). Two popular trellis designs are a crisscross and a regular-square pattern (c). Another type of support, suitable for walls and wooden fences, is a plastic-coated steel mesh secured with vine eyes. As well as plant stems, the mesh can support individual pots mounted in holders (d).

Improvised containers

Plants can be grown in almost any type of container. No matter an object's shape and normal function, provided it is clean, reasonably durable and weatherproof and free of all harmful substances, it can serve as well as a patented pot, planter, tub or trough. Chamber pots, coal scuttles, buckets, copper kettles, saucepans, larger garden objects such as wheelbarrows and watering cans, even such unlikely articles as army steel helmets, all have at some time been used as containers for plants. Wherever possible, drill drainage holes in the base, then crock, fill and plant up in the normal way.

Tree trunks and branches A tree stump or a section of a large branch cut from a tree, if hollowed out with a drill and hammer and chisel, will make an ideal container for several small plants. A large tree stump is best placed vertically on the ground. Make a large hollow in the top and several small ones at angles in the sides, fill and plant up. A section of branch can be similarly treated. Suspend the branch vertically from a bracket or swivel hook using wire or lengths of chain attached to three evenly spaced screw hooks at the top of the branch. Alternatively, use the section of branch in a horizontal position, hollowing out small cavities along its top surface. To suspend the planted-up container horizontally, insert screw hooks at each end of the branch.

Rubber tires These can be camouflaged by painting over with exterior quality paint of a neutral color such as stone or buff. It is best to fill and plant them as one operation. Use two together, stacking one above the other, or just one tire cut in half and hung on a wall. For the former, place one tire flat on the ground, lay a piece of nylon netting inside and across the center, and fill with prepared potting mix. Make sure the hollows round the sides of the tire are filled as well as the center. Place the second tire on top of the first and pack soil between the adjacent tire side walls, planting trailing plants in the space as you do so. Fill the center and tire inners as before, if necessary using more nylon netting to prevent potting mix falling out, and finally plant up with more trailing plants around the edges using taller specimens in the center. The container is best placed on a porous gravel base for drainage. With a half-circle portion of a tire, use an electric drill to make a series of drainage holes in the base and a hole in each of the four corners of the segment. Fill the hollow trough and plant up, again with trailing plants, then thread wire through the four corner holes and suspend the container from a sturdy wall bracket or overhead hook (see p. 15).

Glazed earthenware sinks Although these are becoming something of a rarity, it is still possible to come across one. The first step in refurbishing a sink for use as a plant container is to clean it thoroughly, finally washing with detergent, rinsing and drying. Then paint over the whole surface, inside and out, with a strong adhesive to provide a tacky coat for the surfacing, which is prepared as follows: on a clean, level surface, spread out in a shallow layer two shovelsful of finely screened peat and cover this with a shovelful each of, first, building sand, then cement. Thoroughly work in together, turning at least three times, before adding water to make a fairly stiff mix. (Do not attempt this during either frosty or very hot sunny conditions, both of which may ruin the best of endeavors.) Apply the surfacing to the sink, both inside and out, using a building trowel. Aim to work fairly quickly, completing the covering coat within 30 minutes or so, before hardening begins, to leave a roughened rock- or stonelike finish. Cover the sink with damp sacking to prevent excessively rapid drying out, and protect it from rain for at least three days. By then the surfacing should be hardened and the sink ready for use.

Paint pots Available in a range of sizes that matches that of patented plant pots, these make ideal containers to hang on a fence or to stand on a low wall. Clean pots out thoroughly, if necessary removing oil-based paint with turpentine then warm soapy water, drill or punch drainage holes in the base of each, and paint the outside with a suitable weatherproof paint. Fill and plant up in one operation. If the pot does not have a handle, drill two holes in the sides near the top and suspend with wire or chain.

Wheelbarrows Old wooden wheelbarrows need nothing more than to be cleaned out and drainage holes drilled in their bases to make perfect plant containers. They are suitable for growing a collection of small annuals and biennials, herb or alpine plants. Fill and plant up a wheelbarrow once you have set it in position.

Beer barrels and wine casks These can be used whole or cut vertically or horizontally in half. They need to be suitably cleaned, painted or weatherproofed on the outside, and have drainage holes drilled in the base. With a whole barrel or cask you can cut out holes in the sides (using a keyhole saw); fill these with strawberry plants or a selection of herbs. Use half barrels and casks as tubs or troughs: a half barrel resulting from a vertical cut through the original article will need to be mounted on 'feet' or a suitable base. All are best stood on a gravel bed.

Chimney pots Scrubbed, washed, and placed on a shallow, pebble-filled tray or on gravel, chimney pots make novel planters. For drainage fill the bottom third or so with pebbles, and fill and plant at the same time. Alternatively, use the chimney pot simply as a holder for an ordinary pot or hanging basket, which can be either wedged in the top or suspended from the rim with wire. Protect large clay containers of this type from frosts.

LOOKING AFTER PLANTS AND CONTAINERS

Growing plants in containers can be extremely rewarding as a modicum of effort will guarantee an attractive and lasting display. It is worth taking a little trouble over the important potting stages, and giving regular attention as required, to ensure healthy, long-lived plants that can provide reliable stock for propagating. Short cuts are a form of neglect and the plants will eventually suffer and die.

You will want to extend the useful life of both plants and their containers and their care is closely integrated at several stages. Potting up the plant initially involves using a container of the right size, carefully cleaned and with adequate drainage; it needs to be crocked correctly before being filled with a suitable potting mix. Using the right tools will make potting, planting and related operations much more straightforward; however, the basic requirements for the container gardener are deliberately kept to a minimum and need not take up much storage space.

Routine care is extremely important if your plants are to stay healthy and look their best; this covers tasks such as watering and feeding, as well as supporting and pruning those plants that require it. These needs will vary from season to season. This chapter includes a guide to diagnosing symptoms of neglect (p. 56) and to the pests and diseases likely to attack container-grown plants; the pictures on page 57 will help you to recognize and control the pest or disease in question.

Propagating your own plants is the cheapest and most reliable way to replenish and increase your stock. This is in fact a less daunting prospect than many imagine, and the various means of propagating, including sowing seeds and layering stems, are explained in detail.

You should be able to find all the tools and equipment mentioned in this chapter, as well as the seed, potting and cutting mixes, the fertilizers and plant chemicals, at a large, reputable garden supply store. If you do not have a large one nearby, it should be possible to find them in a seed merchant's or nursery's catalogue and send away for them by post. The same applies to many types of container, and to most of the plants referred to, though you may wish to find out more about the plants, and their suitability for your site, on pp. 94–153, before buying or ordering them. You might need to look in a builders' merchants for some of the equipment suggested, for example that for treating or repairing containers, as well as aggregate such as chippings, and you may know of alternative cheap, local sources for natural materials like bracken or straw.

All of the operations, including planting, pruning and propagating, have been explained in stages, in order to be clear to a beginner; experienced gardeners may in some cases have a preferred method that varies slightly in detail, but this need not conflict with the general advice given.

Tools and equipment

The container gardener needs only a few tools, and what they are will be governed by the number and type of plants grown. Choose your tools carefully, comparing brands and prices, and try them out for lightness and ease of handling. Always clean them after use and store them carefully to prolong their working lives. A tool-rack and wall-hooks are a good idea, especially if you are short of space. Do not leave wooden-handled tools in wet conditions or their handles will crack, making them painful to use. Many tools now have plastic handles, which weigh less and are more durable. Metal tools must be washed or scraped clean of soil, because if this sets hard, it will be very difficult to remove later. Wipe metal surfaces with an oily cloth after cleaning. Keep moving parts lubricated with grease or oil. Whenever tools have locking catches, store them safely locked, and well out of the reach of children.

A trowel is essential for planting and for topdressing, and a hand-fork for loosening the soil if it becomes compressed by heavy rain. You may need a spade to fill larger containers and to make your own potting mixes (see p. 22). It should be light, with the correct balance for your height, since you may be lifting it well above ground level. A small shovel may serve the purpose equally well.

Pruners are needed for pruning roses and hardwooded shrubs, for taking cuttings, and for removing dead blooms and unsightly stems. They must make a clean cut, with no bruising or tearing that might allow disease to enter. Buy ones of reputable make, which will stay sharp – using blunt pruners will damage the plants and blister your hands. For heavy cutting, loppers are used: heavy-duty ones, with handles up to 75 cm/30 in long, cut woody stems up to 2.5 cm/1 in thick, whereas pole pruners, with handles 1.8 m/6 ft or more long, are used to prune trees and tall climbers.

Another essential is a watering can. A plastic can is light to use, but may split if left out in frost; a metal can is heavier but more durable, particularly if it has been painted or has a galvanized finish. If you have many plants to water, you could consider using a hose, fitted with a rose or fine-spray nozzle (see p. 34). To apply pesticides or foliar feed, or to spray foliage with clean water, use a hand-operated pressure sprayer, which releases a fine, mistlike spray that covers the plant.

Unless you have a large number of containers to fill, a carrying sheet or a plastic bucket will be all you require to move soil and other items to your containers. Plastics do not react with fertilizers. A bucket is useful, too, for mixing liquids and for soaking dried-out potted plants. Very heavy items can be placed on a pot-trolley (see p. 25) for moving. If you really need a wheelbarrow, and have space to store it, buy one with a galvanized steel body and tubular steel chassis, which will be light to use and weigh only about 10 kg/22 lb, with a soil capacity of about 71 litres (16 UK or 18½ US gallons) – about half that of most normal wooden garden barrows.

If you intend to propagate your own plants, you will need some additional items of equipment (see p. 46).

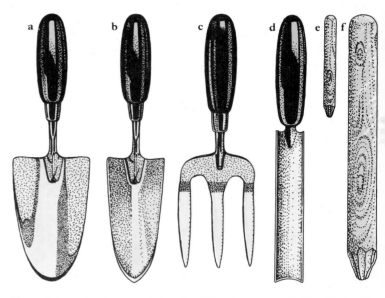

Above A trowel with a rounded end (a) is used for topdressing and to make holes for planting; a narrower one with a pointed end (b) can be used for planting large seedlings and small plants. Use a hand-fork (c) for weeding and for loosening the soil surface. Hand-forks and trowels come in lengths from 15 cm/6 in to 23 cm/9 in. Of the many ways that the handle can be fitted to the blade, the tang and ferrule method, as shown, is the most secure. A weeding knife (d) with a narrow, hollow blade will gouge out weeds in confined spaces. Use a dibble (e) to make small holes in soil for cuttings and seedlings; buy one, or make it from a stick about 10 cm/4 in long, rounding off the end so that it will go easily into soil. Make a pot-presser (f) from a rounded stick – part of a broom-handle, for example. Taper it slightly toward one end. When potting on a plant to a larger container, use the presser to work soil down around the rootball.

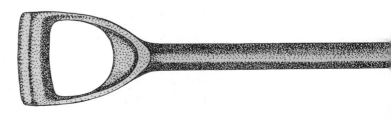

Below and right General-purpose pruners, 20 cm/8 in long, can be used for most plants. The anvil type (**a**), with one blade that chops against a flat plate, is strong, inexpensive and the best for hardwoods. The double-cut type (**b**) is more costly; its slicing action eliminates any bruises or tears.

Right A watering can should have a long spout, to reach window boxes and hanging baskets. It should not be too heavy, so one of 4.5 litres (1 UK or 1⅕ US gallons) is best. Use a fine rose attachment (**a**) to water seedlings, and a coarser one (**b**) for established plants.

Below To fill big containers it is best to use a short-handled spade with a blade of about 23 × 15 cm/9 × 6 in. Larger spaces are much less manageable. Unlike a square one, a rounded blade should not catch on plants when topdressing the potting mix.

Right A garden knife is important for some pruning operations, for cutting out the growing point, removing suckers, and for taking cuttings and layering. Choose one with a good carbon or tungsten steel blade and use a sharpener to preserve its keen edge, because the knife must make a clean cut. The blade should fold back into the handle for safety.

Right A 1½ or 3 litre (2.5 or 5 UK and 3 or 5.5 US pint) sprayer is the best size for container gardening. Certain types have an adjustable nozzle and 'easy squeeze' trigger action control, while a detachable nozzle makes cleaning easy. Cleaning will prolong the sprayer's life, and you must wash out one chemical before filling it with another, which may have a different function. The fluid is generally poured into a ball- or bottle-shaped container after screwing off the nozzle and trigger controller. To reach high containers, the sprayer will need an extension lance (**a**). A root feeder attachment (**b**) is also available.

Below A lightweight knitted polypropylene or nylon fine-mesh net can be draped over woody plants to protect buds and fruit from birds. It also protects against hail and wind. Over other plants it is best attached to a light frame.

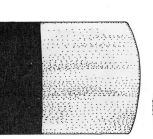

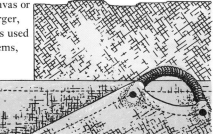

Below A carrying sheet of canvas or burlap 1.2 m/4 ft square, or larger, with a handle at each corner, is used to transport light but bulky items, or to catch clippings.

The planting medium

Sometimes the soil of a garden needs a lot of work before it is fit for planting, and even then you may still be unable to grow the plants that you want. This is not the case if you grow plants in containers – you can give them the exact medium that they need. In fact, if you get the soil balance right in the first place, you will save much time and trouble.

The medium that you use in containers should crumble easily, retain moisture without becoming waterlogged, but permit free drainage and circulation of air, since roots need oxygen. It should have the right balance of nutrients (see pp. 36–37) and the correct level of lime or acid – some plants, such as *Rhododendron*, are acid-lovers, and unable to tolerate lime.

Many gardeners use the mixes known as potting mixes for plants in permanent containers. Do not, by the way, confuse these with the 'garden compost' that results from rotted organic matter (see below). The John Innes Horticultural Institute of Great Britain has devised a series of potting-mix formulations based on loam (that is, good-quality soil). John Innes is not a brand name; it denotes standardized formulations which are a useful guide to the range of potting mixes to be purchased either ready-made or ready to mix at home. When buying choose a supplier with a fast turnover of stock, since the mixes have a short shelf-life, varying from two or three weeks to a year. Buy them just before use and do not keep them for too long – if you have to do so, store them in closed plastic bags in a frost-free place. If it is cold, warm the potting mix up first by bringing it indoors for a day or two.

Each John Innes mix has been prepared for a specific range of plants. The seed mix is for seeds; the cutting mix is made for starting off cuttings. For older plants there are the potting mixes: these are designated nos. 1, 2 or 3 according to their nutrient content – no. 3 being the strongest. Use no. 1 for fine-rooted, slow-growing plants, like young heathers or alpines, for sickly plants, and for tiny seedlings in spring. Standard no. 2 is the multipurpose potting mix used for plants of average vigor except acid-lovers. Quick- or strong-growers, like tomatoes or any climbers that need to gain height, such as sweet peas, require no. 3. Modified potting mixes are available for the acid-lovers. The season also plays a part: use a weaker formula if potting in spring, particularly for young and slow-growing plants, and a strong one later in the year for vigorous plants.

A range of 'soilless' (not based on loam) mixes are available. Many are based on peat – for example, the University of California and Cornell University formulae. They are cleaner to use, cheaper and weigh less than the loam-based ones – important points for the container gardener. They can sometimes fluctuate between being unduly wet or arid; this is an especial problem in areas of high rainfall. Nor, for plants outdoors, do they provide as much root hold or support as the soil-based mixes. They are, however, suitable for acid-loving plants, which like the peat content. Like John Innes potting mixes they come in a variety of strengths and types, including 'ericaceous' or '*Rhododendron*' mixes for acid-lovers.

'Bark fiber-based' potting mixes tend, in fact, to be a mixture of peat and bark. They are probably best avoided, since they present watering, feeding and anchorage problems.

It is better to use an approved potting mix than garden soil – and certainly you should avoid soil from a town garden, which will contain weed seeds and disease spores, may be inert through neglect, and could be acid with deposits of soot and sulphur.

Growing bags, made of plastics and filled with peat, sometimes pulverized tree bark, and added nutrients, are widely used – generally for tomatoes. They will take many other plants, such as lettuce, strawberries or summer-flowering annuals, but are unsuitable for deep-rooted plants like beetroot or turnip. A smaller bag is available for rooting cuttings. The bags are clean to use, and can be placed outdoors for spring and summer crops or indoors in a sunny room.

John Innes formulations

It is cheaper, and less time- and space-consuming, to buy these or similar mixes ready-made, however it is possible to make them up yourself. The ingredients can be bought from a garden supply store although sterilized loam could be expensive and hard to obtain. The basic John Innes mixture consists of:

7 parts (by bulk) sterilized loam
3 parts coarse, dust-free, undecomposed sphagnum peat
2 parts washed, coarse sand,

To make **John Innes no. 1**, add to 36 litres or 131 cu cm of basic mixture (8 UK or 9½ US gallons or 1¼ cu ft):
112 g/4 oz John Innes Base
21 g/¾ oz ground limestone or powdered chalk.

To make **John Innes no. 2**, double the quantities of Base and limestone, and for **John Innes no. 3**, treble them. For lime-hating plants, omit the linestone.

The **John Innes Base** can be be made up according to the following recipe:
2 parts (by weight) hoof and horn 3 mm/⅛ in grist
2 parts calcium phosphate (superphosphate of lime)
1 part potassium sulphate (sulphate of potash).

Making up the potting mixes
Use a screen to sift the loam onto a plastic sheet over a flat surface. Moisten the peat with a watering can. Mix together with a spade. Keep the Base and limestone separate, until the moment when you mix them together with some sand. Add this with the rest of the sand to the loam and peat and, again, mix thoroughly.

Below A growing bag 1 m/3 ft long and 30 cm/12 in wide will take three plants, in three separate holes, or more in one large, rectangular opening. For use, make slits in the sides, under the welt. Stand the bag on a plastic tray, and pour water in the tray. The bag can also be used without a tray and watered gently, with a rose, through the top. Water before inserting the plants.

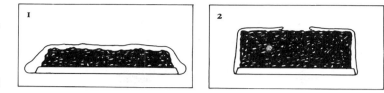

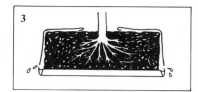

Left and above 1 A growing board consists of a block of dehydrated sphagnum peat in a polythene bag. It is used like a growing bag, but must be rehydrated first – when dry, it is light to transport. **2** Place it on a tray, cut an opening in the top and add water until the peat expands fully. **3** Make holes in the peat and insert the plants. Make slits low in the sides, then pour water into the tray or gently through the top, to collect in the reservoir at the bottom of the bag; any excess will run out of the slits. The plants will take some days to use up the water in the reservoir. Growing boards come in two lengths.

A correctly chosen potting mix cuts out the need for soil-testing. However, once the mix has been in use for a while, you may wish to check its acidity or alkalinity (its pH level), either because a plant growing in it looks sickly, or because the water in your area contains salts, which may have raised the alkalinity of the mix. Simple soil-testing kits are available for this purpose. If a soil proves to be too acid for the plants, add more lime; if it is too alkaline, repot or pot on in a mix for acid-lovers, and when feeding, use an acid fertilizer like sulphate of ammonia.

If you have room on a patio or in a service yard, you could instal a compost bin to produce humus (or decayed organic matter). For hygiene, it should be at least 3.6 m/12 ft from the house. Remember that liquids like amino acids will leech out, and may deeply stain the surface below – even a tray underneath will not stop this entirely. Air must circulate, so that bacterial action can take place to break down all the materials, which may be tea-leaves, eggshells, wet newspapers, vegetable waste – anything organic except diseased or infected material, which should be burnt. Peat and old mix can be added. To encourage the waste to break down faster, sprinkle brand-name activator or compost-maker over the surface. The time taken to make humus will depend on the season – waste laid down in summer may have decomposed sufficiently in three months but in the fall breakdown may take as long as five months.

Below Simple kits are available to test the acidity or alkalinity of soil. A sample of soil is placed in a test-tube, some chemical is poured in, and the tube is stoppered and shaken. Once the contents have settled, the color is compared with the bands of color on a chart that represents different levels of alkalinity or acidity (i.e. pH).

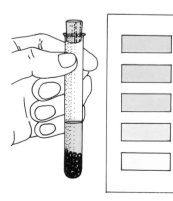

Above A common type of patented compost bin has a hinged top through which material is added, and is made up of plastic panels, drilled with small holes to admit air. The compost is removed through an aperture at the base. A standard bin of this type has a capacity of 0.39 cu m/14 cu ft.

23

Preparing containers for planting

Containers must have enough drainage, be clean and free from disease and pests, and be in a sufficiently good condition to last – the collapse of a rotting tub that holds your favorite plant can be infuriating. Carefully prepared containers go a long way towards ensuring healthy plants.

Drainage

A lack of adequate drainage is probably the greatest single cause of trouble among container-grown plants. Water must escape freely from containers for outdoor use. Rain can soon upset all your calculations, and plants in soil that is water-logged for long periods will sicken and even die. Plants can be grown outdoors in containers without drainage holes only if they are sheltered from rain. Otherwise containers must have holes at or near the base: most manufacturers of plastic and unglazed earthenware pots provide these. Wooden tubs, troughs and window boxes may not come with holes, but it is a simple matter to drill them. You can also drill fiberglass, plastic and concrete containers, using the slow speed on a two-speed electric drill with a 6 mm/¼ in masonry bit. Glazed earthenware containers often come without drainage holes, so add these, using the masonry drill at the slow speed – drill without hurrying, or you may break the container. It can help to place a piece of masking tape on the surface before you drill, to prevent splintering. A sink already provided with a 4–5 cm/1½–2 in outlet needs no further holes, as long as it is filled correctly (see p. 26).

Take steps to prevent fine soil or sand from being washed out of containers and silting up your drains. Do this, first, by filling containers correctly and taking particular care over crocking (see below), second, by using drip trays, and third, if re-laying a service yard or patio, by fitting a sediment trap, obtainable from builders' merchants, to any surface water drain.

Drip trays

While obviously essential in hanging baskets suspended over doorways, these are also worth using wherever stains from escaping water may cause problems. They catch the nutrient-rich drainage water, thus reducing the growth of green algal film on paths, window sills and walls; they trap sediment close to its source, which prevents blocked drains; where they consist of trays filled with moist pebbles, they raise the humidity of the air around the plants and so help them on hot days. Two types of non-drip hanging baskets are available. In one, a drip tray is fitted immediately below the basket; in the other the basket incorporates a small reservoir and drip-chamber within. Well-designed window boxes, raised on feet or runners, allow shallow trays to be slid beneath. A pot in a tray should be raised either on gravel or on small blocks of wood placed in the tray, so that the pot's base is not constantly standing in water.

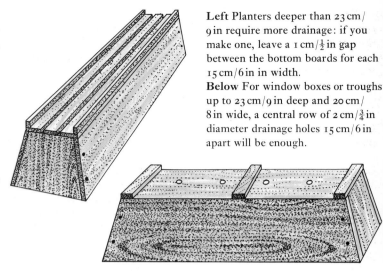

Left Planters deeper than 23 cm/9 in require more drainage: if you make one, leave a 1 cm/½ in gap between the bottom boards for each 15 cm/6 in in width.
Below For window boxes or troughs up to 23 cm/9 in deep and 20 cm/8 in wide, a central row of 2 cm/¾ in diameter drainage holes 15 cm/6 in apart will be enough.

Inspecting and cleaning

If containers have been used before, remove dust and loose dirt with a soft brush. Make sure that no pieces of old root remain inside to start infection. Examine used wooden containers particularly closely for knotted or split wood where rot might set in, and for damage by insects such as woodworm. Check for rot in the corners and base with a penknife; its point will slide easily into rotten wood. Any cracked or broken containers should be set aside for repair, or discarded.

Submerge stained and soil-encrusted containers in water for 12 to 24 hours before washing, to help to loosen the dirt and to speed up cleaning. Carry out any repairs to wooden containers *before* soaking, so that when the wood swells it will hold the fitting nails or screws more firmly.

Scrub used containers in mild detergent, then in disinfectant and finally rinse in clean water. A cresylic-acid type of disinfectant, used as directed, is safe for the user, and leaves no fumes behind to harm plants. Badly stained concrete or stone containers, window sills and paving can all be cleaned using a brand-name stain-remover.

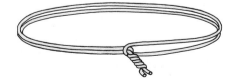

Right Earthenware containers, liable to frost-cracking around the rims, may be made good by inconspicuous wiring.

The aggregate, or chippings, used in trays should be sifted in a screen to remove roots, washed by flooding several times until the water is clean, then drained, disinfected and finally rinsed again with clean water. Drain and rinse the trays. Any self-watering appliances, capillary matting and reservoirs must also be washed out and disinfected before being used for plants again.

New porous or non-glazed containers should be soaked in clean water before use, to dissolve and remove any harmful salts, and to ensure full rehydration, because dried-out porous pots take up moisture from the soil to the detriment of the plants.

Extending the life of containers

Wood, although attractive, is liable to rot, so treat any wooden containers against this before use. Clean them, then paint them inside and out with a safe horticultural preservative – these are available in various colors. Never use creosote since, particularly in warm weather, it gives off fumes that are harmful to plants.

Rotting and badly worm-eaten wood in used containers must be replaced. If the resultant patchwork of old and new wood spoils the appearance, two coats of exterior-quality paint will work wonders.

Tubs intended for use as miniature pools need special care since aquatic plants and fish are very sensitive to oil or mineral contamination. Give the insides of such wooden or metal containers at least two coats of a good rubber-based paint.

Iron and copper alloy containers are always safer for plants when painted inside with rubber-based paint. Go over any metal on their outsides with a wire brush or steel wool and then coat it with liquid tar or rubber-based paint, to make it rust-proof and to prevent chemical reactions between the metal and fertilizers. Aluminum alloy containers are, of course, resistant to rust and corrosion, and should be left untreated. Home improvement centers stock kits that will make good any damaged plastic or fiberglass containers.

Before filling

Make sure that automatic watering systems are clean and in working order, with no blocked nozzles or pipes. Check that watertight trays used with capillary matting or aggregate are level: this ensures even watering, so that none of the plants dry out too quickly. If plants are to be trained up a wall or trellis, make sure that their containers are placed no more than 2 cm/$\frac{3}{4}$ in in front of it, and are firm and level. Where the floor is uneven or sloping, check that containers will not fall over. You may need to re-lay a flagstone or add a skim of cement, to even up the base, or place blocks under one side of the container. Brackets for hanging baskets and wall-mounted containers must be in good condition; if in doubt, renew them.

Left Move a heavy container on boards above pieces of pipe acting as rollers. Tie a strong rope round the container to hold onto as you push. Each time the planks move ahead of the back pipe, slide it under the planks, at the front.
Below To take a planter down steps, lay planks lengthways over the steps, then push the planter down. Use a rope to control its slide.

Left A pot-trolley is a durable circular plastic frame 20–25 cm/ 8–10 in in diameter, set on three casters, on which pots can be placed for moving or be kept in their permanent position.

Mobility

It is usually easier to take the plants and the potting mixes to the container – especially if it is a heavy one. It is also more sensible to carry a small quantity of soil at a time, in a bucket, than to drag a large sack around. Medium-sized planters and tubs may be readily moved on a dolly: this can be rented quite reasonably, and should be worth while if you have a number of containers to transport. To move a pot only a short distance, try dragging it on

Crocking

Carried out correctly, crocking, together with zinc gauze, can help to prevent creatures from coming up through the drainage holes, and stops fine particles being washed out after watering, while improving both drainage and aeration. The type of crocking material can be important, particularly for acid-loving plants like *Rhododendron*, where limestone chippings could contribute to an attack of chlorosis (see p. 56); for these plants, use 1 cm/½ in granite chippings or other neutral aggregate like fired-clay granules. Conversely, the lime-lovers like *Clematis* or *Lychnis* thrive with limestone chippings. Pieces of broken earthenware pot, cleaned and disinfected, can also be used. For containers less than 15 cm/6 in wide use 6 mm/¼ in chippings.

Above Short troughs or window boxes, which can be handled easily, are better than long, unmanageable ones. If a large container is essential to the design, stand smaller pots (**a**) or liners (**b**) inside it, packing moist peat or bark around them to help to slow down

drying out. The plastic baskets used in garden pools, with nylon gauze fillings, make excellent liners. If you have the space, you can even have two sets of liners for each big container – one set on display, while the other is grown on elsewhere for later.

Left A container for a water garden, unlike others, must be watertight. If a wooden tub that is to be used in this way dries out, shrinks, and develops a slight leak, give it a good soaking to swell the wood. Then line it with a flexible plastic or rubber pool liner reaching almost to the top. Paint the barrel's inside rim with rubber solution; press the liner to it along the edge so that it sticks firmly to the inside of the tub.

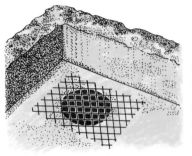

Crocking a pot (below)
1 Insert zinc gauze, if needed.
2 Cover the drainage holes with flat stones or pieces of broken earthenware, concave side down.
3 Sprinkle with chippings – a 1–5 cm/½–2 in layer for a pot 15 cm/6 in wide. 4 For permanent planting, add about 1 cm/½ in of fine, granulated sphagnum peat to stop tiny particles being washed down,

Left In large outdoor containers, place fine zinc gauze over drainage holes 2 cm/¾ in or more wide. This keeps out earthworms and earwigs, and keeps in the gravel, and is particularly important where containers are placed on, or plunged to the rim in, soil. It is not necessary for small containers set on gravel or matting in trays.

and to retain moisture. Pulverized bark can be used instead. In a sink garden, place leaf mold, rather than peat, over a 5–10 cm/2–4 in layer of chippings. In containers 40 cm/16 in wide, or more, place over the peat 2 cm/¾ in of finely chopped fibrous turf, previously stacked for at least six months, for aeration. Make sure this is devoid of yellow wireworms and earthworms.

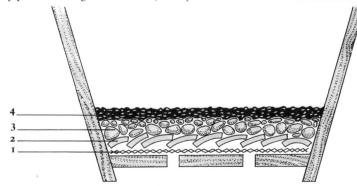

a piece of strong sacking or a large heavy-duty polythene bag, such as those containing peat or potting mix.

Keep the movement of filled containers to a minimum. Apart from the sheer effort of moving bulky objects and materials around, the plants and containers may be damaged. However, there are times when plants must be moved – the overwintering of tender plants indoors, for instance, or the seasonal changeover from spring to summer bedding. Before moving large, tall plants, always take time to tie in the branches, with soft green twine, or wrap the plant in soft netting, to minimize the risk of damage to leaves and stems.

Potting and planting

Good potting can influence plants as much as feeding and pruning. Discerning gardeners employ various potting techniques, together with watering, feeding, pruning and training, to manipulate plant growth and productiveness. 'Potting' covers several related but distinct operations. **Potting up** is the term used for setting bulbs, corms, tubers and young plants into pots of potting mix. If shallow flats or boxes are used instead of pots, it is known as **boxing up**. In **potting on**, an actively growing young plant, or a semimature woody plant or herbaceous perennial, is moved from a small to a larger pot. **Repotting** is reserved for a plant that is growing steadily in its final-sized pot: it is removed, gently shaken out and set back into fresh potting mix in a pot of the same size. The term **planting** is used here for setting out plants in large containers.

When to pot
Some form of potting is normally needed when:
A young plant is starting off
A plant is outgrowing its existing container
Growth is falling off, or a plant is ailing
Renewed vigor needs encouraging
Productivity needs to be induced
Existing levels of flowering and fruiting need to be maintained or increased.

The timing of potting should be related to season, age, condition and type of plant, as well as to considerations of convenience or necessity. For most established perennials, this is an annual task, except for those in very large containers, which can be repotted biennially. Although potting can be carried out at almost any time, it is usually better, unless plants are suffering, to work to the guide given right, which refers to *outdoor* plants.

Containers
These should suit the needs of the plants as well as those of their owners. Make sure that all containers have drainage holes and are properly prepared (see pp. 24–26).

Two common problems are **under-** and **over-potting**; when combined with neglect in potting they can be fatal. Under-potted plants – in very small containers – quickly become pot-bound and fill the potting mix with an impenetrable mass of roots. This also occurs if plants are neglected and not potted on in time. The consequences will be: unduly rapid drying out that adds to the problems of watering in dry weather, starvation, hardening of plant stems and leaves, premature flowering, dropping of leaves and buds, stunting, loss of vigor, and poor flowering and fruiting.

Where plants are over-potted – placed in excessively large containers – one of two things can happen. In slow-growing plants, the roots cannot permeate the potting mix quickly. It therefore remains wet for long periods, stays cold, and eventually becomes sour and causes root problems. Quick-growing plants may make too much leaf growth, which delays and even prevents flowering and fruiting.

Potting mixes
On the choice of potting mix, see page 22. Most container plants can be successfully grown in near-neutral mixes, but some, like *Rhododendron*, need acid conditions, and others, like *Clematis*, prefer alkaline. (For details of the needs of individual plants see pp. 94–153.) As most of the plants under discussion here are being grown outdoors and in their natural season, mainly standard and strong mixes are needed. The plant-food level in mixes varies with the amount of fertilizer in it. Of the John Innes formulae, no. 2 is standard and no. 3 is strong. For *final* potting, even fine-rooted, slow-growing plants, like heathers or alpines, prefer standard strength mixtures, and the quick-growing, vigorous ones like tomatoes need strong mixtures. Soil-based mixes can be firmed down quite hard during potting or planting, but never compact the peat-based ones, or the plants may suffocate; just press them down gently.

Potting timetable	
PLANT GROUP	IDEAL TIME
Conifers	Fall or spring
Evergreen trees and shrubs: spring-flowering	Fall
fall and winter-flowering	Spring
Deciduous trees and shrubs: spring, summer, and winter-flowering	Fall
fall-flowering	Spring
Halfhardy summer bedding and annuals	Late spring after last frost
Spring- and summer-flowering hardy biennials	Fall
Hardy herbaceous perennials	Spring and fall
Hardy summer-flowering bulbs	Late winter and spring
Hardy spring-flowering bulbs	Fall
Plants for water gardens	Late spring
Fruit trees	Fall
Bush fruits, currants and berries	Fall
One-crop strawberry plants	Fall
Remontant and alpine strawberries	Spring or early summer

The semimature and partly grown woody-stemmed trees and shrubs, and the hardy herbaceous plants and bulbs, are all best moved when dormant. However, quick-growing and short-lived subjects like bedding plants, salad crops and vegetables need to be potted on as soon as they show any signs of outgrowing their existing containers.

Simple potting

The various potting and planting techniques relate mainly to the container but also to the plant's habit. Container plants grown singly, or in small groups, require straightforward potting up, as shown below. This is usually the first step for young plants and for bulbs. The size of pot will depend on the type and number of plants to be grown in it. The spacing required between individual plants is given in the plant lists on pages 94–153.

Potting up a bulb

1 Crock the pot well with broken earthenware and chippings, following the instructions on page 26. For most bulbs, which are base-rooting, and for small plants half-fill the pot with moist standard potting mix. (Stem-rooting varieties of lily, which form roots just above the bulb at the base of the stem, require deeper planting – twice the depth of their diameter is a good guide.) **2** Settle the mix by tapping the pot base firmly on the work surface. **3** For bulbs, put a handful of sharp, coarse sand or grit in the center, to improve drainage. Place the bulb level on the sand. Small plants should not require this additional draining medium. **4** Fill the pot with more potting mix up to

about 2 cm/$\frac{3}{4}$ in from the rim, keeping the bulb centered by lightly pressing it with one finger. Firm the mix with your fingers, smooth off the surface and tap the base of the pot to settle the mix again. Water through a rose, and move to a cool, sheltered position to form roots.
5 Protect from mice and other vermin by laying a sheet of glass, plastic, slate or fine gauze over the pot; remove it once the plant has broken through the soil surface.

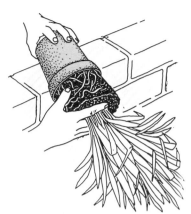

Knocking a plant out of its pot

To check whether a plant has become pot-bound, examine its roots after watering. Place two fingers on top of the potting mix, one on either side of the plant, and invert the pot, holding the base with the other hand. Gently tap the pot rim on the edge of the work surface and remove the rootball. If new roots are encircling the mix, the plant must be potted on. If no roots are visible, put it back in the pot; replace any mix that has fallen away.

Potting on and repotting

For best results, most plants should be moved into progressively larger pots, filled with fresh potting mix. With quick-growing plants, like pelargoniums, examine the roots at weekly intervals – starting about three weeks after potting – to establish when they are ready to pot on. For slow-growing plants, like conifers and maples, potting on is usually carried out, as a matter of course, at the annual potting time. A bought-in plant with the rootball 9 cm/$3\frac{1}{2}$ in wide should usually go into a 13 cm/5 in pot that has been crocked and part-filled with potting mix. Set the plant at about the same depth as in the original pot. Cover the roots with fresh mix and firm it round, leaving a 2 cm/$\frac{3}{4}$ in space at the top for watering. Take care not to push the potting mix down too hard around the rootball as this can lead to waterlogging.

Sooner or later many long-lived plants reach the stage at which a still larger container is out of the question. The usual course of action is to repot them, following the procedure for potting on. The easiest way to loosen the rootball from a large container is usually to tap the pot against a raised surface. Round containers are more manageable than square ones, since they can be rolled over a few times without damage to themselves or their plants. Remove any old crocks, and squeeze out with your fingers or tease out with a pointed stick or a hand-fork as much of the old potting mix as possible from the bottom, sides and top of the roots – taking care not to damage the plant. Cut back any dead, damaged or obviously diseased roots with a garden knife or pruners.

Replace the plant in a crocked container of the same size and shape – or re-use the original one after cleaning and disinfecting (see p. 24). Work fresh mix in and around the roots and onto the surface. The soil should be 13 mm/$\frac{1}{2}$ in higher than in the old container, to allow for settlement. Water the plant enough to fill the space between the rim of the pot and the top of the mix. Adjust or replace stakes and ties and carry out any pruning.

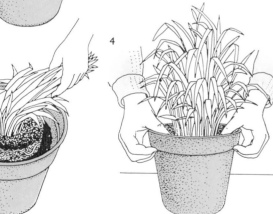

Potting on

Crock and part-fill a pot at least one size larger than the plant's present container, using moist, standard potting mix, preferably soil-based. Remove the plant, as you would to examine its roots. **1** Ease away the old crocks and any loose potting mix, using your hands or a pointed stick. **2** Stand the plant inside the larger pot and add or remove mix so that the top of the rootball is at least 2.5 cm/1 in below the rim. **3** Spread out the roots slightly and add more mix, working it in and around the rootball with a pot-presser. **4** Fill the pot to within 2 cm/¾ in of the rim, firming it as you go. Tap the base of the pot on a hard surface to settle the mix.

Planting in large containers

An entirely permanent planting design of dwarf conifers and evergreens is perhaps the easiest of all. Pot them up in individual pots in the usual way and set them inside the main container (see p. 26). Pot them on in due course. Similarly, by using liners in a trough or window box, the changeover from, say, spring bedding to summer bedding can easily be achieved. Simply plant up a second set of liners with a reserve of plants. This is less easy in a circular planter, which would need to be planted up as a whole, as would any planting design that mixes permanent species with bedding plants. The latter give seasonal color but neeed changing at least twice a year.

Mixed planting in a large container

Prepare the planter as shown on page 26, then fill with moist, standard, preferably soil-based, mix up to 2.5 cm/1 in from the rim, firming it into the corners. If the mix is dry, prepare the container the day before and water gently. **1** Work out the design first by placing plants on the soil surface. As a rule, put taller, more upright plants in the center, with smaller and trailing species round the edges. Water the plants and leave to drain for 20 minutes. **2** With a trowel, make holes for the tallest plants first. **3** Check that each cavity is big enough to take the roots – test it by placing the plant's pot, or one of the same size, in the hole. Enlarge as needed, twisting the pot round in the hole to widen it. **4** Knock each plant out of its pot (see opposite) and set it slightly deeper than it was in the original pot, firming the mix round the roots. Set out the smallest plants last. If you use permanent plants only, a surface layer of fine gravel chippings or pulverized bark will prevent drying out and reduce rain compaction. **5** For a mixed planting, add a surface covering of gravel, peat or fresh green moss. Water the plants.

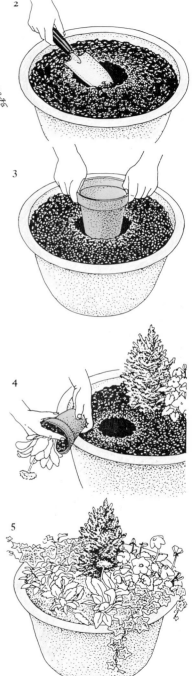

Strawberry barrels and parsley pots

Tall pots and barrels, with numerous openings up the sides, enable heavy crops to be obtained from a small space, which justifies the extra care and attention that they need. As well as the traditional earthenware strawberry pot, patented self-assembly barrels are now widely available. These round plastic tubs have holes in the sides and a central plastic drainage column. Each one can take as many as 30 plants. Turn the tub 15 cm/6 in each week, so that each side may receive an equal amount of sunshine during the growing season; do this just before watering, when it is lightest.

The principles of planting a strawberry barrel also apply to planting up the containers known as parsley or herb pots – although these small pots will not require a central drainage column. They are used, too, for the tower pots, spiral planters or stacked pot arrangements designed for growing strawberries and bedding plants (see p. 13).

Planting a strawberry barrel
Plant up on a calm, overcast day. Stand the barrel on the level and water plants well first. **1** Assemble a patented barrel according to the instructions. **2** Pour gravel into the drainage column, and potting mix up to the lowest hole.

If using a traditional strawberry pot, ensure that there are drainage holes in the bottom; cover with crocks and a thin layer of peat. If the pot is higher than 60 cm/24 in, assist drainage by inserting a central 5–7.5 cm/2–3 in wide vertical column of fine mesh netting up to about 17 cm/7 in from the pot rim– fill this

to the top with pebbles. Set the pot on a pebble-filled tray.

Proceed in the same way for barrel and pot. Cover the drainage column with a small pot, and fill the container up to the lowest openings with moist, preferably soil-based, standard potting mix.
3 Carefully push the roots of a strawberry plant in through a low hole. Cover the roots with more mix, lightly firming round them. Plant up all the lowest openings, before adding more mix to raise the level to the next holes. Continue planting and filling, firming the mix after each layer.

Leave the little pot in place in a traditional strawberry pot; smooth off the soil surface level with it, about 7.5 cm/3 in below the rim. Plant up the top.

Remove the small pot from a barrel and put the lid on. **4** Use a dibble to make depressions through the holes, then remove lid. **5** Set remaining plants in these holes, firming mix round the roots; replace the lid, taking care not to damage the small plants. Leave the central hole empty for watering.
6 and **7** The plants will grow through the holes. When fruit appears, protect it with netting.

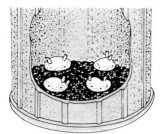

Potato barrels

Worthwhile potato crops can be obtained from plastic barrels about 73 cm/29 in high and 60 cm/24 in wide. Some models come without a base, although a matching tray with drainage holes can be bought. Prepare the barrel for planting as on page 26 (leaving out the turf), then add 10 cm/4 in of standard potting mix. **1** Place four egg-sized, sprouted potato tubers evenly apart on the mix, the pitted and sprouting end upward. Cover with a 10 cm/4 in layer of moist potting mix. Firm and smooth the surface before watering. **2** The potato plants will thrust vigorously through the mix toward the light. **3** Each time the plant stems show 15–20 cm/6–8 in above the soil, add 10–15 cm/4–6 in more mix. When the level is 5 cm/2 in below the rim, add a final layer of peat. **4** Harvest early potatoes when the plants flower; check they are ready by feeling for them under the mix. Dig up maincrop potatoes when the leaves start to die down.

Hanging baskets

Hanging and wall-mounted baskets can add height to planting designs and are very valuable in small spaces. Unfortunately, plants grown in them tend to dry out rapidly so choose only those species that are best able to stand such conditions (see p. 157). Despite dripping and rapid drying out the traditional wire basket, often plastic-coated, offers more scope for plant arranging than the plastic non-drip type. The latter should be crocked and planted up in the usual way, with plants inserted at the top. Frequent watering and deadheading ensure continuous flowering. Pin back long stems with hairpins.

Filling a wire hanging basket
1 Rest the basket on a large pot or bucket. Line the inside base with dampened living sphagnum moss, green side outward – the larger the pieces of moss, the longer it will live. **2** Fit it in place with a little moist, standard potting mix; use peat if you are worried about weight. **3** Push the roots of one trailing plant at a time from the outside into the mix, embedding them firmly, to create a circle of plants on the underside. Add more moss up the sides, more potting mix inside, and perhaps another circle of plants. **4** Work the moss up the edges to the rim, and add mix almost up to the top of the moss. **5** Set the tallest plants in the center, and trailing and edging plants round them, firming more mix in round the plants. For a wall basket, set the tall plants at the back. Water gently. Cover bare mix with moss to prevent drying out. **6** The growing plants should spill out of the basket.

If moss is hard to obtain, use green or black plastic sheeting, cutting slits in it for planting.

Growing bags

Used outdoors, growing bags are best for spring and summer crops; in the fall and winter, frost or heavy rain will cause drainage problems. Lay the growing bag on a tray on a level surface, in a sheltered, sunny spot. Perforate the underside (see p. 23). Slit open the covering plastics either in three separate places or cut out a rectangular panel. If the potting mix is dry, water it first and plant or sow an hour or two later. For tall crops, like some tomatoes, insert a plant-supporting frame – patented models are obtainable – or use bamboo canes (see pp. 38–39).

Plant up and water afterward. Tie tall plants to the supports – but not too tightly, to leave room for stem expansion. Tomato plants should be planted *before* the flowers show on the first truss. Do not grow root crops – except for short-rooted varieties like early carrots – as the results are rarely satisfactory because of the lack of depth. Outdoor varieties of tomato, pepper, cucumber and marrow are usually well worth growing; all need a warm site. Other less fussy crops include strawberries, French beans, lettuce, salad onions, herbs and bedding plants. Plant up growing boards, after they have been rehydrated (see p. 23).

Sink and alpine gardens

A miniature garden in a sink made to look like a stone trough is an excellent way to display diminutive rock and alpine plants, slow-growing dwarf conifers, and dwarf bulbs. Treat the sink to disguise its original use (see p. 17), and raise it securely so that it is off the ground. Bear in mind that some plants, like heather, are acid-lovers and resent limestone, so, if planting these, avoid using limestone materials for crocking or covering, or for any stonework; use an acid, preferably soil-based, potting mix.

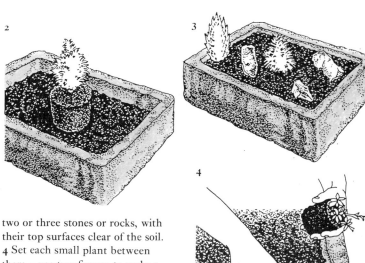

two or three stones or rocks, with their top surfaces clear of the soil. **4** Set each small plant between them – use two fingers to make a hole in the mix and place the root-ball in it. **5** Firm the potting mix back around each plant and smooth off the top. Brush off any loose mix lying on the stones. **6** Cover the exposed potting mix with a layer of fine grit – limestone for limestone-lovers and granite or ironstone for acid-lovers. Water through a fine rose. Protect from cold winds if planting in winter, or from hot sun in late spring (see p. 52).

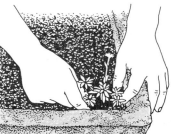

Planting a sink garden

1 Crock the drainage hole carefully (see p. 26), and put a 5–10 cm/2–4 in layer of gravel, stone chippings or clean crocks into the bottom of the sink, followed by 2 cm/¾ in of leaf mold. Half-fill with potting mix, firming it into the corners. Plan out the design by placing the dwarf conifers, alpines and large stones on the soil surface in different arrangements, as for the mixed planting design on page 29. **2** Leave the tallest, deepest-rooted plants upright on the surface. Add more potting mix up to about 2 cm/¾ in of the sink rim. **3** Insert

Planting a water garden

Any large container is suitable for a miniature pool, provided it is made watertight and has a minimum depth of 30 cm/12 in (or 45 cm/18 in if fish are to be included). A tub, lined with plastics, is a particularly appropriate vessel; preparing it for use as a water garden is covered on page 26. Information on specific water plants and their cultivation is given on pages 134–35. 'Marginal' water plants, such as marsh marigolds or water iris, that flourish in saturated soil, can in fact be grown in a bowl or tub as shallow as 20–23 cm/8–9 in, since they need only 15 cm/6 in soil, and 5 cm/2 in water on top of it.

Carry out planting in late spring. While it is possible to set plants directly in prepared soil or mix on the bottom of the water-garden container, it is better to grow them in the perforated plastic baskets that are sold specially for pools. They need less soil, and can easily be lifted out for inspection, root-trimming or replanting. They also prevent fast-growing plants from taking over the miniature pool.

Set the pool container in an open, partially shaded site, not under trees, where falling leaves will foul the water. Excess sunlight on the water will encourage the growth of algae, including those that form green cotton-wool-like masses of submerged threads (sometimes known as blanket weed), or 'pea-soup' – greenish-yellow wads that float on the surface. Chemical treatments will alleviate this temporarily, as will part-emptying and refilling two or three times, but the long-term solution is to allow water-lily leaves to cover up to two-thirds of the surface, and to avoid overfeeding with fertilizer. Rinse new plants thoroughly to remove any traces of algae. Some algae can be controlled by introducing daphnia – water-flea nymphs that feed upon them – each spring; in this case, do not add fish to the pool, as they will eat the daphnia. Insert one water snail, obtainable from a good water-garden supply store, for every 0.2 sq. m/2 sq ft of water surface, to eat the rotting leaves.

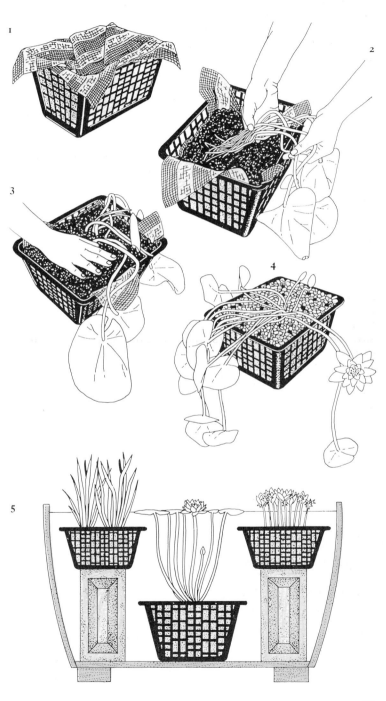

Most of the aquatics require a basket at least 30 cm/12 in square and 20 cm/8 in deep. For pygmy aquatics and for marginals, a 15 cm/6 in deep basket will suffice. **1** Line the basket with a piece of nylon gauze. For the planting medium, use a brand-name water-lily mix as directed by the manufacturers, or a soil-based mix such as John Innes no. 1. Part fill the basket with a layer of potting mix. **2** Set the water plant in it, and fill the basket to within 2.5 cm/1 in of the rim, making sure the crown, or growing point, stays just above the mix. **3** Firm the mix around the roots. To help keep the water clear, lay a few pieces of oxygenating plant like *Elodea* on the soil surface. **4** Top with clean gravel to prevent the soil from muddying the water. **5** Carefully position the basket in the pool container. Shallow baskets containing marginals may be placed on bricks so that they are covered with only 5–7.5 cm/2–3 in of water.

Watering and feeding

Plants obtain their water and nutrient requirements mainly by their roots, but a small proportion is also taken in through their leaves; this is especially true with aquatics. In containers, the plant roots are restricted in their search for water and food, so these needs should never be neglected.

Watering

Always make sure you give enough water to reach down to the plant root; simply wetting the surface of the potting mix is not enough. Provided a suitable mix is used and the container has adequate drainage, you should continue overhead watering until surplus water begins to trickle out at the bottom. With plants stood in shallow water for a short time and those watered by the capillary method (see below), moisture is taken up automatically to replace losses from the plant and potting mix.

The interval between waterings will vary, depending upon many factors such as season, temperature and wind, as well as the type and condition of the individual plant. Actively growing or fruiting plants, warm summer conditions, strong sun and wind, all increase evaporation rates and moisture loss, and therefore more frequent watering is required. However, in calm, cool, overcast or shaded conditions, in drizzle, or during fall and winter when plants are dormant, longer intervals are advisable.

Always aim to water plants before they start wilting or showing other signs of stress. In the height of summer, daily watering may well be necessary, whereas it can be reduced to only two or three times a month, or even less, in winter. Early morning and evening are the best times of day to water in the summer months; never splash water directly on to the leaves in bright sunshine or they will get scorched. Misting and damping are also of benefit in hot weather (see p. 52).

Watering methods

Methods of watering range from the traditional use of a watering can or hose to fully automatic systems. Traditional practices, though effective and often less expensive initially, can be time-consuming where large numbers of plants are involved.

Overhead, low-level watering methods suit many plants, though not all take kindly to having their leaves wetted – hairy-leaved plants, like some alpines, mark or scorch easily and should always be watered from the bottom. Nozzle sprinklers, both fixed and moving, can be used for watering groups of closely set containers; they are most suitable for a large roof terrace or patio. Their drawbacks are the wastage of water that falls between containers, the fact that they spray windows and outside walls as well as the plants, and their dependence on calm, overcast weather conditions to minimize evaporation loss.

Watering from the bottom, either by standing the pot in shallow water or by continuous capillary watering, means the

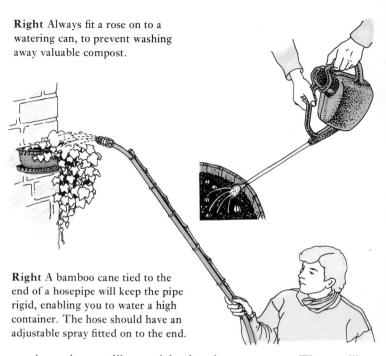

Right Always fit a rose on to a watering can, to prevent washing away valuable compost.

Right A bamboo cane tied to the end of a hosepipe will keep the pipe rigid, enabling you to water a high container. The hose should have an adjustable spray fitted on to the end.

potting mix acts like a wick, drawing water up. The capillary watering system can be used for any small plants, though in pots over $11 \text{ cm}/4\frac{1}{2}$ in it is less efficient. It is a particularly suitable method for plants whose leaves should not be allowed to get wet, and for short holiday periods or where small plants are under cover. A ready-made kit can be bought, supplying a reservoir tray and one in which to stand the small pots, and a length of capillary matting. You could rig up your own system, using an improvised reservoir such as a shallow dish or bowl and either capillary matting bought by the meter, or a moist aggregate such as sand or gravel to stand the plants on. If you are using aggregate, a strip of capillary matting is still needed to conduct the water.

Self-watering planters are the most trouble-free solution. Originally designed for indoor use, they are equally suited to areas such as semienclosed balconies or verandas.

Watering problems

Salts Acid-loving subjects like heathers and azaleas will suffer from an excess of salts in the water supply. In the chalk or limestone areas, collection and storage of rainwater or using distilled water needs to be considered.

Drips Window boxes, troughs and containers placed on window sills, the tops of walls or other surfaces that are liable to stain from drainage water should be provided with a drip tray. Drip trays or 'saucers' made of plastics or terracotta come in

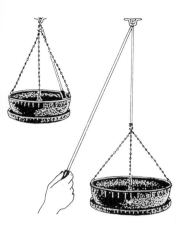

Capillary watering
Right This method of watering involves placing small pots in a tray on capillary matting or wet sand, which is kept moist by an adjacent reservoir (**a**). As an added refinement, wicks, available from garden supply stores, can be inserted in the bottom of each container, to ensure a continuous flow of water (**b**). See that reservoirs are kept full and the wicks clean.

Holiday care
Right Small plants can be watered and put in individual perforated clear plastic bags, sealed, to reduce water loss. Place them in a cool, shaded spot.

Right You could provide an improvised drip feed for larger plants; fill a basin or bucket with water, stand it on a shelf or raise it up on bricks, then use a length of bandage or capillary matting to conduct water to the pots. A stone will keep each bandage in place. Again, keep the plants shaded.

Left A pulley system facilitates watering and feeding hanging baskets. This self-locking pulley is simple to use: it can be lowered to the required working height and locked into place; after watering, it is raised again, locked into place and the excess cord wound round the pull handle.

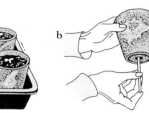

Right Many window boxes or troughs on a window sill or balcony receive no rainwater because of overhanging masonry. The advantage of a self-watering planter

Right Nozzle sprinklers release a spray of fine water drops. They fit onto the end of a hose and either have a stand or can be stuck into a large pot of earth. Both the spike sprinkler (**a**) and the rotating sprinkler (**b**) spray in a circular pattern. Their range is adjustable and they can save a lot of time.

is that the reservoir, once filled, lasts for several weeks.

The reservoir is underneath and is filled through an opening in the side or on the top of the planter; a fiber wick draws moisture up as required. A water level indicator tells you when it needs refilling.

The planters, though functional, are elegant enough to grace any window sill or veranda.

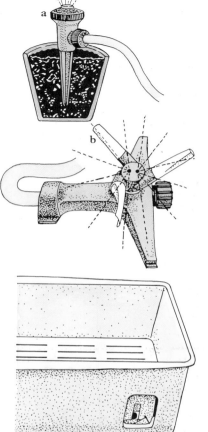

Revival
Left To revive a wilting plant, stand the pot in a watertight tray filled with moist gravel, which will provide local humidity round the plant.

Left Dried-out plants, where the roots and potting mix have shrunk away from the pot, can be resaturated by plunging them up to 2.5 cm/1 in above the pot rim in water. Leave until the bubbles stop rising and the rootball has swollen, which may take about 20 minutes; remove and leave to drain.

several shapes and many sizes. Hanging baskets with a built-in drip tray are also a good idea; in some models the tray acts as a reservoir, thereby cutting down the need for watering.

Accessibility Inaccessible hanging baskets and wall-hung containers can be watered by means of a pressure sprayer with extension lance or by tying something rigid to the end section of a hose. A pulley could also be used; remember that the point of attachment for the pulley must be strong enough to take three times the dry weight of the basket and potting mix – to allow for the weight of the water.

Drying out In hot weather, where frequent watering is a problem, moisture-loving plants can be stood on wet gravel. Wilting plants can also be revived quickly by this means or by a vapor bath: stand the plant on a block of wood or a brick in a sink of warm water, keeping the pot itself out of the water. The roots of dried-out plants should be completely immersed in cold water.

Holidays Small containers tend to dry out more rapidly than large ones such as window boxes, and woody-stemmed shrubs suffer less than thin-leaved plants like ferns and many annuals. Small pots can be placed in sealed plastic bags after a thorough watering, or kept moist by the capillary method.

One way to prevent larger pot plants drying out is to make an improvised drip feed (see p. 35). Stand the odd plant in its pot on a piece of wood or a brick in a bucket of water, to reduce evaporation. Another expedient is to spray smooth-leaved plants with an antidesiccant before placing them in a cool place.

Feeding

In practical terms, plant feeding is the application of fertilizers, in either dry or liquid form. It is particularly important to ensure that container-grown plants are fed regularly, as the small amount of potting mixture in a tub or pot may contain only enough food to supply the plant for a few months. There is also a danger of rain washing away nutrients in the potting mix.

Basic needs

For balanced growth plants need various chemical elements as well as the starches and sugars that they manufacture in their leaves in the presence of sunlight. Those needed in the largest quantities are nitrogen, phosphorus and potassium. Nitrogen is necessary for growth and, in particular, leaf development – too little results in stunted plants and pale yellowish-green leaves, whereas too much delays flowering and fruiting as well as encouraging lush, dark green, disease-prone foliage. Phosphates are essential for root formation, especially in young plants – both deficiency and excess result in stunting. Potash/potassium promotes hardiness, good quality and color, counteracts excess nitrogen and increases disease-resistance. Deficiency often manifests itself as marginal leaf scorching and as a reddish or purplish discoloration round the leaf edges.

Minerals are also needed, though in minute quantities. These include: iron and magnesium, necessary for making the green pigment chlorophyll, and manganese, sulphur and calcium.

Fertilizers and topdressings

Fertilizers may be organic – of animal or plant origin – or man-made/inorganic, from mineral sources. Organic fertilizers are usually more costly, and tend to be slower-acting but longer-lasting. Fertilizers vary considerably in their rate of action, the essential difference between slow- and quick-acting feeds being their solubility in water. Plants can utilize nutrients only when they are dissolved in water and many of the organics, such as bonemeal, are not readily soluble. The gradual-release fertilizers used in potting mixes need about 14 days minimum for plants to show a response, while topdressings of quick-acting fertilizer may start to work in seven to ten days, in warm weather. Liquid fertilizer applied to the roots can show results in five days, and liquid foliar feeding takes about three days to act.

Another consideration when buying fertilizers and liquid feed is their nutrient content. Straight fertilizers such as those based on nitrochalk, supplying nitrogen, provide only one chemical element, whereas compound fertilizers supply two or more and complete or balanced fertilizers contain all three major elements. Complete fertilizers in fact have added trace elements and so contain all or most of the ingredients needed for balanced growth. Homemade, soil-based potting mixes normally contain sufficient trace elements to support growth, while soilless mixtures require them to be added.

The brand-name balanced fertilizers are the most widely used, as they are easy and convenient to handle, save time as well as effort, and are ideal for average use. The labels of most proprietary fertilizers give the percentage of nitrogen (N), phosphorus (P) and potassium (K), showing the relative proportions of each. However, some gardeners prefer to prepare their own mixtures from straight fertilizers. The chief advantage of this is that the nitrogen, phosphate and potash content – or ratio – can be adjusted according to the needs of particular plants.

It is not possible to go into detail about these needs here, as they can vary according to the health of the individual plant and its growing conditions, as well as between different plant groups. However, in very general terms, most container-grown foliage plants benefit from a fertilizer high in nitrogen, while a combination of potash and nitrogen will suit most flowering plants, improving the quality and texture of blooms. Remember that it is safe to apply a general-purpose dilute mix of 1 part nitrogen, 1 part phosphorus and 1 part potash, in either liquid or dry form, to most plants at most times. If you have room for a compost bin, rotted-down vegetable or plant waste makes a good general bulky manure and mulch.

Left Bulky topdressings, consisting of slow-acting dry fertilizer and potting mix, are used to top up the sunken contents of large containers at the beginning of the growing season, and to feed the plants simultaneously. If the original potting mix has become compacted, loosen the top of it first with a pointed stick.

Left A root feeder attachment, used with pressure from a sprayer, will ensure that the food reaches the plant roots as quickly as possible. Insert it down the side of the pot, to avoid damaging the roots themselves. The potting mix should be thoroughly drenched first so that the food becomes evenly dissipated throughout the mix and not concentrated in one area.

Left Highly soluble dilute foliar feed is sprayed directly onto the leaves when overcast. The plant food is absorbed by the leaves and very quickly taken up by the plant.

Left Plant food pellets and nutrient sticks are slow-acting forms of fertilizer; they are simply pushed into the potting mix, and gradually release the nutrients at each watering.

When and how to feed

To ensure good growth, start by adding granular or powder fertilizer to the potting mix, if you are making up your own, to build up an initial reserve of nutrients. The brand-name ready-mixed potting mixes usually contain added chemicals in the form of slow-acting or gradual-release base fertilizers. Subsequent feeding should consist of applying quick-acting fertilizers to replenish nutrients both lost in drainage and taken up by plants through their roots.

Plants should be fed only when they are actively growing, not in their dormant period. Never feed plants that are dry without watering them first, and avoid applying fertilizer in strong sun because of the danger of scorching. Always use fertilizer and liquid feed according to manufacturer's directions, and if any concentrated feed is spilt on the plant, wash it off immediately. Remember to wash out all equipment after using fertilizers.

The most common forms of plant food are:

Granular or powder forms of base fertilizer, usually incorporated when making up potting mixes and bulky top-dressings. The latter are used to top up well-established plants in large pots, at the beginning of the growing season. Light top-dressings of quick-acting synthetic fertilizer can be applied during the growing season to permanent plants such as shrubs, or greedy feeders like chrysanthemums and dahlias.

Liquid fertilizers, which are watered in by can or hose, are ideal for use on container plants generally. They can either be bought as a concentrated liquid, or made up by dissolving granules or powder in a bucket of water. When making up liquid feed, mix it thoroughly and keep well agitated; use tepid, never cold, water.

Foliar feeds are sprayed onto the leaves in overcast weather conditions. Specially formulated foliar feeds will correct specific deficiencies or meet particular needs. Magnesium should be sprayed on tomatoes and peppers, for example, to assist fruiting, and iron on azaleas, hydrangeas and camellias, which are known acid-lovers and tend to be short of iron when grown in a potting mix containing lime.

Pellets and sticks are a convenient form of slow-acting fertilizer; each one will last two to three months.

Keeping plants attractive

Most container-grown plants need regular pruning to keep them healthy, tidy and in good condition. Often they need to be given some form of support as well. These operations are closely interlinked, especially in 'training', when a plant is encouraged to grow in a particular shape.

Supporting plants

Supports not only keep plants looking tidy but also prevent them from flopping and being blown about and so suffering damage. Methods of support vary according to the type and size of plant and the sturdiness of stems.

Stake and tie a plant early, as soon as it is tall enough for you to tie twine round it. For most plants choose a support that will be about two-thirds of the plant's ultimate height. The exceptions are the fast-growers such as tomatoes and climbers, which need supports taller than themselves. As a general rule a stake should be the same thickness as the stem that it is to support, so that it is strong enough to do its job. Make sure that the soil is soft and moist before inserting supports, taking care not to damage the roots.

If possible use rust-, rot- and corrosion-proof supports. Plastics or specially coated metals are ideal, while wood treated with a safe horticultural preservative can last many years. Bamboo canes either whole, or split lengthways, are useful, but should be disinfected before re-use, since they can harbor insects.

Soft twine or 'fillis' is best for tying soft-stemmed plants; wire ties covered with tar-impregnated paper can be used for sturdier stems. Use plastic trees ties for hardwood stems.

Single-stem support

For a plant with one stem only, carefully push in a support close to it and tie it in place. For a standard tree, use a 2.5–4 cm/1–1½ in thick wooden stake treated with a safe, horticultural preservative. The stake top must be 2.5–5 cm/1–2 in below the lowest branches (right). Secure the stem with two adjustable tree ties, one about 4 cm/1½ in from the top of the stake, the other halfway down. Make sure that there is space between stake and stem, to prevent chafing – some tree ties include a square block that automatically preserves this distance, but otherwise you could make your own from odd pieces of wood treated with preservative.

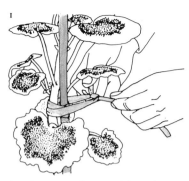
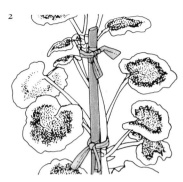

A soft-stemmed perennial needs a bamboo cane or metal rod. **1** Loop soft twine round the support, cross the ends behind it. Bring these round the plant to behind the stem, just above a leaf joint, and knot the ends against the side of the support. **2** Place further ties at 15 cm/6 in intervals, the top one being 4 cm/1½ in from the top of the support.

Supports for multistemmed plants

(a) Support multistemmed annuals like *Clarkia* or dwarf beans by pushing twiggy sticks, obtainable from garden supply stores, into the soil between the young plants, when they are 7.5–10 cm/3–4 in high. Set the sticks slanting slightly inward so that shoots can grow through and conceal them.

(b) Alternatively, use a patented metal support consisting of three legs holding a flat, circular frame of wire mesh through which plants grow up and are held securely.

(c) Another form of multistem support, much used for bulbs and for dwarf beans, consists of three or more split or whole canes, or metal rods, set slanting slightly outward around the edge of a pot. Loop twine around the sticks to keep leaves and stems in place.

(d) Special frames are available for use with growing bags. They contain three or four supports through which canes are slotted down into the potting mix.

(e) Patented support frames, which can be pushed into the potting mix for anchorage, should be positioned in a sheltered spot out of the wind. An improvised version can be made by inserting two or three canes or rods upright into pots, with three or four rods tied or nailed across horizontally. The plant may need tying in at intervals.

(f) Runner beans grown round the edge of a large tub can be trained up 1.8–2.4 m/6–8 ft canes – one per plant – wired or tied together at the top. Patented bean maypoles allow climbers to be trained individually up strings or wires.

(g) You can fix trellis, plastic netting or horizontal wires to a wall or fence to support your plants (see p. 18). On horizontal wires, if the plants already have supports such as rods or canes, tie these to the wires rather than the stems.

(h) Soft-stemmed climbers may be tied to trellis or net with soft twine, and woody ones with paper-covered wire ties, but self-clinging climbers can make their own way without help. When growing climbers against a wall or fence always use flat-sided containers; leave a 2.5 cm/1 in gap between the container and the wall of a building.

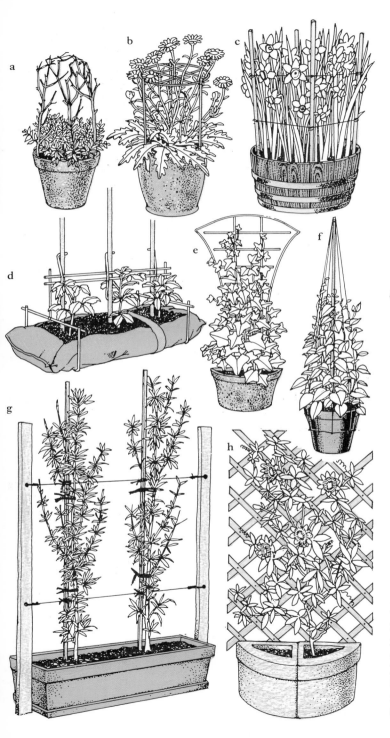

Training and tidying

In order to keep your plants looking their best you may wish to adopt various 'training' techniques which influence their shape and growth habit, and may prolong their flowering period. To maintain a neat appearance you should also deal promptly with dead flowers heads and dying foliage; in addition to tidying up the plant, this reduces the risk of infection and disease, and will not encourage pests (see also pp. 51–52).

The following training and tidying terms apply to particular groups or types of plant.

Stopping and pinching

The removal of the growing points in young plants. This exploits the natural tendency of plants to form new shoots low down and, when carried out early in the growing season, induces bushiness. Done late in the growing season, it hastens the development and improves the size of flowers and fruit. Although the term 'pinching' or 'pinching out' implies the use of finger and thumb, unless you have long nails it may be better to use a knife, in which case the operation is usually known as 'stopping'.

Early in the summer, especially when in shade, zonal pelargoniums, *Browallia*, and some varieties of petunia and *Antirrhinum* may grow tall and spindly. If 10–15 cm/4–6 in high plants are not bushing out, remove each growing point, just above a leaf (above). Use a sharp knife or pair of scissors or, if you have a long thumbnail, pinch out the stems between thumbnail and first finger.

Nicking and notching

Occasionally used on apple or pear trees to influence the behaviour of buds that might otherwise remain dormant. Cutting a small nick with a knife below a dormant bud encourages it to develop into a flower or fruit; carefully cutting a small notch above a similar bud may produce a new shoot (below).

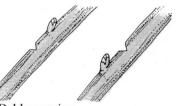

Deblossoming

The removal of premature flower buds and flowers. When nursing along small cuttings of herbaceous plants like *Doronicum* and *Lychnis*, cutting off the flower buds in the first season will ensure larger plants the following year. Winter- and spring-sown sweet peas sometimes produce flower buds when the plants are very small. If allowed to bloom too soon they will do so for only a short season. To prevent this, cut off the first two or three buds, if the plants are less than 13–15 cm/5–6 in high. When going away on holiday, pick every sweet pea flower bud in sight, and you will be rewarded by extra flowers two weeks later.

Deadheading

The removal of dead and faded flowers. If left on the plant they not only look untidy and encourage disease but they also form seeds, weakening the plant. Pick them off with your fingers, or cut them off with scissors or flower-gatherers. The plant can then divert its energies to hastening the development of later flowers.

For many bedding plants, including *Bellis*, *Calendula*, *Impatiens*, petunia and *Salvia*, deadheading lengthens the flowering season and improves the quality of the blooms. If the main spikes on plants such as lupins are promptly cut out as the flowers finish, secondary smaller spikes will be produced. Alpines like *Alyssum* and *Aubrieta* can be lightly clipped over with a pair of shears or scissors, to remove faded flowers and old seed heads. Deadheading is not usually done if fruit, seed or berries are required.

Disbudding

Removing secondary or side buds – those immediately below the main flower bud – will, if done early enough, produce a large, single bloom on, for instance, a carnation plant. Twist the side bud off its stem with your fingers, taking care not to damage the main stem (above).

Leaf-tying

Bulbs that are retained to flower for a second and third season, like *Narcissus*, *Muscari* and species tulips, should be allowed to die down naturally. This will replenish food reserves used up when flowering. As soon as flowering is over, tidy up the leaves by bending them double and tying them with string (above), or, quicker still, slip over a rubber band to hold them in place. Only when they have turned brown should they be removed.

Cutting down

At the end of the growing season cut herbaceous plants down to near the soil surface with pruners or a knife. Those that finish flowering in late summer should be cut down by a half to two-thirds, and those that finish in fall should be cut to 5 cm/2 in above the soil. Do not, however, prune immediately after flowering – deadhead first, and allow the foliage to die down naturally to ensure that the roots obtain the benefit of the starches and sugars manufactured by the leaves.

Pruning

The main aim of pruning is to remove unwanted wood or shoots in order to regulate growth, flowering and cropping. Pruning is carried out at different times of the year depending on its purpose and the nature of the plant. Used together with the right supports, it helps to train, and maintain, the plant's shape.

A young plant often needs pruning to create a good framework of branches, to remove awkwardly growing stems in order to achieve the required shape, and to promote flowering and fruiting. An established plant needs pruning to keep a good shape, to regulate flowering and fruiting, and to maintain plant health and discourage pests and diseases. An old and neglected plant is pruned to remove dead, diseased or overcrowded stems.

Many plants tend naturally to grow vertically with maximum growth nearest the tips. Pruning and training can encourage a proportion of branches to grow more horizontally, which ensures flowering and fruiting, since vertical shoots are vigorous but produce fewer flowers and fruit. When the growing point is removed, the plant is kept short, the less active buds immediately below the cut are stimulated into growth, and the new branches formed lower down the stems will grow out closer to the horizontal. This pruning is used to encourage bushiness as well as fruitfulness in fruit trees and bushes.

As a general rule, severe cutting-back results in vigorous growth, and light pruning in less growth but more flowers.

Pruning guidelines

Ensure that cutting tools are sharp, so they make a clean cut, without tearing or leaving a ragged edge.

Cut branches back flush with the main stem. Cut shoots and stems back to sound, healthy wood or tissue, ideally just above a plump, upward- and outward-facing bud. Do not prune too near (**a**) or too far (**b**) from the bud. The correct cut (**c**) should be about 3 mm/$\frac{1}{8}$ in above the bud, and should slope slightly downward away from it.

First cut out dead, diseased or damaged shoots, and then any that are overcrowded, weak, crossing or inward- or downward-pointing.

After cutting any stem thicker than 2.5 cm/1 in, paint the wound with a horticultural sealing preparation, to help it to heal quickly and cleanly.

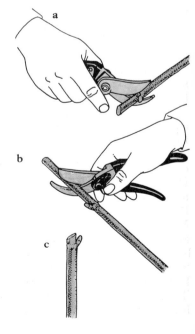

Pruning shrubs

Pruning is the single operation that has the greatest influence on keeping shrubs looking attractive. For convenience, shrubs are grouped together here according to their habit of growth and flowering as well as their pruning needs.

Spring- and summer-flowering shrubs, like *Forsythia suspensa*, *Kerria* and *Philadelphus*, that flower on young wood formed the previous year, are normally pruned as soon as flowering is over. Cut the shoots that have flowered back to the main framework so that only the young, non-flowering growths are left. Thin out weak, spindly, badly placed or crossing growths at the same time.

Late summer-flowering shrubs, like hardy fuchsia and *Buddleia*, that flower on the new season's shoots, should be cut back hard to the main framework of branches just after flowering in fall or in early spring before growth begins again.

Slow-growing evergreens, such as *Rhododendron* and *Camellia*, need little attention. Just after flowering, deadhead to remove faded flowers and seed pods. At the same time shorten straggly or misplaced shoots, to keep the plant in shape. Do not carry this to excess, or next year's flowering may suffer.

Small-leaved evergreens, like heathers and lavender, that form a mass of flowers immediately above the foliage, soon look untidy unless trimmed. Clipping also keeps the plants bushy at the base, prevents them becoming straggly, conserves their strength and stops seeding. Lightly clip the plants over with pruners or shears as soon as flowering is over.

Shrubs used for topiary, like box, privet and bay laurel, need regular clipping every three or four weeks if they are to be kept in first-class condition. In their initial and subsequent training, keep them wider at the base and tapering inward at the top, to avoid having bare stems at the bottom.

Deciduous shrubs like *Viburnum*, that flower mainly on short spurs and on old wood, have a naturally neat habit, and need little pruning other than thinning and cutting out dead wood.

Since plants and their needs differ, a range of forms of pruning and training has been evolved.

Formation pruning

The treatment given to young deciduous trees or shrubs, especially fruit trees, designed to form the branch framework. It is often quite severe: after planting in spring new growths may be cut back to one-third or a half immediately.

Routine pruning

Mainly involves thinning out overcrowded, weak, dead, diseased and crossing shoots and branches on established plants. It may be referred to as 'winter pruning', when ripe wood is cut out, or 'summer pruning', when semiripe new growths are cut away.

Lopping and remedial pruning

Terms for the more drastic treatment needed by old and neglected trees, such as the cutting out of large limbs.

Climbers and other wall-trained plants

Climbers of neat habit, like ivy, need only be trimmed to shape and the odd straggly shoot shortened. Do not prune them at planting time, or growth can be seriously retarded.

Summer-flowering climbing plants, like honeysuckle and common jasmine, flower mainly on short growths on old wood, and need only occasional thinning out. They usually require no pruning at planting time. Tie in stems as necessary.

Many varieties of *Clematis* flower on the previous season's wood, especially those that flower from late spring to mid-summer. Prune the young plants back to 15–20 cm/6–8 in in spring, after planting. Train up and tie in a simple framework of vertical and horizontal branches. The side-shoots that are formed one year bloom the following season, and should then be cut out – back to the main branch just above a pair of buds – after flowering. The replacement growths that then arise should be tied and trained in.

Varieties of late-flowering *Clematis* flower on new wood. Again, the young plants are cut back to 15–20 cm/6–8 in in spring, after planting, and a framework of vertical and horizontal stems tied in. After flowering, cut out the flowered shoots and tie in the replacement growths that are produced in the following spring and early summer.

Pruning roses

In spring, *after planting*, cut bush Hybrid tea roses back to two and Floribunda roses back to three buds from their base, to about 10–15 cm/4–6 in high. Cut back standard and half-standard roses to three buds from the base of the head. Prune shrub roses less severely, cutting them back to 15–20 cm/6–8 in. Miniature roses should be shortened by a half to two-thirds.

Subsequently, shorten the flowered stems of Hybrid tea and Floribunda roses by one-third in the fall in order to reduce wind damage. The following spring, cut back the stems to 15–20 cm/6–8 in. Shrub roses should be lightly pruned or 'tipped' only: cut any stem tips that are soft back to a good bud. Cut old, weak branches back to the base, and remove any remaining hips. Prune miniatures back to about half in spring.

Cut the main stems of *newly planted* climbers and ramblers back to 45–60 cm/18–24 in, and any weak growths back to about 10 cm/4 in. Avoid hard cutting at this stage, or the plants may revert to bush forms. Later, prune climbers and ramblers as soon as possible after flowering in the summer or fall to avoid the risk of damage by winter winds. With climbers, once a framework has been formed by tying in strong shoots from the base, cut side-shoots back to the main stems; then remove the last 10 cm/4 in of the stems. (Climbers can be pruned in spring if in a sheltered site.) On ramblers, cut back the flowered and weak stems to the base and tie in strong new growths.

To get the best results from container-grown roses, you also need to pay prompt attention to disbudding and deadheading (see p. 40), and to sucker removal. Vigorous, different-looking growths that arise from near the base – or on the stems of standard roses – should be cut out cleanly and level with the stem, using a sharp knife. If these growths, or suckers, are left they will crowd out the chosen variety. To distinguish a sucker, count the number of leaflets and compare it with the rest of the plant; the color and texture of the leaves will be different too.

To get bigger blooms on large-flowered Hybrid tea roses, disbud them. Pick off the secondary flower buds as soon as they can be handled. The longer you delay this, the less the benefit.

Deadheading is particularly important for rose varieties grown for their blooms, especially Hybrid tea and Floribunda roses. Do not deadhead roses grown for their autumn hips.

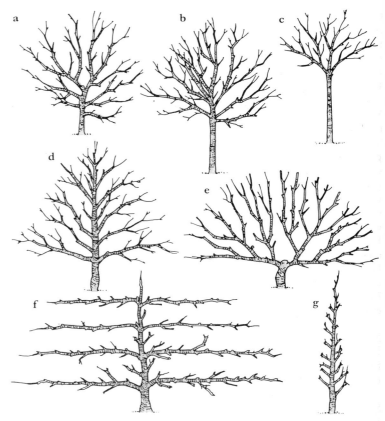

Pruning Hybrid tea roses (below)
1 On a newly planted Hybrid tea rose, you will need to prune each stem back to two buds from the base. **2** Always cut just above a plump, outward-facing bud, using sharp pruners.

Pruning climbing roses (above)
1 After planting a climbing rose, identify the weak and strong stems.
2 Prune weak growths back to about 10 cm/4 in and sturdier stems to about 45–60 cm/18–24 in.

Training for shape

Soft-growth plants can be allowed to develop naturally but woody ones are usually trained into a particular shape. It helps if you can buy them already partly trained. The following forms are commonly used in container-growing, and are achieved by a combination of pruning, clipping and supporting techniques.

(a) Bush
A crown or head of shoots and branches on a short trunk. Ideal form for a freestanding container plant; needs less pruning than other forms. Used for fruit trees, it produces a good weight of fruit.

(b) Half-standard and (c) standard
Simply bush forms with the branches starting much further up the single stem or trunk – a long stem for a standard, an intermediate one for a half-standard. The actual stem lengths vary according to the type of plant. Standards make good specimen plants, but are prone to being blown over. Their height may make them hard to spray and to prune. Half-standards are easier to manage, but are still tall enough for other, lower plants to be grown in the same container.

(d) Pyramid
A popular, compact shape for fruit trees, shrubs like *Prunus* and for decorative plants, this has a wide base, tapering toward the top. Useful for freestanding containers.

Wall-trained: (e) fan and (f) espalier
Training against a wall or fence protects a plant by giving it warmer conditions. It also enables you to get the maximum crop from a narrow space. Fans, with branches radiating out from the base, and espaliers, with opposite pairs of horizontal branches, can be trained on horizontal wires. The main branches of fans are best tied to canes and then fitted to the wires. Flowering and fruiting occurs evenly on these forms.

(g) Cordon
The oblique single-stem cordon, set at an angle of 45°, is little used in containers, since the weight of fruit can overbalance the plant and its pot. The upright single-stem, however, is a popular form for such plants as tomatoes. Cordons can either be grow in freestanding pots, or against a wall or fence, with appropriate support.

Topiary
Clipping tub-grown evergreens into decorative shapes, such as animals or spirals, is an old practice. Keep the shape balanced, and tapering toward the top, so that there is no chance that the container could be blown over.

Supporting, pruning and training fruit
Because of the great variations in habit and cropping among fruit-bearing plants, the methods of support, pruning and training are particularly important.

Support
Bush, standard and half-standard fruit trees are usually supported by a stake and one or two tree ties. Bush apples are sometimes given a tall stake so that the heavily laden branches can be supported with strings, maypole-fashion. Peaches and nectarines can be fan-trained against a wall for protection, but in warm areas and in sheltered sites bush forms are better because they are easier to prune.

Straight-stemmed cane fruits with an upright habit, like raspberry, can be kept in place with a triangle of canes (see p. 38). Train sprawling cane fruits like loganberry along horizontal wires attached to a wall or between posts (see opposite); this method is also sometimes adopted for grape vines. Vine-forming grapes, grown in warm, sheltered sites, can combine considerable beauty with utility when carefully trained on a vertical self-supporting frame.

Pruning
Provided that you choose suitable varieties and trained shapes at the outset, the pruning required by fruit trees and bushes will follow a few broad rules.

Summer pruning
In summer cordon apples and pears and espalier or fan-trained peaches and nectarines need their new growths shortened, to leave three to five leaves on each new shoot (above).

On summer-fruiting raspberries cut canes that have borne fruit and weak growths down to soil level as soon as picking ceases.

Winter pruning
Bush, cordon and espaliered apples and pears are 'spur-pruned'. This means cutting the side-shoots back to within one or two buds of the permanent main branch during fall and winter (a). Leave the main stem of cordon fruits uncut until it reaches the required height, then cut it back cleanly to a well-formed bud.

Berry fruits like cherries and plums grown as bushes should be only lightly pruned, cutting out weak and crossing shoots, and dead, diseased or inward-growing stems.

Train loganberries on wires so that older, fruiting stems grow up and along one side with younger growths on the other. Prune in fall or early winter: cut out the stems that have borne fruit and tie in replacement new growths (b).

The side-shoots of grape vines, when grown with a single main vine, are cut back to within one bud of the main stem, some time between harvesting and leaf fall. Do not leave it later than this, because vines bleed badly when the sap is beginning to rise.

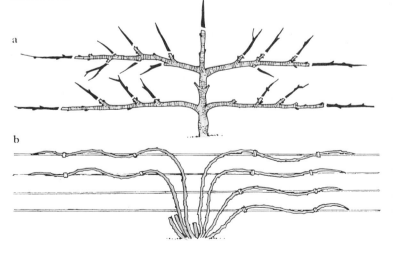

a

b

Supporting, training and tidying vegetables

Certain of the vegetable plants suitable for container growing require special treatment in order to produce their best crops.

TOMATOES

Tall varieties grown as single-stem cordons supported by either a cane or a growing frame need regular tying.

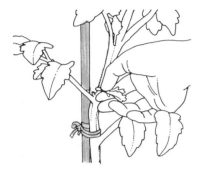

Side-shooting

Carefully cut out side growths that arise from the leaf joints, as soon as you see them, with a sharp, clean knife or pull away with finger and thumb (above). This will ensure early fruiting.

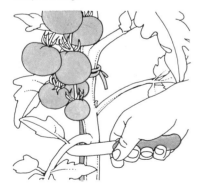

Deleafing

Do this in seasons when the fruits are slow to ripen. When the first fruit does change color, carefully cut upward with a knife to remove all the leaves under the bottom truss *except* the leaf immediately below it. Repeat the process under the second truss as soon as the first fruit on it begins to ripen. Continue the technique up the plant.

Stopping

When the plant has formed four fruit trusses, or reached the top of its support – whichever is the sooner – cut out the growing point at the second leaf above the top fruit truss. This allows the top fruits time to ripen before frosts.

Mulching

Carried out on bush tomatoes as well as squash, ridge cucumbers, and when strawberries are grown on the soil in large containers. Lay slug bait, then place straw, felt or cellulose matting or plastic sheeting on the soil under ripening fruits to keep them clean and to help to conserve moisture (above). It should fit right up against the stem, except on strawberry plants where a 4–5 cm/ 1½–2 in diameter gap should be left around the stem.

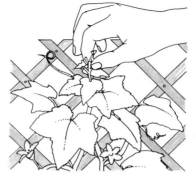

CUCUMBERS

According to the variety and the site, ridge cucumbers can either be grown flat on the soil surface, or can be trained up sticks or netting; the latter will chiefly be used in containers.

Stopping

Stop varieties trained up canes or netting when the leading shoot reaches about 90–120 cm/36–48 in by cutting or pinching out the growing point (above). The resulting side-shoots that arise from the main stem should be stopped at one leaf beyond a fruit, and secondary side-shoots stopped at one leaf.

SQUASH
Pollination

Early in the season, when there are few insects about, the female flowers – those with an embryo fruit below – will need to be pollinated by hand. Use a paint brush to transfer the yellow dust, or pollen, from the male flowers – those without an embryo fruit – to the female. One male flower can pollinate three females. In a cold summer repeat this on two or three successive days to ensure fertilization. (Use the same technique to pollinate flowers of self-sterile fruit plants, see pp. 150–53.)

Pollution problems in town gardens

Shiny-leaved evergreens will benefit from being washed clean of the soot and grime deposits of the winter. Soft soap in water followed by a clean water rinse, sprayed through a hose fitted with a rose, is most effective. If large-leaved plants such as *Fatsia* are very grimy, and the weather is too dry for rain, clean them carefully by hand with a soft cloth, leaf by leaf.

During the middle of winter, when the worst of the grime is deposited in foggy conditions, protect hairy-leaved plants. Set plastic sheeting or muslin on a light framework around the plant. However, it is best not to try to grow hairy-leaved plants in cities, since it is impossible to remove grime from them.

Potting mixes tend to become acid in town conditions, due to sulphur deposits. Unless you are growing acid-lovers, such as *Rhododendron*, you will need to correct the acid with carefully chosen fertilizer (see pp. 36–37) – nitro-chalk, for instance, instead of sulphate of ammonia.

Propagation

To keep containers filled, you must sooner or later replace some of your plants. Buying substitutes will be expensive; providing your own is cheaper and often allows greater choice. But before you start a program of propagation, or plant-increasing, think about the types and number of plants that you will require and whether you can actually produce them. Bear in mind: the time that you must allow between propagation and having plants ready for display (in general, the longer-lived the plant, the longer it takes to reach planting-out size); the availability of seeds, or of plants from which to take cuttings; whether you have the facilities, especially for plants with unusual needs; and the best method to use. Above all, do not underestimate the time and attention that young plants require.

Plant lifespans

If well looked after, kept in the right conditions, and repotted when necessary, many woody-stemmed conifers, trees and shrubs can last at least 20 years. Fruit trees and bushes should be productive for 7 to 15 years. Strawberries are best replaced after two or three years. Many herbaceous perennials, including alpines and water plants, need lifting, dividing and replanting after between two and five years. Seed-raised bedding plants are usually grown for a season only, then discarded, like many vegetables grown and consumed in the same year.

In other words, the plants you will need to propagate regularly are the short-term bedding plants and vegetables, and strawberries, although you will also need to propagate to replace shrubs and trees, once past their best.

Growing from seed

Many plants cannot be raised by any other method. Those grown from seed are usually genetically different from each other as well as from their parents, and can show visible variations. The seeds known as F_1 hybrid, which usually cost more than the standard strains, produce vigorous, healthy and reasonably uniform seedlings that crop well. Their own progeny, however, are variable and often inferior, so never bother to save the seed of F_1 hybrids.

By using seed, you can raise large numbers of plants, and you will not need to keep stock plants to provide cuttings. Seeds need a minimum of storage space.

Vegetative methods

These techniques – cuttings, division, using bulbs or tubers – become necessary with those plants that will not flower, or do not breed true, from seed. Plants increased in these ways are usually identical to the parent plant, and can be faithfully reproduced generation after generation, which means that a particularly fine plant can be reliably increased.

Since bad features as well as good are repeated, you must propagate only from plants with the right characteristics, and which are healthy, because certain virus and other diseases, such as wilt, can pass in the sap from one generation to the next. The number of plants that you can raise is limited by the availability of suitable propagating material. You will, of course, need access to good stock plants, and should always select young, vigorous, growing parts of the plants. Plants raised by vegetative methods take a shorter time to reach maturity than those raised from seed.

Choosing the best method

Exploit the natural tendencies of plants. Herbaceous perennials, for instance, form clumps, which can be lifted during the resting stage in the fall or spring, split up into several pieces, and replanted. Most bulbs and corms form small replicas, which can be pulled away from them, and grown on, but some bulbs, such as *Muscari*, also simply seed themselves. While many tubers form clumps, which can be split up, they also throw up shoots that are suitable for cuttings.

If a plant can be increased by any of several ways, select the method best suited to the season and the circumstances. For example, some varieties of *Rhododendron*, which are commercially increased by the difficult technique of grafting, can also be propagated by layering. This can be done with the minimum of fuss in the open air, and whereas grafting would usually take place in spring, layering can be carried out in spring, summer or fall. Another versatile breeder is *Forsythia*. For normal purposes, take hardwood cuttings in fall and root them outdoors, but semiripe cuttings can be taken too, in summer, and rooted indoors or in a frame.

Budding, bud-grafting and grafting must be used for certain plants such as apples and some roses, but are seldom done by amateurs since it may be difficult to obtain suitable rootstock, and specialized facilities and much skill are needed. For these, it is simpler to buy new plants.

Ferns are increased by means of spores, though some can also be propagated by division (the propagation of ferns is dealt with separately, on page 138).

Facilities and equipment

What you will need for propagation depends on the type and number of plants that you are dealing with. For designs of long-lived trees and shrubs, the replacements should be minimal; plants that can be raised outdoors without protection, like herbaceous perennials, also require only simple propagation facilities.

Self-watering devices and capillary watering kits (see p. 35) are needed for average smallscale use only if you are going to leave plants unattended for long periods in spring and summer.

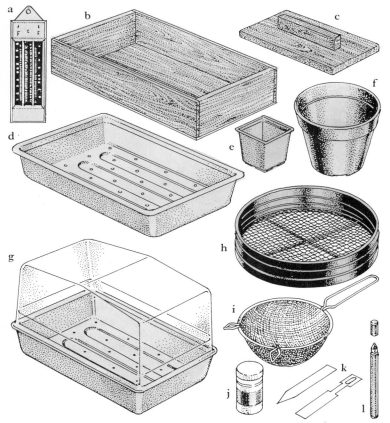

Raising from seed

Choose the best varieties for local conditions, for the season, and for container-growing (see pp. 95–157, and the information on the seed packets). Sow seed at the right time. To avoid later confusion, always label a container with the name of the plant, the variety, and the sowing and potting up dates.

Some seeds are available not only in their natural raw state but also pelleted – coated with a soluble material containing fertilizer and fungicide. This increases their size and makes them easier to space out when sowing, but they are more expensive.

Seed can be collected by cutting off the dry seed pods or capsules just before they open, complete with stalk, and hanging them upside down in a paper bag. Leave until they burst, then shake the dried seeds into the bag. The pods of large-seeded plants, such as beans, can be spread out to dry on paper on a tray.

In situ sowing

Used for hardy plants, mainly vegetables, this involves sowing the seed where the plants will mature – in other words, outdoors. There are slight variations in the technique, depending on the size of seeds and their individual requirements.

Essential propagating equipment

Thermometer (**a**); containers, including seed flats (**b, d, e, f**); presser (**c**); screen for sieving together homemade mix (**h**); kitchen sieve with 3 mm/⅛ in mesh, for sifting mix over seeds (**i**); rooting powder, to stimulate root formation (**j**); labels (**k**); indelible marker (**l**). (See also pp. 20–21.)

A propagator (**g**) can be used to germinate seeds, grow on seedlings, and root cuttings. It will keep them in a warm, moist atmosphere. Either plant directly in its base, or set a number of pots and flats inside it. For seeds, an alternative is to cover their flat or pot with glass or plastics. Pots or flats of cuttings can be enclosed in a clear polythene sheet or bag supported with hoops of wire so as not to touch the plants and encourage fungus.

An electric propagator with a heated base controlled by a thermostat can be used on an indoor window sill to maintain high temperatures at a low cost. In summer, with the heat turned off, it can be used like an ordinary propagator.

A garden frame or a cloche, minimum internal height 30 cm/12 in, may be useful for protecting small plants in seed flats and 'hardening off' indoor-raised plants to outdoor conditions.

Large seeds

Soak the seeds for two hours in tepid water, to help germination. Crock and fill a 20–25 cm/8–10 in diameter pot to within 2 cm/¾ in of the rim with moist standard potting mix. **1** Make six holes 2.5–5 cm/1–2 in deep around the edge of the pot. **2** Drop a seed in each one. **3** Replace mix over the holes with a dibble. Place the pots on a firm surface in a warm, sheltered spot and water them through a rose. **4** Lay a piece of paper over them and cover it with a sheet of plastic or glass weighted down with a stone, to protect from animals and heavy rain. Slow-germinating seeds may need a further watering after several days. Remove glass and paper as soon as seedlings appear.

Medium and small seeds
Prepare a 20–25 cm/8–10 in pot as for large seeds, and lightly firm with a presser, to leave a level surface. Water the mix through a fine rose and allow it to drain. **1** Sow seeds thinly, a pinch at a time between finger and thumb. **2** Sift onto them a layer of mix, double their own depth or, on pelleted seeds, equal to their depth. Damp the surface, using a sprayer. Cover with paper and glass or plastics (remove when seedlings show). Water, as for large seeds, if necessary.

You can sow lettuce, initially quite thickly, in this way, but you should thin the seedlings when about 2 cm/¾ in high, to leave single plants 2.5–5 cm/1–2 in apart. Thin them again when the leaves touch, to leave three or four to a 25 cm/10 in pot. Transplant the thinnings to another pot – or eat them.

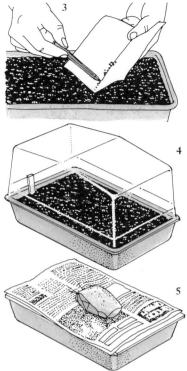

sized seeds in a piece of paper folded to form a chute, and gently ease them off with a pencil, so that they are evenly scattered over the surface. Cover them with a thin sprinkling of sieved seed mix, press lightly and moisten the surface. **4** If using a propagator, put on the lid. **5** Alternatively, lay a sheet of glass on top of the flat, followed by a piece of paper folded double and a stone. Keep warm and moist, watering if necessary by standing the seed flat in water, or using a fine rose in a propagator. When seedlings show, remove the propagator lid, or glass and paper. Shade the seedlings from strong sunlight.

Before sowing very fine seed, scatter fine sand over the surface. This not only helps you to see the seed as you sow it, but also will not stick to the presser when you firm the seeds into the surface; do not cover them with seed mix after sowing. Proceed as above.

Sowing in seed flats and pricking out
The method used for most seed-raised bedding plants. The seeds are sown and placed under cover – in a propagator, frame or cloche, or indoors on a sunny window sill. As soon as they have grown into seedlings large enough to be handled, they are pricked out or potted up into other flats or their outdoor containers.

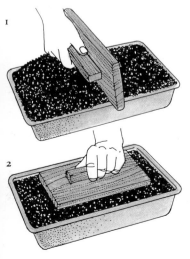

Sowing seeds to grow under cover
Cover the bottom of a clean seed flat or a propagator base with a shallow layer of fine, washed gravel or clean crocks. Fill almost to the rim with seed mix. If this is soil-based, firm it at the edges and corners. **1** Add more seed mix, piling it at one end, then smooth off the surface with a presser. **2** Lightly firm with the presser, to leave the surface at least 3 mm/⅛ in below the rim. Peat-based mixes should be smoothed off without firming. Water through a fine rose, and allow to drain. **3** Place medium-

Pricking out
Water the seedlings by standing their container in a shallow tray of water, and then allow them to drain. Prepare more seed flats, as for sowing, but use moist standard potting mix. **1** With a fine dibble or a label, gently ease out a clump of seedlings, and separate the roots, taking particular care not to damage them. **2** Pick up a seedling by the leaves, never by the stem, since pinching the stem can lead to infection. Transfer each seedling to a dibble hole large enough to take the roots completely – for most flowering annual plants the holes should be 4 cm/1½ in apart. **3** Firm the seedlings in with the dibble. The seedlings of spreading plants should be pricked out into 7.5 cm/3 in pots of standard potting mix.

Division

Perennials such as *Doronicum* and *Hosta* form large clumps that increase in size with age. These can be split up to give a number of plants when they are removed from their containers for repotting in fall, or just before growth begins again in spring. Another form of division involves offsets – single, short, compressed stems that spring up at or just below ground level from some bulbs and a few other plants. They can be separated from the parent with a sharp knife.

Many bulbs, like lilies, *Narcissus* and tulips, and corms such as *Gladiolus* form small new bulbs and corms alongside the parent, from which they can be separated. This is best done when the foliage has died down, or when repotting in the fall. Iris rhizomes can be split up in summer and potted up; ensure that each one has a fan of leaves attached.

Individual tubers, such as potatoes, can be cut into sections to form two or more new plants. Each piece should have at least one shoot, or 'eye'. Carry out the cutting with a sharp knife, at planting time, dusting the cut surfaces with a fungicide to prevent rotting. Plant them as described on page 31 or 149.

Thicket-forming shrubs such as *Kerria* can be increased by means of suckers – rooted shoots that arise from below soil level. In raspberries these are called 'spawn'. Do not, however, try to propagate from the suckers that emanate from *grafted* plants, such as Hybrid tea or Floribunda roses, since they probably spring from the rootstock alone.

fingers or a hand-fork. Cut them from a main root so that they have some root attached (below). Shorten each sucker to a plump bud about 20 cm/8 in above soil level and pot up in fresh potting mix, three or four to a 25 cm/10 in pot, at about the same depth as before. Water, to settle in. Protect from frost.

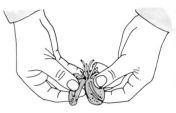

Bulblets and cormlets
Above Separate the new bulbs or corms from the parent by pulling them apart once the bulb has been lifted from the container. Discard any that are soft, spongy or diseased. Pot up the rest in fresh potting mix (see p. 28). Most bulblets and cormlets will need to be grown on for two years before they reach flowering size.

Cuttings

Many garden plants are increased by cuttings, and these are usually best rooted under cover. The methods vary according to the type of plant – cuttings are taken at different stages of development; various parts of the plant may be used but, in practice, stem or tip cuttings are most common (see pp. 94–153 for notes on the type of cutting for individual plants.

Brand-name cutting mixes are available to plant them in. Alternatively, make your own sandy cutting mix by combining equal amounts of sphagnum peat (or good sedge peat), sifted through a screen, and coarse sand that has a low lime content. Half peat and half vermiculite or perlite will also do. It is advisable to crock the pot before filling with cutting mix.

About 12 hours before taking cuttings, give the parent plants a good watering to ensure that the cuttings will be fully charged with moisture. Never use shoots that are flowering or carrying flower buds, or rooting will be poor.

Soft stem or tip cuttings come from plants whose stems are soft enough to be crushed between finger and thumb. They are taken from the base of the plant in spring and from side-shoots in summer.

Semiripe cuttings are young growths, complete with tips, with firm, not fully hardened stems that bend without being brittle. They are taken in summer. Tips and pipings are variations of the technique and are used for specific types of plant.

Hardwood cuttings come from stems that are brittle enough to be snapped, and are taken in fall. Some shrubs, trees, alpines and herbaceous perennials – for instance, *Cordyline* or *Phlox* – can easily be increased by taking root cuttings.

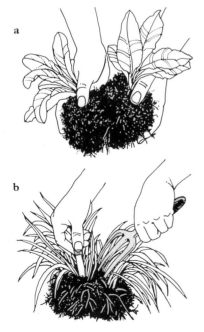

a

b

Division
Left Remove the plant from its container. The roots of a young plant can be pulled apart by hand (a) or with a hand-fork. Check that each of the sections has healthy roots and some new growth, and pot it up in fresh potting mix. Impale a larger plant with a hand-fork, or grasp it firmly in one hand. With the other hand, prise off young, outer, rooted sections using a knife or another hand-fork (b), and pot them up in a crocked pot.

Suckers and spawn
In fall carefully remove the parent plant from its container. Select vigorous young shoots growing near the outside edge of the rootball, and gently tease them out from the root mass with your

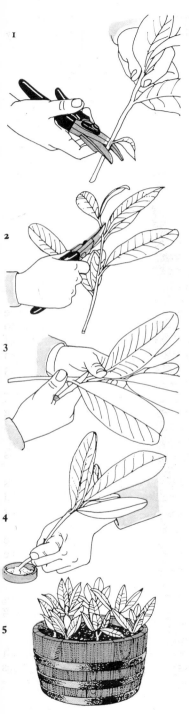

Hardwood and soft cuttings

Taken in the fall, hardwood cuttings are used mainly for deciduous trees and shrubs. With sharp pruners remove mature but young growths about 30 cm/12 in long. **1** Cut each one squarely below the bottom leaf joint. **2** If the stem is immature and soft, shorten the tip to about 3 mm/⅛ in above a bud or shoot. **3** Trim off bottom leaves, if they are still on. **4** Dip the bottom end in rooting powder. **5** Insert cuttings in dibble holes about 15 cm/6 in deep and 10 cm/ 4 in apart in sandy cutting mix in a 25 cm/10 in diameter crocked container. Water them, using a fine rose. Place in sheltered spot and protect from frost. Put in the open when mild conditions return.

Soft stem or tip cuttings are usually taken from shrubs and herbaceous perennials in spring and summer. Use a sharp knife to remove soft new growths about 7–10 cm/2½–4 in long, which should include a growing point. Then cut the stem squarely, immediately below the bottom leaf joint. Remove the lowest two or three leaves flush with the stem, taking care not to tear it. Dip the cut end into rooting powder made for soft cuttings. Prepare a 7.5 cm/3 in diameter crocked pot filled with sandy cutting mix. Insert each cutting in a dibble hole to half its length, three or four of them around the edge of the pot. Water, using a fine rose. Place in a propagator or on an indoor window sill shaded from the sun and maintain moist, warm conditions – 13–16°C/55–60°F. The cuttings should root within 10–21 days: you can tell that they have rooted if they show new green at the center. Pot up singly in 7.5 cm/3 in pots filled with standard mix.

Semiripe heel cuttings

1 Pull away from the parent plant a 7.5–15 cm/3–6 in side-shoot, with a piece of the older stem attached – this is the 'heel'. **2** With a knife, neaten off any stringy rind attached to the heel. **3** Trim the bottom 1–2 cm/½–¾ in of the stem or, on large-leaved evergreens, pull off the two lowest leaves. Dip the heel end in rooting powder and insert in one of three to six dibble holes around the edge of a 7.5–10 cm/3–4 in diameter crocked pot of cutting mix. Water and keep moist, under the same conditions as soft cuttings. Pot up when rooted, which should take three weeks to six months.

A semiripe node cutting is similar to a heel cutting, but is severed from the parent plant with a knife. It can be a side-shoot or a main stem. Cut the end squarely, just below the bottom leaf joint, and remove the lower leaves.

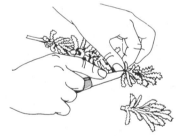

Tips

Above Taken from heather. With a knife, cut off a non-flowering 4–5 cm/1½–2 in side-shoot or main stem, just above a bud or leaf, either squarely across, or with a heel. Do not trim it or remove any leaves, but dip the end in rooting powder. Insert cuttings in 1 cm/½ in dibble holes about 2.5 cm/1 in apart in cutting mix in a 15–20 cm/6–8 in deep pot. Water them in, and keep them shaded and moist. Rooting should take six to eight weeks.

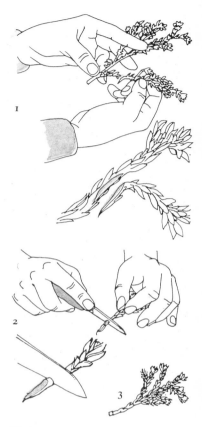

Pipings

Below Taken from pinks and carnations. Gently bend a main, non-flowering stem at the joint 7.5–10 cm/ 3–4 in below the tip and pluck out the top part. Dip the end in rooting preparation, and in a 10–15 cm/ 4–6 in deep pot insert it 2.5 cm/1 in deep in sandy cutting mix. Keep warm on an indoor window sill. Rooting should take 21–28 days.

Root cuttings

In winter, remove the plant from the container and shake off enough mix to expose at least one pencil-thick root. **1** Cut this out carefully with a sharp knife or pruners. **2** Slice the thick piece of root into 4–5 cm/1½–2 in lengths, cut squarely at one end and obliquely at the other. **3** Insert the cuttings in cutting mix in a flat, about 2.5–4 cm/1–1½ in apart, or six to a 13 cm/5 in pot: either drop them vertically into dibble holes, oblique edge to the bottom, or lay them horizontally. Cover them with mix. In both cases, they should be 1–2 cm/½–¾ in below the soil surface. Place on an indoor window sill, potting up singly as soon as you see growth.

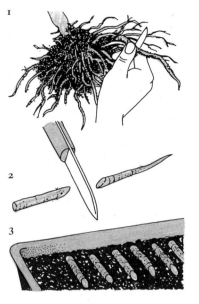

Layering

In this method a young (one- or two-year old) stem is damaged by being bent or scored – carefully – to stimulate root growth from that point. It may be carried out at any time, although the start of the growing season is best. It needs no elaborate equipment, and there is little risk of loss. The two main drawbacks are the time some plants take to root – up to two years – and the fact that suitable young shoots may not be within easy reach.

The technique of air layering, often used for houseplants, is rarely tried outdoors, because wind creates problems.

Layering

To increase shrubs, such as *Rhododendron*. Select a young branch within easy reach of the ground. **1** With a sharp knife remove a 5 cm/2 in long sliver of bark from the underside of a two-year-old stem; do this about 30–40 cm/12–16 in from the tip (10–13 cm/4–5 in for dwarf varieties). Prepare a well-crocked pot or flat of potting mix with a hollow in the surface, and place it under the prepared branch. **2** Peg the cut stem down into the hollow, using a piece of bent wire, and stake it. Cover the stem in the hollow with more mix. Keep it moist and protect it from hard frost. **3** When the new layer is rooted and growing, sever it from the parent plant where the stem enters the mix, preferably just behind a plump underground bud. Pot it up in standard mix in a crocked pot.

Tip layering

For cane fruits such as loganberries. In midsummer select a healthy new rod, cut off the last-formed one or two fully opened leaves and bend the rod down, to thread the growing point 5–7.5 cm/2–3 in down through the hole in the bottom of a 13 cm/5 in pot. **1** Place this pot inside a crocked 20 cm/8 in pot quarter-filled with potting mix. Position the growing point in the space between the two pots, 5–7.5 cm/2–3 in below their rims. The rims should end up level with each other. **2** Press the inner pot down with one hand and fill the cavity between the pots with potting mix. Stand the pots on a firm, level surface and keep the mix moist. **3** After 12–16 weeks new growth should appear above the mix surface, which is a sign that rooting has taken place. Sever the rooted tip layer from the parent with a knife where it enters the hole at the base of the small pot. Remove inner pot. Pot the new plant up in standard mix in a crocked pot.

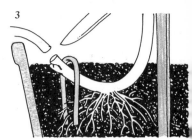

Runners and plantlets

Some plants, such as strawberries (left), saxifrages and some violets, produce embryo plants on long thin stems, or runners. You can easily increase them, in summer, by pegging down the plantlets, as in layering, into individual 7.5 cm/3 in pots of potting mix. As long as the parent plant, the runners and the mix are kept moist, rooting will take place within a few weeks. Then cut through runners and pot on plantlets.

Keeping plants healthy

The key to healthy, vigorous plants lies in good selection, careful cultivation and protection against extreme weather conditions or other forms of injury, as well as against marauders and pests and diseases.

Selecting the right plants

To ensure that you begin with strong, trouble-free plants, obtain both seeds and plants from reputable suppliers and start them off at the correct season. Where possible, inspect plants before buying and avoid any that are weak, spindly, wilted or have poor roots (if these can be seen on removing the plant from its pot). A strong root system is in general a good indication of a healthy plant; beware, however, of pot-bound plants – those with a mass of roots struggling for food and water to sustain a large top. Yellowing and dropping of lower leaves provides an initial clue to an unhealthy condition.

Where practical, select disease-resistant varieties of seeds and plants, especially with vegetable crops like tomato and lettuce; reputable nurseries and seed catalogues indicate the most resistant strains.

Relate your choice of plants to the conditions of your site, particularly as regards their tolerance of sun, shade, wind and drafts, taking into account any local extremes of temperature. Ensure that the plants' size and growth rate are appropriate to the height and space available and also that the containers you select are the right size for the plant being grown. The container itself must have adequate drainage (see p. 24) as waterlogged or poorly drained containers cause root loss. Check that you are using the correct planting medium (see p. 22): that its physical properties and chemical content (acid, alkaline or neutral) suit the plant, that it has adequate food reserves and is free from poisons or pollution. Always buying potting mix of a reputable make is the best way of ensuring that these conditions are met.

If you are propagating your own stock, use only healthy plants and take trouble over careful preparation, planting and spacing of seedlings and cuttings (see pp. 45–50).

Care and cultivation

Neglect and careless cultivation are as much to blame for unhealthy plants as are pests and diseases. To safeguard the health of your plants, pay prompt and meticulous attention to operations such as potting, feeding, watering, pruning, training and timely deadheading, all of which are covered in more detail on pages 22–44. The importance of strict hygiene cannot be underestimated – removing debris and weeds; picking or cutting out any dead and diseased flowers, leaves, shoots, stems and even fruits; using sterile potting mixes; disinfecting knives in particular, as well as re-usable pots and other equipment; and so on. Always use tools carefully.

Diagnosing symptoms of neglect

SYMPTOM	CAUSE
Leaves wilting and drooping (1)	Excess dryness
Scorching of leaf margins Leaf drop and stunted hard growth Seedlings dried off and burnt out Potting mix dry and shrunk, with gaps round the edge of container Flower buds dropping, fruits failing to swell	Lack of watering or haphazard watering
Roots standing in water after heavy persistent rain Leaves wilting and drooping (2) In severe cases blueing or yellowing and dropping of leaves	Inadequate drainage
Reduced plant vigor Leaves small and pale, sometimes yellowing and with reddish, purplish or brownish margins Yellowing between leaf veins Plants – and flowers, if present – small and stunted Fruits, if present, small and highly colored	Starvation
Plants thin, often weak, tall and spindly Leaves of one plant touching and intermingling with those of the next Branches and stems forming an impenetrable mass of shoots and leaves, often accompanied by diseases that thrive on such weakened plants, in dark airless conditions	Overcrowding
Mutilated or straggly plants	Bad pruning, poor training or lack of support
Severe distortion or death of plants (after using hormone-type weedkiller); leaf burn and scorch (after using contact weedkiller).	Careless use of weedkillers

In hot weather, plants may need protection from the sun and should be moved into the shade. Spraying the leaves and the ground around the plants, in the morning before the sun is strong, charges plants with moisture before the heat of the day. This helps to overcome wilting: wilting plants and loss of moisture hinder flower setting and fruit swelling, and often result in bud, flower and fruit dropping. Spraying again in the evening will replenish moisture lost during the day. The moist conditions created by spraying and misting are unfavorable to pests like red spider mites and thrips; however, you should avoid excess moisture on the leaves of crops like tomato at night, especially in late summer as this is when fungus diseases like blight are most likely to attack.

See that plants that may be slightly tender for your area are overwintered correctly and given adequate protection from frost (see individual plant entries in the fourth chapter). Take the necessary precautions against cold weather in good time. A plant may never recover from the effects of an early frost.

Chemical protection

Chemicals give most effective protection against pests and diseases when applied as a preventive measure. It is worth spraying routinely, using a brand-name combined spray to keep the most common threats at bay, or against the most 'likely' problems to attack specific container-grown plants in the hope that you will never need to resort to remedial treatment; for example, on fruit trees, routine spraying against capsid bugs with dormant oil in winter pays dividends by killing off the eggs before they can hatch out into nymphs. However, if your plants *are* threatened – by pests, diseases or disorders – the best method of dealing with it is prompt remedial control. A relatively mild disease like powdery mildew can be reliably controlled by swift treatment; in this case it may be cheaper to take a gamble than to apply preventive sprays.

The table of control measures against pests and diseases on page 56 directs you to the best treatment to adopt. The most commonly used 'protective chemicals' include the following:

Physical protection for plants

WEATHER CONDITIONS	DAMAGE TO PLANTS	FORMS OF PROTECTION
Rain and hail	Rain damages young plants especially; hail cuts leaves to shreds.	Place fine mesh netting or lath screening, supported on a framework, over the plants.
Snow	Weighs down branches; distorts the shape of plants.	Place wide, spreading plants under a tunnel structure made from wood or wire hoops, supporting strong but fine mesh netting. Tie netting round narrow, columnar plants.
Strong sun	Wilting; scorching and scalding of leaves, especially if covered with water droplets left after rain or watering; rapid drying out of porous pots.	Spray the leaves with water at night and early in the mornings; use anti-desiccant sprays on newly potted plants; slow down the rapid drying out of porous pots by standing them inside a larger pot and filling the cavity between the two with wet peat, kept moist by watering.
Winds and draft	Wilting, scorching, browning and leaf loss.	Provide shelter by fences, walls, hedges, or by screens of shrubby, hardy plants, protect with fine mesh netting or burlap attached to light wooden frame. Tie stems of tall plants to horizontal wires or trellis.
Frost	Damaged roots; scorched leaves, shoots, buds and flowers; cracked or burst containers.	Move containers indoors or under cover; outdoors, protect roots and containers by placing a 30 cm/12 in layer of straw or bracken round the sides and top; tie on or hold in place with boards and netting. Lie pots on their sides and cover with 60 cm/24 in layer of straw where winters are very severe; use fine mesh netting or plastic sheeting round plant and container against late spring frost (so long as this is not lower than −2°C/28°F).
Heavy shade and pollution	Reduced vigor.	Use resistant species and varieties (see the fourth chapter), or avoid exposing your plants to extremes of either.

Pesticides and insecticides – used to control insect pests and other creatures at any stage of their life cycle

Fungicides – applied to arrest fungal diseases

Weedkillers and herbicides – for the control of weeds in and around containers

Paints and sealants – prevent rotting in plant wounds such as saw cuts (be sure to use a brand-name sealant or paint approved for plant use)

Antidesiccants – used to prevent wilting in hot weather when moving or repotting large plants

Disinfectants and sterilizers – used to decontaminate tools, containers and soil

Deterrents – used to keep birds and other animals off plants.

When buying pesticides and fungicides, make sure they are not only suitable for control of the problem in question, but also that they are unlikely to harm the plant being protected. Systemic pesticides and fungicides are watered in or sprayed and carried through the plant in the sap; the watered-in type should be considered where it is inadvisable to cover the plant with chemicals, for example on food crops.

Chemicals can be applied dry, as dusts and granules, and in liquid form as sprays, dips, drenches and paints. Dusts are easy to use, need no mixing and normally come in puffer packs. They are particularly suitable for treating seeds, bulbs, corms and tubers as well as plants where liquid preparations are unsuitable or difficult to apply. The only drawback to the outdoor use of dusts is that weather conditions need to be extremely calm. Some herbicides are applied in the form of granules, from a pepper-pot type of dispenser.

Spraying is one of the most economical and popular ways to apply pesticides and fungicides. There are sprayers to suit most purposes, from the small pressurized hand models for a few odd plants, to large sprayers with trigger control and extension lances for high containers. Aerosols are also popular for small-scale spot applications but, although easy and convenient to use, they are an expensive way to apply chemicals.

A quick and effective way of ensuring that prepared cuttings are treated against pests and diseases is to dip them in a chemical solution before inserting them in the cutting mix. Any soil pests that attack plant roots, such as the grubs of the vine weevil, can be checked by drenching the soil around the roots with chemical solution, simply using a watering can with a rose. Drenches are also suitable for sterilizing loam before making up your own potting mix.

Using chemicals safely

1 Read labels before opening containers and always use products strictly as recommended.

2 Use gloves, goggles and protective clothing when handling any poisons. Wash hands and face well after using chemicals. If concentrated chemical gets into eyes or mouth, seek medical advice immediately.

3 Choose calm weather conditions to avoid wind drifts of dusts and sprays; overcast conditions to avoid sun scorch; dry conditions to prevent chemicals being diluted immediately they reach branches and leaves. Avoid spraying when bees, pets and children are around.

4 Mix pesticides outdoors or in a well-ventilated place so that you do not inhale the fumes. Keep them well agitated. Clean and wash equipment thoroughly after use.

5 Seal containers immediately after use, making sure that they are correctly labelled and have their instructions attached. Store chemicals in a safe place, out of the reach of children and pets.

6 Do not use sprayers and containers used to apply herbicides on growing plants, in case any residue remains.

Protecting plants against marauders

Plants are also at risk from bird, pet and slug damage. Although it is not easy to protect fruit trees, bushes and plants from birds completely, they are best netted both during winter, to prevent bud stripping, as well as throughout the fruiting season to protect the crop. Deterrent sprays and bird-scaring devices are all useful for a time, after which birds tend to regain courage and damage ensues. Black thread suspended and intertwined through the branches will deter small birds.

Cats may be another nuisance, causing damage both by their scratching and by using the soil in containers as a cat litter. Seedlings and small plants may be damaged and scratched up as well as the potting mix scratched out of newly planted containers. Small branches and young shoots can also be damaged by cats climbing up trees, shrubs and wall plants. If a cat regularly uses a container as its litter, the plants in it may turn yellow and eventually collapse. The plants themselves can be protected with netting, and deterrents used in the form of cat pepper and scented capsules.

A few common garden pests can be kept in check by the use of baits, like metaldehyde preparations against slugs and snails. Earwigs can be caught in hay-filled, upturned small pots placed on canes among susceptible plants, such as dahlias and chrysanthemums. The traps should be inspected daily, and the earwigs shaken out into a bucket.

Where fruit trees in particular are grown, one effective way to prevent winter moth attack is to place grease bands (from garden supply stores) round the trunks in fall, creating a barrier. The adult, egg-laying female winter moth is wingless and has to crawl up the trunks during the winter in order to lay eggs on the branches. The sticky grease bands trap these pests successfully and so prevent completion of their life cycle.

Pests and diseases

However well you look after your plants, they will always be at risk from pests and diseases. However, plants in containers, being raised off the ground and grown in a specially prepared potting mix, are less at risk than plants growing in beds of garden soil. Paying attention to hygiene and cleanliness (such as sterilizing old pots and always using sterilized potting mixes) will further minimize these risks; you should also inspect your plants regularly, especially the undersides of leaves. If a plant shows signs of being diseased or pest-ridden, isolate it from its neighbors and take prompt action.

PESTS

Container-grown plants may be attacked by a variety of bugs, but their feeding habits give clues both to their identity and to the subsequent methods of their control. Insects, for instance, feed on plants either by chewing or biting – like caterpillars and weevils – leaving stems, leaves and roots holed and eaten, or by sucking – like aphids and scale insects – often leaving plants weak and stunted. Look out for the pests near the damage, or signs like the silvery slime trails of slugs and snails. The time of year may frequently be another reliable clue.

To aid identification, the main pests likely to attack container-grown garden plants, or their characteristic damage, are shown on the following pages; some pests, which attack only specific vegetables or fruit, are described under the particular vegetable or fruit (see Chapter 4). The table on page 56 indicates the plant group(s) chiefly attacked by the individual pests, and the most effective form of control. The pesticides recommended should work well, but if you cannot get hold of them, ask your local garden supply store if there is an alternative.

It is worth remembering that, while some insects attack throughout their life, others only attack plants at certain stages in their life cycle but they are often best dealt with when at a harmless stage. You may also get an indication of the identity of a pest by the part of the plant on which it feeds – some feed only on roots, some on leaves, others on flowers and fruit. But many pests in fact attack several parts of a plant, or one species may favor leaves and growing tips while another tends to attack plant roots and stems. To this extent the divisions below should not be taken too literally – some pests could equally well appear under any one of the following groups.

Sap-sucking pests

1 Aphids Colonies of these greenish, blue or black winged or wingless insects appear on the leaves, buds and growing points of plants – often together with honeydew, a shiny, sticky coating, and sooty molds which grow upon it. Greenfly and blackfly are among the most common species. They cause puckered, deformed and yellowed leaves, distorted shoots, buds, flowers and fruit, while stunting the plant's growth. Most serious of all, they spread virus diseases. Some species feed on the roots of certain plants, like *Primula*, causing them to become stunted and pale and to wilt in the sun.

2 Adelgids These aphidlike insects cause stunted growth in conifers with small 'galls' or swellings on the shoots and stems. Honeydew and sooty molds often appear together with the galls.

3 Mealy bugs Aphidlike insects, covered with a whitish wax, can be seen feeding on and disfiguring leaves as well as stems and berries or fruit. Plants attacked become noticeably stunted and weak.

4 Woolly aphids The affected plants develop conspicuous cotton-wool-like patches on leaves, stems and sometimes roots. Underneath are the woolly aphids, which weaken and disfigure plants by feeding on the sap.

5 Scale insects Hard, brownish or grayish blisterlike scales are formed on the leaves and stems of affected plants; they cover the sap-sucking insects, which cause poor growth and loss of vigor. Honeydew and sooty molds are frequently also present. Scale insects increase rapidly in warm conditions.

6 Whitefly These pests attack many plants, and betray their presence by flying off in quick-moving clouds when disturbed. The nymph stage secretes honeydew on leaves, stems and fruit, followed by the growth of sooty molds, particularly in summer. Severely attacked plants are weak and stunted.

7 Capsid bugs These attack the young leaves and growing points of many plants. Brown spots develop, then enlarge, forming brown-edged holes and distorting and stunting plant growth. Fruit on affected trees like apple and pear are deformed, with sunken areas. It is the sap-sucking, yellowish striped nymphs that do the damage in the early stages; they mature to form bright green, winged insects.

8 Ants These quick-moving blackish or reddish-brown creatures can be clearly seen on plants and on soil, often together with aphids. Ants feed on the honeydew produced by aphids and carry aphids to fresh areas and fresh plants. This usually proves to be a more serious problem than the nuisance of the anthill, though ants also devour and disturb roots in the general vicinity of their nests/hills.

Chewing and biting insects

9 Caterpillars These larvae eat leaves, buds and shoots. They are the immature stage of various moths and butterflies, different species of which attack a wide range of plants.

The caterpillars of some tortrix moths conceal and protect themselves while feeding, with a fine webbing attached to leaves or shoots. The larvae of other moths, including the common cutworm, feed on roots and underground stems, often severing seedling shoots from their roots just below the soil surface.

10 Magpie moths Conspicuous black and white caterpillars of this moth feed on leaves in spring; plants may be left completely defoliated. The adult black and white moth has buff and orange markings.

11 Winter moths The caterpillars of the winter moth have a distinctive looping habit; the color depends on the species. They eat the folige of trees, giving the leaves brownish, curling edges, and in severe cases stripping the tree of foliage, leaving the buds holed and bored. The damage occurs mainly in late spring and early summer.

12 Leaf miners Different species attack different plants, all year round but mainly in late summer. They produce blotches or mines, frequently in the form of meandering pale or whitish lines on the leaves; a maggot-like grub is often found chewing its way through leaf tissue between the upper and lower leaf surface.

13 Vine weevils The adult, dark-colored weevils, about 1 cm/$\frac{1}{2}$ in long with a pronounced snout, hide in debris during the day and attack foliage at night, leaving it holed and eaten around the margins; they attack mainly in fall and early spring. The larvae – ivory-white grubs – feed on the roots and cause the plants to wilt.

14 Froghoppers These yellowish sucking insects are enveloped in frothy patches on leaves and new shoots. They attack mainly in spring and summer, causing wilt and distorted growth.

15 Red spider mites Minute reddish or yellowish mites feeding on leaf undersides and flowers envelop the plants with fine webbing; they cause mottling and in severe cases bronzing of leaves, and take the brightness out of flower colors. They like warm, dry conditions.

Pests that attack flowers and fruit

16 Earwigs These shiny brown creatures with a pincerlike tail feed at night on buds, petals and leaves, especially of *Clematis*, dahlias and chrysanthemums.

17 Thrips In a typical attack, the petals and leaves of summer-flowering bulbs and herbaceous plants are streaked and silvered with whitish speckles. Numerous tiny, black-winged insects are present.

18 Chafers Adult winged chafer beetles of many kinds feed mainly on flowers. The shiny blue-green rose chafer, about 1 cm/$\frac{1}{2}$ in long, feeds on rose blooms in summer, while the May chafer attacks late-flowering apple blossom. The immature whitish chafer grubs with brown heads can feed also on the roots of many plants for two to four years before they emerge as adults.

19 Wasps These familiar insects are well known for their damage to ripe fruit, either by eating out and enlarging holes left by birds or by making fresh cavities. But other forms of damage include part-eaten flower stems of herbaceous plants, usually just below the blooms.

Pests that attack roots, branches and stems

20 Weevils Common forms of damage caused by these clay-colored insects include chewing and removing the bark from shoots of fruiting as well as ornamental trees and bushes. Leaf and bud stalks are gnawed through, causing defoliation in severe cases, and roots may also be eaten. Feeding usually takes place at night and damage is most severe in spring and early summer.

21 Millipedes Slow-moving creatures with four legs to each segment of their wormlike, often coiled, bodies. One type is shiny, black and rounded, another is light gray and flattened. They may attack all year round, in mild climates, and eat roots and stems, resulting in stunted growth and wilting in sun.

22 Snails and slugs Wet conditions favor both shell-carrying snails (a) and soft-backed slugs (b); they eat young plant leaves, shoots and subterranean stems and roots. Telltale silvery slime trails remain above soil level.

In containers, the chief danger is the chewing and biting of tuberous roots, bulbs and corms. Eggs are laid just below the soil surface and are best treated at this stage.

23 Eelworms These microscopic creatures invade the leaves, stems and roots of many plants. They may attack all year round, especially in wet conditions, as they move along on the film of moisture in the sap stream. Dark patches develop on the leaves, which gradually enlarge; the leaves eventually blacken and shrivel. Newly developing shoots become stunted and in severe cases are finally aborted.

The species such as the 'root knot', which attacks plant roots, causes severe stunting and weakening and may even kill the plant. Light-colored, pinhead cysts, each containing numerous eelworms, may be visible near the roots of plants that are affected.

24 Bark- and shoot-boring beetles Stunted growth, with dead shoots and branches, is evidence of these insects. The adult is a small beetle, which in itself rarely causes damage; the chief culprits are the whitish or yellowish grubs, which can do damage all year round. They attack the bark, leaving holes, channels and galleries underneath, or they chew the shoots, which are often hollow with either a grub inside or bearing a small escape hole.

DISEASES

Three main types of organism threaten plants, some of which are fairly easy to recognize.

Fungi

Humid and overcrowded conditions encourage the spread of fungus diseases by air, water or by soil-borne spores. Diseases such as molds and mildew, with a downy or dusty covering on leaves, flowers and fruit, or bright orange and yellow colored rusts, usually on leaves, are typical of fungal damage. Some stem and root rots, together with various wilts, are also caused by fungi. Tomato blight is a specific fungus disease, encouraged by wet conditions, which causes the leaves to go black and slimy and the fruit to turn brown.

25 Gray mold (botrytis) This disease attacks leaves, stems, flowers and fruit, gaining entry by insect damage or injury. The affected tissue turns yellow and, if left, rots and develops a furry mold, which releases clouds of dustlike spores to spread infection. It may attack bulbs, causing withered, blackened leaves and buds.

26 Mildew Plants of many kinds can be attacked by one or other species of mildew, wherever conditions of warmth and moisture prevail. The threat of mildew varies from mild to serious; from powdery mildew, whose spread can be checked relatively easily, to downy mildews that occur as a whitish covering on leaves, buds and shoots, disfiguring foliage and spoiling buds, flowers and fruit. The severe types, occurring on apples and roses, should be controlled by preventive sprays as they can get under the bark and be carried over from one season to the next.

27 Black spot This is a common fungus disease confined to roses. Infection of the new leaves begins in spring as small, usually circular, black spots. These increase in size, often coalescing into large patches, and result in premature leaf fall and weakened plants. Leaves formed later in the season also become infected unless protected by monthly sprays.

28 Peach leaf curl This fungus disease can severely disfigure and weaken peach and nectarine. The first signs appear in the spring as a pale green coloration of new leaves. These turn dull crimson, become puckered, distorted and fall prematurely. Preventive sprays, one before bud burst and again just after natural leaf fall, give reasonable protection.

29 Scab A fungus disease commonly disfiguring fruit trees. The effects occur, usually in spring, as dark discolorations or spots on leaves and fruit; these spots increase in size. Severe attacks result in premature defoliation and weakening of trees.

30 Rust Fungus diseases of this type characteristically form red-brown pustules on leaves and other affected parts, and release into the air yellow and orange powdery spores to spread the disease.

31 Damping-off Warm, moist conditions – such as those necessary for germinating – are very favorable to this fungus attack on seedlings. Damping-off causes seedlings to topple over at soil level, wilt, wither and die. Outbreaks often start in patches, and may wipe out whole pots or boxes of seedlings.

Bacteria

The prevention, as well as the control, of ailments due to bacterial infection is usually more difficult than with fungi – this is due to their resistance to heat and to chemicals. Fortunately, bacterial complaints are encountered less frequently than fungus diseases, but when they strike they are often lethal.

Some of the root rots, various kinds of wilt, and canker are the main bacterial problems encountered in container growing. These diseases are spread in a similar manner to fungal ailments and hygiene is an important preventive factor.

32 Root rot and wilt Plants of most kinds can be attacked by root-rotting bacteria and fungi, resulting in discoloration and final wilting. Even though, on examination, the roots may look healthy, the plants can wilt due to fungi or bacteria blocking or damaging the water-conducting cells or tissues in the plant stems. Dirty soil, containers or tools and careless handling are common causes.

33 Stem canker Many plants with woody stems, including fruit trees, develop shrunken areas surrounded by raised, roughened bark on the main branches and stems. These cankered areas, if left, enlarge and may encircle and gradually kill the branches. Cankers can be caused by fungi as well as bacteria.

34 Virus
Viral diseases are carried in the sap, and can be spread from one plant to another by insects and by contact. There is no practical cure and so prevention is the only course of action. Ensure that you use healthy stock, and immediately destroy any plants where you suspect virus disease, to prevent infection spreading.

Virus affects plants in various ways, often causing stunting, or unusual mottling of both flowers and leaves, sometimes accompanied by severe distortion. Tomato, cucumber and dahlia mosaic and distortion in chrysanthemums are some of the more common virus diseases; all can be carried from one generation to the next in cuttings.

DISORDERS

These are ailments due to seasonal weather variations, cultivation faults or other factors of a non-infectious nature. Examples include:

35 Chlorosis This yellowing of the leaves is a form of malnutrition in acid-loving plants like hydrangeas, *Camellia* or *Rhododendron*, due to an iron deficiency induced by excess lime in the soil, potting mix, or the water supply.

Topple or weak neck This occurs in roses deficient in potash, causing the stems to bend and topple over just below the bloom.

Split fruits In outdoor tomatoes, for example, this may be caused by a wet spell following prolonged hot, dry weather.

Guide to control measures

Refer to key for explanation of plant groups (ABCDEF)

PESTS

1 **Aphids** (ABCDEF) Dust, spray, dip or drench with malathion or fenitrothion

2 **Adelgids** (A) Dust or spray with HCH

3 **Mealy Bugs** (BCDEF) Spray with HCH, malathion or oil emulsion

4 **Woolly aphids** (BCF) Spray with malathion or menazon

5 **Scale insects** (ABCDF) Spray with malathion, oil emulsion or dormant oil

6 **Whitefly** (BCD) Spray with malathion or pirimiphos methyl

7 **Capsid bugs** (BCDEF) Spray with fenitrothion, HCH or dormant oil

8 **Ants** (ABCDEF) Dust with HCH or ant killer

9 **Caterpillars** (ABCDEF) Spray with derris or fenitrothion

10 **Magpie moths** (BCD) Spray with derris, fenitrothion or HCH

11 **Winter moths** (CF) Use grease bands; spray with dormant oil

12 **Leaf miners** (BCD) Spray with diazinon or HCH

13 **Vine weevils** (ABCDEF) Dust or drench with HCH

14 **Froghoppers** (CDEF) Burn affected plants; use clean potting mixes and containers

15 **Red spider mites** (ABCDEF) Spray or dip with derris or malathion

16 **Earwigs** (CDEF) Dust with HCH; hay-pot trapping

17 **Thrips** (BCD) Spray with derris, diazinon or malathion; use dips for bulbs

18 **Chafers** (ABCDEF) Dust with HCH; knock beetles off plant and destroy

19 **Wasps** (BCDF) Destruction of nests by trained operators

20 **Weevils** (ABCDF) Dust or spray with HCH

21 **Millipedes** (ABCDEF) Dust with HCH; bait with pieces of carrot

22 **Snails and slugs** (BCDEF) Metaldehyde baits

23 **Eelworms** (CDEF) Burn affected plants; use clean potting mixes and containers

24 **Bark beetles** (ABCF) Dust with HCH

DISEASES

25 **Gray mold** (ABCDEF) Remove diseased leaves and fruits; dust or spray with benomyl, captan or thiram

26 **Mildew** (ABCDEF) Dust or spray with benomyl, copper or thiram

27 **Black spot** (Roses) Spray with benomyl, captan or copper fungicide

28 **Peach leaf curl** (Nectarine, peach) Spray with benomyl or copper fungicide

29 **Scab** (CF) Spray with benomyl, captan or copper fungicide at bud burst and 4–8 weeks later

30 **Rust** (ABCDF) Apply preventive dusts and sprays; treat affected plants with copper or thiram

31 **Damping-off** (ABCDEF) Dust seeds and potting mixes with thiram; use clean mixes and containers

32 **Root rot and wilt** (ABCDEF) Burn affected plants; propagate from healthy stock; use clean potting mixes and pots

33 **Stem canker** (CF) Cut out infected wood; apply paint or sealant to wound

34 **Virus** (ABCDEF) Remove and burn affected plants; always propagate from healthy stock

35 **Chlorosis** (All acid-lovers) Spray with iron sequestrene

Key to plant groups

A = conifers

B = evergreen trees and shrubs

C = deciduous trees and shrubs; climbers

D = annuals, biennials, perennials, bulbs and succulents

E = vegetables

F = fruit

NOTE Dormant oil should be applied only to deciduous woody plants, only when dormant, not to green leaves or stems. HCH = benzene hexachloride (which may be listed in brand-name pesticides as BHC or Lindane)

1 Aphids (greenfly)

2 Adelgid on spruce

3 Mealy bug

4 Woolly aphids

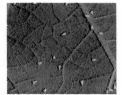
5 Scale insects

6 Whitefly

7 Capsid bug

8 Ants with aphids

9 Caterpillars

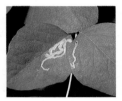
10 Magpie moth

11 Winter moth damage

12 Leaf miner

13 Vine weevil damage

14 Froghoppers in froth

15 Spider mite damage

16 Earwig on dahlia

17 Thrips

18 May chafer

19 Wasp on grapes

20 Weevil

21 Millipede in soil

22a Snail on iris

22b Black slug

23 Onion stem eelworm

24 Bark beetle grub

25 Gray mold (botrytis)

26 Powdery mildew

27 Black spot on rose

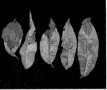
28 Peach leaf curl

29 Scab on pear

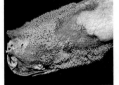
30 Rust on plum

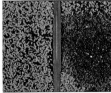
31 Damping-off

32 Tomato wilt

33 Stem canker on apple

34 Color-break virus

35 Chlorosis in cucumber

DESIGNING WITH PLANTS AND CONTAINERS

The successful design of anything, whether it is a piece of furniture, a garden or a group of well-planted containers, relies on following a well-tried set of guidelines. Designing with plants and containers is largely a matter of doing your homework first: analyze the situation, choose plant material with knowledge of its eventual development and keep things simple.

A sensible starting point is to ask yourself why you want to use containers. It could be that you have no garden as such, simply a balcony or roof garden that needs some greenery or a splash of color to furnish it. You may have a paved courtyard with starkly oppressive walls, or perhaps your front door has an austere façade. Alternatively, within a garden, you may wish simply to temper the hard line of a terrace. For all these situations, and many more, a carefully chosen and well planted group of pots can be the perfect solution.

Choosing containers

In many ways, the choice of container is crucial. Not only should it blend with its surroundings but it must also be compatible with others in a group. However, there is often room for an element of surprise and one or two pots of a different character, carefully planted and positioned, can be effective.

Practical considerations must also influence your choice, such as the size and depth needed for the plants you intend to grow, and the space available on your balcony or patio.

Selecting your plants

Having considered your containers, you can think about suitable plant material. Here the choice is even wider, and designs can easily fail through being over-fussy or too complicated. Start by assessing your location from a horticultural point of view – is the position in sun or shade, is it sheltered or exposed? This will narrow down the initial choice of suitable plants (see the lists on pp. 154–7). Then ask yourself questions about what the scheme sets out to do – are you planning a composed group of pots, or one or two single dramatic containers? Do you want instant bright color, in which case you will rely heavily on flowering annuals, or a more permanent display, which will call for the evergreen or variegated foliage of shrubs and perennial species? Does the planting need to provide shelter from wind, or to screen a bad view, in which case you should select from wind-resistant, or fast-growing, species?

The number of plants in a container is obviously governed by its size, but beware of introducing too many different species, which will soon make the design excessively 'busy'. Check that all the plants you intend to group together in one container have compatible requirements, whether they are sun- or shade-loving, prefer a lot of moisture, or like an acid or alkaline soil. Sometimes the underlying shape or style of a container can influence the type of planting – if so, let it; single-species planting in particular should complement the pot. The 'container ideas' on the following pages give examples of different relationships between plants and their pots. But within a planted group, contrasts of shape can be exploited – of rounded and upright outlines, or prostrate and cascading habits.

Seasonal change is an important aspect of planting design and it is well worth mapping out the proposed contents of each container at the outset. Note the time and color of flowers and berries, the color and shape of leaves and what is evergreen, deciduous or variegated. In this way you can plan a scheme in advance, and check that it will work all year round.

Flower color

The color of flowers, though only a single facet of planting design, is probably the most immediately apparent. In basic terms, colors can be hot or cool and in general it is best to group plants within these ranges. In the hot color range are the vibrant reds, oranges and yellows, which demand attention and naturally draw the eye. A tub of bright red flowers, placed at a distance, is therefore immediately obvious, tending to foreshorten a space and make it appear smaller. The cool color range comprises white and the softer pinks, purples and blues, all of which harmonize well and are more restful. They are ideal for a more distant view, leading the eye gently away. In a confined situation this effect is not too critical but it still makes good design sense to keep hot colors close to the building, grading away into the cooler ranges.

Do not underestimate the value of gray foliage in a planting scheme; gray is an essential harmonizer, equally successful in toning down a vivid color scheme or blending pastel shades.

Foliage interest

Permanent displays rely more on foliage to provide color and interest throughout the year. Variegated foliage, in particular, brings life to a container-grown garden in winter when there is often very little in bloom; it also provides exciting contrast within a group of plants. Many shrubs have interesting spring or autumn foliage, or berries, making them valuable then.

The texture and shape of leaves should also be taken into account when juxtaposing permanent species, especially where the contrasts can be appreciated at close quarters. Not only are there enormous shade variations but foliage can also be glossy, hairy, felted, deeply veined or fleshy in texture and spiky, rounded, incised or heart-shaped. Compare, for example, the leaves of lavender with those of rue or an ivy. There are no definite rules here, apart from avoiding the trap of over-complication, so make the infinite permutations of different species one of the pleasures of using plants.

Right A simple example of a harmonious relationship between a plant and its container. The smooth, rounded wine jar is offset by the finely shaped flowers and foliage of a *Clematis macropetala* tumbling down its side.

Below In this boldly modeled planting scheme the containers are secondary to the strong relationship between contrasting plant shapes. The delicate leaves and flowers of the tall *Fuchsia magellanica* and the spreading *Impatiens wallerana* are set off by the leathery, sculptural leaves of the *Colocasia macrorrhiza*.

Above Foliage interest is paramount in this evergreen group. The large-leaved *Datura cornigera*, variegated ivy and low *Helichrysum italicum* contrasts in leaf color and shape.

Below The neat shapes of this collection of low, mound-forming herbs throw attention back onto the container, a fine old decorated lead water tank.

Container ideas

By planting a container you not only bring the receptacle itself to life but you also provide a focus for flowers and foliage that is not nearly so obvious in the more open parts of a garden. Free-standing troughs, pots and bowls direct the eye downward while window boxes, hanging baskets and taller urns are often at eye level, bringing the plants under closer scrutiny and allowing us to appreciate them in greater detail.

Suiting the plant to the container

Whether a container is positioned at ground level, on a parapet wall, hung from a bracket or stood firmly on a window sill, its character will, to a greater or lesser extent, determine its suitability for plants of different kinds. In some planting schemes, the container is almost incidental because foliage and flowers cover the top and tumble down the sides, furnishing the whole effect, and they may in fact entirely conceal the container itself. In such a case, any old or improvised container will suffice, including buckets, cans, oil drums or large saucepans, provided they are fitted with drainage holes and are capable of holding enough soil to sustain growth.

Often, however, the inherent style or shape of a container can influence the planting quite strongly, in which case it should be allowed to do so. Consider the obvious compatibility of low-growing succulents or alpines planted in a stone trough, or brightly flowering and trailing varieties of annuals in a hanging basket; trailing plants are also well-suited to urns but evergreen or more muted species would complement the more formal container better.

Boldly modeled containers, old or new, require dramatic planting, whose large leaves or striking colors will break their outline. Tall urns and vases call for pendulous varieties that can tumble and twist down their sides; such tall pots often look most effective grouped with lower, flatter containers. The traditional terracotta pots and concrete containers in simple shapes are ideally suited to more delicate compositions, their unassuming outline allowing great scope for subtle groupings. Square boxes are ideal for low, bushy shrubs, while other containers specially designed for the plants they hold include strawberry pots, parsley pots and potato barrels. Some idea of the wide range of pots, tubs and boxes commercially available is given on pages 10–13 and there are suggestions for more unusual containers, improvised from domestic or other more unlikely and interesting objects, on pages 18–19.

It is worth bearing in mind that conditions in a container are not always ideal; plants may well be subject to some overcrowding and are likely to dry out quickly; for this reason try to choose pots that are reasonably large. Broadly speaking, any container should be large enough to allow comfortably for plant growth; small pots are obviously unsuitable for rampant species

and very shallow bowls dry out extremely quickly. (See pp. 94–153 for recommended depths of planting for particular species and to give yourself an idea of their eventual height and spread.)

In general terms, the larger freestanding containers really come into their own with shrub planting, as many species need room in which to develop a root system. A number of the larger shrubs and small trees are sufficiently interesting and visually strong to be used alone, whereas annuals frequently need to be planted in a mixed group to look their best. Bulbs in fact often look most effective when a single species is massed together, such as a tub of daffodils or crocus, while a group of upright, more formal-looking tulips can look marvellous in the right modern, geometric type of container.

Grouping the plants

Not only the choice of plants but also their arrangement will, to a certain extent, depend on the shape of the container and how it is positioned. Pots placed against or hung on a wall, for instance, look best planted with taller species at the back, spreading or bushy plants in the center and trailing varieties toward the front; a hanging basket, on the other hand, should look equally attractive from all sides and from below, with perhaps some height in the center. Strawberry or parsley pots are ideal for growing smaller plants and herbs, each pocket or hole allowing an individual species to be planted in it, but they need to stand in an open position so that all sides can be seen.

It is often worth thinking about plant material in three categories – upright plants, which would be used at the back or as the centerpiece of a composition, to give height; bushy or spreading species, which might surround the latter and provide the 'bulk' of the planting; and finally the trailers that tumble over the sides and soften the whole composition. Trailing plants come into their own in any container mounted at eye level, such as window boxes, hanging baskets, urns on a plinth or any pot on a ledge, wall or the edge of a balcony. The idea of three tiers of plants extends to shrubs as well as annuals and perennials, and indeed the categories can often be combined with great success. While both single-specimen planting and compositions in balanced groups are ideal for square or circular containers, asymmetric displays can be very effective in long window boxes or troughs. The taller plants can be placed toward one end, while the lower material is used proportionately to provide balance at the other.

The above guidelines are very general; the photographs on the following pages give specific examples of successful planting designs for different containers, including both simple specimens and mixed-group compositions. In the sections that follow, the container-planting ideas are set in the context of particular locations.

Left Many bulbs look best when a single species is massed together in a simple container. These *Narcissi* stand out sharply against the dark green background of ivy. The concrete container is a quarter-circle; it could form a set piece, with three other sections holding different species, or it could fit in a corner. Being heavy and geometric, it is also dramatic enough to be freestanding. The best modern containers should be as versatile as this pleasing unit.

Below A stone trough blends well into a natural setting, particularly when it is encrusted with lichens and has the texture of age. The subtle planting design uses only three species and simplicity is the keynote of its success. It exploits the contrasting foliage of the fernlike *Corydalis cheilanthifolia* and the *Begonia sutherlandii*; the third species is *Erinus alpinus*, a low-growing alpine perennial that seeds itself freely.

Above right A home-made container can, if suitably planted, look more comfortable in its setting than a bought one. A succulent bed has been constructed by carefully placing stones together which echo those in the dry stone wall behind. The different species of *Sempervivum* have a natural affinity with the stone bed and the eye is drawn down to their interesting shapes.

Above and right The pot may be entirely secondary to the planting if flowers and foliage cascade out of the top and down the sides.

The climbing rose 'Masquerade' (above) has been allowed to trail down, creating a softer effect than if it were trained upward.

This largely evergreen planting design (right) dominates its container. The subtle grouping relies on delicate contrasts of shape and color in the flowers and foliage. The plants are *Senecio maritima*, *Reseda odorata*, fuchsia, *Helichrysum petiolatum* 'Aureum', *Lobelia*.

62

Left A hanging basket should be planted to look attractive when seen from below as well as from all sides. Suspended over a doorway, this colorful basket dramatically brightens the entrance. The lush planting has height and bulk in the center and includes several trailing species: pelargoniums, lobelia, hybrid fuchsia, French and striped marigolds, *Helichrysum petiolatum*, *Nemesia strumosa* and *Verbena ×hybrida*.

Left Strawberry pots are more versatile than their name suggests. Planting in 'pockets' is an excellent way of displaying small plants of an interesting shape, such as succulents. This is a permanent composition of contrasting shapes, colors and textures, which links with the more rampant ground cover. At the top is *Opuntia robusta*, with varieties of *Sempervivum* in the pockets.

Above Improvised containers as dramatic as this old zinc boiler should be allowed to be a feature in their own right. The two hybrid fuchsias and the pelargonium planted in it soften the expanse of metal without detracting from the importance of the container as a focal point in the garden setting. A container this size is ideal for shrubs, allowing room for root development.

Opposite Stone sinks or shallow troughs are the perfect receptacle for planting small, low-growing species. They make a delightful miniature garden in themselves, but also look effective as part of a larger composition, as here. The well-balanced group of plants in the sink offers subtle contrast between the prostrate juniper (*Juniperus* 'Pfitzerana Aurea'), the spreading *Ajuga reptans* and upright miniature conifers (*Juniperus communis* 'Compressa' and *Picea glauca* 'Albertiana Conica').

Right An urn stood on a plinth enables the delicate details of the foliage to be appreciated. The ivy and *Ballota* trail attractively down the sides of the urn, while height is maintained in the center of the planting design. The furry *Ballota* leaves, the variegation in the ivy and the feathery gray foliage of rue contrast strongly with the dark-colored *Perilla* leaves. Floral interest and color is added by the hybrid fuchsia, a trailing pink pelargonium, the daisylike *Felicia amelloides* and the orange-flowered *Mimulus glutinosus*.

Above Various large containers lend themselves to water gardens. The tall *Equisetum hiemale* catches the eye without detracting from the stone trough set at ground level.

Right Large shrubs and small trees need plenty of room for their roots. This half-barrel offers adequate space for the *Pieris japonica* to grow to a dramatic size.

Locations

We have already seen that both pots and plants have particular characters and that, in general terms, they should complement each other. However, only when a well-planted container or group of containers is seen in the context of a specific location can the result really be assessed. An individual combination may well lend itself much better to one setting than to another. Some plants are naturally architectural in shape, forming a link with walls and buildings, and it is possible to choose containers that complement their outline. Other plants are essentially soft and floppy and harmonize with a rural or informal setting. Much will depend on the effect you are trying to create, of course; while a soft composition naturally suits an informal setting, you might equally use it to relieve an excessively austere or formal situation. In the latter context, it would be a good idea to choose more muted flower colors, with perhaps a higher proportion of gray material, in keeping with the dignity of the setting.

It is well worth trying to integrate any planting design into its location as far as possible. The color of exterior walls or paintwork can be echoed in the container itself (particularly if it is painted) or in the color of flowers. Materials, too, deserve careful consideration, as some will be more appropriate to a particular situation. Terracotta and stone, being natural materials, look effective in most settings but particularly in traditional ones. More recent materials such as fiberglass, asbestos-cement and concrete work best in contemporary, strongly architectural situations. Wood is especially versatile – left unpainted, it suits a rural or informal location very well but can be painted to look crisp and eye-catching in an urban, sophisticated one.

Any design should be strongly influenced by practicality, as the most charming or imaginative idea is useless unless it complies with the physical limitations of the site. There is no point thinking in terms of an elaborate design that involves grouping containers of different sizes together, if you have only a narrow balcony with limited floor space. Larger paved areas need a few big, freestanding containers, or a reasonable sized grouping of smaller ones, to break up and soften the expanse of paving, but where floor area is limited, make maximum use of wall space.

Forward planning is important; you have to take into account possible load-bearing problems when considering the size and weight of different containers for a roof, and to assess the practical restrictions involved in getting soil and containers out onto a small fourth-floor balcony. It is just as important to ensure easy access afterward for the maintenance and watering of all your plants, but especially those in wall-hung pots.

Bear the above general observations in mind when you start to survey a range of containers and to select your planting material. The following pages offer a wealth of container-planting ideas, tied in to specific sites or locations, which will give you more precise guidelines.

An individual marriage of plant and container has to work in its location as well as forming a harmonious composition in itself. This strongly modeled chimney pot needs bold planting to complement its outline and the large, heart-shaped leaves of *Begonia haageana* suit it perfectly. The tall, narrow shape of this dramatic container is ideal for the limited space at the side of a doorway, and the weathered terracotta blends well with the warm red brickwork of the house. The shrubby *Begonia* is evergreen, and therefore gives interest all year round; it is in fact planted in a pot suspended inside the chimney pot.

Entrances and steps

An entrance, by its very nature, demands attention and sets a scene. Virtually all entrances will benefit from planting, which can either emphasize their importance or soften their rigid line. Most doors and gates are set in hard surfacing where it is difficult to plant directly into the ground so containers, either freestanding or wall-hung, are ideal and will bring color and interest to an otherwise barren area.

The choice of container and planting will of course depend on the size of the area around the entrance. Space permitting, pots and tubs at ground level can be quite large, as long as they do not visually swamp the area. For permanent planting, you might choose a shrub or small tree of a naturally architectural shape, such as *Acer palmatum*, possibly underplanted with lower-growing species. In very large pots, herbaceous material could be mixed in to 'lighten' the composition.

A formal entrance often needs a little dressing up and containers of a formal style, such as Versailles tubs or an urn, would be ideally suited. Container planting around an entrance in a rural or informal situation can afford to be softer. Hanging baskets and wall-hung terracotta pots blend well with mellow old stone or brick; trailing species are particularly suitable. If support is provided, or a self-clinging species chosen, a climber can be effectively trained to frame a doorway.

Steps, in addition to linking different levels, concentrate attention along a specific route – planting can further emphasize this while accentuating or softening the outline. Ideally, all steps should be as generous as possible, so that they are easy both on the eye and on the feet. Freestanding pots can be placed on the treads, if the steps are wide and deep enough.

As steps are often flanked by walls, climbers may be considered. They are normally heavy feeders, needing large pots or troughs; these could be placed at the bottom of the flight. In a sunny situation leading up to a roof or balcony, *Actinidia kolomicta*, *Clematis × jackmanii* or a climbing rose could be grown, while shade-tolerant climbers suitable for a darker basement include many of the ivies, climbing hydrangea, *Clematis montana* or Virginia creeper.

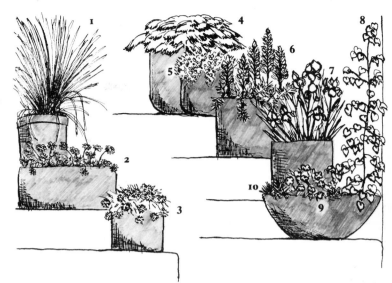

Above Basically architectural planting emphasizes the line of these concrete steps. The permanent species are enlivened by early-summer-flowering annuals. If steps are wide enough, pots can be placed on either side for greater impact.

1 *Miscanthus sinensis* 2 *Arctotis breviscapa* 3 *Caryopteris × clandonensis* 4 *Juniperus chinensis* 'Pfitzerana' 5 Broom 6 *Acanthus spinosus* 7 *Iris germanica* 8 *Actinidia chinensis* trained up the wall 9 *Cistus × cyprius* 10 *Festuca glauca*

Right Traditional planting of shrubs and annuals complements an informal entrance. The *Acer* and low-growing *Hebes* form a classic purple/gray color combination.

1 *Acer palmatum* 'Dissectum Atropurpureum' 2 *Hebe pinguifolia* 'Pagei' 3 Dwarf *Verbena × hybrida* 4 *Gentiana sèptemfida* 5 Sweet peas, trained on canes 6 Zonal pelargoniums 7 Sage

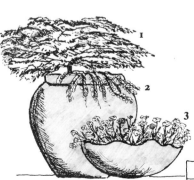

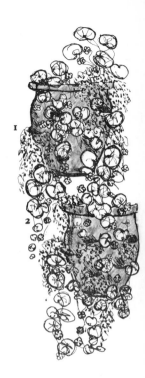

Right Where space around a doorway is limited, one or two wall-hung containers will soften the starkness of a bare wall. Here two half strawberry pots are planted with trailing varieties of summer-flowering annuals.
1 Trailing lobelia **2** Nasturtiums

Below Where the architectural style is not too dominant, a group of modern containers can be teamed with more traditional ones. The angular boxes hung on the wall to one side of the door are each planted with a single species, while those on the ground are filled with a mixture of permanent plants, adding stability and variety to the composition.
1 *Clematis* × *jackmanii* **2** White Marguerite daisies **3** Ivy-leaved trailing pelargonium **4** Rosemary **5** Sage **6** *Hosta fortunei* **7** *Hebe subalpina* **8** *Geum* × *borisii* **9** *Cistus* × *lusitanicus*

Above Steps leading up from a basement will be in shade at the bottom and sun at the top – planting must take account of this. The Virginia creeper planted in the box on the ground could be trained up against a wall, if there is one, or on vertical wooden slats, which would harmonize with the wooden steps and draw the eye upward. Climbers are also a good way of hiding pipes, which is one function of the *Aristolochia* at the top. All the planting is permanent.
1 Virginia creeper **2** *Fatsia japonica* **3** *Euphorbia griffithii* **4** *Cotoneaster dammeri* **5** *Aristolochia durior* **6** Miniature apple **7** *Hibiscus syriacus*

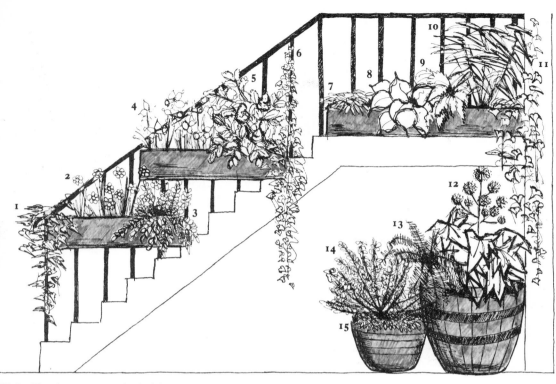

Left It is worth considering hanging troughs and boxes on the outside of railings, where they are well out of the way. They need to be fixed securely (see p. 17).

Shady areas such as basements can pose problems but there are many permanent and annual species that will thrive in shade, such as those in the tubs under the steps. Evergreen and variegated ivies are shade-tolerant climbers chosen to clad the railings themselves; here they are combined with spring-flowering bulbs.

1 *Hedera helix* 'Sagittaefolia'
2 White *Narcissus* 3 *Vinca major*
4 Large trumpet daffodils 5 *Mahonia aquifolium* 6 *Hedera helix* 'Green Ripple' 7 *Sarcococca hookeriana*
8 *Hosta fortunei* 9 *Helleborus argutifolius* 10 *Arundinaria auricoma*
11 *Hedera canariensis* 12 *Fatsia japonica* 13 *Dryopteris filix-mas*
14 *Symphoricarpos racemosus*
15 *Pachysandra terminalis*

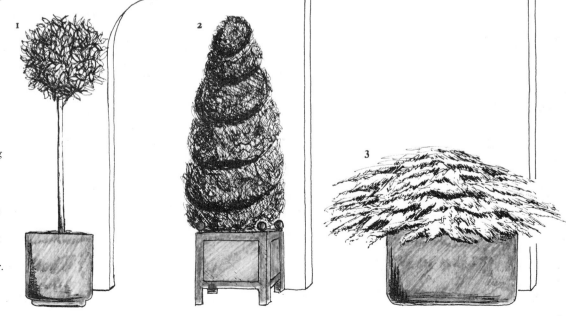

Right Planting on one or both sides of an entrance can be effectively simple if the container is chosen to harmonize with the plant shape.
1 A mop-headed standard bay tree echoes the shape of the circular fiberglass container in which it is planted, making a simple statement that dignifies the entrance. It could be underplanted with low-growing *Muscari* or *Scilla* for a spring display but should be kept clear during the summer, otherwise the composition looks too fussy.
2 A spirally clipped box tree in a wooden Versailles tub emphasizes a formal situation.
3 A large square wooden box is best suited by a low-growing, widely spreading shrub such as this juniper. Its horizontal line could be used to reinforce that of a long, low building.

Right Broad treads allow room for a group of terracotta and china pots. Bold planting of succulents (*Crassula portulacea* and *Aeonium holochrysum*) echoes the architectural line of the wooden steps.

Below right These wooden steps down to a basement are enhanced by the container planting, which also softens them. Ivies are particularly suitable for shady basements and here a large-leaved variegated ivy (*Hedera colchica dentata*) is planted in a box at the top of the flight and trained to conceal the drainpipe, while smaller-leaved ivies are trained up the wooden posts at the bottom, providing year-round greenery. Generous terracotta pots on the treads themselves are filled mainly with petunias and pelargoniums for summer color.

Below A plain concrete container planted with bright blue hyacinths brings color and cheer to a gateway on an overcast winter's day.

Above An orange tree in a wooden tub placed at the bottom of a flight of stone steps softens their rigid outline. Holes have been drilled in the tub to take rope handles, which facilitate moving it. In temperate or cool climates, the tree would have to be overwintered indoors.

Right Placed close to the back door, a large old wooden trough makes an excellent container for a herb garden, readily accessible for the kitchen. The herbs have been chosen for their decorative as well as their culinary values and the variety of leaf shapes, color and texture provides as much interest as a floral display. From left to right: variegated lemon balm, golden lemon thyme, marjoram, red sage, camphor, and pink-flowered *Lychnis* (not a herb).

Walls

In many small outdoor spaces, such as balconies, basements and patios, the surface area of the wall is considerably greater than that of the floor. Such high boundaries, if left bare, can be starkly oppressive whereas in fact they present a wide range of possibilities for container planting, which will clothe them in greenery to give color and interest all year round. Walls also, of course, provide valuable shelter for the plants, allowing the cultivation of more tender species. This is particularly true of southfacing walls.

There is a wide choice of wall-mounted containers, such as wire half-baskets and terracotta pots in a variety of shapes and sizes. In addition hanging baskets and window boxes, with the aid of securely fixed brackets, can effectively decorate a wall. Wall-hung containers are ideal for annuals, which can provide 'instant' color during spring and summer. Do not ignore unusual possibilities, such as old cast-iron cattle mangers (see opposite) – suitably lined, they will hold a generous collection of plants.

Freestanding pots and planters placed against the bottom of a wall can hold climbers (a list of suitable ones will be found on pp. 109–12), which will either cling to the wall or can be trained up it, using suitable means of support. These include wooden trellis, plastic-covered wire netting, and horizontal wires fixed to the wall itself (see p. 18). It is best to grow climbers in a box, trough or other straight-sided container that can stand flat against the wall. Alternatively, if the wall is wide enough and access is easily available, you could place troughs and boxes on the top, allowing trailing foliage to cascade down the wall.

Any container needs frequent watering and for those on the ground this is relatively straightforward, but wall-mounted pots do pose maintenance problems. If a basket or pot can be watered from a window or balcony, this is obviously best, but if not you will have to use step ladders or a hose extension (see p. 35). Whatever the means of access, make sure it is safe and convenient enough to allow regular attention, or else the display suffers. Some baskets and boxes can be lowered by pulley, but the mechanics may be awkward and unsightly. It is also worth bearing in mind that there are a number of self-watering containers that can virtually solve the watering problem altogether. Containers with a built-in drip tray also come into their own here; otherwise, make sure that a wall-hung pot will drip where it does not matter. All fixings must, of course, be sound (see p. 17), as the consequences of a falling container heavy with soil could be serious.

The material and color of a wall may well influence your choice of pot and plant. Color can also visually link the outdoor wall with an adjacent wall inside; if they are separated only by large windows or glass patio doors, it is especially worth while trying to blend indoors and out.

Above A single wall is an ideal background for a group of large wall-hung containers. Permanent and annual, sun-loving plants are combined in a range of colors in a hanging basket and two wall-mounted cattle mangers (large terracotta pots could be substituted). The wisteria can be trained up the wall to give height to the design, while the trailing ivy cascades down.

1 *Wisteria sinensis* 2 *Fuchsia fulgens* 3 Purple zonal pelargonium 4 *Helianthemum* 'Raspberry Ripple' 5 Low-growing bedding chrysanthemums 6 *Hedera helix* 'Chicago' 7 *Senecio laxifolius* 8 *Sedum spectabile*

Right The rendered or concrete wall of a modern building forms an effective backdrop for this simple but very strong spring planting design. The geometrically arranged window boxes are complemented by the upright outline of the bulbs, and the formally balanced colors keep the pattern strong. The color design is hot, apart from the pure white at the head of the triangle and the bright blue at the bottom center. It would be seen to best advantage against a cool background, such as a pale colorwashed wall.

1 White hyacinths 2 and 3 Scarlet early tulips 4 and 6 Trumpet daffodils 5 Blue hyacinths

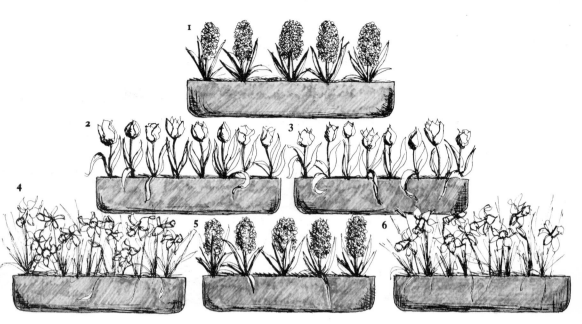

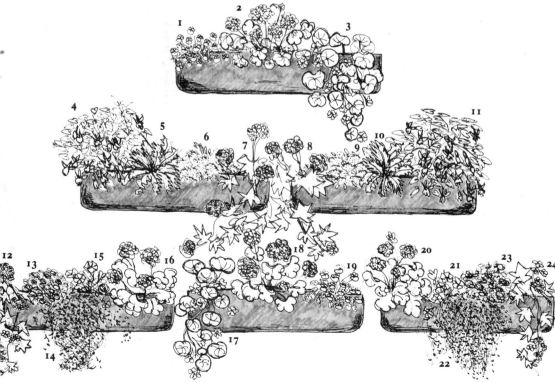

Left The same arrangement of wall-mounted window boxes as shown above reveals a very different treatment. This summer bedding design in cooler colors uses plants that flop and trail softly over the edges of the boxes; it would be suitable for a darker colored wall.

1 and 19 Mauve pansies 2 and 18 White zonal pelargoniums 3 and 17 Pale yellow trailing nasturtiums 4 and 11 Fuchsia 5 and 10 *Cineraria maritima* 6 and 9 *Ageratum* 7 and 8 Pink ivy-leaved pelargoniums 12 and 24 White ivy-leaved pelargoniums 13 and 23 Pink *Begonia semperflorens* 14 and 22 Blue trailing lobelia 15 and 21 Purple petunias 16 and 20 Pink zonal pelargoniums

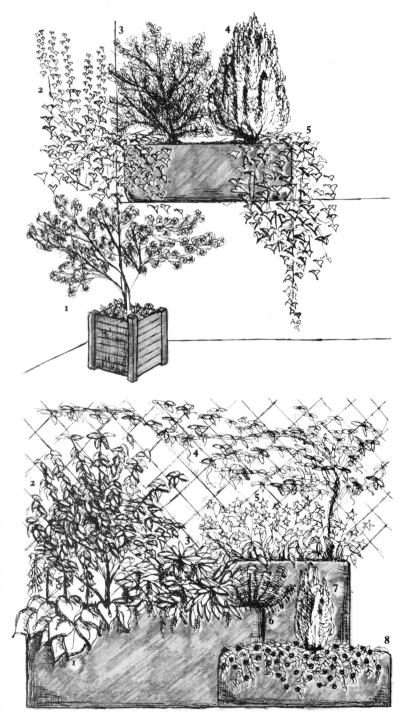

Left If there is enough floor space, a bold arrangement in large planters looks striking against a wall, especially if climbers are included. Here the widest planter holds the dramatic *Clerodendron trichotomum*, while a *Clematis* in a taller container scales the wall at a different height. This arrangement of mainly permanent planting is shade-tolerant.

Where there is earth against the wall, an unusual idea is to paint concrete sewage pipes of different diameters and sink them into the ground to varying depths. They offer ample room for plant roots.
1 *Hosta* 'Thomas Hogg' **2** *Clerodendron trichotomum* **3** *Pieris forestii* **4** *Clematis montana* **5** *Nicotiana affinis* (lime green) **6** *Euphorbia wulfenii* **7** *Taxus baccata* 'Fastigiata' **8** *Vinca minor*

Above and above left A sheltered corner bordered by two walls offers great possibilities for container planting. Climbers are planted in the troughs nearest to the wall of the building, while trailing species are encouraged to cascade down the parapet wall. Use different pots or sets of liners and seasonal planting to ring the changes during the year.

This late-spring-flowering design (above) looks best against a light wall (such as pale stone, brick, or stucco painted white or cream).
1 *Camellia japonica*, underplanted with forget-me-nots **2** *Hedera canariensis* 'Gloire de Marengo' **3** *Fatsia japonica* **4** *Cytisus* × 'Goldfinch' **5** *Clematis armandii*

Again, a pale-colored wall shows off the evergreen and variegated foliage of winter planting to best effect, and allows maximum light on overcast winter days (above left).
1 *Hamamelis mollis*, underplanted with snowdrops **2** *Hedera helix* 'Goldheart' **3** *Elaeagnus pungens* 'Maculata' **4** *Taxus baccata* 'Fastigiata' **5** *Hedera helix* 'Glacier'

Left In a container that will stand against a wall the composition should be graded in height so that taller and more upright species are planted at the back and trailing varieties towards the front. This successful design in cool colors relies on simple planting (fuchsia, *Helichrysum petiolatum*, trailing pelargoniums and lobelia).

Below Maximum use is made of the wall space in this small paved garden. Trellis enables climbers such as *Mandevilla* to be trained up the walls, while built-in brick boxes allow individual plant groups to decorate them. The theme of the garden is white, the color of walls and paintwork being echoed in the predominant flower color, relieved only by occasional splashes of pink.

Most of the flowering plants, such as petunias, *Impatiens* and Marguerite daisies, are annuals but plenty of evergreens are included, like ivies, *Helichrysum microphyllum*, *Hebe* and a *Choisya ternata*.

Left A group of three terracotta wall-hung pots makes a simple but pleasing composition against a mellow brick wall; they are planted with annual, spring-flowering *Campanula* and different ivies.

Right The corner of a low wall is made a dramatic focal point within a garden by standing this large terracotta planter on it. The abundant planting of a single species (a dwarf zonal pelargonium) enhances rather than detracts from the magnificence of the container itself.

Below A climbing shrub trained against a wall adds dignity and interest to an entrance. This spring-flowering *Chaenomeles speciosa* and low-growing *Sedum spectabile* are planted in a built-in container.

Left This group of asbestos-cement containers of different heights and diameters allows a vivid collection of spring bulbs and pansies to be seen to great advantage. The bright colors of hyacinths, tulips and pansies are relieved by the cream *Narcissi*; the warm tone of the wooden fence behind acts as an excellent foil.

Right Fruit benefit from the warmth reflected by a brick wall; this pot-grown peach tree is ripening beautifully.

Above A wooden fence affords shelter for a group of pot-grown food plants; this collection includes a maiden cherry tree, bush tomato and the herbs, bay laurel and thyme.

Right A wall-mounted wire basket lined with moss is planted informally to create a natural effect that blends well with the mellow, old brick wall. The *Fuchsia triphylla* planted at the back gives height, while different varieties of pelargonium appear to tumble out of the top and sides, together with trailing lobelia, variegated ivy and another fuchsia; *Echeveria glauca* adds a harmonizing touch of gray.

Windows and small balconies

Window sills and balconies make excellent locations for a wide range of container-grown plants. They may be in an open position, catching more light than at ground level, where they will also escape the worst frost. If the situation is very open, however, planting part way up a building may be exposed to wind and buffeting, which can strain plant stems and dry the soil out quickly. Low-growing, shrubby species are most suitable.

Regular maintenance is straightforward, provided windows give adequate access by tilting, opening inward or moving up and down. Outward-opening casements obviously present problems, as do fixed panes and louvers; however, window boxes can in fact be suspended below the window itself, supported on wall brackets, provided access is available for fixing, planting and watering. Do not neglect safety considerations – if you do not know the weight a balcony can take, avoid using too many large or heavy containers, and make sure that window sills are in good condition structurally before placing boxes on them. Ensure that boxes on both window sills and brackets, and pots or troughs hung on walls, are fixed securely (see p. 17).

As both window sills and small balcony areas are limited in size, narrow containers, troughs and boxes are most appropriate. If there is room for one or two larger containers on a balcony, these will give any composition greater visual emphasis. Wood is an obvious choice of material for troughs or boxes, being durable if properly treated (see p. 25), and it can be painted to match the color of doors and windows. Troughs made of asbestos-cement, fiberglass and plastics are relatively lightweight, although soil in them will dry out faster than in wooden containers. A small balcony is so strongly linked to indoors that you could also use household objects such as jugs, bowls and glazed pots for more interesting and unusual containers (but ensure adequate drainage), while the more sophisticated plastic and ceramic pots are also fitting.

On a balcony in an exposed situation you can provide some shelter by clothing railings with climbers of a less rampant nature, such as *Clematis × jackmanii*, summer-flowering jasmine or one of the slower-growing honeysuckles, such as *Lonicera japonica*; the last two climbers have the additional advantage of being fragrant. If not grown against railings they can be supported by plastic mesh or trellis.

Some vegetables too will act as a partial windbreak, for example beans or peas, which also bear flowers. Troughs containing vegetables should be not less than 20 cm/8 in deep. Shallow-rooted salad crops, such as radishes, spring onions, lettuce and tomatoes as well as early, short-rooted carrots can also be grown in a window box. The dwarf varieties of these crops are less voracious feeders and will suffer less in a wind.

The plants on a window sill or small balcony will be enjoyed indoors as well as out so it is worth trying to plan a colorful

Planting round a window or on a balcony can do much to cheer up the façade of a building. These lushly planted balconies cascade with foliage, which softens the rigid horizontal lines of concrete.

and eye-catching display. Whether using shrubs or annuals, or a combination of both, think of teaming colors and contrasting shape for maximum impact. Many of the annual or summer bedding plants will be suitable in a sunny situation, especially the more shrubby species such as *Begonia semperflorens*, *Ageratum*, salvias, zonal pelargoniums, petunias and *Verbena*. Avoid the taller varieties that would suffer from wind damage. Nasturtiums are particularly fond of sun and dry conditions, as are ivy-leaved pelargoniums and trailing lobelia. Many plants and shrubs with gray, felted and furry leaves are ideal for sunny but exposed conditions, and thrive, for example, by the sea. Such species include *Helichrysum petiolatum*, *Senecio*, *Phlomis*, rosemary, lavender, *Santolina* and smaller *Hebes*.

If your window box or balcony is in a shady position, or overhung by another balcony above, there are still many appropriate shrubs and perennials from which to choose. Evergreens include *Viburnum davidii* and *Skimmia japonica*, both of which are slow-growing and remain compact in size, and the whole spectrum of ivies, with their range of different sized and patterned leaves; ivies can climb or trail as the situation demands. The shrubs could be underplanted with shade-tolerant ground covers, including *Bergenia*, *Epimedium* or *Hypericum calycinum*, to form a dense, well-modeled group. Hostas look effective grown in pots and will tolerate cool, shady positions. Bulbs are happy in shade if the situation is reasonably open.

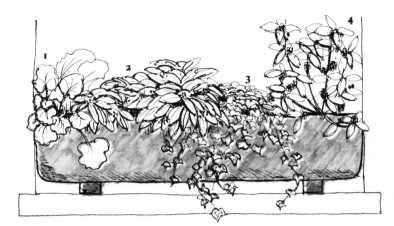

Right Some window sills are in permanent shade, in addition to being exposed. A carefully chosen group of tough, evergreen plants can still produce a great variety of leaf form and color. The *Viburnum* has the advantage of berries, while the *Bergenia* flowers toward the end of winter, when bloom is very welcome.

1 *Bergenia cordifolia* 2 *Viburnum davidii* 3 *Hedera helix* 4 *Aucuba japonica*

Above and right In a sunny and reasonably sheltered position, containers can be fixed to the reveals at the sides of windows if they are wide enough. Herbs are useful here if the window belongs to a kitchen.

In this summer design (above), some of the wall-hung pots are planted with herbs and alpine strawberries, while the window box contains a lush group of plants in a restrained blue, pink and gray color combination.

1 Ivy-leaved pelargonium 2 Mint 3 Chervil 4 Trailing lobelia 5 Pink zonal pelargoniums 6 *Heliotropium × hybridum* 7 *Helichrysum petiolatum* 8 Alpine strawberries.

Late autumn can be dull in flowering terms, but it is possible to select material that is particularly bright in this season (right).

1 *Hedera helix* 'Goldheart' 2 Parsley 3 Lavender 4 *Erica carnea* 'Myretoun Ruby' 5 *Euonymus* 6 *Solanum capsicastrum* 7 *Erica carnea* 'Foxhollow' 8 Chives 9 *Hedera helix* 'Glacier'

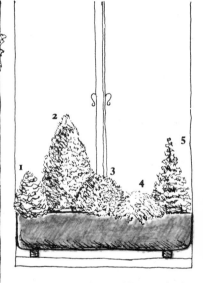

Above Miniature conifers can look lost in the broad sweep of a garden, but their precise outline and often rich colors can be appreciated at close quarters. They tend to look best grouped as a collection, so a window box is an ideal container. Conifers enjoy an open position and, being evergreen, provide year-round interest.

1 *Chamaecyparis obtusa* 'Nana Gracilis' 2 *Picea glauca* 'Albertiana Glauca' 3 *Pinus mugo pumilio* 4 *Juniperus squamata* 5 *Thuja plicata*

Right If you want to block out an unsightly view from your balcony, use the parapet wall to support a trellis or vertical slats. Fill free-standing containers at the foot of the wall with permanent plants that will climb the trellis or that can be trained against it as a screen. This planting is shade-tolerant.
1 *Clematis montana* **2** *Pachysandra terminalis* **3** *Skimmia japonica* **4** *Helleborus corsicus* **5** *Acer palmatum* 'Dissectum' **6** *Hosta fortunei* **7** *Epimedium warlyensis* **8** Honeysuckle

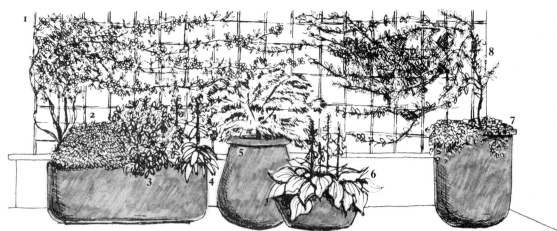

Left A long trough fixed securely on top of the balcony wall allows small shrubs to spread on either side, without blocking a good view. The climber, *Aristolochia durior*, could be trained up a support to the desired height, and then allowed to fall and clothe the wall. All the planting is permanent, and likes full sun.
1 *Potentilla fruticosa* **2** Rosemary **3** *Genista hispanica* **4** *Choisya ternata* **5** *Aristolochia durior*

Right Railings along the edge of a small balcony in a sunny position can be used as support for beans and zucchini. The vegetables are planted in two troughs, which could perhaps be filled with bulbs for a spring display. Other pots are furnished with evergreens, annuals and a fuchsia, to provide winter interest and summer color.
1 Runner beans **2** Zucchini **3** *Hebe pinguifolia* 'Pagei' **4** *Escallonia* 'Apple Blossom' **5** White zonal pelargoniums **6** *Verbena × hybrida* **7** Fuchsia **8** Trailing nasturtiums

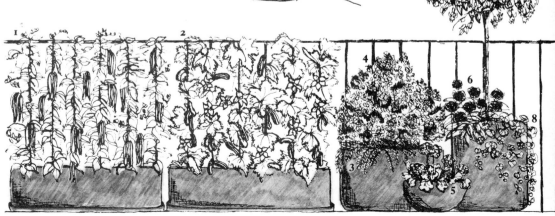

Right and below right Plants selected within a limited color range make an effective composition if it complements the background.

The formal façade of an urban building (right) is enlivened by this judiciously planted window box. The dwarf junipers blend with the stonework, while the *Impatiens* and pelargoniums add summer color.

This restful color design (below right) works well against the cream walls and window frame – it uses gray *Helichrysum petiolatum*, green *Nicotiana*, blue and white *Campanula*.

Far right Planting on a small balcony is often a visual extension of indoors; these pots of zinnias foreshorten the distant view.

Below Be adventurous with containers: beans in a window box are trained up string to a balcony above.

Left Colorful annuals appear to spill out of this window box, virtually concealing the container itself. The warm brown background is a perfect foil for the deep colors of the pelargoniums and petunias.

Below left An imaginatively-planted window box breaks up an expanse of roof tiles. This summer design uses simply two varieties of trailing pelargonium, which cascade over the window box, and a mass of *Impatiens*, which fills the top, all but masking the small window; this would not be advisable without another source of light in the room.

Above The vivid colors of nasturtium and marigold flowers planted in this long trough on a small balcony complement those of the house. The *Dianthus* is the only hardy plant in this summer design. A vine on the trellis above casts dappled shade over the whole area.

Below A formal composition needs careful handling if it is to be successful. The two clipped conifers (*Chamaecyparis lawsoniana* 'Nana Aurea') symmetrically planted at either end of this stone trough standing in front of a window are visually tied together by the variegated ivy.

Above The sublime, but nevertheless effective, understatement. A pelargonium in a single terracotta pot transforms a dull, crumbling façade.

Right The austere brickwork of contemporary architecture demands the softening influence of plants. In this recessed balcony a small-leaved ivy provides a curtain of greenery and interest throughout the year. Scarlet pelargoniums add seasonal color, as will the honeysuckle trained horizontally.

Left If the color of flowers can echo that of architectural features, the effect is more integrated. The white petunias and Marguerite daisies in this summer design pick up the color of the window frame, shutters, and of the window box.

Below Early-flowering plants on a small balcony bring a welcome splash of color, which can be appreciated from indoors. The startling yellow of the *Iris danfordiae* is echoed by the yellow pansies.

The patio garden

Moving away from small, intimate outdoor areas and into larger flat areas such as patios, courtyards, roof gardens and basements, the possibilities and the problems change quite dramatically. Because there is more room to move about, you might want to work out an overall design for the space, which may have to take into account various different factors, such as the inclusion or screening of a view and the provision of shelter.

Container planting again comes into its own in larger paved gardens because these are outdoor 'rooms' in the fullest sense of the word, and as such will need furnishing. A visual link between indoors and out is likely to be desirable, so the color of pots and plants becomes particularly important. There is far greater scope for grouping containers together than, for example, on a window sill or tiny balcony, simply because there is much more floor space.

Space permitting, you may feel inclined to try some more specialized, or experimental, planting, such as a collection of alpines or succulents in a sink or trough. You may also be encouraged to grow some fruit or vegetables that need larger pots, such as potatoes in a special barrel; there should at least be room for a collection of pot-grown herbs, preferably positioned near a door for convenient cutting.

Planning the space
Initially it is sensible to make a scale drawing of the area on graph or squared paper, marking anything that might influence the layout. This will include the overall dimensions of the space together with any changes of level, and the possible location of a sitting-out area. Note down the movement of the sun throughout the day, and the direction of a prevailing wind and you should have all the basic information needed to work out a feasible plan. By doing this initial research you will immediately pinpoint any difficulties and this in turn will influence the distribution of containers. Different viewpoints will also affect the way in which the pots are grouped.

You also need to consider the microclimate, that is, the localized climate of your patio or terrace. Even in a harsh climate, your own site could be fairly sheltered if you are surrounded by tall buildings on all sides; on the other hand, these could create excessively shady conditions. In this way, the microclimate can have quite a telling influence on your choice of plants – its effects may be beneficial, allowing the cultivation of more tender species, or harsh, which will limit your selection. The planting can always be arranged in such a way that tougher, more resilient species give shelter to more delicate neighbors.

Roof gardens
Each situation will be different, of course. Roof gardens often need a great deal of shelter and, because they are high above the ground, they also need a feeling of intimacy to be created that might involve the grouping of pots to enclose a sitting area. While pastel shades of flower and foliage may be exactly what is needed in a dark courtyard, they will be swamped by bright light on a roof. The type of container also has to be chosen with regard to the limited load-bearing capacity of a roof (if you are unsure how much weight your roof or large balcony can take, you might need to consult an architect or surveyor). Here the lightweight materials such as fiberglass and plastics come into their own; often available in bright colors and with patterned or textured surfaces they are ideal for counteracting the deadening effects of strong sunlight.

Screening and shelter
Roof gardens in particular are frequently very exposed. To provide shelter, height is invariably needed. This can be achieved by using tall plants of a densely growing habit; however, they do take time to grow and species must be chosen that do not mind the constriction of a pot. Another way is to use containers that link and stack together, allowing you to build up a planting design in tiers. Screening is provided by the bulk of the stacked containers themselves and young or naturally small plants can still be used, as they are given the necessary elevation.

A screen can alternatively be provided by erecting railings, slats or a length of trellis, which will act as host for climbing plants grown in containers. Overhead beams can also be useful, both for casting light shade and blocking off the view from windows at a higher level. Climbers can be grown to clad the beams and hanging baskets can be suspended from them, creating color and interest at eye level.

Basements and courtyards
The main problem affecting basement areas and enclosed yards is that they are invariably shady; plant material has to be chosen with this in mind (see the lists on pp. 154–7). It makes sense to grow suitable climbers in large containers at ground level – they will partially clad the expanse of high walls and will have the benefit of extra light and sun the higher they grow. Many basements incorporate a flight of steps and these can add an extra dimension for container planting – suggestions are given in the section on entrances and steps on pages 67–71.

Where the paved area is large, containers can be used to form divisions and points of emphasis within the overall boundaries, as is suggested in the context of larger gardens (see pp. 92–3). In a square patio or courtyard, a diagonal line drawn between two opposite corners is the longest available measurement. If you wish to emphasize the space, a well-planted pot or group of pots positioned on the diagonal will act as a focal point, drawing the eye over the greatest linear distance.

These hexagonal fiberglass stacking containers are extremely versatile. They could be used to enclose a sitting area or make an effective screen and, being lightweight, are especially appropriate for a roof or larger balcony.

This permanent design will provide color and interest throughout the year, the shapes created by the shrubs being as important as flower or leaf color; it is suitable for an open position and would tolerate partial shade.
1 *Juniperus* 'Pfitzerana' **2** *Calluna vulgaris* **3** *Pinus sylvestris* 'Fastigiata', with *Geranium macrorrhizum* planted round it **4** *Salvia officinalis* 'Purpurascens' **5** *Senecio laxifolius* **6** *Cotoneaster salicifolius* **7** *Hypericum elatum* **8** *Phormium cookianum*

Left Large, freestanding pots soften and bring interest to a paved terrace or patio. Manholes in the middle of a paved area can be an eyesore but a group of mixed pots and tubs, surrounded by boulders and loose cobbles, will mask them effectively. Planting in the pots is mainly evergreen but would be most suitable for a mild, sunny, sheltered position.
1 Night-scented stocks 2 *Camellia* 'Alba simplex' 3 *Geranium cinereum* 4 *Grevillea rosmarinifolia* 5 *Cistus* × *lusitanicus* 6 *Raphiolepis delacourii*

Below Where there is enough space on a patio or in a roof garden, the corner between two adjacent walls could be used to build up an interesting arrangement of interlocking containers. You could even use hollow concrete building blocks, which easily stack together; they might be painted to tone in with a color used outdoors.

To make productive use of a limited area, plant a herb garden, which mixes well with salad crops. The individual pockets, filled with potting mix, are ideal for the often rampant herbs; most herbs prefer a sunny position.
1 Garlic 2 and 13 Radishes 3 and 5 Lettuces 4 Rue 6 Basil 7 Summer savory 8 Balm 9 Spearmint 10 Mint 11 Thyme 12 Chives

Left The distribution of weight has to be considered carefully on a roof, and here the heavy containers are situated near load-bearing walls. On the most exposed side a row of fast-growing *Cupressocyparis leylandii* provides year-round screening and shelter. Placing floor-standing pots on bricks assists drainage.

Troughs of *Hebe × franciscana* on top of the wall soften the outline of urban rooftops. The wooden staging below echoes the wooden-slatted floor and provides space for a massed group of pots.

Below A spacious roof terrace allows scope for planting trees and shrubs. Large containers should be of lightweight material. In this boldly planted central group, the weeping birch gives height needed to counteract the dreary view of chimneys and roofs; *Rhododendron* and the ornamental grass *Cortaderia* provide contrasts of foliage and outline. The collection of shrubs at one end includes *Acer palmatum*, *Ligustrum ovalifolium* and *Cytisus scoparius*. Smaller subjects are seen to better effect in wall-mounted pots.

Above and right The use of a
single material, such as terracotta or
plastics, harmonizes a group of pots
of different shapes and sizes.

In this group at the edge of a
patio (above), subtle foliage
contrasts are achieved through the
juxtaposition of different varieties
of *Helichrysum* (*H. petiolatum*, *H.p.*
'Aureum' and *H. microphyllum*) and
pelargonium (*P. peltatum*, *P. crispum*
'Variegatum' and *P. odorantissimum*).
White Marguerite daisies and lilac
daisies (*Dimorphotheca*) add simple
flower shapes to the composition.

A collection of small, mainly
plastic, pots planted with flowering
annuals (right) acts almost as
'underplanting' for the taller
climbing roses and *Philadelphus* in
the ground behind. The rich variety
of colorful subjects includes
marigolds, petunias, pelargoniums
and *Antirrhinum*. The small pots
would need frequent watering.

Left A random collection of pots softens the line of a long, narrow paved yard. Maximum use is made of the space, with a trellis providing a fixing-point for wall-hung pots as well as support for climbers. The rich variety of planting includes permanent species such as *Camellia*, *Senecio maritima*, *Helleborus niger*, *Hydrangea*, *Hosta* and lilies as well as annuals like nasturtiums, pelargoniums, petunias, lobelia. Herbs are placed near the door.

Below The planting is graded in height so that the tall *Agapanthus* and lilies at the back of this group echo the high column, descending through *Nicotiana alata*, *Salpiglossis sinuata* and *Convolvulus cneorum* to the dwarf juniper, *Sempervivum tectorum* and *Euryops acraeus* in smaller pots at the front.

Right A studied plant group can be most effective on a terrace or patio, where it can be seen to advantage. The tall lilies (*Lilium longiflorum*) and the *Begonia haageana* in this composition are balanced by lower-growing ferns planted in a small trough. The lilies and ferns are only halfhardy and may need to be overwintered indoors.

Right The siting and grouping of
containers in this enclosed
courtyard has been carefully
planned to break up and soften the
paved expanse while maintaining
the continuity of an overall design.
The largely evergreen planting gains
in impact by being grouped to
exploit foliage contrast; for example,
the *Pittosporum tobira* 'Variegata'
and *Cotoneaster microphylla* in the
large pot on the left are balanced by
the variegated *Euonymus japonicus*
and *Prunus laurocerasus* in the
planter on the right.

The variety of different containers
used is entirely successful as the
shapes chosen, and those of the
plants, are very simple. Interest at
all levels mitigates the totally
enclosed feeling of a courtyard that
is surrounded by high walls on all
sides. The tall chimney pots,
planted with *Hebe* and a variegated
ivy, add height to the design,
balanced by a *Rhododendron* in the
adjacent corner. Two stone troughs
are fittingly planted with low-
growing species such as *Campanula*,
drawing attention down to ground
level. An old coal scuttle makes a
pleasing, individual container for
the flowering *Dianthus*.

Right Planted pots create an oasis
of greenery in a city garden, making
a pleasant sitting area in this shady
basement. The hardy shrubs
chosen, such as *Weigela florida* and
Laurus nobilis, are shade-tolerant,
but the large pot of Marguerite
daisies on the verandah at the top
of the steps is positioned so that it
will receive more sun. The use of a
basketweave plant holder links the
verandah with indoors, though both
it and the cane furniture would
need to be brought inside during
wet weather.

Containers in gardens

Planted containers are a decorative and mobile addition to any garden, whatever its size; their value is not limited to situations where there are no flower beds. Nor are they necessarily best grouped in the vicinity of a house or intimate 'outdoor room', but they can play an equally important role in the more distant parts of a larger garden. The versatility of containers really proves itself in the garden in fact. Their role can be 'structural', or architectural, or equally that of 'furnishing' the garden.

Pots may be used to provide seasonal bright spots of color to be seen, for example, against a mainly evergreen shrub border. They may be of particular value during the winter months, when many gardens are devoid of color. Imaginatively planted window boxes or wall-hung pots can add an individual, decorative touch and brighten an expanse of wall, while arbors and pergolas offer endless scope for hanging baskets. A group of planted containers brings a softening influence to the hard edge of paved areas; a single large container can provide a focal point. Well-planted pots are especially useful in a newly-created garden, where they can bring a dull corner to life or fill a gap in a shrub border while young plant material is maturing and beginning to spread.

Larger pots can be used to divide up a garden visually, which may be especially desirable in a long, narrow plot, or to demarcate different parts of it, for example to give a seating area a semienclosed feel, or to separate lawn from terrace, while masking the hard edge of paving. Containers may also be useful as deterrents, perhaps placed at the edge of a path to prevent people cutting corners over grass or delicate planting.

Swimming pools are one of the most awkward features to blend into the overall design of a garden, and it is often difficult to plant directly into the ground close to a pool; planted containers can break up the monotonous horizontal line of paving and water, giving vertical emphasis, as well as providing color and interest.

In a formal garden layout the use of planted urns can be valuable, framing a view, flanking a walk or forming a centerpiece to a lawn or rose garden. In a strongly modeled layout, pots act as an intermediate stage between purely artificial, man-made shapes and the softer, more informal planted areas.

Containers also provide an opportunity for trying out new plants, for creating a miniature alpine or water garden, for growing annuals or vegetables and fruit without disturbing the permanently planted flower beds. Alternatively they can be used for bringing on bulbs and tender perennials such as pelargoniums, which can then be planted out in borders to bridge any gaps. Similarly, tender plants can be overwintered indoors, space permitting, if they are in pots. Gardening in containers also allows the gardener to use the right type of soil for a plant that may otherwise not grow in the garden.

Above Container-grown planting can provide demarcation within a large garden. A partial screen is created by this straight line of pot-grown *Hibiscus rosa-sinensis*.

Below An urn can be a significant feature in the garden. The centrally-planted *Euonymus japonicus* gives height, surrounded by densely planted *Impatiens* and gray-leaved

Hebe 'Pagei'; the trailing ivy links with the *Rhododendron* foliage.

Right An informal grouping of traditional terracotta pots softens the hard edge of a paved terrace. The mainly foliage planting includes: *Prunus* 'Amanogawa', *Fragaria vesca*, rosemary, *Hosta sieboldiana*, *Convolvulus cneorum* and *Phlomis fruticosa*.

PLANTS FOR CONTAINERS

This section of the book comprises a description plus cultivation requirements for more than 400 commercially available plants suitable for growing in containers. The list is by no means fully comprehensive, but contains a wide selection of recommended species, cultivars and hybrids. Plants are grouped on the basis of either common stem, leaf or flower characteristics or common life cycle. Thus, while there is a section **Annuals and Biennials** and another **Perennials**, which in fact cover all plants except trees and shrubs, there are individual sections for **Succulents**, **Alpines** and **Ferns**.

Each section begins with a general introduction. This defines the general characteristics of plants within the section and highlights important cultivation needs. Bear in mind that where specific details of care and attention are the same for all plants in the section, these are included in the introduction, rather than under each individual entry.

The individual plant entries follow a standard pattern. Each entry is headed by the botanical name and, if any, the common name(s) of the plant. (Occasionally, a second Latin name is given in brackets. This is a previous, but perhaps better-known name for the plant.) Botanical names of plants usually consist of two elements. The first is that of the genus, e.g. *Geranium*. A genus contains several species – *Geranium endressii*, *G. ibericum*, *G. pratense*. Cultivars, which are distinct forms within a plant species maintained only in cultivation, are given a third name that is printed in Roman type inside single quotation marks, for example *G. endresii* 'Claridge Druce'. Hybrids bear a name with a multiplication sign ×. *Geranium × magnificum* is a cross between species within the same genus. Crosses between species of different genera bear a name with the multiplication sign first, e.g. × *Fatshedera lizei*, a cross between *Fatsia japonica* and *Hedera helix hibernica*. An entry may be concerned with a genus as a whole or with one particular species that is ideally suited for containers.

The first subheading in an entry – ZONES – relates to the hardiness of the plant. Based on a standard zonal system of annual average minimum temperatures – the coldest area being zone 1, the hottest zone 10 – this is an indication of the suitability of the plant for growing in a container in your area. A map of hardiness zones is given on page 154. Interpret this broadly: plants designated, say, zones 5–8 may be grown in zones 3 and 4 provided they can be kept in a frost-free position in winter. As a suffix to the zonal range is one of the following terms: 'easy', 'moderately easy' or, rarely, 'difficult'. This refers to cultivation of the plant in a container.

The HEIGHT and SPREAD given for each plant are the maximum attainable for a container specimen in favorable weather conditions. In some cases, qualification is made if the plant has a trailing habit or reaches maximum height only when in bloom.

The last of the introductory details concerns FLOWERS – flowering time and color range. With plants such as Ferns, where flowers are not produced, or with vegetables and fruits, where flowers are not of primary concern, this subheading is omitted. For conifers, details of foliage, not flowers, are given.

The general description of the plant's growth habit includes details of whether the plant is erect or trailing, a bush or shrub, clump- or mat-forming, and the shape, size and color of leaves and flowers. For precision and brevity a number of botanical descriptive terms are used; an explanation of these can be found in the Glossary, pages 161–62. CONTAINER SIZE gives dimensions of the ideal size or range of sizes of pot, tub or box for the plant, and SOIL the best potting mix to use. (These may be omitted if already mentioned in the section's introduction.) Under PLANTING information is given about when to plant seeds or young rooted plants, how many to place in a container and, if in groups, how far apart individual plants should be spaced. For example, 'in groups at 20 cm/8 in apart in the larger containers', suggests that, for decorative reasons, you grow the stated number of plants in one container. Arrange the plants in a circle (closer to the edge of the container than to its center), the distance between plants being measured around the circumference of the circle, not the straight-line distance. The ideal location for the plant is given as 'in sun', 'in sun or partial shade' or 'in full shade'.

Where applicable, PROPAGATION indicates the method(s) and recommended times for multiplication of the plant. The paragraph CARE gives details of watering, feeding, repotting, pruning and support of plants and outlines any special attention required during the winter and any major pests and diseases.

The last paragraph in each entry is concerned with SPECIES AND CULTIVARS recommended for growing in containers. In entries relating to only one species, this usually comprises a list of important cultivar names. In other entries, species, together with their cultivars, are listed; a brief description of each is included.

Each main plant entry is illustrated in color to show the plant's overall appearance, its shape and growth habit, its flowers (or vegetables/fruit), if any, and its relative size within the particular group. (A variety, not the type plant, may be shown.)

In this list of plants, each entry can give only a general description of habit, care and cultivation of the plant. For further details of specific cultivation techniques see the appropriate section within the second chapter **Looking after Plants and Containers**, pages 20–57.

At the end of the chapter is a section designed to help you choose the ideal plants to grow in a particular outdoor site, and another to give you a comparison of the time and care needed to maintain the different plants in containers. Finally, a container gardener's year-planner comprises summary information of when to sow seeds, pot, repot, prune and so forth.

Conifers

Conifers, or cone-bearing trees, grow well in containers since they tolerate root restriction and need much less food from the soil than larger-leaved plants. A few deciduous conifers exist, but they are seldom grown in containers; all the conifers listed here are evergreen.

Conifers vary in shape – from neat globes to cones and spires – and in foliage. Some, like false cypress (*Chamaecyparis*), have minute, scale-like leaves. Most junipers bear awl-shaped foliage, while the firs (*Abies*) have needles. Nor is it as simple as that: all junipers, for example, start off with awl-shaped leaves: this is 'juvenile' foliage, and later gives way to the 'adult' scale leaves. But some junipers keep their juvenile foliage for life, while others, like *Juniperus chinensis*, bear a mixture of awl-shaped and scale leaves. Sometimes, juvenile foliage becomes fixed through a mutation, as in some arbor-vitae (*Thuja*) cultivars.

For most containers and sites, the slower-growing conifers are best. Fast-growing, ultimately large ones can become leggy or untidy. Conifers do not thrive in areas with the sulphurous air pollution of industry, but there are species and cultivars to suit most other locations, including shady and drafty ones. Conifers look best as specimen plants grown singly in large tubs, but smaller ones can go with bulbs and annuals in bigger containers.

Conifers need minimal maintenance. Grow them, unless otherwise stated, in any approved potting mix. It is best to top dress them every spring with fresh potting mix, but this can be done every other spring and a slow-release fertilizer applied during alternate years (see pp. 36–7). Pruning should not be necessary, except to cut out stems that mar the overall shape. Some dwarf conifers may revert, that is, produce stems of the tall-growing tree. Cut these out right to their bases as soon as you recognize them (see pp. 39–41).

Abies Fir
ZONES 3–8   Easy
HEIGHT 0.6–10 m/2–33 ft
SPREAD 1–3 m/3–10 ft
FOLIAGE Dark green or blue-white Pyramidal trees with branches in regular tiers. Broad needle-shaped leaves. Barrel-shaped, erect cones, attractively colored when young.
CONTAINER SIZE 25–60 cm/10–24 in wide by 25–40 cm/10–16 in deep.
SOIL Any approved potting mix, preferably without added lime.
PLANTING Singly, or as a focal point in a mixed planting arrangement, in sun or partial shade.
PROPAGATION By seeds sown in spring; *A. balsamea* 'Hudsonia' by cuttings in late summer.
CARE Water regularly, particularly in hot weather. Apply liquid feed monthly from spring to midsummer.
SPECIES AND CULTIVAR *A. balsamea* 'Hudsonia': to 60 cm/24 in tall and wide, a slow-growing, bushy dwarf form of the seldom cultivated balsam fir. *A. koreana*: to 3 m/10 ft tall by 75–105 cm/30–42 in wide; young cones are rich violet-purple.

Juniperus chinensis 'Pfitzerana'

Chamaecyparis False cypress
ZONES 3–8   Easy
HEIGHT 1–3 m/3–10 ft
SPREAD 30–75 cm/12–30 in
FOLIAGE Green to gray-green and yellow
Variable in habit but basically flame-shaped to columnar; rounded or irregular in the dwarf forms. Scale-like leaves in flattened sprays.
CONTAINER SIZE 25–60 cm/10–24 in wide by 25–40 cm/10–16 in deep.
PLANTING Singly, or as a focal point in a mixed planting arrangement, in sun or partial shade.
PROPAGATION By seeds in spring or cuttings late summer or early fall.
CARE Water regularly, particularly in hot weather. Apply liquid feed to long-established specimens monthly from spring to fall.
SPECIES AND CULTIVARS *C. lawsoniana* Lawson cypress (zones 5–8) can be used for a specimen plant, but it will soon outgrow even a big container. Its dwarf forms are more useful –

Chamaecyparis lawsoniana

Chamaecyparis pisifera

'Ellwoodii': to 1.8 m/6 ft, slow-growing to start with, columnar habit, deep gray-green foliage of juvenile awl-shaped type in fluffy sprays; 'Minima Glauca': 1 m/3 ft tall, slow-growing, conical habit, blue-green foliage. *C. obtusa*, Hinoki cypress, is similar but more graceful. It has many smaller cultivars – 'Nana': to 1.8 m/6 ft tall, dark green foliage in rounded sprays; 'Pygmaea': to 60 cm/24 in, wide-spreading habit with branches in tiers; 'Aurea': to 3 m/10 ft tall, slow-growing, irregular habit, golden-yellow foliage in mossy sprays. *C. pisifera* Sawara cypress: similar to Lawson cypress; dwarf or slow-growing forms are best for containers – 'Plumosa Compressa': to 25 cm/10 in tall, extremely compact, yellow-green foliage.

Juniperus Juniper
ZONES 4–8   Easy
HEIGHT 15–90 cm/36 in or more
SPREAD 10–90 cm/4–36 in
FOLIAGE Mainly gray to blue-green
CONTAINER SIZE 20–60 cm/8–24 in wide by 20–30 cm/8–12 in deep.
PLANTING Singly, or smaller ones in groups at 45 cm/18 in apart; or used as focal points in mixed planting

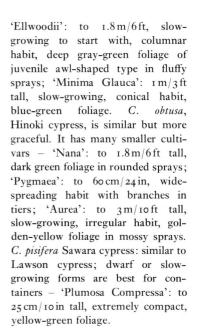

Abies koreana

Abies balsamea 'Hudsonia'

arrangements. Grows best in sun.
PROPAGATION By cuttings in early
fall.
CARE Water regularly, but avoid over-
wet soil. Apply liquid feed monthly
during late spring and summer to
long-established specimens.
SPECIES AND CULTIVARS *J. chinensis*
(inc. *J. × media*) varies in habit, from
conical and columnar to wide-spreading; green to gray-green foliage mixes
juvenile and adult forms. *J.c.* 'Colum-
naris': to 3.6 m/12 ft tall, erect
habit, blue-green foliage; 'Kaizuka':
to 1.8 m/6 ft, bushy spreading habit,
bright green adult leaves; 'Pfitzerana': 1–1.8 m/3–6 ft wide, spreading,
grayish-green juvenile leaves; 'Pfitzerana Aurea': to 1.5 m/5 ft, spreading habit, green with yellow tips in
summer; 'Pfitzerana Old Gold':
more compact, with bronzy-yellow
foliage; *J. communis* Common juniper: erect to spreading with awl-
shaped leaves. Best cultivars for containers are: *J.c.* 'Compressa' Noah's
Ark juniper: to 45 cm/18 in tall in 20
years, compact columnar habit, gray-
green foliage; 'San Jose': to 30 cm/
12 in tall, spreading habit, sage-green
foliage, very hardy; *J. sabina* is similar to *J. chinensis* but always a bush –
'Blue Danube': almost prostrate with
scalelike, blue-gray leaves; 'Tamaris-
cifolia': wide-spreading, flat-topped

hummock, green juvenile leaves. *J.
squamata* 'Meyeri': to 1.8 m/6 ft tall,
erect to semierect, with arching to
pendent stem tips, blue-gray leaves.

Pinus Pine
ZONES 2–8 Easy
HEIGHT 1–3 m/3–10 ft
SPREAD 30–60 cm/12–24 in or more
FOLIAGE Green to gray or blue-
green
Erect pyramidal trees, at least when
young, with long slender needles
carried in pairs or clusters of three
or five. Woody cones, often pendent
and decorative. Although most pines
are too big, the dwarfs or semidwarfs
make excellent container plants.
CONTAINER SIZE 25–60 cm/10–24 in
wide by 25–40 cm/10–16 in deep.
SOIL Any approved potting mix, but
preferably a loam-based one.
PLANTING Singly, or as focal point in
big container of mixed plants. Best
in sun but will tolerate light shade.
PROPAGATION By seeds sown in spring.
(Cuttings of pines are hard to root
and grafting is a skilled operation).

CARE Water regularly, particularly in
hot weather. Apply liquid feed to
well-established specimens monthly
from late spring to late summer.
SPECIES AND CULTIVARS *P. mugo* Dwarf
or mountain pine: bushy, to 1.8 m/
6 ft tall, rich green leaves; 'Gnome',
small, condensed globular form. *P.
parviflora* Japanese white pine (zones
5–8): to 3 m/10 ft tall but slow-
growing, conical to columnar, its
twisted, blue-green leaves carried in
fives. *P. sylvestris*, Scots pine, soon
outgrows containers. Its cultivars
are better – 'Beuvronensis': tiny
dense shrub, growing about 2 cm/
¾ in per year, with short, gray-green
leaves in pairs; 'Watereri': broad
pyramidal, slow-growing shrub,
1.2 m/4 ft or more, with bluish-
green leaves. *P. thunbergii* Black pine:
3 m/10 ft or more tall but slow-
growing in containers, with gray-
green leaves in pairs.

Taxus Yew
ZONES 4–8 Easy
HEIGHT 1–3 m/3–10 ft
SPREAD 60–150 cm/24–60 in
FOLIAGE Dark green or yellow-green
Bushy trees with broad needle-
shaped leaves. Use smaller cultivars.
CONTAINER SIZE 45–90 cm/18–36 in
wide by 25–40 cm/10–16 in deep.
PLANTING Singly; ideal for shade but
will tolerate sun.
PROPAGATION By cuttings in early
fall.
CARE Water regularly, particularly
during hot weather. Apply liquid
feed to long-established specimens
monthly from late spring to fall.
SPECIES AND CULTIVARS *T. baccata*
Common yew (zones 6–8): 3 m/10 ft
or more tall, can be clipped for
topiary; 'Fastigiata', Irish yew: erect,
compact, but only for largest containers; 'Fastigiata Aurea': has
yellow-margined leaves; 'Standishii':

similar to 'Aurea' but narrow and
slow growing. *T. × media*: similar to
T. baccata but hardier (zones 4–8).
T. × m. 'Hatfieldii': erect dense habit,
can be clipped.

Thuja Arbor-vitae
ZONES 2–8 Easy
HEIGHT 3 m/10 ft or more
SPREAD 30–75 cm/12–30 in
FOLIAGE Green, yellow, bronze
Similar in foliage to false cypress,
but scale leaves larger and cones
ovoid to cylindrical. Dwarf or slow-
growing sorts are best.
CONTAINER SIZE 45–60 cm/18–24 in
wide by 25–40 cm/10–16 in deep.
PLANTING Singly, sun or partial shade.
PROPAGATION Cuttings early fall.
CARE Water freely in hot weather,
less at other times. Apply liquid feed
to long-established specimens monthly from late spring to late summer.
SPECIES AND CULTIVARS *T. occidentalis*, American arbor-vitae, yellow-
green aromatic foliage. The species
itself is too large for containers, and
the following cultivars are better –
'Compacta': dense, pyramidal, to
1.5 m/5 ft but slow growing; 'Little
Gem': globular, to 45 cm/18 in, very
slow growing, rich green foliage;
'Rheingold': broadly conical, 1 m/3 ft
or more, old-gold shaded bronze
foliage. *T. orientalis* (*Biota orientalis*)
Chinese arbor-vitae (zones 6–8):
large, rounded shrub, 3 m/10 ft or
more tall, with vertical foliage sprays
– cones, sometimes abundant, are
blue-white when young. The best
cultivars for containers are 'Aurea
Nana': to 75 cm/30 in, dense ovoid
bush, golden-green; 'Elegantissima':
columnar habit to 1.8 m/6 ft, yellow
in summer, bronze in winter; 'Minima Glauca': globular bushlet to
30 cm/12 in, sea-green leaves of a
semijuvenile form, tinted bronze in
winter.

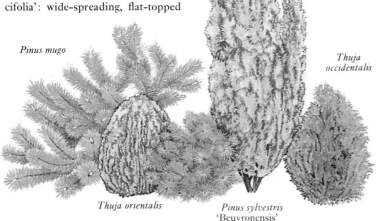

Pinus mugo

Thuja orientalis

Taxus baccata
Fastigiata

*Thuja
occidentalis*

Pinus sylvestris
'Beuvronensis'

Broad-leaved trees and shrubs: evergreen

A shrub is a plant that does not die back to the soil surface in winter, but retains its woody stems. A tree has a single woody stem unbranched for half to two-thirds of its height, and all its branches above that point. All trees and shrubs that are not conifers are termed 'broad-leaved'. They have recognizable leaves, not the needles, awls and scales of conifers.

Small or medium-sized shrubs are the easiest to grow in containers. Many trees and larger shrubs will also grow well, if you can cope with the annual or biennial root pruning and repotting (see below). Where you have enough room, it is worth trying, say, a small tree up to 3 m/10 ft to make a focal point.

The general care of broad-leaved shrubs and trees is similar to that of conifers (see p. 95). Most thrive in an approved potting mix. The smaller and slower-growing species must be top dressed with fresh compost in spring, annually or biennially, and given liquid feed in the summer. The larger shrubs – those ultimately 1.8 m/6 ft or more high – will need potting-on and then repotting at least every other year. To do this, remove the plant from its container during the dormant season, and shake off or tease away with a hand-fork as much of the rooting medium as possible. Cut away all diseased or damaged roots. In order to grow the plant on to a larger size, put it back into a bigger container each time. Once it has reached the size you want, return it either to a container of similar size, or to the same one after cleaning (see pp. 28–9).

Vigorous, strong-growing, shrubs and trees are best treated thus annually. If left longer, the root system becomes totally enmeshed and much damage may be done when transferring it over to another container.

Annual repotting maintains healthy growth, without excessive vigour. Root-pruning – the cutting out of coarse roots to leave only the fibrous feeding ones – is often recommended to restrict the size of strong-growing shrubs, but it is hard for an amateur to do successfully. Propagate from a large shrub *before* it outgrows its last container, then discard it, and concentrate on raising its progeny instead.

Container-grown broad-leaved shrubs and trees need fairly regular pruning to maintain their shape and size (see pp. 39–43). For most evergreens you need remove only dead stems or small branches that spoil the overall appearance. Deciduous flowering shrubs benefit from more rigorous and controlled annual pruning. Those that bloom on the previous season's growth, such as *Forsythia* or *Weigela*, should have the flowering stems cut back to the young leafy shoots at their bases. Shrubs that flower in summer, on the current season's growth, should be similarly pruned in winter or early spring.

Buxus sempervirens Box
ZONES 5–8 Easy
HEIGHT 60–120 cm/24–48 in or more
SPREAD 30–90 cm/12–36 in or more
Very bushy habit; slow-growing. Small, ovate to oblong, rich, glossy green leaves. Insignificant flowers, in spring. Will tolerate some neglect, stands clipping well and can therefore be used for topiary.
CONTAINER SIZE 25–60 cm/10–24 in wide by 25–30 cm/10–12 in deep.
PLANTING Singly, in sun or shade; the dwarf 'Suffruticosa' in groups 30 cm/12 in apart.
PROPAGATION By cuttings, in late summer or fall.
CARE Water freely in hot weather, less at other times.

CULTIVARS 'Aureovariegata' ('Aurea Maculata'): leaves splashed and mottled creamy-yellow; 'Gold Tip': young shoots yellow when young – rather variable; 'Handsworthensis': erect, vigorous habit, rounded leaves; 'Latifolia': spreading habit, larger leaves. *B.s.* 'Suffruticosa' Edging box: dwarf, densely twiggy, small leaves.

Camellia
ZONES 7–9 Moderately easy
HEIGHT 90–180 cm/36–72 in
SPREAD Generally two-thirds of height
FLOWERS Winter to late spring: red, pink, white
Erect to spreading habit. Elliptic to broad oval, toothed, glossy, leathery leaves; the roselike flowers have five thick petals and a central boss of yellow stamens.
CONTAINER SIZE 20–45 cm/8–18 in wide and deep.
SOIL Any free-draining neutral to acid potting mix, particularly the lime-free all-peat ones.
PLANTING Singly, in the fall, in partial shade.
PROPAGATION By seeds under glass, sown as soon as obtained; or by stem cuttings in fall.
CARE Water daily in hot weather, less at other times. If potting mix dries out, flowers will not develop. Apply liquid feed every two weeks from early summer to fall. Repot every third year. If necessary, after flowering, prune back previous year's stems by one-third to one-half. Frost turns flowers brown, so in cold areas bring plants into a cool room.
SPECIES AND CULTIVARS *C. japonica*, the hardiest (zone 7), has oval leaves 6–12 cm/$2\frac{1}{2}$–$4\frac{3}{4}$ in long, and red flowers 5–8 cm/2–$3\frac{1}{4}$ in wide. Most of the many cultivars have double flowers – 'Adolphe Audusson': semidouble, blood-red, large flowers; 'Drama Girl': semidouble, salmon pink, very large; 'Eleanor Hagood': single, shell pink; 'Magnolieflora': semidouble, magnolialike, shell-pink flowers; 'Purity': fully double, neat and formal shape, white; 'Tomorrow': spreading habit, formal double, strawberry-red flowers.

Cordyline australis
New Zealand cabbage palm
ZONES 8–10 Easy
HEIGHT 1.8 m/6 ft or more
SPREAD 90 cm/36 in
FLOWERS Early summer: white
Palmlike habit, slow-growing, with an unbranched stem for the first years, and a terminal rosette of narrow leaves 45–90 cm/18–36 in or

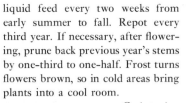

Cordyline australis

Camellia japonica

Buxus sempervirens

more long. In containers may retain this habit, but branching usually occurs at the top after the first flowering.

CONTAINER SIZE 30–60cm/12–24in wide by 25–30cm/10–12in deep.

PLANTING Singly, in sun.

PROPAGATION By seeds sown in warmth in spring.

CARE Water regularly but avoid overwet soil. Apply liquid feed monthly to long-established plants. In areas of hard frost bring indoors in fall.

CULTIVARS 'Atropurpurea': leaves suffused bronze to purple; 'Rubra': leaves coppery-red.

Erica Heath, Heather

ZONES 5–8 Easy

HEIGHT 30–90cm/12–36in

SPREAD 30–45cm/12–18in

FLOWERS Spring to fall: red, pink, purple, white

Mainly bushy habit, with wiry stems set with short needlelike leaves. Bell- to urn-shaped flowers in terminal spikes or clusters.

CONTAINER SIZE 60cm/24in wide, and 20cm/8in deep, or more.

SOIL Approved potting mixes, lime-free for *E. cinerea*, *E. tetralix* and *E. vagans*.

PLANTING In groups of three to five or more, in sun.

PROPAGATION By cuttings in late summer.

CARE Water regularly but avoid overwet soil. Remove old flowering stems once blossoms fade. Apply liquid feed monthly during growing season.

SPECIES AND CULTIVARS *E. carnea* Spring heath: to 25cm/10in tall, with narrow, urn-shaped flowers in dense racemes, fall to spring; many cultivars in shades of pink, red or white. *E. cinerea* Twisted heather: 15–45cm/6–18in tall, rose-purple, red, pink or white flowers, summer to fall; wide range of

cultivars available. *E.×darleyensis*: like a robust *E. carnea*, to 45cm/18in tall, white or pink flowers, fall to spring. *E. mediterranea* (*erigena*) Mediterranean heath: 60–180cm/24–72in tall, fragrant, pink, rose-purple or white flowers, early spring to early summer. *E. tetralix* Cross-leaved heath: 15–40cm/6–16in tall, hairy leaves in whorls of four or more, urn-shaped, white or pink flowers, in small terminal clusters, summer to fall. *E. vagans* Cornish heath: 30–60cm/12–24in tall, broad bell-shaped flowers in dense spikes; many cultivars from lilac-pink to purple and white, summer to fall.

Euonymus

ZONES 5–9 Easy

HEIGHT 60–180cm/24–72in

SPREAD 60–120cm/24–48in

Bushy habit. Oval to elliptic, glossy green leaves. Small greenish flowers, pink and orange fruits sometimes borne on large specimens.

CONTAINER SIZE 40–60cm/16–24in wide by 25–30cm/10–12in deep.

PLANTING Singly, in sun or shade.

PROPAGATION By cuttings in late summer.

CARE Water freely in warm weather, less at other times.

SPECIES AND CULTIVARS *E. fortunei* is basically a trailing or climbing species but the following grow as shrubs 60–90cm/24–36in tall – 'Carrierei': taller, larger, rich green leaves; 'Silver Queen': compact habit, pale yellow leaves when young, turning green with cream margins. *E. japonicus* (zones 7–9): bushy shrub to 1.8m/6ft or more tall, with several striking variegated forms – 'Aureo-variegata': bearing large, central gold-blotched leaves; 'Grandifolia': large dark green leaves, compact, good for shearing or topiary; 'Microphyllus' ('Myrtifolius'): dwarf habit, 90–

120cm/36–48in tall, small leaves; 'Microphyllus Variegatus': white-margined leaves; 'Microphyllus Pulchellus': gold-variegated leaves.

× Fatshedera lizei

ZONES 7–9 Easy

HEIGHT 1.8m/6ft or more

SPREAD 90cm/36in

A hybrid between *Hedera helix hibernica* (Irish ivy) and *Fatsia japonica* (see below). Loosely branched erect habit. Five-lobed handsome leaves up to 25cm/10in wide, of a lustrous, rich green. Small, starry, pale green flowers in terminal clusters, late fall.

CONTAINER SIZE 40–60cm/16–24in wide by 30cm/12in deep.

PLANTING Singly, in partial or full shade.

PROPAGATION By cuttings in summer and fall.

CARE Water freely in warm weather, less at other times. Apply liquid feed monthly during growing season. Pinch out tips of all shoots when 15cm/6in long to create a free-standing plant, otherwise a tall thin plant needing staking will result.

CULTIVAR × *F.l.* 'Variegata': irregularly white-margined leaves.

Fatsia japonica (*Aralia sieboldii*)

ZONES 8–9 Easy

HEIGHT 1.8m/6ft or more

SPREAD 1.2–1.5m/4–5ft

FLOWERS Late fall: white

Myrtus communis

Erect habit, robust and sparingly branched. Deeply fingered, leathery, lustrous leaves, up to 40cm/16in wide. Small, starry, frost-tender flowers in large terminal clusters. Tolerates salty air.

CONTAINER SIZE 45–90cm/18–36in wide by 30cm/12in or more deep.

PLANTING Singly, in partial to full shade.

PROPAGATION By seeds sown in warmth in spring, by cuttings in late summer, or by air-layering in spring.

CARE Water freely in warm weather, less at other times. Apply liquid feed monthly during growing season. Protect from frost in colder parts of zone 8.

CULTIVAR *F.j.* 'Variegata': white-margined leaves.

Hebe Shrubby veronica

ZONES 8–9 Easy

HEIGHT 30–150cm/12–60in

SPREAD 30–90cm/12–36in or more

FLOWERS Early summer to late fall: pink, red, purple, white

Bushy rounded habit. Foliage comes in two types: the 'whipcord' group have tiny scalelike leaves, while the rest have larger, lance-shaped to oval ones. Small, four-petaled flowers in dense spikes from upper leaf axils.

CONTAINER SIZE 30–60cm/12–24in wide by 25–30cm/10–12in deep.

Fatsia japonica

Erica carnea

PLANTING. Singly, in sun or partial shade. Not suitable for areas with hot, dry summers.

PROPAGATION By cuttings from spring to fall.

CARE Water freely in warm weather, less at other times. Apply liquid feed monthly from late spring to fall. Protect from severe frost in zone 8.

SPECIES AND CULTIVARS H. × *andersonii* 'Variegata': 90 cm/36 in or more tall, narrow oblong leaves, in shades of gray-green, margined creamy-white, with violet flowers that fade to white. *H. cupressoides*: 60 cm/24 in or more tall, gray-green foliage of whipcord type, pale bluish-purple flowers. The rest of the species listed here have the larger leaves. *H.* × *franciscana* 'Blue Gem': 60 cm/24 in or more tall, elliptic, lustrous leaves, violet flowers; 'Variegata': leaves with broad cream margins. *H. glaucophylla*': 60–90 cm/24–36 in or more tall, compact, rounded form, blue-green lanceolate-shaped leaves, white flowers. *H. salicifolia*: 1.2 m/4 ft or more tall, willowlike leaves, 10 cm/4 in or more long, white flowers in long spikes; many hybrids with other species, some with colored flowers.

Ilex Holly
ZONES 6–9   Easy
HEIGHT 1.8 m/6 ft or more
SPREAD 1.2 m/4 ft
FLOWERS Spring: white
Erect bushy habit. Broad oval, hard-textured, prickly, glossy leaves. Tiny, starry flowers, in clusters in leaf axils. Usually unisexual, so plants of both sexes are needed for a good berry crop; any male holly will pollinate. Red, shiny berries in the fall last well where birds are not a nuisance.

CONTAINER SIZE 45–90 cm/18–36 in wide and at least 30 cm/12 in deep.
PLANTING Singly, in shade or sun.
PROPAGATION By cuttings in fall.
CARE Water freely in hot weather, less at other times. Apply liquid feed monthly during growing season.
SPECIES AND CULTIVARS *I.* × *altaclarensis*: similar to *I. aquifolium* (below) but more robust, with larger, less spiny foliage. Recommended cultivars: 'Lawsoniana' (female), leaves with bold central yellow blotch. *I. aquifolium*, Common holly, has produced many good groups of cultivars, such as: 'Argenteomarginata', with white-margined leaves. Several forms of this are available, the best being 'Handsworth New Silver' (female) with purple stems and broadly mar-

gined leaves. The 'Aureomarginata' group have yellow or creamy-yellow-margined leaves – 'Ovata Aurea' (male) has a neat, compact habit; 'Pendula' (female): weeping habit. *I.a.* 'Gold King' (female) has yellow-margined leaves, fruits large but few.

Lavandula angustifolia (spica)
Common lavender, Old English lavender
ZONES 5–9   Easy
HEIGHT 40–75 cm/16–30 in
SPREAD 30–60 cm/12–24 in
FLOWERS Late summer: shades of purple-blue, pink and white
Erect bushy habit at first, spreading later. Sweetly aromatic, very narrow, gray leaves. Small, tubular flowers in dense wheatlike spikes.
CONTAINER SIZE 40–60 cm/16–24 in wide by 25–30 cm/10–12 in deep.
SOIL Any approved potting mix, preferably loam-based.
PLANTING Singly in small containers, or in groups of three or more, 25–30 cm/10–12 in apart, in sun.
PROPAGATION By seeds in warmth in spring or by cuttings in late summer.
CARE Water regularly but avoid over-wet soil. Cut off flower spikes when dead and clip in spring to maintain compact habit.
CULTIVARS 'Alba': white flowers; 'Hidcote' ('Nana Atropurpurea'):

compact habit, violet-purple flowers; 'Munstead': compact habit, greener leaves, bright mauve-blue flowers; 'Twickel Purple': 60–90 cm/24–36 in, flower spikes in fanned clusters.

Ligustrum Privet
ZONES 5–9   Easy
HEIGHT 1.8 m/6 ft or more
SPREAD 1.2–1.5 m/4–5 ft
FLOWERS Late summer to the fall: white
Bushy habit. Elliptic, glossy leaves. Small, tubular, four-petaled flowers, in dense clusters.
CONTAINER SIZE 60–90 cm/24–36 in wide by 30 cm/12 in or more deep.
PLANTING Singly, in sun or partial shade.
PROPAGATION By cuttings in late summer.
CARE Water freely in warm weather, less at other times. Apply liquid feed monthly, late spring to late summer.
SPECIES AND CULTIVAR *L. japonicum* Japanese privet: very dark, lustrous green leaves, 5–8 cm/2–3¾ in long – good foliage plant. *L. ovalifolium* 'Aureum' Golden privet: grown for its leaves, either yellow or with green central zone.

Myrtus communis
Common myrtle
ZONES 8–10   Easy
HEIGHT 1.2–1.5 m/4–5 ft
SPREAD 90–120 cm/36–48 in
FLOWERS Late summer: white
Bushy habit. Aromatic, broad lance-shaped, glossy, green leaves. Flowers 2–2.5 cm/¾–1 in wide, five-petaled

Ilex aquifolium

× *Fatshedera lizei*

Ligustrum ovalifolium

Euonymus fortunei

Hebe cupressoides

Lavandula angustifolia

with prominent boss of white, yellow-tipped stamens. Purple-black berries.
CONTAINER SIZE 40–60 cm/16–24 in wide by 30 cm/12 in deep.
PLANTING Singly, in sun, but tolerates partial shade.
PROPAGATION By cuttings in summer.
CARE Water regularly but avoid over-wet soil. Apply liquid feed monthly during growing season. Needs protection in areas of sharp frost.
CULTIVARS 'Compacta': dwarf habit, small leaves; 'Flore Pleno': double flowers; 'Tarentina' ('Jenny Reitenbach'): narrower and somewhat shorter leaves, white berries, hardier than the species itself; 'Variegata': creamy-white margined leaves.

Pieris
ZONES 5–9 Moderately easy
HEIGHT 1.2–1.5 m/4–5 ft
SPREAD 90–120 cm/36–48 in
FLOWERS Spring: white or pink-tinted
Bushy habit. Oblong to lance-shaped, glossy, green leaves. Small, urn-shaped flowers, in pendent sprays.
CONTAINER SIZE 40–60 cm/16–24 in wide by 30 cm/12 in deep.
SOIL An approved *Rhododendron* mix or one of the all-peat rooting mixes, without lime.
PLANTING One per container, in partial shade.
PROPAGATION By cuttings in late summer.

Pieris formosa forrestii

CARE Water freely in warm weather, but avoid over-wet soil. In areas of spring frost (zones 5–8), protect or set in a sheltered corner, as flowers and young leaves are tender.
SPECIES AND CULTIVARS *P. formosa* (zones 8–9): leaves up to 10 cm/4 in long, bright coppery-red when young. *P.f. forrestii*: somewhat pendent habit, young leaves rich red. *P. japonica*: bushier habit and slower growing than *P. formosa*, but hardier (zones 5–9) – young leaves are copper-tinted; 'Christmas Cheer': flowers flushed pink; 'Variegata': slower-growing, cream-edged leaves, often pink-flushed when young.

Pittosporum
ZONES 8–10 Easy
HEIGHT 1.2–1.8 m/4–6 ft
SPREAD 90–120 cm/36–48 in
FLOWERS Spring: chocolate to red-purple
Erect, fairly bushy habit. Oval, glossy, firm-textured leaves. Small, five-petaled flowers in leaf axils.
CONTAINER SIZE 40–60 cm/16–24 in wide by 30 cm/12 in deep.
PLANTING Singly, in sun or very light shade.
PROPAGATION By seeds in warmth in spring or by cuttings in late summer. (Seeds are often slow to germinate and cuttings do not root easily.)

Pittosporum tobira

CARE Water freely in warm weather, but avoid over-wet soil. Apply liquid feed monthly during growing season. Protect from severe frost in colder parts of zone 8. *P. tenuifolium* can be kept as a short, bushy foliage plant by hard pruning in late spring.
SPECIES AND CULTIVARS *P. eugenioides* (zones 9–10) has glossy leaves with wavy edges, smooth gray bark, fragrant, yellow flowers in spring, good screening plant. *P. tenuifolium* more slimly erect with wiry purple-black twigs, wavy, pale, lustrous leaves and fragrant, chocolate-purple flowers; 'Atropurpureum' (purple-flushed leaves), 'Garettii' (variegated white leaves, flushed pink) and 'Warnham Gold' (golden-yellow leaves) are all less hardy than the green-leaved type. *P. tobira* (zones 8–9) is bushy and more wide-spreading, white to pale yellow, fragrant flowers. *P.t.* 'Wheeler's Dwarf' is a dwarf form (to 60 cm/24 in tall).

Prunus Cherry laurel
ZONES 6–9 Easy
HEIGHT 1.2–1.8 m/4–6 ft
SPREAD 90–150 cm/36–60 in
FLOWERS Spring to early summer: white
Bushy habit. Oblong to oval, leathery, lustrous leaves. Small, five-petaled flowers, in axillary spikes.
CONTAINER SIZE 40–90 cm/16–36 in wide by at least 30 cm/12 in deep.
PLANTING Singly, in sun or shade.
PROPAGATION Cuttings, late summer.
CARE Water freely in warm weather,

Senecio × 'Sunshine'

Rhododendron yakushimanum

less at other times. Apply liquid feed monthly from spring to early fall. Can be pruned drastically in spring, to keep neat shape.
SPECIES AND CULTIVARS *P. illicifolia* (zones 8–10) leaves to 5 cm/2 in long, with creamy-white flowers in spring, drought tolerant. *P. laurocerasus* Cherry laurel or Common laurel: vigorous, leaves to 15 cm/6 in long, with 7–13 cm/3–5 in flower spikes in spring. *P. lusitanica* leaves 6–13 cm/2½–5 in long, and flowers from early to midsummer; 'Variegata': white-margined leaves.

Rhododendron including Azalea
ZONES 5–9 Moderately easy
HEIGHT 30–120 cm/12–48 in
SPREAD 30–90 cm/12–36 in
FLOWERS Spring to summer: red, pink, yellow, purple, white
Wide habit range, from prostrate to bushy shrubs and trees. Hundreds of different species and cultivars, both evergreen and deciduous, most growing well in containers.
CONTAINER SIZE 25–40 cm/10–16 in wide by 25–30 cm/10–12 in deep.
SOIL An approved *Rhododendron* or ericaceous potting mix, or any acid peaty soil.
PLANTING Singly, or if small, in groups of three or more, in partial shade. Dwarf small-leaved sorts prefer sun.
PROPAGATION By layering in spring,

Prunus laurocerasus

or by cuttings in late summer or fall (not always easy).

CARE Water freely in warm weather but avoid over-wet soil. Spray over with soft or rainwater daily during dry warm spells. Apply liquid feed monthly during growing season.

SPECIES AND CULTIVARS **Evergreen species and hybrids** R. *cinnabarinum* (zones 6–9): 1.5 m/5 ft tall, gray-green leaves up to 10 cm/4 in, narrow, bell-shaped, pendent, buff-red flowers. R. *indicum* (*Azalea indica*) Indian azalea (zones 8–10): 90 cm/36 in or more tall, small leaves, with broad, funnel-shaped, red flowers; needs protection during winter in zone 8. R. *kaempferi* (R. *obtusum*) Japanese azalea (zones 6–9): 1.2 m/4 ft or more tall, but slow-growing, similar to R. *indicum* but semi-deciduous, red or pink flowers; main parent of Kurume azaleas which include 'Hinodegiri' (crimson), 'Kureno-yuki' (white), 'Sherwood Red' (orange-red), 'Ward's Ruby' (dark red). R. *racemosum*: erect habit, 1.2 m/4 ft tall, small leaves, with blue-white undersides, funnel-shaped pink to red flowers. R. *russatum* (zones 7–9): 60 cm/24 in tall, compact habit, slow-growing, wide funnel-shaped, deep purple-blue flowers. R. *wardii* (zones 7–9): 1.5 m/5 ft or more tall, leaves almost round, to 10 cm/4 in long, with gray undersides, shallow cup-

Rhododendron luteum

Viburnum davidii

Skimmia japonica

Santolina chamaecyparissus

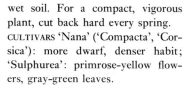

shaped, bright yellow flowers. R. *yakushimanum*: compact habit, 90 cm/36 in or more and wider than tall, narrow leaves, buff-felted beneath and dark, smooth, green above, bell-shaped flowers, pale pink turning to white. **Deciduous azalea types** R. *luteum* (*Azalea pontica*): to 1.8 m/6 ft tall, bright, deep yellow flowers, heavily fragrant, in spring. An important parent of the Ghent azaleas of which there are many fine cultivars, e.g. 'Gloria Mundi', bright orange and yellow; 'Nancy Waterer', gold. The Knap Hill azalea group is similar to Ghent, in yellow, orange, red, pink, e.g. 'Cecile', salmon-pink with yellow flare.

Santolina chamaecyparissus (incana)
Lavender cotton
ZONES 8–9   Easy
HEIGHT 40–60 cm/16–24 in
SPREAD 40–60 cm/16–24 in or more
FLOWERS Late summer: lemon-yellow
Bushy, hummock-forming habit; small, narrow, ferny, gray-white downy leaves. Button-shaped flower heads, well above foliage, can be removed in bud stage if the plant is grown for foliage only.
CONTAINER SIZE 30–40 cm/12–16 in wide by 30 cm/12 in deep.
PLANTING Singly, or in small groups in larger containers, in sun.
PROPAGATION By cuttings in late summer.
CARE Water regularly, but avoid over-

wet soil. For a compact, vigorous plant, cut back hard every spring.
CULTIVARS 'Nana' ('Compacta', 'Corsica'): more dwarf, denser habit; 'Sulphurea': primrose-yellow flowers, gray-green leaves.

Senecio × 'Sunshine'
ZONES 8–10   Easy
HEIGHT 60–90 cm/24–36 in
SPREAD 90 cm/36 in or more
FLOWERS Summer to the fall: yellow
Often sold as S. *greyi* or S. *laxifolius*. Bushy, hummock-forming habit. Elliptic leaves, up to 6 cm/2½ in long, densely white-felted beneath. Daisy-like flower heads, in large clusters above the foliage.
CONTAINER SIZE 40–60 cm/16–24 in.
PLANTING Singly, in sun.
PROPAGATION By cuttings in late summer.
CARE Water regularly but avoid over-wet soil. Remove spent flowering stems promptly to maintain neat appearance. Give well-established plants liquid feed monthly during growing season.

Skimmia japonica
ZONES 7–9   Easy
HEIGHT 90 cm/36 in or more
SPREAD 90 cm/36 in or more
FLOWERS Spring: white
Bushy rounded habit, thinner if in full shade. Narrow elliptic leaves to 10 cm/4 in long, aromatic when bruised. Unisexual, fragrant flowers in dense terminal clusters. Plants of both sexes are needed for a crop of pea-sized, glossy red berries, lasting throughout the winter.
CONTAINER SIZE 40–60 cm/16–24 in wide by at least 30 cm/12 in deep.
PLANTING Singly, in partial shade or full sun; also tolerates full shade.
PROPAGATION By layering in spring, or by cuttings in late summer.

CARE Water freely in warm weather, less at other times. Apply liquid feed monthly from late spring to fall.
CULTIVARS One male cultivar pollinates several females. 'Foremanii' (female): fruit in large clusters; 'Fragrans' (male): free-flowering and strongly scented; 'Macrophylla' (male): rounded form, spreading to 1.8 m/6 ft, large leaves; 'Rubella' (male): free-blooming, red buds.

Viburnum
ZONES 7–9   Easy
HEIGHT 90–180 cm/36–72 in
SPREAD 90–120 cm/36–48 in
FLOWERS Winter to early summer: white
Bushy habit, elliptic to oval, leathery, glossy leaves. Small flowers in dense flattened, terminal heads. Blue berry-like fruits.
CONTAINER SIZE 40–60 cm/16–24 in wide by at least 30 cm/12 in deep, larger for big specimens of V. *tinus*.
PLANTING Singly, in sun or partial shade.
PROPAGATION By cuttings in late summer.
CARE Water freely in warm weather, less at other times. Give well-established specimens liquid feed monthly during growing season.
SPECIES AND CULTIVARS V. *davidii*: domed habit, 90 cm/36 in or more tall. Boldly veined, dark green leaves 6–13 cm/2½–5 in long. Plants usually bear flowers of one sex only, opening early summer. To make sure that the bright blue fruits are produced, grow two or more plants close together. V. *tinus* Laurustinus (zones 8–9) is taller, to 1.8 m/6 ft, with smaller leaves, not boldly veined, and pink-budded flowers, usually profuse, from winter to spring; 'Dwarf': dense habit, large flower heads. V.t. *lucidum*: less hardy, leaves marked creamy-yellow.

Broad-leaved trees and shrubs: deciduous

Acer Maple
ZONES 2–8   Easy
HEIGHT 3 m/10 ft or more
SPREAD 1.2–1.8 m/4–6 ft
Small trees of well-branched habit. Leaves deeply lobed or formed of several separate leaflets.
CONTAINER SIZE 60–90 cm/24–36 in wide by 30–40 cm/12–16 in deep.
SOIL Any approved potting mix, lime-free for *A. palmatum*.
PLANTING Singly, in sun or partial shade.
PROPAGATION By seeds when ripe, by grafting cultivars in late winter, or by softwood cuttings in late spring to early summer (not easy).
CARE Water freely in warm weather, less at other times. Apply liquid feed monthly during growing season.
SPECIES AND CULTIVARS *A. negundo*, Ash-leaved maple or Box elder, has pinnate, ash-tree like foliage of three to seven leaflets; 'Aureomarginatum': variegated, pale yellow leaves; 'Californium': pale green leaves, very drought tolerant; 'Variegatum' ('Argenteovariegatum'): white-margined leaves, not recommended for areas with hot, dry summers. *A. palmatum* Japanese maple: often a bushy shrub

Amelanchier canadensis

or dwarf tree, slow-growing, with bright green leaves cut into five to seven deep lobes, turning red in the fall. Many cultivars available, e.g. 'Atropurpureum': red-purple to bronze-crimson leaves; 'Aureum': soft-yellow leaves; 'Dissectum' (green) and 'Dissectum Atropurpureum' (purple): shrubby, leaves cut into seven to ten very narrow lobes; 'Sangokaku': fall foliage yellow with rose tints; its red twigs give good color in winter; 'Tricolor': leaves spotted red, pink and white.

Amelanchier June berry, Service berry, Shadbush, Snowy mespilus
ZONES 4–8   Easy
HEIGHT 2–3 m/6½–10 ft
SPREAD 1.2–1.5 m/4–5 ft
FLOWERS Spring: white
Small tree or large shrub of bushy habit. Oblong, toothed leaves, turning to shades of red and orange in the fall. Five-petaled flowers, in short spikes, opening with the un-

furling leaves. Berrylike fruits.
CONTAINER SIZE 60–90 cm/24–36 in wide by 30–40 cm/12–16 in deep.
SOIL Any approved neutral to acid potting mix.
PLANTING Singly, in sun or light shade.
PROPAGATION By layering in spring or by suckers in fall.
CARE Water freely in warm weather, less at other times. Apply liquid feed monthly during growing season.
SPECIES *A. canadensis* is erect in habit, with leaves to 6 cm/2½ in long, white-felted when young. *A. laevis* is similar and coppery-red. Both flower profusely when established. *A. florida*: 1.2–4.5 m/4–15 ft tall, leaves turn yellow in the fall. *A.f.* 'Altaglow' has neat columnar habit.

Azalea see under **Rhododendron**, pp. 100–101.

Buddleia davidii
ZONES 5–9   Easy
HEIGHT 1.5–2.1 m/5–7 ft
SPREAD 1.2–1.5 m/4–5 ft
FLOWERS Summer to fall: lilac, purple, white
Erect to spreading habit; vigorous. Lance-shaped leaves to 20 cm/8 in long, with gray-white felted undersides. Small, tubular flowers, in dense, tapered trusses.

CONTAINER SIZE 60–90 cm/24–36 in wide by at least 30 cm/12 in deep.
PLANTING Singly, in sun or very light shade.
PROPAGATION By cuttings in late summer.
CARE Water freely during warm weather, less at other times. Apply liquid feed monthly from spring to fall. Prune annually in late winter, cutting back the previous season's growth to 10–15 cm/4–6 in.
CULTIVARS 'Black Knight': flowers deep violet; 'Charming': pink flowers and grayish foliage; 'Fascinating': violet-pink flowers; 'Peace': large white flower trusses.

Deutzia
ZONES 4–9   Easy
HEIGHT 1.5–1.8 m/5–6 ft
SPREAD 1.2–1.5 m/4–5 ft
FLOWERS Late spring and summer: white, pink, rose-purple
Well-branched shrub, of erect to semierect habit, with lance-shaped leaves, and five-petaled flowers in lateral clusters.
CONTAINER SIZE 40–60 cm/16–24 in wide and 30 cm/12 in deep, or more.
PLANTING Singly, in sun or very light shade.
PROPAGATION By cuttings in late summer.
CARE Water freely in warm weather, less at other times. Apply liquid feed monthly during growing season.
SPECIES AND CULTIVARS *D. gracilis*: to 1.5 m/5 ft tall, with abundant, pure white flowers; needs protection from late spring frosts but flowers ahead of season on an enclosed balcony or patio. *D.* × 'Mont Rose': robust habit, large leaves, and big rose-purple flowers that open in summer. *D. scabra*: erect habit, 1.8 m/6 ft or more tall, white, bell-shaped flowers in mid- to late summer; 'Candidissima': double flowers; 'Flore Pleno':

Acer negundo

Buddleia davidii

Deutzia scabra

double flowers, tinted rose-purple. Other species and cultivars are available, all suitable for containers.

Forsythia Golden bells

ZONES 4–8 Easy
HEIGHT 1.5–1.8 m/5–6 ft
SPREAD 1.2–1.5 m/4–5 ft
FLOWERS Late winter and spring: yellow

Erect to spreading or arching habit. Oval to lance-shaped, toothed leaves sometimes three-lobed or trifoliate. Four-petaled, belllike flowers, borne before the leaves.
CONTAINER SIZE 40–60 cm/16–24 in wide by at least 30 cm/12 in deep.
PLANTING Singly, in sun or very light shade.
PROPAGATION By cuttings in late summer or fall.
CARE Water freely in warm weather, less at other times. Apply liquid feed monthly during growing season. Cut back flowering stems after blooming to maintain a well-branched habit.
SPECIES AND CULTIVAR F. × intermedia: semierect habit, vigorous, profusely borne flowers; F. × i. 'Spring Glory': bright sulphur-yellow flowers, the best cultivar for containers. F. suspensa (F.s. seiboldii) (zones 5–8):

Gleditsia triacanthos

spreading, semipendulous habit, leaves often trifoliate, golden-yellow flowers in early spring. F.s. atrocaulis: purple-black stems, lemon-yellow flowers, opening later than other cultivars. F.s. fortunei: arching to semierect habit.

Fuchsia magellanica

Hardy fuchsia
ZONES 8–10 Easy
HEIGHT 90–150 cm/36–60 in
SPREAD 60–120 cm/24–48 in
FLOWERS Summer to fall: red, pink, purple

Erect, moderately bushy habit. Oval to lance-shaped leaves. Flowers, pendent from leaf axils, composed of four narrow, spreading sepals and four broad petals to form a bell.
CONTAINER SIZE 30–60 cm/12–24 in wide by 30 cm/12 in deep.
PLANTING Singly, in sun, but in particularly hot, dry areas light shade is preferable.
PROPAGATION By cuttings at any time from spring to early fall.
CARE Water freely in warm weather, less at other times, avoiding over-wet soil. Apply liquid feed every two weeks from late spring to early fall. Protect plants from severe frost in the colder parts of zone 8. Can be cut back close to ground level each spring to maintain low, bushy plants that flower mainly in late summer and the fall. If grown as a larger shrub,

thin out a little each spring, removing completely the weaker, twiggy, two-to three-year-old stems.
CULTIVARS AND VARIETIES 'Riccartonii': like the species itself but hardier and more robust, with fuller flowers in richer hues. F.m. gracilis (macrostemma): the hardiest form, of slender, arching habit, with narrow tubular flowers; 'Alba' ('Molinae'): white flowers, tinted rose-pink; 'Versicolor': grayish leaves, pink-tinted when young, then white-margined. Many hybrid fuchsias are available in a wider range of colors; those described as 'hardy' can be grown like F. magellanica.

Gleditsia triacanthos 'Sunburst'

ZONES 4–9 Moderately easy
HEIGHT 3 m/10 ft or more
SPREAD 1.5–1.8 m/5–6 ft or more
Smallish tree with spreading branches, ferny leaves, both pinnate and bipinnate, 10–20 cm/4–8 in long, rich yellow when young, turning to yellow-green. The small, pale yellow flowers are seldom produced.
CONTAINER SIZE 90 cm/36 in wide and 40 cm/16 in deep, or more.
PLANTING Singly, sun or light shade.
PROPAGATION By bud-grafting on green-leaved seedlings.
CARE Water freely in warm weather, less at other times. Apply liquid feed monthly during growing season.

Hibiscus syriacus Hardy hibiscus

ZONES 5–9 Moderately easy
HEIGHT 1.5 m/5 ft or more
SPREAD 1.2 m/4 ft or more
FLOWERS Late summer to fall: pink, red, purple, blue-purple
Moderately bushy habit. Triangular-oval leaves, usually three-lobed. Five-petaled flowers, 5–7.5 cm/2–3 in wide, in upper leaf axils.
CONTAINER SIZE 40–60 cm/16–24 in wide by 30 cm/12 in or more deep.
PLANTING Singly, in sun.
PROPAGATION By cuttings in late summer.
CARE Water freely in warm weather but avoid over-wet soil. Apply liquid feed monthly from late spring to early fall.
CULTIVARS 'Albus': single, white flowers; 'Blue Bird': violet-blue; 'Duc de Brabant': double, deep rose-purple; 'Woodbridge': rich rose-pink, with carmine eye.

Hydrangea macrophylla (hortensis)

ZONES 6–9 Easy
HEIGHT 90–120 cm/36–48 in
SPREAD 75–105 cm/30–42 in
FLOWERS Summer to fall: pink, red, purple, blue
Semierect habit, domed outline.

Hibiscus syriacus

Fuchsia magellanica *Hydrangea macrophylla*

Forsythia × intermedia

Broad oval leaves, deeply veined. Bears two kinds of flower, one kind small and fertile, the other larger and sterile. In wild species and similar forms – known as 'Lacecap' – tiny fertile flowers form flattened clusters surrounded by conspicuous sterile flowers. More popular are mopheaded 'Hortensia' cultivars, whose flower clusters are mainly composed of sterile flowers. Cultivars of both groups produce blue or rich purple-blue coloring only in acid soil. In alkaline soil, the same cultivars will be red or pink.
CONTAINER SIZE 40–60 cm/16–24 in wide by at least 30 cm/12 in deep.
SOIL Any approved potting mix, lime-free for blue-flowered cultivars.
PLANTING Singly, in partial shade, or in sun in areas with cool summers.
PROPAGATION By cuttings in spring or late summer to early fall.
CARE Water freely in warm weather, less at other times. Apply liquid feed every two weeks in growing season. To maintain a plant under 90 cm/36 in with good heads of bloom, remove flowered stems at their bases each spring.
CULTIVARS **Lacecap group** – 'Blue Wave': blue or pink; 'Lanarth White':

fertile flowers blue or pink, sterile ones white; 'Mariesii': large sterile flowers, pink to blue.
Hortensia group – 'Altona': rose-pink or blue; 'Ami Pasquier': crimson; 'Domotoi': pink or blue, double, sterile flowers; 'Hamburg': large, deep pink or purple flowers.

Hypericum
ZONES 6–9 Easy
HEIGHT 60–90 cm/24–36 in
SPREAD 60–75 cm/24–30 in
FLOWERS Summer to the fall: yellow
Bushy habit, rounded outline. Lance-shaped to elliptic, smooth leaves. Five-petaled flowers, with a central boss of slender stamens, of good size and rather like a wild species rose.
CONTAINER SIZE 40–60 cm/16–24 in wide by 30 cm/12 in or more deep.
PLANTING Singly, sun or light shade.
PROPAGATION By cuttings in late summer.
CARE Water freely in warm weather, less at other times. Apply liquid feed monthly during growing season. Thin out twiggy, three-year-old stems each spring.
SPECIES AND CULTIVAR H. × 'Hidcote': rich green leaves, long-lasting in mild winters. Saucer-shaped flowers, 7 cm/2¾ in wide. *H. patulum* covers several closely related species, e.g. *H. forrestii*, *pseudohenryi*, similar to

'Hidcote' but of more compact habit and very freely flowering.

Kerria japonica
ZONES 4–8 Easy
HEIGHT 1.2–1.8 m/4–6 ft
SPREAD 1.2–1.5 m/4–5 ft
FLOWERS Spring to summer: yellow
Spreading to erect habit. Oval to lance-shaped leaves, double-toothed. Five-petaled flowers, like small, single roses.
CONTAINER SIZE 40–60 cm/16–24 in wide by at least 30 cm/12 in deep.
PLANTING Singly, in sun or shade.
PROPAGATION By division when re-potting or by cuttings late summer.
CARE Water regularly. Apply liquid feed monthly during growing season.
CULTIVARS 'Pleniflora' ('Flore Pleno') Bachelor's buttons: the most commonly cultivated *Kerria*, erect, robust stems, fully double flowers; 'Picta' ('Variegata'): white-margined leaves.

Philadelphus Mock orange, 'Syringa' (see also *Syringa*, p. 105)
ZONES 5–8 Easy
HEIGHT 1.2–1.8 m/4–6 ft
SPREAD 1.2–1.5 m/4–5 ft
FLOWERS Summer: white
Bushy habit. Oval to lance-shaped leaves, prominently veined. Four-petaled, cup-shaped flowers, often

fragrant, in profusely borne clusters.
CONTAINER SIZE 40–60 cm/16–24 in wide by at least 30 cm/12 in deep.
PLANTING Singly, in sun or very light shade.
PROPAGATION By cuttings in late summer.
CARE Water freely in warm weather, less at other times. Apply liquid feed monthly during growing season. Remove twiggy three-year-old stems at base each winter.
CULTIVARS 'Avalanche': arching habit, flowers strongly scented; 'Belle Etoile': very sweetly scented flowers flushed purple at centre; 'Bouquet Blanc': lance-shaped leaves, double orange-scented flowers; 'Silver Showers': compact, pointed elliptic leaves, fragrant flowers; 'Sybille': arching habit, orange-scented flowers purple flushed at center.

Prunus Ornamental cherry
ZONES 2–8 Easy
HEIGHT 1.5–3 m/5–10 ft or more
SPREAD 1.2–1.8 m/4–6 ft or more
FLOWERS Spring: white or pink
Well-branched small trees or large shrubs. Oval to lance-shaped leaves. Five-petaled flowers, in clusters with very young leaves.
CONTAINER SIZE 60–90 cm/24–36 in wide by 40 cm/16 in deep. P. × 'Cistena' will grow in smaller containers 30–45 cm/12–18 in wide and 30 cm/12 in deep.
PLANTING Singly, in sun or partial shade.
PROPAGATION By cuttings in late fall (not easy).
CARE Water freely in dry warm weather, less at other times. Apply liquid feed monthly from late spring to late summer.
SPECIES AND CULTIVARS P. cerasifera Cherry plum (zones 3–8): rounded habit, white flowers appearing before leaves; 'Thundercloud': pink flowers,

Prunus × 'Cistena'

Philadelphus 'Avalanche'

Hypericum × 'Hidcote'

Kerria japonica

purple leaves; 'Pissardii' ('Atropurpurea'): white flowers, purple leaves; 'Vesuvius': deep purple leaves. *P.* × 'Cistena': large shrub, fairly slow-growing, deep red leaves, white flowers. *P. incisa* Fuji cherry (zones 5–8): large shrub or small tree, leaves coloring shades of red and yellow in fall, white or pale pink flowers, usually abundant. *P. subhirtella* (*P.s. ascendens*) Rosebud cherry: small erect tree, abundant pink flowers; 'Autumnalis': spreading habit, semi-double flowers opening from fall to spring in areas of mild winters. *P. triloba* 'Multiplex': shrub or small tree, large, fully double, light rose-pink flowers, before leaves. Can be grown as a shrub under 1.2 m/4 ft tall by pollarding annually immediately after blooming.

Spiraea

ZONES 4–9 Easy
HEIGHT 90–150 cm/36–60 in
SPREAD 90–120 cm/36–48 in
FLOWERS Spring to late summer: white, pink, red
Bushy habit. Very narrow to oval leaves. Five-petaled, tiny flowers, in dense clusters.
CONTAINER SIZE 40–60 cm/16–24 in wide by at least 30 cm/12 in deep.
PLANTING Singly, sun or light shade.
PROPAGATION Cuttings, late summer.
CARE Water freely in warm weather, less at other times. Apply liquid feed monthly during summer.
SPECIES AND HYBRIDS *S.* × *arguta* Bridal wreath (zones 4–8): graceful habit, very slender twigs, very narrow, pointed leaves, pure white flowers, before leaves. *S. japonica* (including *S. bumalda*) (zones 5–9): rounded habit, if pruned hard each spring, lance-shaped leaves, with whitish-green undersides, pink to red flowers, in wide, flat heads, late summer, 'Anthony Waterer': cream

and pink-tinted shoots, crimson flowers. *S.* × *vanhouttei*: erect to arching habit, oval, shallowly lobed leaves, white flowers in early summer.

Syringa Lilac

ZONES 3–9 Easy
HEIGHT 1.2–2.4 m/4–8 ft
SPREAD 90–150 cm/36–60 in
FLOWERS Spring to summer: white, red, blue-purple, yellow
More or less erect, well-branched habit. Broad, oval to heart-shaped leaves, in opposite pairs. Tubular, four-petaled flowers, usually fragrant, in dense terminal trusses.
CONTAINER SIZE 45–75 cm/18–30 in wide by 40 cm/16 in deep. For *S. microphylla*, 30–40 cm/12–16 in wide and deep.
SOIL Any approved potting mix, preferably loam-based.
PLANTING Singly, in sun.
PROPAGATION By layering in spring or by cuttings in late summer.
CARE Water freely in warm weather.
SPECIES AND CULTIVARS *S. microphylla*: bushy, twiggy habit to 1.2 m/4 ft tall, rose-pink flowers in small trusses; 'Superba': flowers produced from early summer to the fall. *S. vulgaris* Common lilac: erect habit to 2.4 m/8 ft or more, bluish-purple flowers in large trusses. There are many cultivars, e.g. 'Primrose' (pale yellow), 'Sensation' (purple and white bicolor). Double-flowered cultivars in similar colors.

Viburnum

ZONES 3–9 Easy
HEIGHT 1.2–1.8 m/4–6 ft
SPREAD 1.2–1.5 m/4–5 ft
FLOWERS Spring to summer: white and pink
Bushy, spreading to erect habit. Toothed, prominently veined, narrow to broad oval leaves. Small, tubular, five-petaled flowers, mainly in large, flattened heads. Red, black or yellow berries.
CONTAINER SIZE 40–60 cm/16–24 in wide by 30–40 cm/12–16 in deep.
PLANTING Singly, in sun or very light shade.
PROPAGATION By cuttings in late summer.
CARE Water freely in warm weather, less at other times. Apply liquid feed monthly from late spring to late summer.
SPECIES AND CULTIVARS *V.* × *bodnantense*: erect habit, fragrant pink-tinted white flowers, from fall to spring in areas of mild winters. *V. opulus*: spreading habit, lobed, maplelike leaves, bright red fruits, white, pendent blooms in summer – like Lacecap hydrangeas (see pp. 101–2) bears small fertile and larger sterile flowers; 'Sterile' ('Roseum'):

all flowers in mop-heads sterile, turning to pink; 'Fructuluteo': chrome-yellow fruits. *V. plicatum tomentosum*: spreading habit, flowerheads like those of *V. opulus*, borne erect; 'Mariesii': horizontal branches, creating a tiered habit.

Weigela florida (Diervilla florida)

ZONES 5–9 Easy
HEIGHT 1.2–1.8 m/4–6 ft
SPREAD 1.2–1.5 m/4–5 ft
FLOWERS Summer: white, pink, red
Bushy habit. Oval-oblong, slender-pointed leaves, to 10 cm/4 in long. Tubular flowers, with five-petal lobes, in lateral clusters.
CONTAINER SIZE 45–60 cm/18–24 in wide by at least 30 cm/12 in deep.
PLANTING Singly, sun or light shade.
PROPAGATION By cuttings, in late summer or fall.
CARE Water freely in warm weather, less at other times. Apply liquid feed monthly from late spring to early fall. Thin out congested growth after flowering, removing at bases some or all three-year-old stems.
CULTIVARS 'Bristol Ruby': erect habit, ruby-red flowers; 'Bristol Snowflake': white; 'Foliis Purpureis': purple leaves, slow-growing purplish-pink flowers; 'Perle': cream colored, edged with pink; 'Variegata': leaves margined pale yellow, pink flowers.

Syringa vulgaris

Weigela florida

Spiraea × *arguta*

Viburnum opulus

Roses

The container gardener need not be without roses. Indeed although most roses do best in the open ground in clay soil, they perform remarkably well in a patented potting mix in containers. They respond to the same regime of repotting, top dressing and feeding as that outlined on p. 95. Pruning requirements vary and will be discussed in more detail under the groups described below, and on pp. 40–3.

All the really popular roses are of hybrid origin, some of them of ancient lineage, others very recent. Many thousands of cultivars are known and it is convenient to classify them into six very broad groupings: Old-fashioned shrub, Modern shrub, Floribunda (Cluster-flowered), Hybrid tea (Large-flowered), Climbers and ramblers, and Species shrub roses.

The knowledgeable rose enthusiast will recognize a few other smaller groups, but for the beginner, these can be fitted easily into the first two groups.

Old-fashioned shrub roses

ZONES 5–9 Easy
HEIGHT 1.2–1.8 m/4–6 ft
SPREAD 90–120 cm/36–48 in
FLOWERS Summer: white, pink, red, violet-red

Erect to spreading habit, often somewhat gaunt or thin when old. Fragrant, semidouble or double flowers, opening out flat at maturity. The buds of some cultivars are covered with a sticky, green, mosslike growth – these are the so-called 'moss roses'.
CONTAINER SIZE 40–60 cm/16–24 in wide by 40 cm/16 in deep.
PLANTING Singly, sun or partial shade.
PROPAGATION By bud grafting in summer or by cuttings in fall.
CARE Water freely in warm weather, less at other times. Apply liquid feed monthly from late spring to early fall. Very little pruning is needed, but in spring, very old, twiggy or weak stems should be cut out at the base to stimulate new growth.
CULTIVARS 'Cardinal de Richelieu': to 1.5 m/5 ft tall, velvety maroon rolled petals; 'Céleste' ('Celestial'): clear pink flowers, grayish leaves; 'Königin von Dänemark' ('Queen of Denmark'): open habit, shapely crimson-pink flowers; 'Nuits de Young': moss rose with small, neat maroon flowers; 'Tour de Malakoff': lax habit, best tied to a support, cerise-magenta, violet and mauve blooms; 'William Lobb' ('Old Velvet Moss'): gaunt habit, crimson-purple flowers.

Modern shrub roses

ZONES 5–9 Easy
HEIGHT 1.2–2.1 m/4–7 ft
SPREAD 90–150 cm/36–60 in
FLOWERS Summer to fall: white, pink, red, yellow, purple

Habits vary from low and compact to tall and loose, usually very well branched. Single, semidouble or double flowers, sometimes fragrant, in certain cases followed by attractive fruits, or hips.
CONTAINER SIZE 40–60 cm/16–24 in wide by 40 cm/16 in deep.
PLANTING Singly, in sun or partial shade.
PROPAGATION By bud grafting or cuttings in fall.
CARE As Old-fashioned shrub roses.
CULTIVARS 'Canary Bird': to 1.8 m/6 ft tall, single, bright yellow flowers; 'Constance Spry': to 2.1 m/7 ft, double, cupped, clear rose-pink flowers; 'Frühlingsmorgen': to 2.4 m/8 ft, widespreading if in a large container, single, pink flowers with yellow eye and maroon stamens; 'Kassel': 2.1 m/7 ft, dark, glossy foliage, buff-red and cherry-red flowers, will grow taller if trained against a wall; 'Maigold': to 2.4 m/8 ft, dark, glossy leaves, semidouble, deep yellow, richly scented flowers; 'Scarlet Fire': to 1.8 m/6 ft, arching habit, with single, velvety, bright scarlet flowers. **Hybrid Musk roses** – 'Buff Beauty': to 1.8 m/6 ft tall, double, apricot-yellow, fragrant flowers; 'Cornelia': 1.5 m/5 ft, double, rosette-like, coppery-pink flowers; 'Will Scarlet', to 1.8 m/6 ft, semidouble, crimson flowers with white eye. **Rugosa roses**, derived from the species *R. rugosa* (see below) – 'Pink Grootendorst': to 2.1 m/7 ft tall, clear pink flowers with fringed petals; 'Schneezwerg' ('Snow Dwarf'): to 1.8 m/6 ft, bushy habit, semidouble, pure white flowers.

Floribunda (Cluster-flowered) roses

ZONES 5–9 Easy
HEIGHT 75–150 cm/30–60 in
SPREAD 45–75 cm/18–30 in
FLOWERS Summer to fall: pink, red, yellow, white, purple

Mainly erect habit, vigorous. Single, semidouble or double flowers in large clusters.
CONTAINER SIZE 40–45 cm/16–18 in wide by 40 cm/16 in deep.
PLANTING Singly, in sun.
PROPAGATION By bud grafting in summer or by cuttings in fall.
CARE As for Old-fashioned shrub roses, but vigorous annual pruning is necessary. In the fall shorten flowered stems by one-third and in spring cut stems back to 15–20 cm/6–8 in. From time to time cut out old or weak branches near the base, to stimulate new growth.
CULTIVARS All these are double-flowered, and 60–90 cm/24–36 in tall if pruned annually. 'All Gold': deep golden-yellow flowers; 'Circus': orange, buff or pink (All-American selection); 'Dearest': salmon-rose; 'Evelyn Fison': bright red; 'Iceberg': pure white; 'Lavender Lassie': lavender-purple; 'Orange Sensation': orange-vermilion; 'Pink Parfait': two shades of soft pink, each petal orange at the base; 'Saratoga': white, scented (All-American selection); 'Topsi': dwarf habit, 45 cm/18 in tall, luminous orange-scarlet; 'Topsi's Friend': shell-pink.

Hybrid tea (Large-flowered) roses

ZONES 5–9 Easy
HEIGHT 75–150 cm/30–60 in
SPREAD 60–75 cm/24–30 in
FLOWERS Summer to fall: red, pink, white, yellow, lilac
Mainly erect habit, often rather sparsely branched. Large, often fragrant flowers, usually fully double

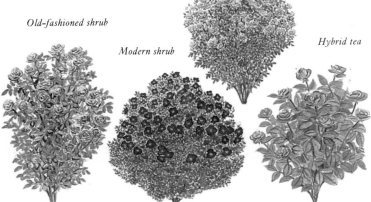

Old-fashioned shrub

Modern shrub

Floribunda

Hybrid tea

with high centers, but singles are known, borne alone or in small clusters.

CONTAINER SIZE 40–45cm/16–18in wide by 40cm/16in deep.

PLANTING Singly, in sun or partial shade.

PROPAGATION By bud grafting in summer.

CARE As for Old-fashioned shrub roses but vigorous annual pruning is necessary. In the fall, shorten flowered stems by one-third and in spring cut stems back to 15–20cm/ 6–8in. Thin out congested bushes by removing at least one complete branch when necessary.

CULTIVARS All 75–90cm/30–36in tall, with fragrant double flowers. 'Blue Moon': pink in bud, blue-lilac when open; 'Caribia': red, striped with gold; 'Ernest H. Morse': bright crimson; 'Fragrant Cloud': orange-red; 'King's Ransom': clear, bright yellow; 'Lowell Thomas': yellow, scented (All-American selection); 'Peace': yellow shaded pink (All-American selection); 'Piccadilly': scarlet with gold reverse to petals; 'Prima Ballerina': deep pink.

Old-fashioned shrub
1 'Cardinal de Richelieu'
2 'Céleste'
3 'Königin von Dänemark'

Modern shrub
4 'Frühlingsmorgen'
5 'Scarlet Fire'
6 'Pink Grootendorst'

Floribunda
7 'All Gold'
8 'Dearest'
9 'Iceberg'
10 'Pink Parfait'
11 'Orange Sensation'

Hybrid tea
12 'Fragrant Cloud'
13 'Caribia'
14 'King's Ransom'
15 'Piccadilly'

Climbing and rambling roses

ZONES 5–9 Easy
HEIGHT 3 m/10 ft or more
SPREAD 90–150 cm/36–60 in or more
FLOWERS Summer to fall:
white, pink, red and yellow
Tall habit with long stems that need support. Single or double flowers, in small to large clusters.
CONTAINER SIZE 40–60 cm/16–24 in wide by 40 cm/16 in deep.
PLANTING Singly, in sun or partial shade.
PROPAGATION By cuttings in fall.
CARE As for Old-fashioned shrub roses but requiring special pruning.
Climbers: on planting, cut back the main stems to 45–60 cm/18–24 in and all other thin growth to 10 cm/4 in. In subsequent years, remove the soft and thin tips of all leading stems and reduce all laterals to two or three buds. All the main leading stems must be secured to a support. **Ramblers:** on planting, cut back all stems

Climbers and Ramblers

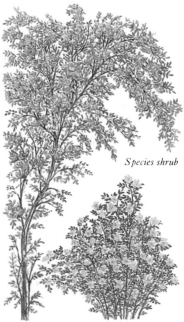

Species shrub

to 30 cm/12 in above the soil. At the end of the first flowering season cut out all flowered stems near their point of origin and tie in the young stems in their places. Some so-called 'ramblers', e.g. 'Albéric Barbier', are midway between ramblers and climbers. To prune them, remove some two- and three-year-old stems annually. Like climbers, ramblers must be tied to a support.
CULTIVARS **Climbers** – 'Danse de Feu': double, vivid red flowers; 'Dr H.J. Nicholas': double rose-pink flowers everblooming; 'Golden Showers': double, bright golden-yellow; 'The New Dawn': semi-rambler type, vigorous, with flowers semidouble, silver-pink. **Ramblers** – 'Albéric Barbier': semi-climber, vigorous, semidouble, with creamy-yellow, apple-scented flowers; 'Don Juan': deep red, scented; 'Dorothy Perkins': double, bright pink; 'Violette': vigorous, thornless, with flowers double, deep crimson turning maroon-gray.

Species shrub roses

ZONES 2–9 Easy
HEIGHT 1.2–2.4 m/4–8 ft
SPREAD 90–150 cm/36–60 in
FLOWERS Summer to fall:
white, red, pink, rose-purple
Erect or arching to bushy and spreading habits. Single flowers in small clusters; red to black, often showy, hips. This group covers some of the more popular wild species roses.
CONTAINER SIZE 40–60 cm/16–24 in wide by at least 30 cm/12 in deep.
PLANTING Singly, in sun or partial shade.
PROPAGATION By cuttings, suckers or seeds in fall.
CARE As Old-fashioned shrub roses.
SPECIES AND CULTIVARS *R. hugonis* (zones 5–9): arching habit, to 1.8 m/6 ft tall, straight spines, bright yellow

flowers in late spring, one of the very few early-blooming roses. *R. moyesii* (zones 6–9): to 2.4 m/8 ft tall, open habit, straight spines, blood-red flowers to 6 cm/2½ in wide, large, flask-shaped crimson to orange-red hips. *R.m.* 'Geranium': slightly more compact, geranium-red flowers; bears the same hips as the species itself. *R. rubrifolia*: bushy habit, 1.5 m/5 ft or more tall, bears a few straight or curved spines, grayish leaves flushed purple, with small, deep pink to purple-red flowers, 4 cm/1½ in wide, in summer. *R. rugosa* Japanese or Ramanas rose: erect, suckering habit, to 1.5 m/5 ft tall, with finely wrinkled, leathery, glossy leaves, butter-yellow in the fall; rose-purple flowers 6–9 cm/2½–3½ in wide, and large, round, flattened, polished, red hips; 'Blanc Double de Coubert': semi-double, white flowers; 'Frau Dagmar Hastrup': more compact habit, pink flowers. *R. spinosissima* (*R. pimpinellifolia*) Burnet or Scotch rose (zones 4–9): bushy habit to 1.2 m/4 ft or more tall, stems thickly set with straight, bristly spines, creamy-white flowers 4 cm/1½ in long, in summer, and purple-black hips. *R. willmottiae* (zones 6–9): to 1.8 m/6 ft tall, small, straight spines, neat, ferny leaves, rose-purple flowers 3 cm/1¼ in wide.

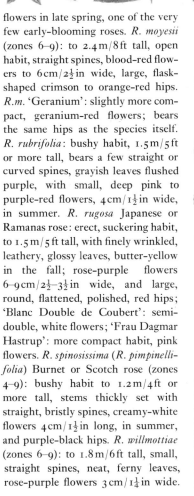

Climbers and Ramblers
1 'Golden Showers'
2 'Handel'
3 'The New Dawn'
4 'Albéric Barbier'
5 'Dorothy Perkins'

Species shrub
6 *R. moyesii*
7 *R. spinosissima*

Climbing plants

Most homes have bare exterior walls which may be dull and even ugly. An ideal camouflage is the tapestry of foliage and flowers provided by climbing plants.

Climbers cling to their supports by various means; these may influence you in your choice. Broadly speaking, there are two main groups: twiners and tendril-bearers. Both require the support of sticks, wires, strings, netting or trellis (see pp. 38–9). Where supports of this kind would be untidy or inconvenient, you could use one of the small group of self-clingers. These adhere to fences and walls either by sucker roots, like ivy, or by sucker-tipped tendrils, like Virginia creeper. None of the self-clingers will harm brick-work or masonry, but an unsightly pattern of sucker roots will be left if you decide to strip them away later.

Supports for the smaller climbers can be pushed into, or attached to, the containers. Larger climbers will need stronger and more extensive supports fixed to walls – galvanized wire, heavy-duty netting or trellis.

The general care of climbers is the same as that outlined on p. 95 and, for the annuals, on p. 113. A beginner may sometimes find problems with pruning (see pp. 40–3), especially of the very bushy, vigorous, fast-growing climbers, like honeysuckle, clematis and jasmine. Where space is restricted, it is important to do some thinning annually, to prevent the build-up of tangled thickets. In general the self-clingers are the easiest to manage – you just need to prune away shoots that wander into window ledges or doorways.

Actinidia

ZONES 7–10   Moderately easy
HEIGHT 5 m/16 ft
SPREAD 1.8–2.4 m/6–8 ft
FLOWERS Summer: white to buff
Twining habit. Fast-growing, once established. Attractive foliage; deciduous, oval, medium to large leaves. Five-petaled, bowl-shaped, fragrant flowers, often rather hidden by leaves. Large, brown to yellowish edible berries.
CONTAINER SIZE 40–60 cm/16–24 in wide by 40 cm/16 in deep.
PLANTING Singly, in sun or light shade.
PROPAGATION By layering in spring or by cuttings in late summer.
CARE Water freely during warm weather, less at other times. Apply liquid feed every two weeks from late spring to late summer.
SPECIES A. chinensis Chinese gooseberry, Kiwi fruit: robust stems, leaves to 13 cm/5 in long, cream to buff flowers 4 cm/1½ in wide; brown, hairy fruits tasting rather like gooseberries, rarely produced on solitary plants. A. kolomikta: slender stems, pointed leaves to 10 cm/4 in long, the upper halves white or white-flushed pink; small, white flowers, smooth, yellowish fruits.

Akebia quinata

ZONES 4–9   Easy
HEIGHT 5 m/16 ft
SPREAD 1.2–1.8 m/4–6 ft
FLOWERS Spring: chocolate-purple
Twining habit; vigorous. Stays semi-

Actinidia chinensis

evergreen in mild winters. Leaves composed of five oblong to oval leaflets. Unisexual, three-petaled flowers, in pendent spikes, larger female ones at the base of each spike. The fruit, a dark purple berry 5–10 cm/2–4 in long, is seldom produced.
CONTAINER SIZE 40–60 cm/16–24 in wide by 30–40 cm/12–16 in deep.
PLANTING Singly, in sun or partial shade.
PROPAGATION By layering in spring, by cuttings in late summer.
CARE Water freely in warm weather, less at other times. Apply liquid feed monthly during the growing season.

Aristolochia macrophylla (durior, sipho) Dutchman's pipe

ZONES 4–9   Moderately easy
HEIGHT 3–5 m/10–16 ft
SPREAD 1.8 m/6 ft or more
FLOWERS Summer: yellow-green and purple-brown
Twining habit; vigorous. Rich green, heart- to kidney-shaped leaves, up to 25 cm/10 in long. Small, pipe-shaped flowers, hidden by foliage.
CONTAINER SIZE 40–60 cm/16–24 in wide by 30–40 cm/12–16 in deep.
PLANTING Singly, in sun or light shade.

PROPAGATION By cuttings in summer.
CARE Water freely in warm weather, less at other times. Apply liquid feed monthly from late spring to late summer.

Clematis

ZONES 5–9   Easy
HEIGHT 1.8–3 m/6–10 ft
SPREAD 90–150 cm/36–60 in
FLOWERS Late spring to late summer: purple, red, pink
Leaf-tendril climbing habit; vigorous. Deciduous leaves, composed of several oval to lance-shaped leaflets. Flowers with four to six or more petals, nodding and bell-shaped, or erect and flat.
CONTAINER SIZE 40–60 cm/16–24 in wide by 40 cm/16 in deep.
PLANTING Singly, in sun or partial

Aristolochia macrophylla

Clematis × jackmanii

Akebia quinata

shade. Screen the container from direct sunlight to keep roots cool.

PROPAGATION By layering in spring or by cuttings in late summer.

CARE Water freely in warm weather, less at other times. Apply liquid feed every two weeks during growing season. Cut back stems of C. × jackmanii and C. viticella to near soil level each winter.

SPECIES AND CULTIVARS C. × jackmanii (zones 5–9): to 3 m/10 ft tall, simple to trifoliate leaves, deep violet-purple. four- to six-petaled flowers, 10–13 cm/4–5 in wide. C. × jackmanii is also used as a group name for most of the popular large-flowered cultivars, e.g. 'Comtesse de Bouchard' (rose-pink, to 15 cm/6 in wide), 'Henryi' (white), 'Lasurstern' (deep lavender), 'Madame Edouard Andre' (purplish-red), 'Nelly Moser' (bluish-white, central carmine stripe to each petal). C. macropetala (zones 5–9): 1.8 m/6 ft tall, leaves of three to nine leaflets, lavender and white semi-double, nodding flowers, 6–8 cm/2½–3 in wide; 'Maidwell Hall': deeper lavender blue; 'Markhamii': mauve-pink. C. viticella Virgin's bower (zones 5–9): 3 m/10 ft tall, leaves of three or more leaflets, four-petaled, bell-shaped, nodding, purple-blue flowers; 'Albiflora'; white; 'Minuet': white and mauve-purple bicolor; 'Nana': only 1 m/3 ft tall.

Cobaea scandens
Cup and saucer vine
ZONES 9–10   Easy
HEIGHT 5 m/16 ft or more
SPREAD 1.2–1.8 m/4–6 ft
FLOWERS Summer to fall: yellow-green and purple
Tendril climbing habit; very vigorous. Pinnate leaves, composed of four to six elliptic leaflets and a long, branched tendril. Broad bell-shaped, nodding flowers, 6–8 cm/2½–3 in long.

Grow as an annual in zones 5–8.
CONTAINER SIZE 40–60 cm/16–24 in wide by at least 30 cm/12 in deep.
PLANTING Singly, in sun or very light shade.
PROPAGATION By seeds in warmth in early to midspring.
CARE Water freely, particularly in warm weather. Apply liquid feed at 10–14 day intervals throughout summer. Plants grown as perennials in zones 9–10 are best cut back by one-third to one half in spring.

Eccremocarpus scaber
Chilean glory flower
ZONES 8–10   Easy
HEIGHT 5 m/16 ft or more
SPREAD 1.2–1.8 m/4–6 ft
FLOWERS Summer to fall: orange, red, yellow
Tendril-climbing habit, vigorous. Bipinnate leaves, composed of several small leaflets and a terminal, branched tendril. Flowers tubular, somewhat inflated, about 2.5 cm/1 in, in axillary spikes. Can be grown as an annual in zones 4–8.
CONTAINER SIZE 40–50 cm/16–20 in wide by 30 cm/12 in or more deep.
PLANTING Singly, in sun.
PROPAGATION By seeds in spring.
CARE Water freely in warm weather, less at other times. Apply liquid feed every two weeks during summer. In zone 8 plants need shelter in winter. If top of plant becomes frosted, young growth generally arises from base if root system was protected.
CULTIVARS 'Aureus': yellow flowers; 'Carmineus': crimson flowers.

Hedera helix

Eccremocarpus scaber

Hedera Ivy
ZONES 6–9   Easy
HEIGHT 1.8–5 m/6–16 ft
SPREAD 90–180 cm/36–72 in or more
Sucker-root climbing habit. Vigorous, once established. Leaves are broad oval or three- to five-lobed, leathery and usually lustrous. Small, yellow-green flowers in globular clusters, in autumn; berries are black or, rarely, yellow. Flowers and fruits are borne only on well-established specimens, generally when they have reached the top of their supports. The flowering stems are non-climbing and branched, with usually narrower, unlobed leaves.
CONTAINER SIZE 25–45 cm/10–18 in wide by at least 30 cm/12 in deep.
PLANTING Singly, in partial or full shade, though sun is tolerated.
PROPAGATION By cuttings at any time, especially late summer to early autumn.
CARE Water freely in warm weather, less at other times. Monthly liquid feeds will maintain vigorous growth. A flattish, roughened surface is best for the clinging roots. Pruning can be done in spring or late summer.
SPECIES AND CULTIVARS H. canariensis (zones 8–10): purplish-red stems, and lustrous leaves, 6–15 cm/2½–6 in

Cobaea scandens

long, oval or cut into three to five shallow lobes; 'Gloire de Marengo': leaves mostly unlobed, green and gray-green with a creamy-white margin. H. helix English ivy: leaves usually three- to five-lobed, up to 10 cm/4 in wide; many cultivars are known, e.g. 'Buttercup' (golden-yellow leaves turning to yellow-green), 'Glacier' (slow-growing, small, mottled gray leaves, margined white), 'Goldheart' (small, dark green leaves with central yellow blotch), 'Green Ripple' (small leaves, with three to five very narrow, pointed lobes). H.h. hibernica Irish ivy: robust, very vigorous stems, thick textured leaves to 15 cm/6 in wide, usually five-lobed.

Lathyrus oderatus

Jasminum officinale

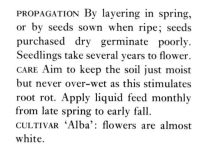

Lapageria rosea

Ipomoea purpurea

Ipomoea (Pharbitis)
Morning glory
ZONES 4–10   Moderately easy
HEIGHT 2.1–3 m/7–10 ft
SPREAD 60–120 cm/24–48 in
FLOWERS Summer to fall: pink, purple, red, blue
Annual with stem twining habit, vigorous. Heart-shaped leaves, sometimes lobed; funnel-shaped, relatively large flowers.
CONTAINER SIZE 25–40 cm/10–16 in wide by 30 cm/12 in deep.
SOIL Any approved potting mix, ideally lime-free.
PLANTING Singly in minimum-sized containers, two or three in larger ones, in sun.
PROPAGATION By seeds in warmth in spring, ideally pre-soaked in tepid water for 12 hours and sown singly in 6–8 cm/2½–3 in pots.
CARE Water freely in warm weather, less at other times, but always with care to avoid root rot. Apply liquid feed every two weeks once flower buds show.
SPECIES AND CULTIVAR *I. hederacea*: leaves to 9 cm/3½ in long, heart-shaped or cut into three lobes; blue to pale purple flowers, 5 cm/2 in long, wider at the mouth. *I. purpurea*: leaves always heart-shaped, to 13 cm/5 in long, blue, purple, pink or white flowers to 8 cm/3 in long. *I. tricolor*: perennial grown as an annual, similar to *I. purpurea* but larger in all parts, with white and purple-blue or lavender flowers; 'Heavenly Blue': sky-blue flowers.

Jasminum Jasmine
ZONES 7–10   Easy
HEIGHT 5 m/16 ft or more
SPREAD 1.5–2.1 m/5–7 ft
FLOWERS Spring to the fall: white and pink
Twining habit, evergreen or deciduous, depending on the degree of cold; vigorous, once established. Pinnate leaves, composed of several oval, pointed leaflets. Tubular flowers, with five to six petal lobes, in axillary and terminal trusses.
CONTAINER SIZE 40–60 cm/16–24 in wide by 30–40 cm/12–16 in deep.
PLANTING Singly, in sun or partial shade.

PROPAGATION By cuttings in late summer to early fall.
CARE Water freely in warm weather, less at other times, avoiding over-wet soil conditions. Apply liquid feed monthly from late spring to early fall. Thin out congested growth after flowering, or in spring.
SPECIES AND CULTIVAR *J. officinale* Common jasmine (zones 7–9): deciduous leaves that fall in early winter, fragrant, white flowers, summer to the fall; 'Aureovariegatum' ('Aureum'): yellow-blotched leaves and shoots. *J. polyanthum* (zones 9–10): evergreen leaves, fragrant flowers, spring to summer, pink in bud, opening white; can be grown in colder zones if brought indoors or into a frost-free area for winter, and will then flower earlier.

Lapageria rosea
Chilean bell flower
ZONES 8–10   Moderately easy
HEIGHT 2.4–3 m/8–10 ft
SPREAD 90–150 cm/36–60 in
FLOWERS Late summer to fall: rose-pink to crimson
Twining habit, slower-growing. Narrow heart-shaped, leathery, glossy, deep green leaves. Narrow bell-shaped, waxy flowers, to 7 cm/2¾ in long.
CONTAINER SIZE 30–45 cm/12–18 in wide by at least 30 cm/12 in deep.
SOIL One of the all-peat mixes, ideally lime-free.
PLANTING Singly, in partial shade.

PROPAGATION By layering in spring, or by seeds sown when ripe; seeds purchased dry germinate poorly. Seedlings take several years to flower.
CARE Aim to keep the soil just moist but never over-wet as this stimulates root rot. Apply liquid feed monthly from late spring to early fall.
CULTIVAR 'Alba': flowers are almost white.

Lathyrus
ZONES 3–9   Easy
HEIGHT 1.8–3 m/6–10 ft
SPREAD 60–90 cm/24–36 in
FLOWERS Summer to fall: wide color range
Annual and herbaceous perennial tendril-climbers of erect habit; vigorous. Leaves composed of two oval leaflets and a branched tendril. Flowers consist of an erect standard, two flared lower petals and a narrow keel beneath, borne in small clusters on stems from the upper leaf axils.
CONTAINER SIZE 25–40 cm/10–16 in wide by at least 30 cm/12 in deep.
PLANTING *L. latifolius* singly. *L. odoratus* singly in minimum-sized containers, three to four together in larger ones. Both species in sun.
PROPAGATION By seeds in fall or spring; protect seedlings of fall sowing from severe frost. Fall-raised plants grow bigger and flower earlier. *L. latifolius* may also be propagated by division from late fall to early spring.
CARE Water freely in warm weather, less at other times, avoiding over-wet soil. Apply liquid feed at 7–10 day intervals once flower buds show. Twiggy sticks are the best supports; canes and green plastic netting a good alternative. Cut off dead stems of *L. latifolius* during winter or early spring.
SPECIES AND CULTIVARS *L. latifolius* Everlasting pea: perennial, to 3 m/

10ft tall, 4–10cm/1½–4in long leaflets, rose-purple or white flowers, 3cm/1¼in wide in spikes of five to fifteen. *L. odoratus* Sweet pea: annual, to 1.8m/6ft tall, leaflets to 6cm/2½in long, fragrant flowers to 4cm/1½in wide, in spikes of three to six or more. Almost every color is represented and dozens of cultivars are available. Particularly good for containers are the strongly scented old-fashioned strains, e.g. 'Bijou Mixed' (30cm/12in non-climbing dwarf), 'Knee Hi' (mixed colors, self-supporting bush type to 75cm/30in), 'Royal' (mixed colors, heat resistant).

Lonicera Honeysuckle
ZONES 5–9   Easy
HEIGHT 3–5m/10–16ft
SPREAD 1.5–2.4m/5–8ft
FLOWERS Late spring to fall: white, yellow, red, purple-red
Stem twining habit; vigorous. Deciduous or evergreen, oval to elliptic leaves. Tubular flowers, gaping at the mouth, usually fragrant, in terminal spikes or clusters.
CONTAINER SIZE 40–60cm/16–24in wide by 40cm/16in deep.
PLANTING Singly, in sun or partial shade.
PROPAGATION By cuttings from late summer to fall.
CARE Water freely, especially in warm weather. Apply liquid feed monthly during the growing period.
SPECIES AND CULTIVARS *L. caprifolium*: deciduous, elliptic leaves, those at the tips of the flowering stems in fused pairs; white to deep cream flowers. *L. perichymenum* Woodbine: deciduous, oval, somewhat hairy leaves, flowers creamy-white deepening with age, summer-blooming; 'Belgica' Dutch honeysuckle: purple-red flower buds; 'Serotina': like 'Belgica' but it starts flowering later. *L. sempervirens* Trumpet honeysuckle: partially evergreen, elliptic leaves, blue-white beneath, those at the tips of the flowering stems in fused pairs; narrow trumpet-shaped, rich orange-scarlet flowers from summer to fall.

Mandevilla suaveolens (laxa)
Chilean jasmine
ZONES 8–10   Moderately easy
HEIGHT 3–5m/10–16ft
SPREAD 1.5–2.1m/5–7ft
FLOWERS Summer to early fall: white
Stem twining habit; vigorous. Deciduous, parallel-sided oval, slender-pointed leaves. Fragrant, funnel-shaped flowers, 5cm/2in long, in small clusters.
CONTAINER SIZE 40–60cm/16–24in wide by 30cm/12in deep.
PLANTING Singly, in sun.
PROPAGATION By seeds in warmth in spring, by cuttings in summer.
CARE Water freely in warm weather, less at other times. Apply liquid feed monthly during the growing season. Thin out congested growth annually in early spring. In all but the mildest parts of zone 8 and above, protection from severe frost is needed.

Parthenocissus
ZONES 3–9   Easy
HEIGHT 5m/16ft or more
SPREAD 3m/10ft or more
Self-clinging habit, the tendrils bearing sucker tips; vigorous. Broad oval leaves, lobed or composed of several

Mandevilla suaveolens

lance-shaped leaflets, turning bright red in the fall. Tiny, greenish flowers, followed by small grapelike berries, but mainly hidden in foliage.
CONTAINER SIZE 45–60cm/18–24in wide by 40cm/16in deep.
PLANTING Singly, sun or partial shade.
PROPAGATION By layering in spring; by cuttings in late summer or fall.
CARE Water freely, especially in warm weather. Apply liquid feed monthly during the growing season.
SPECIES AND CULTIVAR *P. henryana* (zones 8–9): less than 5m/16ft tall, leaves composed of three to five leaflets, rich velvety green with contrasting silver vein pattern, dark blue fruits. *P. quinquefolia* True Virginia creeper: at least 5m/16ft tall, leaves composed of five leaflets, matt-green above, slightly bluish-white beneath, turning bright red in the fall. *P. tricuspidata*, at least 5m/16ft tall, maplelike, lobed, somewhat glossy leaves, coloring bright crimson; 'Veitchii' (*Ampelopsis veitchii*): smaller leaves, purplish when young.

Passiflora caerulea
Common passion flower
ZONES 8–10   Easy
HEIGHT 5m/16ft or more
SPREAD 1.5–2.1m/5–7ft
FLOWERS Summer to fall: white and blue

Parthenocissus henryana

Passiflora caerulea

Tendril climbing habit, vigorous; 10–15cm/4–6in wide leaves cut into between five and nine deep lobes. Flowers are 6–10cm/2½–4in wide, with eight to ten white petals surrounding a corona of blue filaments. Ovoid, yellow to orange fruits, 3–4cm/1¼–1½in long.
CONTAINER SIZE 30–45cm/12–18in wide by 30–40cm/12–16in deep.
PLANTING Singly, in sun.
PROPAGATION By seeds in spring in warmth or by cuttings in summer.
CARE Water freely, especially in warm weather. Apply liquid feed every two weeks in summer. In all but the mildest parts of zone 8 and above, protection from severe winter frosts must be given. If the top is killed by frost, young growth will come from the base. If necessary, plants can be drastically thinned in late spring.
CULTIVAR 'Constance Elliott': flowers entirely white.

Lonicera periclymenum

Annuals and biennials

Of all the plants suitable for container growing, annuals are the most accommodating, and their ease and speed of growth makes them ideal for a quick display. They are particularly useful for filling gaps among the dying leaves of spring bulbs or around specimen shrubs and climbers. If you like plenty of color, and wish to ring the changes from year to year, they are indispensable.

Annuals grow from seed, flower a few months after and later die in one growing season. Generally, they are best sown where they are to bloom, but, if this is not convenient, they can be grown on in smaller pots or boxes (see pp.46–7), and planted out into permanent containers later. Some annuals – known as halfhardy – may suffer damage by frost and in colder areas (from zone 8 downward) their seeds can be sown outside only in late spring or early summer. However, an earlier sowing can be made indoors on a sunny window sill. Fully hardy annuals can be sown outside in spring or early fall. Plants from the fall sowing will provide some winter greenery and flower much earlier than usual the following summer.

Biennials also make colorful gap-fillers. They make their root systems and leaves in one year, flowering and dying the following year. This can make growing them a problem if container room is limited, since they produce no display until the second year. Their seeds must be sown in early summer and the subsequent plants grown on somewhere until the fall, when they can be transferred to their flowering quarters for the next year. If you have no facilities for growing on plants, either purchase biennials ready to plant out, or use annuals instead.

A number of plants, although technically perennials (plants that live three or more seasons), look their best in their first year and are therefore treated as annuals or, like wallflowers, as biennials. Cuttings can be taken from some (see pp. 49–50).

To get the best from both annuals and biennials, a good, well-balanced soil or potting mix must be used. The latter can be one of the all-peat mixes, or a loam-based type, such as John Innes no. 2 or 3 (see p. 22). Watering must be carried out regularly. If the soil dries out, growth will be severely checked and flowering delayed. It pays to start applying a liquid feed (see pp. 36–7) at 7–10 day intervals once flower buds are visible. General maintenance other than watering and feeding is usually minimal, but much depends on the sort of plants grown. The main task is regular deadheading (see p. 40), which, as well as removing the faded flowers, prevents seeding and thus stimulates the formation of more buds, prolonging the display. Tall plants may need the support of twiggy sticks or trellis (see p. 39).

Ageratum houstonianum
Floss flower
ZONES 5–10   Easy
HEIGHT 15–60 cm/6–24 in
SPREAD 15–30 cm/6–12 in
FLOWERS Summer to fall: blue, pink, white
Erect to bushy habit. Heart-shaped, somewhat corrugated, mid-green leaves; small, pompon-shaped flower heads, in large fluffy clusters.
CONTAINER SIZE Any diameter, at least 10 cm/4 in deep.
PLANTING In groups of at least three, 15 cm/6 in apart, in sun or light shade.
PROPAGATION By seeds *in situ* when danger of frost is past, or earlier in warmth.

CARE Water freely in hot weather; enough to keep soil just moist at other times. Apply liquid feed at 10–14 day intervals once flower buds show.
CULTIVARS 'Blue Bouquet': bright lavender blue flowers, 45 cm/18 in tall; 'Fairy Pink': lavender-pink, 15 cm/6 in tall; 'Midget Blue': mauvish-blue, 12 cm/5 in tall, All-American selection; 'Summer Snow': white, 12 cm/5 in tall.

Alyssum see Lobularia

Amaranthus
ZONES 5–10   Easy
HEIGHT 60–90 cm/24–36 in
SPREAD 20–40 cm/8–16 in
FLOWERS Summer to fall: red or greenish
Erect, with ovate, mid-green or variegated leaves. Minute flowers in tail-like spikes.
CONTAINER SIZE Diameter and depth at least 25 cm/10 in.
PLANTING One per minimum-sized container or in groups in a larger one, 25 cm/10 in apart, in sun.
PROPAGATION By seeds sown in warmth in midspring; plant seedlings out when danger of frost is past.
CARE Water every day or two in hot weather, less at other times. Apply liquid feed at 7–10 day intervals once flower spikes show.
SPECIES AND CULTIVARS *A. caudatus* Love-lies-bleeding: mid-green leaves and terminal clusters of pendent, thick, catkinlike, crimson flower spikes 40 cm/16 in or more long; 'Viridus': palest green flowers. *A. hypochondriacus* Prince's feather: bears erect, deep red flower spikes and often exceeds 1.2 m/4 ft in rich soil. *A. tricolor* (*gangeticus*): grown for its colored leaves; 'Early Splendor': crimson upper and coppery-red lower leaves; 'Joseph's Coat' is patterned bronze, red, yellow and green; 'Salicifolius': to 60 cm/24 in tall, very narrow, orange-red and bronze drooping leaves.

Antirrhinum majus
Snapdragon
ZONES 5–10   Easy
HEIGHT 15–60 cm/6–24 in
SPREAD 15–30 cm/6–12 in
FLOWERS Summer to fall: mainly red, pink, white, yellow
Erect to bushy habit. Lance-shaped, mid- to deep green leaves. Tubular flowers with closed mouth and five flared petal-lobes, in terminal spikes. A perennial grown as an annual.
CONTAINER SIZE At least 30 cm/12 in wide by 15 cm/6 in deep.

Amaranthus caudatus

Antirrhinum majus

Ageratum houstonianum

Amaranthus tricolor

PLANTING Preferably in groups of no fewer than three, 15–20 cm/6–8 in apart, in sun.

PROPAGATION By seeds sown in warmth in early spring, or outside in late spring.

CARE Water every day or two in hot weather, less often at other times. Apply liquid feed at 10–14 day intervals once flower spikes show.

CULTIVARS **Tall**, 50–75 cm/20–30 in – 'Coronette': large weather-resistant flowers in all colors; 'Madame Butterfly': azalealike double flowers in wide color range; 'Scarlet Supreme': weather-resistant orange-scarlet flowers with bronze tint; 'Wedding Bell's: open-mouthed flowers resembling those of *Penstemon*, in wide color range. **Intermediate**, 35–45 cm/14–18 in – 'Liberty Bell': mixed colors; its white throat gives unique two-tone effect; sturdy habit yet good for cutting. **Dwarf**, 15–30 cm/6–12 in – 'Floral Carpet': 30 cm/12 in, compact habit, good color mixture; 'Tom Thumb': 15 cm/6 in, bright color mix.

Arctotis African daisy
ZONES 5–10   Easy
HEIGHT 15–60 cm/6–24 in
SPREAD 15–30 cm/6–12 in
FLOWERS Summer to fall: white, blue, red, orange, yellow

Annual and perennial, tufted and erect to spreading, according to species. Deeply lobed leaves and daisy-like flowers, opening flat in sun.

CONTAINER SIZE At least 30 cm/12 in wide by 20 cm/8 in deep.

PLANTING Preferably in groups of no fewer than three, about 20 cm/8 in apart, in sun.

PROPAGATION By seeds sown in warmth in spring, or by cuttings taken from tender perennials in late summer; young plants will need protection from frost.

CARE Water regularly, especially in warm weather, but avoid over-watering. Apply liquid feed every two weeks once the flower buds appear.

SPECIES AND CULTIVARS *A. breviscapa* (*speciosa*): tufted annual to 15 cm/6 in tall, with white woolly undersides to leaves and orange-yellow flowers. *A. hybrida*: perennial grown as annual, about 45 cm/18 in tall, gray-green leaves; yellow, orange, red or white flowers, often with contrasting darker central zone. *A. stoechadifolia*: perennial grown as annual, 60 cm/24 in or more tall, with gray-green leaves and blue-budded, white flowers. *A.s. grandis*: larger, white to yellow flowers.

Bellis perennis Common daisy
ZONES 3–8   Easy
HEIGHT 10–20 cm/4–8 in
SPREAD 10–20 cm/4–8 in
FLOWERS Spring to summer: white, pink, red

Tufted rosette habit with spoon-shaped leaves all arising from ground level. Cultivated forms have double or semidouble, pomponlike flowers. A perennial grown as a biennial.

CONTAINER SIZE At least 30 cm/12 in wide by 15 cm/6 in deep.

PLANTING In groups of no fewer than three, 10–15 cm/4–6 in apart, in sun or partial shade.

PROPAGATION By seeds sown in late spring or by division in early fall.

CARE Water freely in hot weather, less at other times. Apply liquid feed once flower buds show.

CULTIVARS Monstrosa group, large flowers, 5 cm/2 in or more wide – 'Giant-Flowered Red' (crimson), 'Giant-Flowered White', 'Giant-Flowered Mixed' (red, pink, salmon, white). Miniature group, double flowers up to 2 cm/¾ in wide with quilled florets – 'Pomponette' and 'Pink Buttons' (shades of red, pink).

Browallia Bush violet
ZONES 3–9   Easy
HEIGHT 20–45 cm/8–18 in
SPREAD 20–30 cm/8–12 in
FLOWERS Summer to fall: purple, blue and white

Erect, mainly bushy habit. Narrow, somewhat corrugated, deep green leaves. Flowers resembling large violets, borne in short, leafy, terminal spikes. A tropical perennial grown as an annual.

CONTAINER SIZE At least 30 cm/12 in wide by 15 cm/6 in deep.

PLANTING In groups of at least three or four, 20 cm/8 in apart, in sun or partial shade. In areas of cool summers a warm sheltered site is best.

PROPAGATION By seeds sown in warmth in spring.

CARE Water freely in hot weather, less at other times. Apply liquid feed every two weeks once the flower buds show color.

SPECIES AND CULTIVARS *B. speciosa*: tallest species generally cultivated, 45–90 cm/18–36 in with rich purple-blue flowers; *B.s. major* has larger flowers; 'Jingle Bells Mixed': blue, white and lavender. *B. viscosa*: 30–45 cm/12–18 in tall, with violet-blue, white-throated flowers; 'Blue Troll': compact habit to 25 cm/10 in; 'White Troll': the same with white flowers; 'Sapphire': similar to 'Blue Troll' but with slightly paler flowers.

Calendula officinalis Pot marigold
ZONES 3–9   Easy
HEIGHT 30–60 cm/12–24 in
SPREAD 25–40 cm/10–16 in
FLOWERS Summer to fall: yellow and orange

Robust bushy habit. Wide, spoon-shaped, bright green leaves. Daisy-like flowers, double or semidouble in all cultivated forms.

CONTAINER SIZE At least 30 cm/12 in

wide by 15–20 cm/6–8 in deep.

PLANTING Ideally in groups of three, 20–25 cm/8–10 in apart, in sun.

PROPAGATION By seeds sown *in situ* in spring or, in zones 7–9, in fall for spring flowering.

CARE Water freely in hot weather, less at other times. Apply liquid feed at 10–14 day intervals once buds show color.

CULTIVARS 'Apricot Beauty': 45–60 cm/18–24 in tall; 'Dwarf Gems': 30 cm/12 in compact habit, double flowers in shades from creamy-yellow to bright orange; 'Orange Coronet': 30–38 cm/12–15 in, flowers are fully or semidouble; 'Pacific Beauty': to 60 cm/24 in, yellow, orange and apricot double flowers on long stems; 'Radio': 45 cm/18 in, fully double flowers with quilled orange petals.

Callistephus chinensis China aster
ZONES 3–9   Easy
HEIGHT 25–75 cm/10–30 in
SPREAD 25–40 cm/10–16 in
FLOWERS Summer to fall: purple, red, pink, yellow, white

Erect habit, dwarf types bushy. Ovate, prominently toothed, mid-green leaves. In most of the cultivars, the daisylike flowers are double or semidouble.

CONTAINER SIZE At least 30 cm/12 in wide by 15–20 cm/6–8 in deep.

PLANTING Ideally in groups of three to five or more, 20–25 cm/8–10 in apart, in sun.

PROPAGATION By seeds sown in warmth in spring.

CARE Water freely in hot weather, less at other times, avoiding over-wet soil for long periods. Apply liquid feed at 7–10 day intervals once flower buds show.

CULTIVARS 'Ostrich Plume Mixed': 60 cm/24 in tall, fully double flowers with long, curled florets in wide range of colors; 'Super Princess Mixed': 60cm/24in, double heads formed of short, quilled florets, resistant to bad weather; 'Gloriette': 25–30cm/10–12in compact flower heads in wide color range, early blooming and resistant to wilt disease; 'Pinocchio': 20cm/8in tall and wide, very bushy, with small and abundant double flowers in wide color range; 'American Beauty' ('Ball Mixture'): 60–75cm/24–30in, double flowers that appear in midsummer; 'Chater's Erfurt': 23cm/9in with deep rose, chrysanthemumlike flowers.

Catharanthus roseus (Vinca rosea) Malagasy periwinkle

ZONES 3–9 Easy
HEIGHT 25–60cm/10–24in
SPREAD 25–45cm/10–18in
FLOWERS Summer to fall: pink, red, white

Bushy habit. Oblong and glossy, mid- to deep green leaves. Flowers resembling *Phlox* in terminal clusters. Tropical, shrubby perennial grown as an annual.

CONTAINER SIZE At least 30cm/12in wide by 20cm/8in deep. Can grow singly in 18–20cm/7–8in wide pots.
PLANTING In groups of three to four or more, 20–25cm/8–10in apart, in sun. In areas where summers are cool, a warm, sheltered site is necessary. Will flower all winter, in zones 3–8, if brought indoors in fall.
PROPAGATION By seeds sown in warmth in early to midspring, or by cuttings in spring, from over-wintered plants.
CARE Water freely in hot weather, but avoid over-wet soil. Apply liquid feed every two weeks once plants start to bloom.
CULTIVARS 'Bright Eyes': 30–60cm/12–24in tall, compact habit, white flower with rose-red eye; 'Coquette': dwarf habit, rose flowers.

Cheiranthus cheiri Wallflower

ZONES 7–9 Easy
HEIGHT 30–60cm/12–24in
SPREAD 25–45cm/10–18in
FLOWERS Spring to early summer: red-brown, crimson, carmine, yellow, ivory

Erect, usually bushy habit, with willowlike leaves. Four-petaled, fragrant flowers in terminal spikes. Shrubby perennial grown as biennial.

CONTAINER SIZE At least 30cm/12in wide by 15cm/6in deep.
SOIL Any approved potting mix, preferably with lime.
PLANTING In groups, 20–25cm/8–10in apart, in sun.
PROPAGATION By seeds sown in late spring or by heel cuttings in summer. Grow young plants in a reserve container, transplanting them to flowering positions in fall.
CARE Water regularly, avoiding over-wet soil. Apply liquid feed every two weeks once flowering starts.
CULTIVARS Tall, 40–50cm/16–20in – 'Biennial Mix': full color range; 'Harpur Crewe': golden yellow; 'Moonlight': pale yellow; 'Rufus': coppery-red; 'Wenlock Beauty': coppery-red. Dwarf bedding cultivars at 30cm/12in tall, e.g. 'Double Early Wonder' (fragrant flowers), and 'Tomb Thumb' strain 15–23cm/6–9in, in similar or wider color range.

Clarkia (including Godetia)

ZONES 4–9 Easy
HEIGHT 30–60cm/12–24in
SPREAD 20–40cm/8–16in
FLOWERS Summer: pink, red, mauve, purple

Erect, moderately bushy habit. Narrow, pale to mid-green leaves. Four-petaled or double flowers, in terminal spikes.

CONTAINER SIZE At least 30cm/12in wide by 15cm/6in deep.
PLANTING In groups, 10–15cm/4–6in apart, in sun.
PROPAGATION By seeds sown *in situ* in spring; or in fall, in zones 7–9, for larger, earlier-blooming plants.
CARE Water regularly, particularly in hot weather. Apply liquid feed at 10–14 day intervals once flower buds show.
SPECIES AND CULTIVARS *C. amoena* (*Godetia amoena*) – 'Dwarf Bedding Mixed': 25–30cm/10–12in tall, compact habit, cup-shaped flowers in wide color range, some bicolored; 'Sybil Sherwood': to 45cm/18in, single, salmon-pink flowers, edged with white; *C. elegans* (*C. unguiculata*): to 60cm/24in tall, widely opening flowers, with triangular, waved petals: 'Double Mixed': long spikes of azalealike double flowers. similar to *C. elegans* but with three-lobed petals; 'Filigree': 30–40cm/12–16in, double or semidouble flowers of lacy appearance of various colors.

Callistephus chinensis

Clarkia amoena

Cheiranthus cheiri

Clarkia pulchella

Catharanthus roseus

Browallia viscosa

Arctotis

Calendula officinalis

Browallia speciosa

Bellis perennis

Coleus blumei
Painted or flame nettle
ZONES 6–9 Easy
HEIGHT to 60 cm/24 in
SPREAD to 45 cm/18 in
FOLIAGE Richly patterned, yellow, red and purple
Bushy habit: nettle-shaped, toothed, plain or variegated leaves. The small blue flowers are not attractive and are best pinched out when young. Tropical shrubby perennial grown as an annual.
CONTAINER SIZE At least 20 cm/8 in wide by 15–20 cm/6–8 in deep.
PLANTING Singly or, more effectively, in groups of three to five, 25–30 cm/10–12 in apart, in sun or partial shade, sheltered from strong, cold winds. In areas with cool summers, it grows best on enclosed balconies or patios.
PROPAGATION By seeds sown in warmth, or by cuttings from over-wintered plants, both in spring.
CARE Water freely in hot weather, less at other times. Apply liquid feed every two weeks once the plants are about 25 cm/10 in tall.
CULTIVARS Seed-raised – 'Carefree': dwarf compact strain 25–30 cm/10–12 in tall, lobed leaves in good color range; 'Multicolor Rainbow': 38 cm/15 in, leaves in a variety of shapes and colors; 'Sabre': 30 cm/12 in, with long, very narrow leaves; 'Salmon Lace': 38 cm/15 in, salmon-red center, broad green edge.

Cosmos Cosmea
ZONES 4–9 Easy
HEIGHT 90 cm/36 in or more
SPREAD to 30 cm/12 in
FLOWERS Summer to fall: pink, red, white, yellow, orange
Slim, erect habit with finely dissected, ferny leaves. Flowers basically daisylike, with about eight broad outer florets.

CONTAINER SIZE At least 30 cm/12 in wide by 15–20 cm/6–8 in deep.
PLANTING In groups of three to five at 15–20 cm/6–8 in apart, in sun.
PROPAGATION By seeds sown in warmth in spring.
CARE Water freely in hot weather, less at other times. Avoid over-watering.
SPECIES AND CULTIVARS C. bipinnatus: to 90 cm/36 in tall, flowers rose-purple; 'Bright Lights': to 75 cm/30 in tall, yellow, orange, gold and red; 'Sensation Early-Flowering Mixed': 90 cm/36 in, pink, crimson, white Dahlia-like flowers, C. sulphureus: about 60 cm/24 in tall, yellow flowers; 'Diablo': to 75 cm/30 in tall, red-orange flowers, All-American selection.

Dorotheanthus bellidiformis (Mesembryanthemum criniflorum)
Livingstone daisy
ZONES 4–9 Easy
HEIGHT 5 cm/2 in
SPREAD 20 cm/8 in or more
FLOWERS Summer to early fall: red, pink, yellow, orange, bicolored
Mat-forming habit, with almost cylindrical leaves covered with glistening, sugar-grainlike protuberances. Daisylike flowers.
CONTAINER SIZE At least 30 cm/12 in wide by 10–15 cm/4–6 in deep.
PLANTING In large groups for maximum effect, or as an edging to window boxes or other containers, at 15 cm/6 in apart, in sun.
PROPAGATION By seeds sown in warmth, in early spring for an early display, or in situ when danger of frost is past.
CARE Water regularly but moderately, avoiding over-wet potting mix.
CULTIVARS Several mixed-color strains, all equally good for container cultivation.

Gazania hybrids Treasure flower
ZONES 4–9 Easy
HEIGHT 20–30 cm/8–12 in
SPREAD 30–40 cm/12–16 in
FLOWERS Summer to fall: yellow, orange, red-bronze, mauve
Mat-forming habit with prostrate stems and erect flower stalks. Narrow leaves, sometimes deeply lobed, and gray-felted (on undersides only). Daisylike flowers, often with areas of contrasting color.
CONTAINER SIZE At least 30 cm/12 in wide by 15 cm/6 in deep.
PLANTING Ideally in groups of three or more, 20–30 cm/8–12 in apart, in sun. Plants can be overwintered in a cool room.
PROPAGATION By seeds sown in warmth or by cuttings from over-wintered plants, both in spring.
CARE Water regularly, particularly in hot weather, but avoid over-wet soil. Apply liquid feed every two weeks once the plants start to flower.
CULTIVARS 'Golden Margarita Hybrid': 25–30 cm/10–12 in tall, yellow flowers with dark center; 'Sunshine': 15 cm/6 in, wild multicolor array, gray-green foliage.

Godetia see Clarkia

Gomphrena globosa
Globe amaranth
ZONES 4–9 Easy
HEIGHT 15–20 cm/6–8 in
SPREAD 15–30 cm/6–12 in
FLOWERS Summer: purple, pink, white
Erect, moderately bushy habit. Oblong to elliptic leaves. Very small flowers hidden by bracts (large, colored leaves) in clusters.
CONTAINER SIZE At least 30 cm/12 in wide by 15 cm/6 in deep.
PLANTING In groups of three to six or more, 15 cm/6 in apart, in sun. In areas with cool summers, place in a

warm, preferably sheltered site.
PROPAGATION By seeds sown in warmth, early to midspring.
CARE Water regularly, especially in hot weather, but avoid over-wet soil. Apply liquid feed every two weeks once flower heads show color.
CULTIVARS 'Buddy': 15 cm/6 in tall, dwarf and very bushy with rose-purple flowers.

Heliotropium × hybridum
Heliotrope
ZONES 4–9 Easy
HEIGHT 45–90 cm/18–36 in
SPREAD 30–45 cm/12–18 in
FLOWERS Summer to fall: lavender to violet-purple
Bushy, fairly erect habit; ovate, finely corrugated, deep green leaves. Small, very fragrant flowers in large clusters. Subtropical shrub grown as an annual.
CONTAINER SIZE At least 20 cm/8 in wide and deep.
PLANTING Singly, or in groups of three or more at 25–30 cm/10–12 in apart, in sun. Plants can be overwintered in a cool, sunny room.
PROPAGATION By seeds sown in warmth in late winter, or by cuttings from overwintered plants in spring.
CARE Water freely in hot weather, less at other times. Apply liquid feed at 10-day intervals once flowering starts.
CULTIVARS 'Marine': 45–60 cm/18–24 in tall, compact habit, deep violet-purple flowers. Several mixed strains available, with flowers ranging from violet to lavender and white.

Iberis Candytuft
ZONES 4–8 Easy
HEIGHT 15–30 cm/6–12 in
SPREAD 13–20 cm/5–8 in
FLOWERS Summer: white, purple, pink, red
Erect branching habit; very narrow,

Cosmos bipinnatus

Cosmos sulphureus

sometimes lobed or toothed leaves. Fragrant flowers in domed heads or spikes with four petals, two long and two short.

CONTAINER SIZE At least 25 cm/10 in wide by 15 cm/6 in deep.

PLANTING In groups at 10–15 cm/ 4–5 in apart, in sun.

PROPAGATION By seeds sown *in situ* in spring; also in fall, zones 7–8, for larger, earlier-flowering plants.

CARE Water regularly, especially in hot weather, but avoid over-wet soil. Apply liquid feed every two weeks once flower buds show color.

SPECIES AND CULTIVARS *I. amara*: 30–40 cm/12–16 in tall, the flowers in spikelike clusters; 'Giant Empress' and 'Giant Hyacinth Flowered': robust, long and dense flower spikes. *I. umbellata*: 20–25 cm/8–10 in tall, the flowers in domed heads; 'Fairy Mixture': 23 cm/9 in, well-branched plant, wide color range; 'Mt Hood' ('Ruffled White'): 60 cm/24 in, white; 'White Pinnacle': 50 cm/20 in, white.

Impatiens Touch-me-not

ZONES 4–9 Easy

HEIGHT 30–60 cm/12–24 in or more

SPREAD 20–40 cm/8–16 in

FLOWERS Summer to fall: purple, red, pink, yellow, white

Erect to spreading habit; ovate to lance-shaped leaves. Spurred flowers, resembling pansies (*Viola* × *wittrockiana*) in shape.

CONTAINER SIZE At least 20 cm/8 in wide by 18 cm/7 in deep.

PLANTING Singly, or preferably in groups of three or more, 15–20 cm/ 6–8 in apart, in sun, sheltered from cold winds. *I. wallerana* can be brought indoors in the fall to continue flowering.

PROPAGATION By seeds sown in warmth in midspring; *I. wallerana* also by cuttings taken in spring from overwintered plants; *I. balsamina* can also be sown *in situ* in late spring.

CARE Water freely in hot weather, less at other times. Apply liquid feed at 7–10 day intervals once flower buds are visible.

SPECIES AND CULTIVARS *I. balsamina* Balsam: annual, erect, sparingly branched, 45 cm/18 in tall or more, double and semidouble cultivated strains; 'Camellia-Flowered': robust strain, good color mix;

'Tom Thumb': similar strain, but only 25–30 cm/10–12 in tall. *I. wallerana* (*sultanii, holstii*) Busy Lizzie: well-branched tender perennial often grown as annual, with scarlet, orange, carmine, purple, white and bicolored flowers; 'Blitz': 30 cm/12 in tall, compact and abundantly flowering, in bright orange-scarlet; 'Super Elfin Mixed': 15 cm/6 in, good color range; 'Grande': 30 cm/12 in, very large-flowered, fine color mixture; 'Imp': similar to 'Grande' but grows to 40 cm/16 in.

Kochia scoparia trichophylla

Summer cypress, Burning bush

ZONES 4–9 Easy

HEIGHT to 60 cm/24 in

SPREAD to 30 cm/12 in

FOLIAGE Bright green, turning red in autumn

Erect and bushy, cypresslike. Slender leaves and tiny, petalless flowers.

CONTAINER SIZE At least 20 cm/8 in wide and deep.

PLANTING Singly or, more effectively, in groups of three or more, 20–25 cm/ 8–10 in apart, in sun.

PROPAGATION By seeds sown in warmth in early to midspring, or *in situ* in late spring.

CARE Water regularly, especially in hot weather, but avoid over-wet soil. Apply liquid feed at 10–14 day intervals once the plants are 20–25 cm/8–10 in tall.

CULTIVARS 'Childsii': neater and more compact than main species, with brighter, more reliable autumn color.

Heliotropium × *hybridum*

Coleus blumei

Impatiens balsamina

Kochia scoparia trichophylla

Impatiens wallerana

Iberis amara

Gazania hybrid

Gomphrena globosa

Dorotheanthus bellidiformis

Iberis umbellata

Lavatera trimestris Mallow
ZONES 3–9 Easy
HEIGHT 60–90 cm/24–36 in
SPREAD 30–40 cm/12–16 in
FLOWERS Summer to fall: pink, white
Robust, erect habit. Rounded, shallowly lobed leaves. Wide funnel-shaped, satin-textured flowers, in short, terminal spikes.
CONTAINER SIZE At least 30 cm/12 in wide by 20 cm/8 in deep.
PLANTING In groups of three or more, 15–20 cm/6–8 in apart each way, in sun or light shade.

Lavatera trimestris

Nicotiana × sanderae

Myosotis sylvatica

Lobelia erinus

PROPAGATION By seeds *in situ* in spring.
CARE Water freely in hot weather, less at other times. Apply liquid feed at 10–14 day intervals once the flower buds show color.
CULTIVARS 'Loveliness': 75 cm/30 in, rich rose-pink; 'Mont Blanc': 50 cm/20 in tall, pure white; 'Silver Cup': glowing pink, paler in the center; 'Tanagra': to 1.2 m/4 ft, glistening cerise-pink.

Lobelia erinus
ZONES 4–9 Easy
HEIGHT 15 cm/6 in
SPREAD 15–25 cm/6–10 in
FLOWERS Summer to fall: blue, red, white
Tufted, spreading habit. Small, slender leaves, some narrowly spoon-shaped. Fan-shaped flowers with three board petals and two small, narrow ones.

Matthiola incana

Phlox drummondii

Nemesia strumosa

CONTAINER SIZE At least 25 cm/10 in wide by 15 cm/6 in deep.
PLANTING In groups of at least five, 15 cm/6 in apart, in sun or light shade. Good for hanging baskets and useful for edging large containers.
PROPAGATION By seeds sown in warmth in late winter to early spring.
CARE Water freely in hot weather.
CULTIVARS 'Cambridge Blue': azure flowers; 'Crystal Palace': dark blue flowers, bronzy foliage; 'Mrs Clibran Improved': deep blue, with white eye; 'Rosamund': wine-red, with white eye; 'Snowball': compact habit, white; 'Hamburgia': long trailing stems, pale blue, the best for hanging baskets; 'Sapphire': habit of 'Hamburgia', deep blue with white eye.

Lobularia maritima (Alyssum maritimum) Sweet alyssum
ZONES 3–9 Easy
HEIGHT 10–15 cm/4–6 in
SPREAD 15–25 cm/6–10 in
FLOWERS Summer to fall: white, red, purple
Tufted, spreading habit. Small, very narrow leaves. Four-petaled flowers in short, spiky heads.
CONTAINER SIZE At least 30 cm/12 in wide by 15 cm/6 in deep.

Pelargonium × hortorum

Petunia × hybrida

Lobularia maritima

PLANTING In groups of six or more, or as an edging, 13–15 cm/5–6 in apart, in sun.
PROPAGATION By seeds *in situ* or in reserve containers in spring.
CARE Water regularly but avoid over-wet soil.
CULTIVARS 'Carpet of Snow': 10–13 cm/4–5 in tall, creeping habit; 'Little Dorrit': 15 cm/6 in, is similar, but more erect; 'Little Gem': 7.5 cm/3 in, white; 'Rosie O'Day': 10 cm/4 in, lilac pink; 'Violet King': 10 cm/4 in, deep violet-purple; 'Wonderland': 7.5 cm/3 in, flat habit, deep carmine-red flowers.

Matthiola incana Stock
ZONES 4–9 Easy
HEIGHT 30–75 cm/12–30 in
SPREAD 20–45 cm/8–18 in
FLOWERS Spring, summer, fall: white, pink, purple, red, yellow
Erect, often moderately bushy habit; narrow, gray-white downy leaves. Fragrant four-petaled or double flowers, in spikes. Perennial grown as an annual or biennial.
CONTAINER SIZE At least 30 cm/12 in wide by 20 cm/8 in deep.
SOIL Any approved potting mix with lime.
PLANTING In groups of three or more, at a distance apart equal to half total height, in sun.
PROPAGATION By seeds sown in warmth in spring (for summer flowering) or in late summer (for spring flowering).
CARE Water regularly, especially in warm weather; avoid over-wet soil.
CULTIVARS 'Ten Week Mixed': 30 cm/12 in tall, good color range; 'Beauty of Nice Mixed': similar but taller (45 cm/18 in) and late blooming; 'Brompton Mixed': 40–45 cm/16–18 in, good color mixture, grown as a biennial – the young plants need winter protection in zones 4–7.

Myosotis sylvatica Forget-me-not
ZONES 4–8 Easy
HEIGHT 30–45 cm/12–18 in
SPREAD 20–30 cm/8–12 in
FLOWERS Spring to summer: blue, pink, white
Tufted habit, most of the spoon-shaped leaves arising from ground level. Small flowers, in airy sprays. Most of the compact cultivars listed below are of hybrid origin with the alpine, *M. alpestris*.
CONTAINER SIZE At least 25 cm/10 in wide by 15 cm/6 in deep.
PLANTING In groups of five or more, 15 cm/6 in apart, in partial shade or sun.
PROPAGATION By seeds sown in a reserve container in summer, with the young plants set in permanent position in fall.
CARE Water freely, particularly in warm, dry spells. Apply liquid feed at 10-day intervals once the flower spikes show.
CULTIVARS 'Blue Ball': 15–20 cm/6–8 in tall, compact habit, bright, indigo-blue flowers; 'Blue Bouquet': to 40 cm/16 in, large, deep blue flowers in long sprays; 'Carmine King': 15 cm/6 in, pink; 'Royal Blue': 23–30 cm/9–12 in, dark blue; 'Ultramarine': 15 cm/6 in, dark blue flowers.

Nemesia strumosa
ZONES 4–9 Easy
HEIGHT 20–30 cm/8–12 in
SPREAD 15 cm/6 in
FLOWERS Summer: blue, purple, red, pink, orange, yellow, white
Erect, moderately bushy habit. Lance-shaped, pale green leaves, coarsely toothed. Somewhat orchid-like flowers, in showy clusters.
CONTAINER SIZE At least 25 cm/10 in wide by 15–20 cm/6–8 in deep.
PLANTING In groups of no fewer than five at 10–15 cm/4–6 in apart, in sun.

PROPAGATION By seeds sown in warmth in early to midspring.
CARE Water regularly, particularly in hot weather, but avoid over-wet soil.
CULTIVARS 'Blue Gem': small, abundant lavender-blue flowers; 'Fire King': larger, orange-scarlet flowers; 'Orange King': rich orange; 'Carnival': extra large flowers in wide color range; 'Triumph': similar to 'Carnival', but more compact, to 23 cm/9 in tall.

Nicotiana Flowering tobacco
ZONES 4–9 Easy
HEIGHT 45–75 cm/18–30 in
SPREAD 30–45 cm/12–18 in
FLOWERS Summer to fall: white, lime, pink, red
Erect habit, branching in the lower part only. Large, ovate, stickily hairy, pale green leaves. Long, tubular flowers with five broad petal lobes, opening and fragrant at dusk. Tender perennials grown as annuals.
CONTAINER SIZE At least 30 cm/12 in wide by 20 cm/8 in deep.
PLANTING Singly or, ideally, in groups of at least three, 25–30 cm/10–12 in apart, in sun.
PROPAGATION By seeds sown in warmth in early to midspring.
CARE Water freely in hot weather, less at other times. Apply liquid feed at 10–14 day intervals once flower buds are visible.
SPECIES AND CULTIVARS *N. affinis* (*N. alata grandiflora*): about 75 cm/30 in tall, with white flowers; 'Dwarf White Bedder': 30–40 cm/12–16 in, the flowers staying open all day; 'Lime Green': 65 cm/26 in, pale greenish-yellow flowers. *N. × sanderae* (*affinis × forgetiana*) covers the red and pink shades often listed under *N. affinis* or *N. alata*, and is usually sold mixed with the white parent; 'Dwarf Crimson Bedder': 40 cm/16 in tall, with red flowers.

Pelargonium
ZONES 4–9 Easy
HEIGHT 15–45 cm/6–18 in or more
SPREAD 30–60 cm/12–24 in or more
FLOWERS Summer to fall: red, pink, white, purple, bicolored
Erect or trailing habit. Five-petaled flowers often in dense clusters. A tender shrub or shrubby perennial grown as an annual or pot plant.
CONTAINER SIZE At least 18 cm/7 in wide by 15 cm/6 in deep.
PLANTING In sun, singly, or in groups, *P. × hortorum* 30–40 cm/12–16 in apart, *P. peltatum* 25 cm/10 in apart.
PROPAGATION By cuttings from over-wintered plants in spring; *P. peltatum* also by cuttings in late summer to early fall; *P. × hortorum* by seeds sown in warmth in early spring.
CARE Water regularly, but avoid over-wet soil. Apply liquid feed at 10–14 day intervals once flower buds show. In zones lower than 9, overwinter indoors on a sunny window sill.
SPECIES AND CULTIVARS *P. × hortorum* Pot geranium: erect, often bushy habit, circular leaves sometimes with a dark horseshoe-shaped mark; seed-raised cultivars only, mixed colors. *P. peltatum* Ivy-leaved geranium: trailing habit, ivylike leaves, but fleshy. 'Galilee': double, rose-pink flowers; 'L'elegant': single, pink flowers, variegated leaves.

Petunia × hybrida
ZONES 4–9 Easy
HEIGHT 20–30 cm/8–12 in
SPREAD to 30 cm/12 in or more
FLOWERS Summer to fall: purple, pink, red, yellow, white
Spreading, freely branching habit. Ovate, light to mid-green leaves. Wide, funnel-shaped flowers.
CONTAINER SIZE At least 25 cm/10 in wide by 15–20 cm/6–8 in deep.
PLANTING In groups of at least three, 23 cm/9 in apart, in sun.

PROPAGATION By seeds sown in warmth in midspring.
CARE Water freely in hot weather, less at other times. Apply liquid feed at 10–14 day intervals once flower buds show.
CULTIVARS **Multiflora** groups: bushy, very free-flowering – 'Satin' series in single colors, e.g. 'Pink Satin', 'Red Satin', 'Purple Plum', 'Summer Sun'; double-flowered cultivars include 'Apple Tart' (scarlet); 'Blue Empress' (violet-blue); 'Cherry Tart' (pink and white bicolor); 'Snowberry Tart' (white). **Nana Compacta** group: similar but smaller and more compact. **Grandiflora** group: loose habit, longer stems and larger flowers, good for boxes and hanging baskets.

Phlox drummondii
ZONES 4–9 Easy
HEIGHT 25–37 cm/10–15 in
SPREAD 15–25 cm/6–10 in
FLOWERS Summer to fall: red, pink, purple, buff, white
Erect, branching habit. Pale green, ovate to lance-shaped leaves. Tubular flowers with five broad petal lobes, in clusters.
CONTAINER SIZE 30 cm/12 in wide by 15 cm/6 in deep, or more.
PLANTING In groups of at least five at 15 cm/6 in apart, in sun.
PROPAGATION By seeds sown in warmth in spring.
CARE Water freely in hot weather, less at other times, but avoid over-wet soil, which can foster root rot. Apply liquid feed at 10–14 day intervals when flower buds show.
CULTIVARS **Grandiflora** group: large, round flowers – 'Carnival': 30 cm/12 in tall, good color mixture; 'Dwarf Beauty', similar but very compact, to 20 cm/8 in. **Cuspidata**, or Star phlox, group: starry flowers with pointed tips – 'Cuspidata Twinkle': 20 cm/8 in tall, good color range.

Reseda odorata Mignonette
ZONES 4–9   Easy
HEIGHT 30–40cm/12–16in
SPREAD 15–25cm/6–10in
FLOWERS Summer to fall: yellowish to reddish

Erect, moderately bushy habit. Narrow, midgreen leaves, often three-lobed. Small, strongly and sweetly scented flowers with six-lobed whitish petals and prominent, colored stamens.
CONTAINER SIZE At least 25cm/10in wide by 15–20cm/6–8in deep. A single plant can be grown in a 15cm/6in wide pot.
PLANTING In groups of at least three, 15–20cm/6–8in apart, in sun.
PROPAGATION By seeds *in situ* in spring.
CARE Water regularly, particularly in hot weather, but avoid over-wet soil.
CULTIVARS 'Machet': reddish flowers in broad spikes, with rich yellowish stamens; 'Red Monarch'; deep red flowers.

Salpiglossis sinuata
Painted tongue
ZONES 7–9   Easy
HEIGHT 60–90cm/24–36in
SPREAD 20–30cm/8–12in
FLOWERS Summer to fall: pink, red, yellow, purple, blue; bicolored and patterned

Erect, slim plants, branching low down. Narrow, midgreen, stickily hairy leaves, lobed or wavy-edged. Obliquely funnel-shaped flowers in terminal spikes.
CONTAINER SIZE At least 25cm/10in wide by 20cm/8in deep.
PLANTING In groups of three or more, 20cm/8in apart, in sun.
PROPAGATION By seeds sown in warmth in spring.
CARE Water regularly but avoid over-wet soil, which can foster root rot.
CULTIVARS 'Bolero': large velvety flowers, good color range; 'Splash': 45–60cm/18–24in tall, good strong colors, takes heat well.

Salvia
ZONES 4–9   Easy
HEIGHT 25–75cm/10–30in
SPREAD 20–30cm/8–12in
FLOWERS Summer to fall: red, purple, pink, blue, white

Erect habit, usually well branched. Ovate to lance-shaped leaves; tubular, hooded flowers, in spikes.
CONTAINER SIZE 30cm/12in wide by at least 20cm/8in deep.
PLANTING In groups of three to five or more, 20cm/8in apart, in sun.
PROPAGATION By seeds sown in warmth in spring. *S. horminum* may be sown *in situ*.
CARE Water freely during hot spells, less at other times. Apply liquid feed at 10–14 day intervals once flower spikes are well developed.
SPECIES AND CULTIVARS *S. farinacea*: 60–80cm/24–32in tall, violet-blue flowers with woolly calyces, in dense spikes – a halfhardy perennial grown as an annual; 'Blue Bedder': 60cm/24in, midnight blue. *S. horminum*: 45cm/18in tall, small, pale lilac flower spikes, topped by large, colored leaves (bracts) in showy tufts; 'Bouquet Mixed': good color mixture. *S. splendens* Scarlet sage: 30cm/12in tall as an annual, 90cm/36in or more in the tropics, vivid scarlet flowers and bracts; 'Blaze of Fire': 25cm/10in, compact; 'Flamenco': 30cm/12in, compact, deep red color.

Tagetes
ZONES 4–9   Easy
HEIGHT 15–90cm/6–36in
SPREAD 15–40cm/6–16in
FLOWERS Summer to fall: yellow, orange, red-brown

Variable in habit; some species erect with few branches, others low and bushy. All species given here have dissected or lobed leaves and daisy-like flowers, with very broad outer petals, often double.
CONTAINER SIZE 30cm/12in wide or more by 20cm/8in deep.
PLANTING In groups of at least five (short cultivars) or three (tall ones), 23cm/9in apart, in sun.
PROPAGATION By seeds sown in warmth, midspring, or *in situ* when danger of frost is past.
CARE Water freely in hot weather, less at other times. Apply liquid feed at 7–10 day intervals once flower buds show color.
SPECIES AND CULTIVARS *T. erecta* African marigold: 90cm/36in tall or more, branching but not bushy. All those commonly grown have large double flowers – 'Golden Jubilee': 65cm/26in, light yellow, All-American selection; 'Orange Hawaii': 60cm/24in, rich orange; 'Sunset Giants': 60cm/24in, dark and light yellows, and orange; 'Yellow Climax': lemon yellow. Many African marigolds are of hybrid origin with *T. patula*, being shorter and bushier, e.g. 'First Lady': 40cm/16in, clear yellow; 'Pineapple Crush': 20cm/8in, buttercup yellow; 'Pumpkin Crush': 20cm/8in, rich orange. *T. patula* French marigold: 15–40cm/6–16in tall, bushy habit; single and double flowered cultivars have yellow to orange petals sometimes marked or suffused red-brown; 'Cinnabar': 30cm/12in, single burgundy-red, with yellow center; 'Goldie': 25cm/10in, golden yellow with red markings at base;

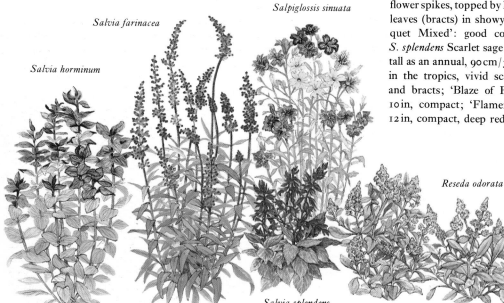

Salvia farinacea

Salvia horminum

Salpiglossis sinuata

Reseda odorata

Salvia splendens

'Naughty Marietta': to 40 cm/16 in, single, gold, red-brown; 'Crested Mixed': 30–35 cm/12–14 in, double in good color range; 'Petite Mixed': 15 cm/6 in, orange, canary and gold. *T. signata pumila* (*T. tenuifolia pumila*) Signet or Striped marigold: 15–30 cm/6–12 in, very bushy, leaves finely cut, with small, single flowers, profusely borne; 'Lulu': 20 cm/8 in, rich canary yellow; 'Paprika': 15 cm/6 in, copper-brown and golden yellow; 'Tangerine Gem': 20 cm/8 in, larger flowered, deep orange.

Tropaeolum majus Nasturtium
ZONES 4–9 Easy
HEIGHT 23–180 cm/9–72 in or more
SPREAD 30–90 cm/12–36 in
FLOWERS Summer to fall: yellow, orange, red
Bushy and spreading, climbing or trailing, depending on support available. Circular, long-stalked leaves, and flowers with five spreading, rounded petals and a prominent spur.
CONTAINER SIZE At least 25 cm/10 in wide by 20 cm/8 in deep.
PLANTING Long trailing or climbing varieties singly or in small groups, 60 cm/24 in apart, compact ones in groups of five or so, 25–30 cm/10–12 in apart, in sun or partial shade.
PROPAGATION By seeds *in situ* when danger of frost is past, or earlier in warmth.
CARE Water freely in hot weather, less at other times. Apply liquid feed at 10–14 day intervals when flower buds show.
CULTIVARS 'Tall Mixed': trailing or climbing to 1.8 m/6 ft or more, good range of orange and yellow shades; 'Gleam Hybrids': bushy habit to 30 cm/12 in, semidouble flowers in varied shades of orange and yellow; 'Dwarf Jewel Mixture': similar to 'Gleam' but of a rather more compact habit.

Verbena × hybrida
Garden or annual verbena
ZONES 4–9 Easy
HEIGHT 20–30 cm/8–12 in
SPREAD 25–40 cm/10–16 in
FLOWERS Summer to fall: red, purple, pale yellow, white
Spreading, fairly bushy habit with erect flowering stems. Oblong to lance-shaped leaves, prominently toothed and veined. Flowers are primroselike, but smaller and in compact clusters. Tender perennial grown as an annual.
CONTAINER SIZE At least 30 cm/12 in wide by 15–20 cm/6–8 in deep.
PLANTING In groups of three or more at 20 cm/8 in apart, in sun.
PROPAGATION By seeds sown in warmth in midspring.
CARE Water regularly but avoid over-wet soil, which fosters root rot. Verbenas can stand short spells of drought. Apply liquid feed every two weeks once flower buds show.
CULTIVARS 'Rainbow Mixture' and 'Springtime Mix': both well-branched in a good color range; 'Sparkle Mix': similar, but shorter and more compact; single-colored cultivars are also available, e.g. 'Amethyst', 'Blaze' (scarlet), 'Miss Susie' (coral-pink), 'Splendor' (royal purple), 'White Ball'.

Tagetes patula

Verbena × hybrida

Viola × wittrockiana (tricolor)
Pansy
ZONES 4–9 Easy
HEIGHT 10–15 cm/4–6 in
SPREAD 15–20 cm/6–8 in
FLOWERS All year: purple, blue, red, yellow, white, ivory and bicolored
Tufted, spreading habit. Oval to lance-shaped leaves, usually rich green; flat-faced flowers, generally with a black masklike blotch in the center. Short-lived perennial, grown as an annual or a biennial.
CONTAINER SIZE At least 30 cm/12 in wide by 15–20 cm/6–8 in deep.
PLANTING In groups of five or more, 15 cm/6 in apart, in sun or partial shade.
PROPAGATION By seeds sown in warmth in early spring for summer or fall blooming; sow in a reserve container outside in late summer for winter or spring flowering in zones 8–9.
CARE Water regularly, especially during hot spells, but avoid over-wet soil.

Tagetes erecta

Viola × wittrockiana

CULTIVARS 'Engelmann's Giant', 'Majestic Giants Mixed', 'Roggli Giant Mixed', 'Swiss Giants Mixed': all large-flowered mixtures with good color range, for summer flowering. Many single-color cultivars are available – 'Alpine Glow': crimson with black blotch; 'Beacon' (coppery-red), 'Celestial Queen' (light blue), 'Helios' (golden-yellow), 'Ice King' (white), 'Mars' (ultramarine-blue). Several other cultivar groups are available, including miniature-flowered ones, and the plain-faced 'Clear Crystals'.

Tropaeolum majus

Tagetes signata pumila

Perennials

Hardy perennials respond well to culture in containers, but as plants to grow under this regime they are invariably overlooked. If chosen carefully, however, they can provide flower and/or foliage interest for most of the year. Unlike their close relatives, the annuals, they do not need continually replacing from seed or cuttings. Once a plant is established in its container, it needs only a top dressing of fresh potting mix in spring and a series of liquid-feed applications during the summer. Should a plant become noticeably congested in its container it should be divided, with the healthiest sections replanted with fresh soil.

With respect to perennials, the hardiness zones indicate how much cold a plant will stand when resting or dormant in winter. In the coldest zones (1–5), the containers of many normally hardy perennials will need protecting in a cellar or on a covered balcony where temperatures do not drop much below freezing. In the open ground, roots are protected by the soil cover, whereas in a container frost can freeze solid the whole root system and surrounding soil, severely damaging both roots and dormant buds.

Perennials can be roughly divided into two groups, the herbaceous, which die back to ground level each fall or winter, and those that are evergreen or winter green. (Species included in this section are herbaceous unless otherwise stated.) Plants from the latter group, especially those with decorative foliage, such as *Bergenia* and *Pulmonaria*, are particularly desirable. But do not ignore the true herbaceous perennials. These often give the best summer or fall showing of flowers and can be planted around spring bulbs or annuals for an earlier dis-

play. In large containers, herbaceous and evergreen perennials can be effectively combined, or mixed with shrubs and other plants.

For those who appreciate the overall shape and texture of a plant, rather than the massed color effect that annuals supply so admirably, perennials have much to offer. For example, a well-constructed wooden tub set with a single plant of *Acanthus*, *Bergenia* or *Hosta* will give grace and distinction to any patio or balcony and will look good for years with minimal basic care. Groups of smaller plants can look equally attractive, but much depends on the site and decorative requirements. If the plants are chosen with care, there need be no staking chores or maintenance other than regular watering.

Container gardening provides an ideal cultural regime for the less hardy perennials too, for example African lily (*Agapanthus*). In areas with cold winters, they can be kept in a cool room during the late fall to spring period.

Most of the commercial pre-packed potting mixes can be used for perennials, though the loam-based ones, such as John Innes no. 2 or 3, generally give the best results. However, all the plants described here will grow perfectly well in the readily obtainable all-peat based mixes.

In this section, the heights given are for plants in full bloom or, where foliage is the primary interest, the height with fully expanded leaves. The term 'clump-forming' denotes a plant with a number of shoots arising close together. 'Colony-forming' indicates that the plant spreads sideways underground, annually sending up a less crowded and well-spaced colony of stems. A 'mat-forming' plant has a dense, prostrate habit.

Acanthus Bear's breeches
ZONES 8–9 Easy
HEIGHT 90–120 cm/36–48 in
SPREAD 60–90 cm/24–36 in
FLOWERS Summer: white to purple
Clump-forming habit, robust and statuesque. Large, arching leaves, deeply lobed. Tubular flowers, with protruding three-lobed lip, borne in spikes from among spiny, ornamental bracts. Explosive seed capsules.
CONTAINER SIZE 40–50 cm/16–20 in wide by 30–40 cm/12–16 in deep.
PLANTING Singly, in sun or, in hot summer areas, partial shade.
PROPAGATION By division in fall or early spring, by seeds in spring, by root cuttings in late winter.
CARE Water freely, especially in hot weather, but avoid over-wet soil. Apply liquid feed monthly to established specimens, from late spring to early fall.
SPECIES *A. mollis*: glossy, mid-green leaves to 60 cm/24 in long, wavy-margined, deeply but coarsely lobed, flowers white or purple-flushed, spikes 30 cm/12 in long. *A. m. latifolius* is more robust and the most commonly grown. *A. spinosus*: deep glossy-green leaves more elaborately cut into narrow, spine-tipped segments, light purple-mauve flowers, spikes 45 cm/18 in long.

Agapanthus African lily
ZONES 8–10 Easy
HEIGHT 60–120 cm/24–48 in
SPREAD 30–60 cm/12–24 in
FLOWERS Late summer to early fall: shades of blue to blue-purple, white
Densely clump-forming. Erect stems, resistant to wind. Leaves all basal, broadly strap-shaped. Six-petaled, funnel-shaped flowers, in dense, rounded terminal heads.
CONTAINER SIZE 30–45 cm/12–18 in wide by 30–40 cm/12–16 in deep.
PLANTING Singly, or in groups of three at 30 cm/12 in apart in the larger containers, in sun.
PROPAGATION By division or by seeds sown in warmth in spring.
CARE Water regularly, especially in warm weather, but avoid over-wet soil. Apply liquid feed monthly during the growing season.
SPECIES AND CULTIVARS *A. campanulatus*: deciduous leaves, 4 cm/1½ in long flowers, mid-blue or white. *A. ×* 'Headbourne Hybrids': a race of hybrids, mostly robust, up to 1.2 m/4 ft tall, flowers in a wide range of blue to purple shades and white; *A. umbellatus* 'Peter Pan': 45 cm/18 in tall, very compact, evergreen leaves.

Agapanthus campanulatus

Acanthus mollis

Aquilegia × hybrida

Aquilegia Columbine
ZONES 3–9 Easy
HEIGHT 45–70 cm / 18–28 in
SPREAD 30–45 cm / 12–18 in
FLOWERS Spring to summer:
various colors
Clump-forming habit. Erect stems, usually resistant to wind. Coarsely fernlike, decorative leaves, composed of several lobed leaflets. Cup-shaped flowers, with five colored sepals and five spurred petals.
CONTAINER SIZE 30–40 cm / 12–16 in wide by 30 cm / 12 in deep.
PLANTING Singly, or in groups of three at 25 cm / 10 in apart in the larger containers, in sun or partial shade.
PROPAGATION By division, fall to early spring, or by seeds in spring or when ripe.
CARE Water freely, especially in warm weather. Apply liquid feed every two weeks from spring to midsummer.
CULTIVARS A. × hybrida: covers a wide range of flower types and colors, all plants about 60 cm / 24 in or so tall. Long-spurred hybrids have large flowers with very long, flared spurs. Short-spurred hybrids have shorter, hooked spurs. Both come in shades of red, pink, yellow, purple and near-blue.

Astilbe
ZONES 5–9 Easy
HEIGHT 45–150 cm / 18–60 in
SPREAD 20–60 cm / 8–24 in
FLOWERS Summer to fall: pink, red, purple, white

Clump-forming habit. Erect stems, resistant to wind. Fernlike leaves, composed of oval, toothed leaflets. Tiny flowers, densely borne in erect, terminal plumes.
CONTAINER SIZE 30–60 cm / 12–24 in wide by 30 cm / 12 in deep.
PLANTING Singly in small containers, but ideally in groups of three to five in larger ones, setting plants 20–30 cm / 8–12 in apart, depending on ultimate size, in sun or partial shade.
PROPAGATION By division, fall to early spring.
CARE Water freely during the growing season, ideally placing the container in a tray kept filled with water. Apply liquid feed monthly from late spring to late summer.
SPECIES AND CULTIVARS A. × arendsii: covers a large group of named hybrids of multi-parentage differing greatly in height and flower color. A. chinensis (sinensis) pumila: colony-forming, 30 cm / 12 in tall, flowers mauve-pink, long-lasting, late summer to fall, needs less moisture.

Bergenia (Megasea)
ZONES 5–9 Easy
HEIGHT 30–40 cm / 12–16 in
SPREAD 45–60 cm / 18–24 in or more
FLOWERS Winter to late spring: pink to red-purple, white
Slowly spreading habit. Thick stems, more or less prostrate. Large, paddle-

shaped, thick-textured, shiny, evergreen leaves. Five- to six-petaled flowers, in clusters above the leaves.
CONTAINER SIZE 30–60 cm / 12–24 in wide by 30 cm / 12 in deep.
PLANTING Singly, or in groups of three to five at 30 cm / 12 in apart in the larger containers, in sun or partial shade.
PROPAGATION By division in fall or early spring, by seeds in spring.
CARE Water freely in warm weather, less at other times. Apply liquid feed monthly from late spring to late summer.
SPECIES AND CULTIVARS B. cordifolia: rounded leaves, to 30 cm / 12 in long, often crinkly-margined and heart-shaped at base. Pink flowers, on stems 30 cm / 12 in or more tall, in spring. B.c. purpurea: leaves flushed purple, especially in winter, rose-magenta flowers. B. crassifolia: oval leaves, 20 cm / 8 in or more long, flowers like those of B. cordifolia, rose-purple, late winter–early spring. B.c. pacifica: purple flowers. Several named cultivars are available.

Doronicum Leopard's bane
ZONES 4–9 Easy
HEIGHT 30–75 cm / 12–30 in
SPREAD 25–45 cm / 10–18 in
FLOWERS Spring: yellow
Clump-forming habit. Erect stems, fairly resistant to wind. Mainly basal, elliptic to heart-shaped leaves. Daisy-like flowers at the end of main stems

and their branches.
CONTAINER SIZE 25–45 cm / 10–18 in wide by 30–40 cm / 12–16 in deep.
PLANTING Singly, or in groups of three to five at 30 cm / 12 in apart in the larger containers, in sun or partial shade.
PROPAGATION By division in the fall or winter.
CARE Water regularly, especially in warm weather. Apply liquid feed every two weeks from late spring to late summer.
SPECIES AND CULTIVARS D. orientale (D. caucasicum, and listed by some nurserymen under D. cordatum): stems to 30 cm / 12 in tall, broadly oval to heart-shaped leaves, 5 cm / 2 in wide flowers; 'Magnificum' is a finer, taller, more robust hybrid; 'Spring Beauty': flowers fully double. D. plantagineum: stems to 75 cm / 30 in tall, oval to elliptic leaves, flowers about 5 cm / 2 in wide; 'Harpur Crewe' ('Excelsum'): 1–2 m / 3–6½ ft tall, flowers to 7.5 cm / 3 in wide.

Geranium Crane's bill
ZONES 4–9 Easy
HEIGHT 30–60 cm / 12–24 in
SPREAD 30–60 cm / 12–24 in
FLOWERS Summer to fall: pink or violet-blue
Clump-forming to spreading habit. Long-stalked, rounded leaves, five- to seven-lobed. Five-petaled flowers, shallowly bowl-shaped or flat, in loose terminal clusters. They are true hardy perennials, not to be confused with the semishrubby pot geranium, which botanically is classified in the genus Pelargonium.
CONTAINER SIZE 40–60 cm / 16–24 in wide by 30–40 cm / 12–16 in deep.
PLANTING Singly, or in groups of three or four at 25–30 cm / 10–12 in apart, in sun or partial shade.
PROPAGATION By division, fall to late winter/early spring.

Geranium pratense

Doronicum orientale

Geranium endressii

Astilbe chinensis pumila

Bergenia cordifolia

CARE Water freely in warm weather, less at other times. Apply liquid feed monthly from late spring to late summer.

SPECIES G. *endressii*: spreading habit, erect stems, 30 cm/12 in or more in height, five-lobed leaves to 8 cm/3¼ in wide, pink flowers, 3 cm/1¼ in wide, early to late summer. 'Claridge Druce', derived from this species, is more robust, with larger leaves and rose-purple flowers. G. × *magnificum* (often erroneously listed as G. *ibericum* and G. *platypetalum*): clump-forming, stems to 60 cm/24 in, boldly veined, deep-cut five- to seven-lobed leaves, 10 cm/4 in or more wide, flowers 3–4 cm/1¼–1½ in wide, violet-blue with reddish veins, summer only. G. *pratense*: clump-forming, to 75 cm/30 in tall, very deep-cut seven-lobed leaves, long-stalked, to 13 cm/5 in wide, flowers 4 cm/1½ in wide, purple-blue, summer to fall; 'Caeruleum Plenum': flowers double, deep violet-blue; 'Johnson's Blue': dwarf, about 30 cm/12 in tall, flowers 5 cm/2 in wide, lavender-blue with violet veins.

Geum chiloense (G. coccineum)
ZONES 6–9   Easy
HEIGHT 60 cm/24 in
SPREAD 30–40 cm/12–16 in
FLOWERS Summer to fall: red, yellow, orange

Clump-forming habit. Erect, wiry stems, largely resistant to wind. Leaves 20 cm/8 in long, pinnately divided with an extra large terminal leaflet. Flowers basically five-petaled, but in cultivation there are semidouble forms, 5 cm/2 in wide.

CONTAINER SIZE 40–60 cm/16–24 in wide by 30 cm/12 in or more deep.

PLANTING In groups of three or four at 25–30 cm/10–12 in apart, in sun or partial shade.

PROPAGATION By division in fall or early spring.

CARE Water regularly, especially in warm weather, less at other times. Apply liquid feed monthly from late spring to early summer.

CULTIVARS G.c. 'Fire Opal' (flowers rich bronze-scarlet), 'Lady Stratheden' (yellow), 'Mrs Bradshaw' (bright brick-red), 'Princess Juliana' (double orange-scarlet).

Helleborus
ZONES 3–9   Moderately easy
HEIGHT 25–45 cm/10–18 in
SPREAD 30–50 cm/12–20 in
FLOWERS Winter, spring: yellow-green, white, pink to purple

Clump-forming habit. Erect stems, resistant to wind. Relatively large leaves, cut into three to eleven leaflets. Five-petaled, saucer- to bowl-shaped flowers, inclined or nodding in loose clusters.

CONTAINER SIZE 30–45 cm/12–18 in wide by 30–40 cm/12–16 in deep.

PLANTING Singly, or in groups of three or four at 30 cm/12 in apart in the larger containers, in sun or partial shade.

PROPAGATION By careful division immediately after flowering.

CARE Water freely during warm weather, less at other times. Apply liquid feed monthly from spring to midsummer. Remove flowering stems once blooms have faded.

SPECIES AND CULTIVARS H. *lividus corsicus* (H. *corsicus*) (zones 7–9): has robust, semiwoody stems that carry all the leaves and flowers; evergreen, trifoliate leaves, each leaflet 14 cm/5½ in long, waved, toothed and glossy, flowers yellow-green, winter to spring. H. *niger* Christmas rose (zones 3–9): 30 cm/12 in tall, evergreen leaves, most of which rise at ground level, divided into seven to nine leaflets, flowers 5–10 cm/2–4 in wide, white, winter to spring. H. *orientalis* Lenten rose (zones 6–9): like H. *niger*, but with bigger, usually evergreen leaves composed of five to eleven leaflets. Most plants sold under this name are hybrids.

Hemerocallis Day lily
ZONES 3–9   Easy
HEIGHT 60–90 cm/24–36 in or more
SPREAD 40–60 cm/16–24 in
FLOWERS Summer: yellow, orange, red, pink

Clump-forming habit. Erect stems, resistant to wind. Strap-shaped, arching leaves, mostly basal. Six-petaled, lilylike flowers, in terminal sprays.

CONTAINER SIZE 40–60 cm/16–24 in wide by 40 cm/16 in deep.

PLANTING Singly, or in groups of three to five at 40 cm/16 in apart in the larger containers, in sun.

PROPAGATION By division in fall or early spring.

CARE Water freely in warm weather, less at other times. Apply liquid feed monthly from late spring to late summer.

SPECIES AND CULTIVARS H. *fulva*: 10 cm/4 in long, buff-orange flowers; 'Kwanso' (H. *disticha* 'Flore Pleno'): double, strongly colored flowers. H. *lilioasphodelus* (H. *flava*): clear-yellow, fragrant flowers, late spring to early summer.

Many hybrid cultivars now available with generally larger flowers in a wide color range.

Heuchera Alum root, Coral bells
ZONES 4–9   Easy
HEIGHT 45–75 cm/18–30 in
SPREAD 30–45 cm/12–18 in
FLOWERS Early to late summer: red, pink, near white

Clump-forming to slow spreading habit. Slim, wiry stems, resistant to wind. Decorative, evergreen, basal foliage, maplelike, sometimes paler marbled or bronze-tinted. Small bell-shaped flowers, in spikes or clusters.

CONTAINER SIZE 40–60 cm/16–24 in wide by 20–30 cm/8–12 in deep.

PLANTING In groups of three to five at 20–25 cm/8–10 in apart, in sun or light shade.

PROPAGATION By division, fall to early spring, or by seeds in spring.

CARE Water regularly but avoid over-wet soil. Benefits from occasional applications of liquid feed during the growing season.

Hemerocallis fulva

Heuchera × brizoides

Helleborus orientalis

Helleborus lividus corsicus

Geum chiloense

SPECIES AND CULTIVARS H. × *brizoides* covers a race of cultivars with the bell-shaped flowers carried in elegant airy sprays, e.g. 'Bressingham Hybrids': mixed shades; 'Garnet': coral-red, leaves bronze-marbled; 'Gloriana': rosy-crimson; H. *cylindrica* 'Greenfinch': greenish flowers, in slim, pokerlike spikes.

Hosta (Funkia) Plantain lily
ZONES 3–9 Easy
HEIGHT 45–90 cm/18–36 in
SPREAD 45–90 cm/18–36 in
FLOWERS Summer: lilac to purple
Clump-forming habit. Ornamental foliage. Lance-shaped to rounded, boldly veined leaves, often variegated, arching and overlapping to form decorative mounds. Six-petaled, trumpet-shaped flowers, in spikes above the leaves.
CONTAINER SIZE 40–60 cm/16–24 in wide by 40 cm/16 in deep.
PLANTING Singly, or in groups of three or four at 40 cm/16 in apart in the larger containers, in sun or light shade.
PROPAGATION By division in fall or early spring.
CARE Water freely in warm weather, less at other times, but soil must always be moist. Apply liquid feed monthly from late spring to late summer.
SPECIES AND CULTIVARS H. *fortunei*: oval leaves, heart-shaped at base, usually grayish-green, 13 cm/5 in long, stems to 90 cm/36 in tall, flowers 4 cm/1½ in long, lilac to violet, summer. H. *lancifolia*: broadly lance-shaped, glossy leaves, to 18 cm/7 in long, stems to 60 cm/24 in tall, pale purple flowers, 4 cm/1½ in long, late summer. H. *sieboldiana*: 25–38 cm/10–13 in long, very strongly veined, blue-gray leaves, 60 cm/24 in tall stems, barely topping the leaf clump, pale lilac flowers, 4 cm/1½ in long,

summer. H.s. *elegans*: somewhat corrugated, more intensely blue-gray leaves. H. *undulata*: elliptic, strongly waved leaves, to 15 cm/6 in long, with a bold central white zone, stems 60 cm/24 in tall, pale violet flowers, 5 cm/2 in long, late summer. H. *ventricosa*: heart-shaped leaves, to 24 cm/9½ in long, stems to 90 cm/36 in tall, deep violet flowers, to 5 cm/2 in long, late summer.

Iris
ZONES 3–10 Easy
HEIGHT 30–120 cm/12–48 in
SPREAD 30–60 cm/12–24 in
FLOWERS Winter to summer: blue, purple, red, white
Clump-forming habit. Erect stems, mainly resistant to wind. Sword-shaped leaves. Flowers of six petals, three outer – known as falls – generally larger, arching out or hanging down, and three inner – called standards – narrower, erect. Also there are three central, petallike styles that alternate with the standards.
CONTAINER SIZE 30–60 cm/12–24 in wide by 30–40 cm/12–16 in deep.
PLANTING Singly, or in groups of three to five at 30 cm/12 in apart in the larger containers, in sun.
PROPAGATION By division after flowering, fall or early spring.
CARE Keep *Iris sibirica* moist at all times. Water the others regularly but avoid over-wet soil. Apply liquid feed monthly from late spring to

late summer. Remove stems when last flower fades, unless seed is required.
SPECIES AND CULTIVARS I. *germanica* Flag iris (zones 4–10): stems to 75 cm/30 in tall, broad, gray-green leaves, large flowers, falls 7.5 cm/3 in long, deep purple with yellow 'beard', standards paler. Very similar in overall appearance are the many cultivars known as 'Bearded' or June-flowering hybrids (zones 5–10). These are the familiar flag-type irises with flowers in a vast array of colors and shades, some bicolors. I. *pallida dalmatica* (zones 5–10): like I. *germanica*, but leaves more gray, and larger, lavender-blue, fragrant flowers, early summer. I.p. 'Aurea-variegata' (zones 5–10): leaves striped yellow; 'Variegata': leaves striped creamy-white. I. *sibirica* (zones 3–9): densely clump-forming, stems to 120 cm/48 in tall, narrow, green leaves, flowers 6–7.5 cm/2½–3 in wide, lilac to purple-blue, summer. Several named cultivars are available. I. *tectorum* Japanese roof iris (zones 5–10): clump-forming, stems 40 cm/16 in or more tall, evergreen, flowers to 10 cm/4 in wide, blue-lilac with darker veins, early summer; stands a fair amount of neglect. I. *unguicularis* (*stylosa*) (zones 8–10): clump-forming, stemless, evergreen leaves, to 60 cm/24 in long, flowers narrow, arching, lilac to lavender, fragrant,

7.5 cm/3 in wide, on tube 15 cm/6 in or more long, winter to spring in mild winter areas; keep somewhat dry in late summer and early fall.
See also *Iris* p. 130 and p. 134.

Lamium maculatum
Spotted dead-nettle
ZONES 3–9 Easy
HEIGHT About 30 cm/12 in
SPREAD 60 cm/24 in
FLOWERS Early to late summer: red-purple, pink, white
Mat-forming habit. Heart-shaped, 4–8 cm/1½–3¼ in long leaves, each with a silvery-white central band. Tubular flowers, two-lipped, the upper one hooded, in whorls in the upper leaf axils.
CONTAINER SIZE 25–60 cm/10–24 in wide by 20–30 cm/8–12 in deep.
PLANTING Singly, or in groups of three to five at 25 cm/10 in apart in the larger containers, in sun or partial shade. Effective as ground cover.
PROPAGATION By division, fall to spring.
CARE Water regularly, especially during warm weather, less at other times. Apply liquid feed monthly from late spring to late summer.

Hosta ventricosa

Hosta lancifolia

Lamium maculatum

Iris sibirica

CULTIVARS *L.m.* 'Album': pure white flowers; 'Aureum': yellow leaves, pink-purple flowers, weaker growing and needs partial shade; 'Beacon Silver': entirely silvery gray-white leaves, purple flowers; 'Roseum': soft, clear pink flowers.

Lupinus polyphyllus
Border lupin
ZONES 3–9   Easy
HEIGHT 60–90 cm/24–36 in
SPREAD 45–60 cm/18–24 in
FLOWERS Mainly summer: wide color range
Clump-forming habit. Erect stems, mainly resistant to wind. Leaves composed of 10–17 narrowly elliptic leaflets radiating from the tip of each leaf stalk. Pealike flowers, in terminal, minaret-shaped spikes.
CONTAINER SIZE 30–60 cm/12–24 in wide by 30–40 cm/12–16 in deep.
PLANTING Singly, or in groups of four or five at 25–35 cm/10–14 in apart in the larger containers, in sun.
PROPAGATION By division, fall to early spring, or by cuttings of basal shoots, mid- to late spring.
CARE Water freely in warm weather, less at other times. Apply liquid feed monthly from late spring to late summer. Remove spent flowering stems as soon as possible.
CULTIVARS Many self- and bicolored cultivars are available, the best being sold under the general name of Russell lupins. 'Little Lulu' is a compact, weather-resistant selection to 60 cm/24 in tall.

Nepeta × faasenii
Catmint, Catnip
ZONES 3–9   Easy
HEIGHT 30 cm/12 in
SPREAD 60 cm/24 in
FLOWERS Early summer to fall: violet-blue
Clump-forming habit, but stems semiprostrate, the flowering tips ascending. Aromatic, grayish-downy, narrowly oval leaves. Small, tubular flowers, two-lipped, in interrupted spikes.
CONTAINER SIZE 25–45 cm/10–18 in wide by 30 cm/12 in deep.
PLANTING Singly, or in groups of up to five at 30 cm/12 in apart in the larger containers, in sun. Best used around the base of trees and larger shrubs in large containers.
PROPAGATION By division in early spring.
CARE Water regularly but avoid over-wet soil. Benefits from occasional applications of liquid feed during the summer. Shear plants over each early spring. Prompt removal of flowering heads in summer will stimulate the production of more.

Phormium tenax
New Zealand flax
ZONES 8–10   Moderately easy
HEIGHT 1.2–2.1 m/4–7 ft
SPREAD 1.2–1.8 m/4–6 ft
FLOWERS Summer: reddish; mainly grown for foliage
Clump-forming habit. Evergreen, sword-shaped, leathery leaves, often lightly bluish-white beneath. Tubular flowers, in stiff, branched clusters above the leaves, not commonly produced on specimens grown in containers.
CONTAINER SIZE 45–75 cm/18–30 in wide by 40 cm/16 in or more deep.
PLANTING Singly, in sun.
PROPAGATION By division or by seeds in spring.
CARE Water freely throughout the growing season, less at other times, but avoid over-wet soil for long periods. Apply liquid feed monthly from early summer to early fall. In the colder parts of zone 8, at least the rootball should be lagged against severe frost.

CULTIVARS *P.t.* 'Purpureum': bronze-purple leaves; 'Variegatum': leaves cream-margined; 'Veitchii': cream-striped leaves. All variegated and colored-leaf cultivars less hardy than the plain green type.

Primula
ZONES 4–9   Easy
HEIGHT 15–30 cm/6–12 in
SPREAD 20–40 cm/8–16 in
FLOWERS Winter to late spring: lilac, purple, red, yellow, white, cream, pink
Clump-forming habit. Erect, short stems. Leaves all basal, oblong to broadly lance-shaped, the tip broadest, somewhat corrugated. Tubular flowers, with five broad, notched petals.
CONTAINER SIZE 40–60 cm/16–24 in wide by 30 cm/12 in deep.
PLANTING In groups of three or four at 25 cm/10 in apart, in partial shade or, in cool areas, full sun.
PROPAGATION By division in late summer or fall or by seeds when ripe or in spring.
CARE Water freely while in full growth, less at other times. Apply liquid feed every two weeks, spring to midsummer. Polyanthus and primrose cultivars best divided annually in late summer.
SPECIES AND CULTIVARS *P. denticulata* Drumstick primrose: leaves to 30 cm/12 in long when fully grown, flowers in dense globular heads 5–7.5 cm/2–3 in wide, lilac to red or blue-purple or white, starting to open low down among the leaves in early spring, stems finally to 30 cm/12 in tall. *P. × pruhoniciana* (*P. × juliana*) 'Wanda': dwarf primrose with claret-crimson flowers; 'Garryarde Guinevere': cowsliplike, flushed bronze-crimson leaves, pink flowers. *P. × tommasinii* (*P. × polyantha*) Polyanthus: 15–20 cm/6–8 in or more tall, each stem bearing a truss of large, primroselike flowers in shades of yellow, red, cream, purple. *P. vulgaris* Common primrose: along with the familiar pale yellow primrose, there are now named strains in a color range equal to the polyanthus.

Phormium tenax

Lupinus polyphyllus

Nepeta × faasenii

Pulmonaria Lungwort
ZONES 3–9   Easy
HEIGHT 15–30 cm/6–12 in
SPREAD 30–60 cm/12–24 in
FLOWERS Late winter to summer:
red, purple, blue
Clump-forming to slowly spreading
habit. Large, winter green, mainly
basal leaves, oblong to oval. Tubular
flowers, with five rounded petal-
lobes, in clusters above the leaves.
CONTAINER SIZE 40–60 cm/16–24 in
wide by 30–40 cm/12–16 in deep.
PLANTING In groups of three to six
at least 30 cm/12 in apart, in partial
shade.
PROPAGATION By division, fall to
spring.
CARE Water freely in warm weather,
less at other times. Apply liquid
feed monthly from late spring to late
summer.
SPECIES AND CULTIVARS *P. angustifolia*
(*P. azurea*) Blue cowslip: widely
clump-forming to spreading, 20–
30 cm/8–12 in tall, lance-shaped
leaves, bright blue flowers. *P. officinalis* Jerusalem cowslip: clump-
forming, to 30 cm/12 in tall, oval
leaves, boldly spotted silvery-white,
flowers reddish to bluish-violet. *P.
rubra*: widely clump-forming, about
20 cm/8 in tall, oblong-oval leaves,
sometimes faintly spotted, flowers
brick-red.

Pyrethrum roseum
(*Chrysanthemum coccineum*)
ZONES 3–9   Easy
HEIGHT 60 cm/24 in
SPREAD 30–45 cm/12–18 in
FLOWERS Summer: pink, red, white
Clump-forming habit. Erect stems,
moderately resistant to wind. Finely
dissected, ferny leaves. Daisylike
flowers, to 7.5 cm/3 in wide, on long
stems.
CONTAINER SIZE 30–60 cm/12–24 in
wide by 30–40 cm/12–16 in deep.
PLANTING Singly, or in groups of
four or five at 30 cm/12 in apart in the
larger containers, in sun.
PROPAGATION By division, fall to
early spring.
CARE Water freely in warm weather,
less at other times. Apply liquid feed
monthly from late spring to late
summer. Remove spent flowering
stems promptly.
CULTIVARS *P.r.* 'Avalanche': white
flowers; 'Bressingham Red': deep
red; 'Eileen May Robinson': salmon-
pink, large; 'Kelway's Glorious': rich
scarlet, early; 'Madeleine': double,
pale pink.

Rudbeckia fulgida
ZONES 4–9   Easy
HEIGHT 60 cm/24 in or more
SPREAD 45 cm/18 in or more
FLOWERS Summer to fall: yellow and
brown-purple
Clump-forming habit. Erect stems.
Mid-green, oblong to lance-shaped
leaves. Yellow flowers, 7.5 cm/3 in
across, with brown-purple cones.
CONTAINER SIZE 30–60 cm/12–24 in
wide by 30–40 cm/12–16 in deep.
PLANTING Singly, or in groups of four
at 30 cm/12 in apart in the larger
containers, in sun or partial shade.
PROPAGATION By division, fall to
early spring.
CARE Water freely in warm weather,
less at other times. Apply liquid feed
monthly from the spring to late
summer.
CULTIVAR *R.f.* 'Goldsturm': larger,
finer flowers.

Salvia Flowering sage
ZONES 5–9   Easy
HEIGHT 60–90 cm/24–36 in
SPREAD 30–45 cm/12–18 in
FLOWERS Summer: blue to violet-
purple, white, pink
Clump-forming habit. Erect stems,
moderately resistant to wind. Variable, usually wrinkled or corrugated
leaves. Tubular, hooded flowers, in
long spikes.
CONTAINER SIZE 30–60 cm/12–24 in
wide by 30–40 cm/12–16 in deep.
PLANTING Singly, or in groups of
three to five at 30–35 cm/12–14 in
apart in the larger containers, in sun.
PROPAGATION By division in fall or
spring. *S. haematodes* best by seeds
in spring.
CARE Water freely in warm weather,
less at other times. Apply liquid feed
monthly from late spring to late
summer. Remove spent flowering
stems in late fall.
SPECIES AND CULTIVARS *S. argentea*
Silver sage: 75 cm/30 cm or more
tall, handsome, silvery-white woolly,
oval leaves, to 20 cm/8 in long, flowers
white or pink tinted. *S. haematodes*:
to 90 cm/36 in tall, 20–25 cm/8–10 in
long, corrugated leaves, blue-violet
flowers, in large, dense, narrowly
pyramidal clusters; very showy but
short-lived and best raised afresh
from seeds every two years. *S.×
superba* (*Virgata nemorosa*): 60–
90 cm/24–36 in tall, oblong, finely
wrinkled leaves, flowers violet-
purple, surrounded by short, reddish
bracts; 'Lubeca': compact habit, to
45 cm/18 in tall, violet-blue flowers;
'May Night': 60 cm/24 in tall, dark
blue flowers.

Stachys byzantina
(*S. lanata*, *S. olympica*) Lamb's ears,
Lamb's tongue
ZONES 7–9   Easy
HEIGHT 30–45 cm/12–18 in
SPREAD 45 cm/18 in or more
FLOWERS Summer: purple; mainly a
foliage plant
Widely clump-forming to spreading
habit. Erect stems, resistant to wind.
Oblong to elliptic leaves, to 10 cm/
4 in long, densely silvery-white,
woolly. Small, tubular flowers, in
interrupted spikes.
CONTAINER SIZE 40–60 cm/16–24 in
wide by 30 cm/12 in deep.
PLANTING In groups of three or four
at 30 cm/12 in apart, in sun. Can also
be used as ground cover around trees.
PROPAGATION By division in fall or
spring.
CARE Water regularly but avoid over-
wet soil. Benefits from occasional
applications of liquid feed during the
growing season.

Salvia × superba

Pyrethrum roseum

Rudbeckia fulgida

Pulmonaria angustifolia

Stachys byzantina

Primula denticulata

Bulbs, corms and tubers

Bulbs, corms and tubers are food storage organs and a means by which plants survive inclement weather, both winter cold and dry summer heat. They are very suitable for container growing; when planted in the right conditions, they produce leaves and flowers in a comparatively short time. In addition, they are easy to cultivate and many are among the most decorative of plants. In temperate climates, the most useful bulbous plants are those that bloom in spring from a fall planting, growing rapidly with the first warmth of the new year. Several of the most welcome bulbs actually flower in winter, for example some crocuses, snowdrops, winter aconites and certain dwarf bulbous irises. There are also the summer flowering subjects (*Gladiolus* being the best known example) that are planted in spring.

The majority of bulbs, corms and tubers spend at least half of each year below ground, so they must be used in conjunction with other plants. They provide a superb massed show when in bloom, but once the flowers fade there will be no further display and it is best to remove and replace them without delay. Grown in this way they are treated like annuals. It is more rewarding and less expensive in terms of potting mix and numbers of containers required to plant them around trees and shrubs or between hardy perennials. If not planted too thickly, they can also be interplanted with annuals.

All the plants mentioned in this section will thrive in any commercial potting mix. Some may need to be lifted and dried off after flowering. When grown with other plants, the feeding they receive will suffice. Where they are grown by themselves, an annual dressing of bonemeal in late fall is recommended.

When buying bulbs, corms and tubers, look for those that are heavy for their size, firm to the touch, plump, and free from scars.

Begonia × tuberhybrida
ZONES 9–10   Easy
HEIGHT 30–45 cm/12–18 in
SPREAD 30–40 cm/12–16 in
FLOWERS Summer to early fall: red, pink, white, yellow, orange
Erect to pendulous habit. Ear-shaped leaves. Flowers single or double, the latter roselike. Pendulous cultivars make excellent hanging basket plants.
CONTAINER SIZE 25–45 cm/10–18 in wide by 15–25 cm/6–10 in deep.
PLANTING Preferably in groups of at least three, the plants 20–30 cm/8–12 in apart, in sun or partial shade.
PROPAGATION By division, or by cuttings in warmth, in spring.
CARE In areas where spring frosts are usual (zones lower than 9), do not plant the corms out until the weather warms up, usually in early summer. Corms should be potted in spring and started off indoors at not less than 13–16°C/55–61°F. In the fall, the plants must be lifted and dried off, the corms cleaned, and stored at 7–10°C/45–50°F. During the growing season, water regularly and apply liquid feed every two weeks until the last flowers fade.
CULTIVARS Camellia-flowered: robust, erect, to 30 cm/12 in or more tall, large, double flowers; commonly available as a mixture of cultivars of various flower colors, but some single cultivars are obtainable, e.g. 'Diana Wynford': double white; 'Festiva': rich yellow; 'Guardsman': orange-scarlet; 'Ray Hartley': pink, salmon-tinted. Pendula: prostrate to pendulous habit, flowers smaller than Camellia-flowered types, mainly semi-double; available as mixtures plus a few single cultivars.

Chionodoxa Glory of the snow
ZONES 4–9   Easy
HEIGHT 10–20 cm/4–8 in
SPREAD 5–10 cm/2–4 in
FLOWERS Early spring: blue to lilac-blue, pink, white
Erect habit, with short, strap-shaped, mid-green leaves that are often bronze-margined when young and later elongate and lie flat. Six-petaled, starry flowers, in short spikes.
CONTAINER SIZE Any size.
PLANTING In the fall, in groups, bulbs at 5 cm/2 in apart, in sun. Best used around shrubs and trees or followed by annuals.
PROPAGATION By removing offsets in summer.
CARE Water regularly. Make sure foliage is not smothered by other plants until it dies down.
SPECIES AND CULTIVARS C. *gigantea*: 15–20 cm/6–8 in tall, flowers 3 cm/1¼ in wide, lilac-blue with small white center; 'Alba': pure white flowers. C. *luciliae*: to 13 cm/5 in tall, flowers 2–2.5 cm/¾–1 in wide, rich blue with large white eye; 'Pink Giant' and 'Rosea': pink flowers. C. *sardensis*: 10 cm/4 in tall, flowers 2 cm/¾ in wide, deep blue with or without a very small white eye.

Crocosmia Montbretia
ZONES 7–9   Easy
HEIGHT 60–120 cm/24–48 in
SPREAD 30–40 cm/12–16 in
FLOWERS Late summer to fall: yellow, orange, red
Erect, clump-forming habit. Sword-shaped leaves. Obliquely funnel-shaped flowers, with six flared petal lobes, carried in branched spikes.
CONTAINER SIZE 30–40 cm/12–16 in wide by 30 cm/12 in deep.
PLANTING In fall or early spring, ideally in groups, corms at 20 cm/8 in apart, in sun.
PROPAGATION By separating clumps, late fall or early spring.
CARE Water regularly but avoid over-wet soil. Apply liquid feed monthly from early summer to early fall. Corms may be lifted and kept dry for the winter but are best left *in situ* unless prolonged frosty winter conditions are expected. Divide clumps every three or four years, or when congested.
SPECIES AND CULTIVARS C. × *crocosmiiflora* (*Montbretia crocosmiiflora*) Common montbretia: to 60 cm/24 in tall, bright green leaves, flowers 3 cm/1¼ in long, orange-red, on 90 cm/36 in long stems. C. × c. 'Citronella': soft lemon-yellow flowers; 'Emily McKenzie': red and deep orange; 'Jackanapes': dark red and yellow bicolor: 'Solfatare': orange-yellow flowers and bronze-flushed leaves. C. *masonorum* (*Tritonia masonorum*): 90–120 cm/36–48 in tall, leaves strongly pleated longitudinally, flowers 4 cm/1½ in long, vermilion-orange, in elegantly arching sprays. Several excellent hybrid cultivars have recently become available, e.g. 'Bressingham Blaze': deep, bright flame red flowers; 'Emberglow': burnt orange; 'Lucifer': particularly intense scarlet.

Crocus
ZONES 4–9   Easy
HEIGHT 7.5–13 cm/3–5 in
SPREAD 5–10 cm/2–4 in
FLOWERS Fall to spring: purple, lilac, blue, cream, yellow, white, orange
Erect habit, eventually forming small clumps. Grassy leaves, with a central white line. Six-petaled, chalice-shaped flowers that expand widely in the sun. The 'stalk' of the flower is in fact its tubular base and the seed pod forms underground.
CONTAINER SIZE Minimum size 15–30 cm/6–12 in by 10–15 cm/4–6 in

deep for a massed display of crocus alone.

PLANTING Fall-flowering species in late summer, winter- and spring-flowering species in fall. Set corms at 5–7.5 cm/2–3 in apart, in sun. Best used around trees and shrubs or among other plants.

PROPAGATION By separating clumps, or by removing offsets during dormant summer period.

CARE During the growing period, water regularly and, with mass-planted containers, apply liquid feed every 10–14 days.

SPECIES AND CULTIVARS C. biflorus: to 10 cm/4 in tall, flowers white, or blue with purple veining, usually with yellow throat, spring. C.b. weldenii 'Albus': pure white flowers. C. chrysanthus: 5–7.5 cm/2–3 in tall, orange flowers, late winter; many cultivars are available, some hybrids with C. biflorus, e.g. 'Blue Pearl': pale blue; 'Canary Bird': deep yellow suffused purple-brown in bud; 'Cream Beauty': pale creamy yellow; 'E. P. Bowles': deep butter-yellow flowers; 'Snow Bunting': white and cream flowers. C. flavus (C. aureus): 7.5–10 cm/3–4 in tall, orange-yellow to lemon flowers, winter to early spring; 'Dutch Yellow': bright orange-yellow; the best known spring crocus of this color. C. kotschyanus (C. zonatus): 6–8 cm/2½–3¼ in tall, lilac flowers, with a ring of deep yellow

spots in the throat, early fall. C. speciosus: 10 cm/4 in or more tall, bright lilac to purple-blue flowers with darker veining, mid fall; 'Aitchisonii': lavender blue, large; 'Albus': white; 'Oxonian': deep purple-blue. C. vernus: 10–13 cm/4–5 in tall, purple-blue to white flowers, spring; the most familiar large spring crocus; 'Pickwick': white and deep purple-striped; 'Purpureus Grandiflorus': purple-blue, large; 'Queen of the Blues': soft mauve-blue; 'Snow Storm': pure white; 'Vanguard': gray-blue outside, pale gray inside, early spring flowering.

Cyclamen neapolitanum (hederifolium)
ZONES 6–9   Easy
HEIGHT 10–13 cm/4–5 in
SPREAD 15–25 cm/6–10 in
FLOWERS Fall: pink to carmine, mauve, white

Semi mat-forming habit. Attractive, broadly oval, shallowly to deeply lobed leaves, somewhat ivylike with a variable amount of silvery patterning. Shuttlecock-shaped flowers, on

Crocosmia masonorum

Begonia × tuberhybrida

Chionodoxa luciliae

Crocus chrysanthus

erect stalks, the reflexed petals about 2.5 cm/1 in long.

CONTAINER SIZE 20–40 cm/8–16 in wide by about 15 cm/6 in deep.

PLANTING Plant in summer, covering shallowly. Singly in the smaller container, but best in groups, the corms at 20 cm/8 in apart, in partial shade. Best used with other plants to provide fall and winter interest.

PROPAGATION By seeds, when ripe or in spring.

CARE Water regularly but avoid over-wet soil. Top dress annually in late summer with leaf-mold, or peat and bonemeal.

CULTIVAR C.n. 'Album': pure white flowers.

Endymion (Scilla) Bluebell
ZONES 5–9   Easy
HEIGHT 30–40 cm/12–16 in
SPREAD 30 cm/12 in or more
FLOWERS Spring: blue, purple-blue, pink, white

Clump-forming habit. Stems erect or arching at tip. Strap-shaped, arching, glossy leaves. Six-petaled, narrowly to widely bell-shaped flowers, in spikes.

CONTAINER SIZE 30–45 cm/12–18 in wide by 15–20 cm/6–8 in deep.

PLANTING In fall, bulbs 10 cm/4 in apart for a quick effect, or 20–25 cm/8–10 in apart to form long-term clumps, in partial shade.

PROPAGATION By removing offsets or separating clumps, during the dormant period.

Endymion hispanicus

Eranthis × tubergenii

Cyclamen neapolitanum

CARE During the growing period, water regularly and apply occasional doses of liquid feed. Divide clumps that are congested or fail to flower satisfactorily.

SPECIES AND CULTIVARS E. hispanicus (Scilla campanulata): broad leaves, widely bell-shaped, blue flowers, more or less horizontal, in erect spikes. E. nonscriptus (Scilla nutans) Common or English bluebell: slender leaves, narrowly bell-shaped, nodding, blue flowers, in arching spikes. The following popular cultivars are technically hybrids: 'Alba Maxima': white, large; 'Blue Queen': light blue, late flowering; 'Excelsior': deep blue, large; 'Rose Beauty': lilac-pink.

Eranthis Winter aconite
ZONES 4–9   Easy
HEIGHT 7.5–13 cm/3–5 in
SPREAD 10–20 cm/4–8 in
FLOWERS Winter to early spring: yellow

Clump-forming. Umbrella-shaped leaves on erect stalks. Buttercuplike flowers, appearing to sit in the center of a leaf.

CONTAINER SIZE Any size.

PLANTING In fall, turberous roots 6–10 cm/2½–4 in apart, in partial shade. Best used in large groups among late-developing perennials or around trees and shrubs.

PROPAGATION By separating clumps or removing offsets, during the dormant period.

CARE Make sure mix does not become dry. Apply bonemeal annually in late fall.

SPECIES AND CULTIVARS E. hyemalis Common winter aconite: 7.5–10 cm/3–4 in tall, flowers 3 cm/1¼ in wide, bright yellow. E. × tubergenii: more robust than E. hyemalis, leaves somewhat bronze-flushed when young; 'Guinea Gold' is the finest cultivar.

Fritillaria Fritillary
ZONES 5–9   Easy
HEIGHT 25–105 cm/10–42 in
SPREAD 15–30 cm/6–12 in or more
FLOWERS Spring: red, yellow, purple, white
Erect habit, eventually forming small clumps. Narrow to grassy leaves. Six-petaled, bell-shaped, pendent flowers.
CONTAINER SIZE 25–45 cm/10–18 in wide by 30 cm/12 in deep.
PLANTING In the fall, F. imperialis singly, F. meleagris in groups at 10–15 cm/4–6 in apart, in sun or partial shade.
PROPAGATION By removing offsets or separating clumps during the dormant season.
CARE Water regularly, especially in warm or drying windy weather. Apply liquid feed every two to three weeks once flower buds are visible. Divide clumps every three or four years or when congested.
SPECIES AND CULTIVARS F. imperialis Crown imperial: 75–105 cm/30–42 in tall, robust, leafy stem, flowers to 6 cm/2½ in long, in terminal heads topped by a crown of erect leaves; 'Aurora': deep reddish-orange flowers; 'Lutea Maxima': deep lemon-yellow. F. meleagris Snake's head fritillary: 20–30 cm/8–12 in tall, slender stem with a few grassy leaves, solitary flowers 4 cm/1½ in long, red-purple with a darker checkering; forms are available in shades of dusky purple to purple-rose and white.

Galanthus Snowdrop
ZONES 3–9   Easy
HEIGHT 10–20 cm/4–8 in
SPREAD 7.5–10 cm/3–4 in or more
FLOWERS Winter to early spring: white and green
Clump-forming. Erect stems. Strap-shaped, arching leaves. Pendent, soli-

tary flowers, six-petaled, the inner three petals much smaller.
CONTAINER SIZE Any size.
PLANTING In early fall, as soon as possible, bulbs at 6–10 cm/2½–4 in apart, in partial shade or sun. Best used in groups around trees or shrubs or among perennials.
PROPAGATION By removing offsets or separating clumps during the dormant season.
CARE During active growth, make sure the soil does not dry out and occasionally apply liquid feed from the time the flower buds show. Divide clumps once they get congested.
SPECIES AND CULTIVARS G. elwesii: 15–20 cm/6–8 in tall, broad, strongly gray-green leaves, 4–5 cm/1½–2 in wide flowers with deep green inner petals. G. nivalis Common snowdrop: 10–15 cm/4–6 in tall, narrow, grayish-green leaves, flowers to 3 cm/1¼ in wide, with green markings; 'Plena': flowers double.

Galtonia candicans
Summer hyacinth
ZONES 6–9   Easy
HEIGHT to 60 cm/24 in
SPREAD to 30 cm/12 in
FLOWERS Summer: white
Erect habit. Robust stems, usually resistant to wind. Strap-shaped, arching leaves. Bell-shaped flowers, 4 cm/1½ in long, pendent, in loose spikes.
CONTAINER SIZE 30–40 cm/12–16 in wide by 30 cm/12 in deep.
PLANTING In spring or fall, in groups of at least three at 15–20 cm/6–8 in apart, in sun.
PROPAGATION By removing offsets during the dormant season.
CARE Water regularly when in full growth but avoid over-wet soil. Apply liquid feed every two weeks once flowers show. Except in zone 9 and the milder areas of zone 8, bulbs must be kept frost-free during winter.

Gladiolus
ZONES 7–10   Easy
HEIGHT 45–90 cm/18–36 in
SPREAD 15–30 cm/6–12 in
FLOWERS Early summer to early fall: red, pink, purple, yellow, white
Erect, sometimes clump-forming habit. Slim to robust stems, needing support in windy sites. Rigid, sword-shaped leaves. Obliquely funnel-shaped flowers, the upper petal sometimes forming a hood, in spikes.
CONTAINER SIZE 25–45 cm/10–18 in wide by 25 cm/10 in or more deep.
PLANTING In spring, in groups of six or more at 10–20 cm/4–8 in apart, in sun. G. byzantinus, G. × colvillei and G. × nanus can be planted in fall in zones 8–9.
PROPAGATION By separating offsets or removing cormlets, during the dormant period.
CARE Water regularly during active growth but avoid over-wet soil. Apply liquid feed every two weeks once the flower spikes show until last bloom falls. Six to eight weeks later, lift plants, cut off foliage just above new corms and dry off corms as rapidly as possible. Ideally, dry at 24°C/75°F for the first three days and at 13–15°C/55–59°F for the following ten days. Clean off withered old corms, separate offsets and store these dry at not less than 10°C/50°F. Divide corms of 'hardy' species when the clumps get congested.
SPECIES AND CULTIVARS G. byzantinus: clump-forming, 60–75 cm/24–30 in tall, rose-purple to magenta flowers, 5 cm/2 in long, early summer; the hardiest Gladiolus but the corms must not stay frozen for long periods. G. × colvillei: about 45 cm/18 in tall, scarlet flowers, early summer; 'The Bride' ('Albus'): white flowers. Large-flowered (Exhibition) hybrids: 60–90 cm/24–36 in tall, large flowers,

in long, dense spikes, summer; it is the most popular race of Gladiolus, represented by hundreds of cultivars, e.g. 'Blue Conqueror': deep purple-blue; 'Carmen': bright scarlet, large; 'Chopin': rose; 'Flower Song': yellow, large; 'Morning Bride': pure white; 'Red Beauty': blood-red, frilled; 'Rose Supreme': salmon-pink; 'Ultima': light lavender; 'Yellow Supreme': mimosa yellow. G. × nanus: to 60 cm/24 in tall, rather like smaller, more graceful versions of the Large-flowered group, but hardier, e.g. 'Amanda Mahy': salmon-pink and violet; 'Comet': bright red; 'Impressive': orange-pink; 'Spitfire': scarlet with purple blotches.

Hyacinthus orientalis Hyacinth
ZONES 7–9   Easy
HEIGHT 20–30 cm/8–12 in
SPREAD 15–20 cm/6–8 in
FLOWERS Spring: blue, purple, red, pink, white, yellow
Erect habit, eventually clump-forming. Strap-shaped leaves. Bell-shaped flowers with six long, recurving petals, in spikes.
CONTAINER SIZE 25–45 cm/10–18 in wide by 25 cm/10 in or more deep.
PLANTING In the fall, in groups of six or more, bulbs at 20 cm/8 in apart, in sun.
PROPAGATION By removing offsets, during the dormant period.
CARE Water regularly, particularly in warm weather. Apply liquid feed every two weeks once the flower buds show until leaves start to yellow. To maintain large flower spikes lift annually in late summer and replant only the biggest bulbs. Offsets can be grown on in separate containers.
CULTIVARS 'City of Haarlem': primrose yellow flowers; 'Delft Blue': bright porcelain-blue; 'Innocence': white; 'Jan Bos': scarlet; 'Lady Derby' and 'Pink Pearl': rose-pink.

Iris Iris
ZONES 5–9 Easy
HEIGHT 10–60 cm/4–24 in
SPREAD 10–20 cm/4–8 in
FLOWERS Late winter to summer: blue, purple, yellow, white, orange Erect habit, eventually clump-forming. Stems wiry, usually resistant to wind. Grassy or rushlike leaves. For flower details see *Iris* p. 125.
CONTAINER SIZE 20–45 cm/8–18 in wide by 20–30 cm/8–12 in deep.
PLANTING In fall, in groups of five or more, bulbs at 10–15 cm/4–6 in apart, in sun.
PROPAGATION By removing offsets, during the dormant period.
CARE Water regularly, especially while in full growth. Apply liquid feed every two to three weeks while foliage actively growing. *I. xiphioides* needs protection from severe frost.
SPECIES AND CULTIVARS *I. histrioides major*: about 10 cm/4 in tall in bloom, flowers 7 cm/2¾ in wide, purple-blue, winter, before the leaves. *I. reticulata*: 15 cm/6 in tall in bloom, flowers 6 cm/2½ in wide, purple to pale blue, early spring, appear with young short leaves; 'J. S. Dijt': red-purple; 'Cantab': pale blue. *I. xiphioides* English iris: 45–60 cm/12–24 in tall, flowers about 10 cm/4 in wide, deep purple-blue or white, mid- to late summer. *I. xiphium* Spanish iris: much like *I. xiphioides* but more slender, flowers about 9 cm/3½ in wide, two to four

weeks earlier; best known is the hybrid race known as Dutch iris, e.g. 'H. C. van Vleit': bright blue; 'Imperator': purple to azure blue; 'Pride of Holland': deep yellow.

Lilium Lily
ZONES 3–9 Easy
HEIGHT 60–150 cm/24–60 in or more
SPREAD 30–45 cm/12–18 in
FLOWERS Summer to fall: red, pink, orange, yellow, white Erect habit, usually forming clumps. Strong stems, mostly resistant to wind. Relatively short, very narrow leaves. Six-petaled flowers, trumpet to Turk's-cap shaped, in short to long terminal spikes or clusters.
CONTAINER SIZE 20–45 cm/8–18 in wide by 25 cm/10 in or more deep.
PLANTING In fall or winter, the larger ones singly in the smaller containers, but ideally in groups of three or more, the bulbs at 20–30 cm/8–12 in apart, in sun or partial shade.
PROPAGATION By removing offsets or bulblets during the dormant period; stem bulbils in late summer; scales in winter to early spring.
CARE Water regularly, particularly during warm weather, but avoid over-

wet soil. Apply liquid feed every two weeks once the flower buds show until a month after the last flower fades. Remove stems when the last leaf has withered.
SPECIES AND CULTIVARS *L. candidum* Madonna lily (zones 5–9): to 120 cm/48 in tall, widely trumpet-shaped, pure white, fragrant flowers, summer. *L. henryi*: 120–180 cm/48–72 in tall, flowers Turk's-cap shaped, 6–7.5 cm/2½–3 in wide, orange, late summer. *L. martagon*: 90–120 cm/36–48 in tall, leaves in succession of whorls, Turk's-cap shaped, purple, black-purple or white flowers, early summer. *L. regale* Regal lily: 75–120 cm/30–48 in tall, trumpet-shaped, 12–15 cm/4¾–6 in long flowers, white within, red-purple without, heavily fragrant, summer; the easiest and best of trumpet lilies. The following hybrid cultivars are generally vigorous and perform well in containers: 'Black Dragon': dark purple and white, fragrant; 'Bright Star': white and orange, purple spotted; 'Destiny': yellow, brown spotted; 'Enchantment': Nasturtium-red, vigorous; 'Golden Splendor': deep yellow; 'Green Magic': green-white; 'Pink Perfection': lilac-pink; 'Tabasco': dark red, erect flowers.

Muscari Grape hyacinth
ZONES 4–9 Easy
HEIGHT 20–30 cm/8–12 in
SPREAD 10–15 cm/4–6 in
FLOWERS Spring: blue to blue-purple Clump-forming habit. Erect stems. Narrow, strap-shaped, channeled leaves. Small, bell-shaped flowers, in dense spikes.
CONTAINER SIZE 20–40 cm/8–16 in wide by 20 cm/8 in deep.
PLANTING In the fall, in groups of eight or more, bulbs at 6–10 cm/2½–4 in apart, in sun. *M. armeniacum* can be used effectively around shrubs.
PROPAGATION By removing offsets or bulblets during dormant period.
CARE Water regularly, but avoid over-wet soil. Benefits from occasional doses of liquid feed during the growing season.
SPECIES AND CULTIVARS *M. armeniacum*: 15–20 cm/6–8 in tall, leaves appearing in the fall, flowers bright violet-blue. *M. comosum* 'Monstrosum': 30 cm/12 in tall, flowers all sterile, reduced to a feathery mass of purple-blue filaments.

Galtonia candicans

Galanthus elwesii

Fritillaria imperialis

Hyacinthus orientalis

Gladiolus byzantinus

Iris xiphium

Lilium henryi

Muscari armeniacum

Narcissus Daffodil, Narcissus
ZONES 4–9   Easy
HEIGHT 15–40 cm/6–16 in
SPREAD 10–20 cm/4–8 in
FLOWERS Spring: yellow, orange, orange-red, white

Mainly clump-forming habit. Erect stems, generally resistant to wind. Strap-shaped or rushlike leaves. Flowers composed of a central cup and six narrow to broad spreading petals, solitary or in small terminal clusters. There are three groups:
Daffodils: solitary flowers with trumpet-shaped cups equal in length to, or longer than, the petals; Narcissi: solitary flowers with broad cups shorter than petals; Tazetta or Polyanthus narcissi: flowers in a cluster, small, short-cupped.
CONTAINER SIZE 25–45 cm/10–18 in wide by 20–30 cm/8–12 in deep.
PLANTING In fall, in groups of six or more, bulbs at 10–15 cm/4–6 in apart, in sun or shade.
PROPAGATION By removing offsets during the dormant period.
CARE Water regularly, especially during growing season. Apply liquid feed every two weeks once the flower buds are clearly visible until one month after they fade. Divide clumps when dense.
SPECIES AND CULTIVARS *N. bulbocodium* Hoop petticoat daffodil: 10–15 cm/4–6 in tall, dark green, rush-like leaves, yellow flowers to 3 cm/1¼ in long, with a large trumpet and small narrow petals, early spring. *N. poeticus* Pheasant-eye narcissus: to 37 cm/15 in tall, 5–6.5 cm/2–2¾ in wide, white flowers, with very small orange, red or crimson-edged cup, late spring–early summer; 'Actaea' is the largest and best known cultivar. Hybrids between this and the trumpet daffodils provide the many popular narcissus cultivars with short- to medium-sized cups, e.g. 'Flower Record': bright orange cup, white petals; 'Ice Follies': cup and petals white; 'Pomona': green, apricot and orange-red cup, white petals; 'Sun Chariot': orange-red cup, deep yellow petals; 'Texas': fully double flowers, yellow and orange-red; 'White Lion': double flowers, white with soft yellow in the center.
N. pseudonarcissus Wild daffodil: about 30 cm/12 in tall, gray-green leaves, somewhat nodding flowers, to 6.5 cm/2¾ in long, with a deep yellow trumpet and paler yellow, waved petals. Hybrids of this and allied species provide the many very popular daffodil cultivars which make excellent container plants, e.g. 'Golden Harvest': golden-yellow trumpet and petals, early; 'King Alfred': rich yellow, late; 'Mount Hood': cream aging to pure white; 'Spring Glory': gold trumpet, white petals, fragrant.
N. tazetta Polyanthus narcissus (zones 8–9): 30–40 cm/12–16 in tall, flowers 2.5–4 cm/1–1½ in wide, white, with small white or yellow cup, in clusters of four to eight; 'Geranium': white with orange cup, is the best known cultivar.

Scilla sibirica Siberian squill
ZONES 3–9   Easy
HEIGHT to 15 cm/6 in
SPREAD 10–15 cm/4–6 in
FLOWERS Spring: blue, white
Clump-forming habit. Strap-shaped leaves. Six-petaled bell-shaped, nodding flowers, in short spikes.
CONTAINER SIZE 20–30 cm/8–12 in wide by 20 cm/8 in or more deep.
PLANTING In fall, in groups of six or more, bulbs at 10 cm/4 in apart, in sun or partial shade. Very effective around trees, shrubs, perennials, or with annuals.
PROPAGATION By removing offsets during summer dormant period.
CARE Water regularly. Benefits from a few applications of liquid feed during active growth.
CULTIVARS 'Alba': white flowers; 'Spring Beauty': brilliant deep blue, early flowering.

Tulipa Tulip
ZONES 4–9   Easy
HEIGHT 15–75 cm/6–30 in
SPREAD 10–25 cm/4–10 in
FLOWERS Spring to early summer: red, pink, purple, yellow, white
Erect habit, eventually clump-forming if not regularly lifted. Sturdy stems, usually resistant to wind. Lance-shaped to oblong leaves. Six-petaled, erect, cup- or chalice-shaped flowers, opening out flat on warm days.
CONTAINER SIZE 20–40 cm/8–16 in wide by 20–25 cm/8–10 in deep.
PLANTING In late fall, in groups of four or more, bulbs at 15–30 cm/6–12 in apart, in sun.
PROPAGATION By removing offsets during the dormant period.
CARE Water regularly but avoid over-wet soil. Apply liquid feed every two weeks from time flower buds show until one month after flowers fade. When leaves yellow, bulbs can be lifted and stored dry until planting time. Even if left *in situ*, bulbs should be lifted and divided at least every three years.
SPECIES AND CULTIVARS *T. kaufmanniana* Water-lily tulip: 15–20 cm/6–8 in tall, flowers to 7.5 cm/3 in long, cream to yellow, pink or red-flushed in bud, early to midspring. There are many named hybrid cultivars. *T. fosteriana*: 25–35 cm/10–14 in tall, strongly gray-green leaves, flowers to 10 cm/4 in long, brilliant scarlet with black and yellow basal blotch, mid- to late spring; 'Princeps': compact, sturdy habit to 20 cm/8 in tall. Hybrid cultivars include 'Red Emperor' ('Mme Lefeber'): to 45 cm/18 in tall, bright scarlet flowers.

The following are particularly useful cultivars for container growing – Single-early: 15–38 cm/6–15 in tall, relatively large flowers, e.g. 'Brilliant Star': bright red; 'Pink Beauty': carmine-pink and white. Double-early: as for Single-early but flowers double, e.g. 'Madame Testout': deep pink; 'Orange Nassau': orange-brown. Lily-flowered: 45–60 cm/18–24 in tall, slender flowers, petals with flared, pointed tips, e.g. 'Dyanito': bright red; 'Mariette': rose-pink.

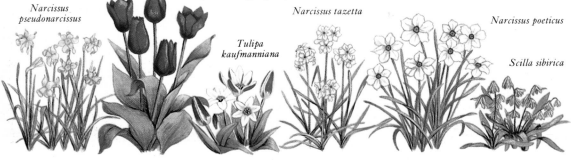

Tulipa fosteriana

Narcissus pseudonarcissus

Tulipa kaufmanniana

Narcissus tazetta

Narcissus poeticus

Scilla sibirica

Succulents

For the container gardener who has to be away from home much of the time, succulent plants are ideal. Having a built-in water supply, they can survive long periods without watering and still look good. Their often rather formal shapes contrast well with modern architecture and outside décor. There are two main types, stem and leaf succulents. Stem succulents have their main stem or stems swollen with water storage tissue. Examples are the familiar, often spiny, cacti. Swollen leaves from more or less normal stems are characteristic of the leaf succulents. These include stonecrops, house-leeks and agaves.

Succulent plants will grow well in any standard potting mix, ideally mixed with one-third part extra-coarse sand, grit or perlite for drainage. They should be watered regularly during the growing season, but the soil should be allowed almost to dry out between applications. Plants will do best if given a liquid feed at monthly intervals during the summer growing season. Repot every three years or when plants become congested. All the succulents described below will stand a little frost. In colder areas (zones 3–8) they will need housing away from the worst cold in a frost-free but well-lit room.

Agave americana
Common century plant
ZONES 9–10   Easy
HEIGHT to 90 cm/36 in or more
SPREAD to 90 cm/36 in or more
Foliage plant
Rosette-forming habit. Gray-green, strap-shaped, fleshy leaves, spine-tipped, arching. Flower stems not normally produced by plants grown in containers.
CONTAINER SIZE 30–60 cm/12–24 in wide by at least 30 cm/12 in deep.

PLANTING Singly, in sun.
PROPAGATION By offsets in early summer.
CARE Can be grown outside in colder zones in summer.
CULTIVAR *A.a.* 'Marginata': broadly yellow- to cream-margined leaves.

Echeveria
ZONES 8–10   Easy
HEIGHT 20–30 cm/8–12 in
SPREAD 15–20 cm/6–8 in
FLOWERS Summer: red and yellow
Rosette and branched habits. Green to gray, lance-shaped to oval leaves, broadest at tip. Tubular flowers, in four- to many-flowered spikes.
CONTAINER SIZE 30 cm/12 in or more wide by 10–20 cm/4–8 in deep.
PLANTING In groups of three to five at 15 cm/6 in apart, in sun.
PROPAGATION By offsets or by cuttings, in summer.
CARE In zone 8, keep dry during winter and protect from hard frost.
SPECIES *E. glauca*: rosette-forming, about 10 cm/4 in wide, stemless, leaves blue-gray, flower stems 20–30 cm/8–12 in long, crooked, red flowers. *E. harmsii*: somewhat shrubby habit, to 30 cm/12 in tall, grayish, reddish-tipped leaves, crowded toward stem tips, large, bright orange-red flowers, in small clusters.

Sedum Stonecrop
ZONES 3–9   Easy
HEIGHT 5–60 cm/2–24 in
SPREAD 20–40 cm/8–16 in
FLOWERS Summer to fall: yellow, purple, red

Clump-forming and spreading habits. Erect or prostrate stems. Fleshy leaves, cylindrical to rounded or oval. Five-petaled, starry flowers, in flattened heads.
CONTAINER SIZE 25–40 cm/10–16 in wide by 20–30 cm/8–12 in deep.
PLANTING In groups of three or more at 20–30 cm/8–12 in apart, the greater distance for the clump-formers, in sun or partial shade.
PROPAGATION By division, fall or spring, or by cuttings, spring or summer.
CARE Water regularly during the growing season, and keep moderately moist in winter.
SPECIES AND CULTIVARS *S. cauticolum*: clump-forming, low-arching, loosely mat-forming stems, small, rounded, gray-green leaves, rose-purple flowers, in 4–6 cm/$1\frac{1}{2}$–$2\frac{1}{2}$ in wide heads. *S. maximum* 'Atropurpureum': clump-forming, robust, erect stems 60 cm/24 in or more tall, oval, deep red-purple leaves 5–10 cm/2–4 in long, pink flowers, in branched terminal heads. *S. spathulifolium* (zones 5–9): low, hummock-forming, 10 cm/4 in tall in bloom, small, spoon-shaped, gray-green flushed red-purple leaves, in rosettes, yellow flowers. *S. spectabile* Ice plant: clump-form-ing, erect stems, 35–45 cm/14–18 in tall, pale gray-green oval leaves 5–7.5 cm/2–3 in long, pink flowers, in heads 10–15 cm/4–6 in wide. *S.s.* 'Autumn Joy': salmon-pink flowers; 'September Ruby': dark rose-pink.

Sempervivum House-leek
ZONES 4–9   Easy
HEIGHT 5–30 cm/2–12 in
SPREAD 20–30 cm/8–12 in
FLOWERS Summer: pink to red-purple

Low, hummock-forming habit. Narrowly oblong leaves, in dense circular rosettes. Flowers with nine to twenty narrow petals, in terminal clusters well above rosettes.
CONTAINER SIZE 20–40 cm/8–16 in wide by 15–20 cm/6–8 in deep.
PLANTING In groups of up to six at 15–20 cm/6–8 in apart, in sun, but light shade tolerated.
PROPAGATION By division or offsets, in spring.
CARE Will grow more vigorously if watered regularly during the growing season. Remove stems immediately flowers fade.
SPECIES *S. arachnoideum* Cobweb house-leek: rosettes 1–2 cm/$\frac{1}{2}$–$\frac{3}{4}$ in wide, often red-flushed leaves, the tips spun together with white hairs, flower stems to 13 cm/5 in tall, rose-red flowers. *S. tectorum* Common or roof house-leek: rosettes 9–15 cm/$3\frac{1}{2}$–6 in wide, leaves tipped red-brown, flower stems to 30 cm/12 in tall, pink to purple-red flowers.

Agave americana

Sempervivum tectorum

Sedum cauticolum

Sedum spectabile

Echeveria glauca

Water-garden plants

Water plants are well suited to container growing. Needing permanently moist or wet soil, they present no problems of watering. They can be planted in any watertight container, though half-barrels are the most useful and aesthetically pleasing. Many water-loving plants are distinctive in appearance and can add just that touch of class to a container garden.

There are two main groups of water plants: marginals and aquatics. The marginal plants are those that inhabit the zone of wet soil just in and just above the water line of a natural pond or river. They can be grown in ordinary plant containers stood in trays kept filled with water. The aquatics live under water, though some kinds, for example water lilies, have floating leaves. All except the smallest species require at least a 30 cm/12 in depth of water in which to grow.

The ideal soil for water plants is a good-quality medium to heavy loam with the addition of a generous handful of bonemeal to each 9-litre (2 UK and 2½ US gallon) bucketful of loam. Alternatively, a loam-based potting mix, such as John Innes no. 1, can be used. The loam or potting mix is spread as a 15 cm/6 in layer over the bottom of the watertight container, and the plants are inserted and mulched with a layer of clean gravel. This will prevent water becoming cloudy when it is poured into the container. A watering can fitted with a fine rose is best for filling. Failing this, place a layer of newspaper on the gravel and pour the water onto it. For marginal species, an alternative and easier method is to grow the plants in pots or the plastic baskets sold specifically for the purpose. Acceptable baskets can also be made from pieces of fine-mesh

chicken-wire netting, held together with galvanized wire. Before filling and planting, these baskets should be lined with fine-mesh nylon gauze or a single thickness of paper, moss or rotted turf to prevent loose soil from fouling the water.

Planting of both marginals and aquatics is best carried out in late spring. Although some species grow best in sun, it is often advisable to keep containers in partial shade: in full sun, the water can warm up excessively, stimulating undesirable growth of the green, slimy algae known as blanket weed. After the first year, feed plants using brand-name water-lily fertilizer pellets. These are simply pushed into the soil around each plant, in spring. Some water plants grow with great vigor in the first season and will need thinning either during, or at the end of, the growing season. Plants grown in pots or baskets should be repotted every two years, and those grown directly in the soil layer, every three or four years. Where hard winters are regularly experienced (zones 3–5), the water level should be lowered or allowed to drain down to soil level in late fall and the containers stored away from frost. In less cold areas, regularly break any ice that forms, or float a block of wood on the water, which will prevent ice pressure from severely cracking the container.

In the descriptions of aquatic plants that follow, container size refers to the pot or basket for the root system, not the water-holding container. The latter must be at least equal to the plant's spread. With respect to the aquatics, height refers to the distance between the base of the stem and the tip of the leaves when the plant is growing in rooting medium not free-floating.

Aponogeton distachyos
Water hawthorn
ZONES 8–10   Easy
HEIGHT 30 cm/12 in or more
SPREAD 30–60 cm/12–24 in
FLOWERS Throughout summer: white
Aquatic; clump-forming habit. Oblong-elliptic, light green, 7.5–15 cm/3–6 in long leaves, on slender stalks equal to water depth. Small, fragrant flowers, in forked spikes 5–10 cm/2–4 in long. Flowers pure white when first open, gradually fading to green.
CONTAINER SIZE At least 25–30 cm/10–12 in wide by 25 cm/10 in deep.
PLANTING Singly, in sun or partial shade.
PROPAGATION By division in spring.
CARE Protect from frost in the colder parts of zone 8. Divide and repot every three years.

Eichhornia crassipes
Water hyacinth
ZONES 9–10   Easy
HEIGHT 15–25 cm/6–10 in
SPREAD 60 cm/24 in or more
FLOWERS Summer: lavender-purple
Aquatic; spreading, free-floating habit. Rounded, glossy, dark green leaves, to 10 cm/4 in wide, attached to short inflated stalks that act as floats. Roots, purplish and feathery, to 20 cm/8 in long, hang down in water. Widely funnel-shaped, orchid-like flowers, each with a yellow eye on the uppermost petal, to 5 cm/2 in wide, in spikes 7.5–10 cm/3–4 in long.
CONTAINER SIZE Container not necessary for root system.
PLANTING Singly, in sun.
PROPAGATION By division in summer.
CARE Can grow very vigorously in warm sites and should be thinned as necessary. May be grown outside during the summer in colder zones. Easily overwintered indoors by keeping in shallow water over a layer of soil, in a sunny window.

Elodea
ZONES 3–10   Easy
HEIGHT 30–60 cm/12–24 in
SPREAD 30–60 cm/12–24 in
FLOWERS Summer: tiny, grayish to white; a foliage plant
Aquatic; spreading habit, totally submerged. Can live as free-floating mass. Small, semitranslucent leaves, in whorls. Three-petaled flowers, seldom produced or insignificant.
CONTAINER SIZE 15 cm/6 in wide by 10–15 cm/4–6 in deep. If free-floating, rooting medium unnecessary.
PLANTING Singly, in partial shade.
PROPAGATION By division in spring or summer.
CARE Can spread with great vigor and must occasionally be thinned.
SPECIES *E. canadensis* Canadian pondweed: oblong, arching leaves, 6–13 mm/¼–½ in long. *E. crispa* (*Anacharis crispa*, *Lagarosiphon major*) (zones 8–10): like *E. canadensis* but more robust, the leaves rolled back in complete rings. *E. densa* (*Anacharis densa*, *Egeria densa*) Brazilian pondweed (zones 8–10): like a robust *E. canadensis* with leaves 2–3 cm/¾–1¼ in long.

Iris kaempferi
Japanese or clematis iris
ZONES 6–9   Easy
HEIGHT 60 cm/24 in or more
SPREAD 30–40 cm/12–16 in
FLOWERS Summer: red, purple, blue, white
Marginal; clump-forming habit. Erect stems, resistant to wind. Sword-shaped leaves. Flowers as described under *Iris* (p. 125), but standard petals as large as falls and carried in the same plane.
CONTAINER SIZE 30–40 cm/12–16 in wide by 30 cm/12 in deep.
PLANTING Singly, or in groups at 30 cm/12 in apart in the larger containers, in sun or partial shade.

PROPAGATION By division in spring, or by seeds sown in spring.
CARE Best grown in a pot stood in a tray of water, from spring to fall.
CULTIVARS *I.k.* 'Blue Heaven', with rich purple-blue flowers, is one of several named cultivars; 'Higo' is a mixed-color seed strain.

Menyanthes trifoliata
Bog or buck bean
ZONES 3–9 Easy
HEIGHT to 30 cm/12 in
SPREAD 30 cm/12 in or more
FLOWERS Late spring to summer: white, from pinkish buds
Marginal; spreading habit. Leaves composed of three elliptic leaflets, each to 7.5 cm/3 in long. Tubular flowers, with five or six spreading petals with long, beaded hairs.
CONTAINER SIZE 30–40 cm/12–16 in wide by 20–30 cm/8–12 in deep.
PLANTING Singly, or in groups of two or three at 25–30 cm/10–12 in apart in the larger containers, in sun or partial shade.
PROPAGATION By division in spring.
CARE Can be grown in wet soil or shallow water.

Myriophyllum aquaticum (proserpinacoides)
Water mifoil or feather
ZONES 9–10 Easy
HEIGHT 90 cm/36 in or more
SPREAD 60–90 cm/24–36 in
Grown as a foliage plant
Aquatic; spreading habit. Leaves 2–3 cm/¾–1¼ in long, deeply segmented, bright green. Shoot tips grow above water, with more compact, blue-green foliage.
CONTAINER SIZE 13–15 cm/5–6 in wide by 10–13 cm/4–5 in deep.
PLANTING Using three to four shoot cuttings as one plant, in sun.
PROPAGATION By cuttings late spring or summer.

CARE Can be grown outside during summer in colder zones than 9. Young plants or cuttings can be over-wintered in an aquarium indoors.

Nymphaea Water lily
ZONES 5–9 Easy
HEIGHT to 60 cm/24 in
SPREAD to 60 cm/24 in or more
FLOWERS Summer: pink, red, yellow
Aquatic; clump-forming to spreading habit. Floating, circular leaves, 10–30 cm/4–12 in wide. Cup-shaped, many-petaled flowers, 5–15 cm/2–6 in wide, floating or carried just above water surface.
CONTAINER SIZE 15–30 cm/6–12 in or more wide by 15–25 cm/6–10 in deep.
PLANTING Singly, in sun or partial shade.
PROPAGATION By division in spring.
CARE If possible, site container so that only the top of the plant gets direct sunlight.
SPECIES AND CULTIVARS *N. × helvola* (*N. pygmaea helvola*): small growing, leaves blotched purple-brown, flowers sulphur-yellow, ideal for containers to 30 cm/12 in wide. *N. × marliacea*: vigorous, leaves to 25 cm/10 in wide, flowers 10–13 cm/4–5 in wide. *M. × m.* 'Carnea' (pale pink), 'Chromatella' (pale yellow); need tubs 60 cm/24 in or more wide.

Pontederia cordata Pickerel weed
ZONES 3–9 Easy
HEIGHT 45–60 cm/18–24 in
SPREAD to 60 cm/24 in or more
FLOWERS Summer to fall: blue
Marginal; colony-forming habit. Narrowly oval, glossy rich green leaves, 7.5–20 cm/3–8 in long, long-stalked. Funnel-shaped, six-lobed flowers, in spikes 10 cm/4 in long.
CONTAINER SIZE 30–60 cm/12–24 in wide by 20–30 cm/8–12 in deep.
PLANTING Singly, in sun or partial shade.
PROPAGATION By division in spring.
CARE Divide only when congested.

Potamogeton
ZONES 7–9 Easy
HEIGHT 30–60 cm/12–24 in
SPREAD 30–60 cm/12–24 in or more
FLOWERS Summer: green or brownish; a foliage plant
Aquatic; spreading habit. Stems much branched. Lance-shaped, semi-translucent leaves. Tiny, four-petaled flowers, insignificant.
CONTAINER SIZE 13–15 cm/5–6 in wide by 10–13 cm/4–5 in deep.
PLANTING Singly, or three to four cuttings together, in sun or partial shade.
PROPAGATION By cuttings, spring or summer.
CARE Growth can be fast, and thinning must be carried out regularly.
SPECIES *P. crispus* Curled pondweed: angled stems, toothed, strongly waved leaves, 4–9 cm/1½–3½ in long, carried in two opposite ranks. *P. densus* (*Groenlandia densa*) Frog's lettuce: stems to 30 cm/12 in long, branching low down, leaves to 2.5 cm/1 in long, in opposite ranks or whorls.

Iris kaempferi

Pontederia cordata

Myriophyllum aquaticum

Nymphaea × marliacea

Aponogeton distachyos

Menyanthes trifoliata

Nymphaea × helvola

Elodea canadensis

Potamogeton crispus

Eichhornia crassipes

Alpines and rock-garden plants

For those with limited container space but who wish to grow as many different plants as possible, rock and alpine subjects are a perfect answer. Though mostly small, they have a wide variety of form; mats, rosettes, trailers, tufts and cushions in all shades of green and gray, and with flowers large and small in all the colors of the rainbow. They are herbaceous perennials but are treated separately on account of their ability to grow in small pockets of soil, often in cold climates, and their need for sharp drainage. (Those that grow from bulbs or corms are dealt with under the appropriate section, pp. 128–32.)

Most rock and alpine plants will grow happily in containers. Those described below will do well provided they are watered regularly but are not allowed to become over-wet at the roots. Any approved potting mix is suitable, ideally blended with a quarter part by bulk of extra-coarse sand, grit or perlite. The container size given is for a single specimen plant, but the most effective way to display these small plants is to arrange several different species in a large container, for example a stone trough or sink, ideally among several pieces of natural stone.

Aethionema 'Warley Rose'
ZONES 6–9   Easy
HEIGHT 10–15 cm/4–6 in
SPREAD 20–25 cm/8–10 in
FLOWERS Early summer: pink
Spreading, bushy habit. Narrow, small, gray-green leaves. Four-petaled flowers, in profusely borne short spikes.
CONTAINER SIZE 15–25 cm/6–10 in wide by at least 15 cm/6 in deep.
PLANTING In sun.
PROPAGATION By cuttings in summer.
CARE Remove spent flowering stems.

Apply a light dressing of slow-release general fertilizer annually in early spring.

Alyssum saxatile (Aurinia saxatile) Gold dust
ZONES 3–8   Easy
HEIGHT 20 cm/8 in
SPREAD 30 cm/12 in or more
FLOWERS Spring: golden yellow
Low mound or deep mat-forming. Gray-green, spoon-shaped leaves. Small flowers, in profuse spikes.
CONTAINER SIZE 20–25 cm/8–10 in wide by 15–20 cm/6–8 in deep.
PLANTING In sun.
PROPAGATION By cuttings in late summer, by seeds in spring.
CARE Thrives best in alkaline conditions, with limestone chippings mixed in the soil.
CULTIVARS A.s. 'Citrinum': bright lemon-yellow flowers; 'Compactum': dwarf habit; 'Dudley Neville': biscuit-yellow flowers; 'Plenum' ('Flore Pleno'): flowers double.

Aubrieta deltoidea Aubretia
ZONES 4–8   Easy
HEIGHT 10–15 cm/4–6 in
SPREAD 25 cm/10 in or more
FLOWERS Spring: lilac, purple, red, pink
Mat-forming habit. Spoon-shaped, somewhat hoary leaves. Four-petaled, cross-shaped flowers, to 2 cm/¾ in wide, with rounded petals, in profusely borne short spikes.
CONTAINER SIZE 20–25 cm/8–10 in wide by 15–20 cm/6–8 in deep.
PLANTING In sun.

Helianthemum nummularium

PROPAGATION By cuttings in summer, by seeds in spring.
CARE To maintain a plant 20–25 cm/8–10 in wide, cut back hard immediately after flowering. Apply a slow-release general fertilizer annually at this time.

Campanula Bellflower
ZONES 3–8   Easy
HEIGHT 10–25 cm/4–10 in
SPREAD 15–30 cm/6–12 in
FLOWERS Summer to fall: blue, purple, white
Clump-forming to colonizing habit. Small, rounded leaves. Narrowish to widely bell-shaped flowers.
CONTAINER SIZE 15–20 cm/6–8 in wide by 15 cm/6 in deep.
PLANTING In sun or partial shade.
PROPAGATION By division in spring.
CARE Divide and replant every three years in spring.
SPECIES AND CULTIVARS C. carpatica: clump-forming, stems erect, 15–25 cm/6–10 in tall, bowl-shaped, erect flowers, about 3 cm/1¼ in wide, purple-blue; 'Alba': white flowers; 'Turbinata': dwarf form, 10 cm/4 in tall. C. cochleariifolia (C. pusilla): colonizing, semi mat-forming, stems very slender, 10 cm/4 in tall, bell-shaped, nodding flowers, 16 mm/⅝ in long, lavender-blue; 'Alba': white flowers. C. muralis (C. portenschlagiana):

Campanula carpatica

colonizing, semi mat-forming, dense, stems 10–15 cm/4–6 in tall, nodding, 2 cm/¾ in long flowers, lilac-blue, very freely borne.

Dianthus Pinks
ZONES 3–8   Easy
HEIGHT 15–25 cm/6–10 in
SPREAD 20–25 cm/8–10 in
FLOWERS Summer: pink, red, white
Low cushion to mat-forming habit. Short, grassy, often gray-green leaves. Five-petaled flowers, opening flat, one to several per stem.
CONTAINER SIZE 15–20 cm/6–8 in wide by 15 cm/6 in deep.
PLANTING In sun or light shade.
PROPAGATION By cuttings in summer, by seeds in spring.
CARE Best with limestone chippings mixed in the potting soil. Remove spent flowering stems promptly to promote further bloom.
SPECIES D. caesius (D. gratianopolitanus) (zones 5–8) Cheddar pink: mat-forming, stems 15 cm/6 in or more tall, gray leaves, pink flowers to 2.5 cm/1 in wide. D. deltoides Maiden pink: mat-forming, 15–25 cm/6–10 in tall stems, very short, rich green leaves, 1.2–2 cm/⅓–¾ in wide flowers, deep pink to red with a darker ring in center, profusely borne; 'Albus': white flowers. D. neglectus: tufted to small cushion-forming, stems about 10 cm/4 in tall, green leaves, flowers 2–3 cm/¾–1¼ in wide, buff in bud, opening pink or crimson.

Alyssum saxatile

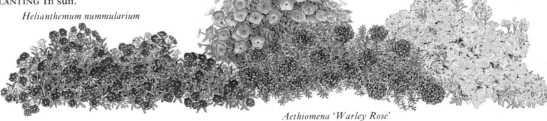

Aethiomena 'Warley Rose'

Helianthemum nummularium (chamaecistus) Rock-rose
ZONES 6–9 Easy
HEIGHT 15 cm/6 in
SPREAD 30–45 cm/12–18 in
FLOWERS Summer: white, yellow, pink, orange, red
Shrubby, mat-forming habit. Small, oval to oblong, gray or green leaves. Five-petaled flowers, opening flat, in profusely borne sprays.
CONTAINER SIZE 20–30 cm/8–12 in wide by at least 15 cm/6 in deep.
PLANTING In sun.
PROPAGATION By cuttings in late summer.
CARE Clip or shear off spent flowering stems and tops of leafy stems that bear them, to maintain a neat, compact habit. At the same time, apply a slow-release fertilizer.
CULTIVARS Several named varieties of wide range of flower colors are available.

Morisia hypogaea (M. monanthos)
ZONES 7–9 Easy
HEIGHT 2–3 cm/$\frac{3}{4}$–1$\frac{1}{4}$ in
SPREAD 10 cm/4 in
FLOWERS Spring: yellow
Tufted, rosette-forming habit. Rich glossy green, lance-shaped leaves, to 5 cm/2 in long, deeply pinnately lobed. Four-petaled flowers, 1.5 cm/$\frac{3}{5}$ in wide, in stemless clusters.

CONTAINER SIZE 10–15 cm/4–6 in wide and deep.
PLANTING In sun.
PROPAGATION By careful division or by root cuttings in spring.
CARE Needs a gritty potting soil with limestone chippings mixed in. Repot every three years in early fall.

Phlox subulata
Moss or mountain phlox
ZONES 3–8 Easy
HEIGHT 7.5–10 cm/3–4 in
SPREAD 25–40 cm/10–16 in
FLOWERS Late spring to summer: red, pink, violet, blue, white
Mat-forming habit. Small, awl-shaped, mid-green leaves. Tubular flowers, 1–2 cm/$\frac{1}{2}$–$\frac{3}{4}$ in wide, with five notched petals in profuse clusters above the leaves.
CONTAINER SIZE 20–25 cm/8–10 in wide by at least 15 cm/6 in deep.
PLANTING In sun.
PROPAGATION By cuttings in late summer.
CARE To maintain a neat, smallish plant, cut back hard immediately after flowering. Apply a slow-release general fertilizer annually in spring.

Dianthus deltoides

Dianthus caesius

Saxifraga moschata

Campanula muralis

Aubretia deltoidea

CULTIVARS *P.s.* 'Alexander's Surprise': flowers large, rich salmon-pink; 'Apple Blossom': pale pink; 'Avalon White': white; 'G. F. Wilson': lavender-blue; 'Temiscaming': brilliant magenta-red.

Primula auricula Auricula
ZONES 3–8 Easy
HEIGHT 10–15 cm/4–6 in
SPREAD 10–15 cm/4–6 in or more
FLOWERS Spring: yellow, white, red, purple
Tufted habit, composed of short-stemmed rosettes. Oval, 5–10 cm/2–4 in long leaves, usually covered with a yellowish waxy powder (farina). Flowers primroselike, but more rounded, fragrant, 2 cm/$\frac{3}{4}$ in wide, in terminal clusters.
CONTAINER SIZE 15 cm/6 in wide and deep.
PLANTING In sun or partial shade.
PROPAGATION By division in spring.
CARE Repot every two to three years in late summer, setting the plants deeper to cover the elongating stem. Apply a general slow-release fertilizer annually in spring.
CULTIVARS *P.a.* 'Blairside Yellow': miniature, to 5 cm/2 in tall, yellow flowers. The following are of hybrid origin: 'Alba': white; 'Falconside': crimson; 'Mrs J. H. Wilson': violet; 'Rufus': brick-red.

Primula auricula

Morisia hypogaea

Phlox subulata

Saxifraga Rockfoil or saxifrage
ZONES 2–8 Easy
HEIGHT 5–30 cm/2–12 in
SPREAD 15–30 cm/6–12 in
FLOWERS Spring: yellow, white, pink, red
Low hummock, or cushion to mat-forming habit. Small, oblong to spoon-shaped leaves, in rosettes. Small, five-petaled flowers, in small to large sprays.
CONTAINER SIZE 15–20 cm/6–8 in wide and deep.
PLANTING In sun or partial shade. Especially effective in groups in larger containers or among rocks.
PROPAGATION By division after flowering, or by cuttings of single rosettes in late summer.
CARE Best in a gritty soil. Apply a light application of slow-release general fertilizer annually in spring.
SPECIES AND CULTIVARS *S.* × *apiculata*: low hummock to mat-forming, awl-shaped leaves, 1 cm/$\frac{1}{2}$ in wide, flowers, primrose-yellow, on stems 6–10 cm/2$\frac{1}{2}$–4 in tall. *S.* × *jenkinsae*: similar to *apiculata* but smaller, leaves gray-green, pink flowers. *S. longifolia*: large rosettes solitary or in small groups, silvery lime-encrusted leaves, narrowly spoon-shaped, to 7.5 cm/3 in long, flowers 1.5 cm/$\frac{3}{5}$ in wide, white, often red-dotted, in large airy sprays 30 cm/12 in or more long. *S. moschata* Mossy saxifrage: mat-forming, leaves fan-shaped, deeply-lobed, rich green, 1 cm/$\frac{1}{2}$ in wide flowers, white, pink or red, in small clusters on 10 cm/4 in tall stems; 'Triumph': scarlet flowers. *S. paniculata* (*S. aizoon*): low hummock-forming, silvery lime-encrusted leaves, to 4 cm/1$\frac{1}{2}$ in long, flowers 1–1.5 cm/$\frac{1}{2}$–$\frac{3}{5}$ in wide, white, in airy sprays 15–30 cm/6–12 in long; 'Lutea': soft yellow flowers; 'Rosea': deep green encrusted leaves, vivid deep pink flowers.

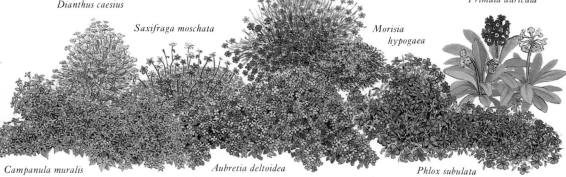

Ferns

All too often the container gardener has to cope with sunless corners, some dark, others dry and drafty, and here ferns come into their own. Among the many species there is an astonishing variety of foliage, from the typical finely cut fronds, arranged in vaselike rosettes, to stiff, leathery, paddle-shaped leaf blades, usually in tight clumps. Some species thrive in full sun and dry situations, others need deep shade and high humidity. Here we are mostly concerned with shade tolerance and adaptability to container culture. Ferns will grow well in any standard potting mix. Each spring, dead fronds should be removed to encourage new growth. Repot every three years or when congested. (Ferns could have been included in the Perennials section, but their distinctive appearance and shade tolerance make them worthy of separate treatment.)

Ferns are primitive plants, inhabiting the earth long before the more familiar flowering plants evolved. In the wild, they reproduce by spores, dustlike specks of matter smaller and more rudimentary than seeds. The spores give rise to tiny leaflike bodies known as prothalli (singular, prothallus), upon which are borne male and female cells. Only on the fusion of these cells does a new fern plant start to develop.

Growing ferns from spores is somewhat more exacting than raising plants from seed. Spores are collected in fall by wrapping fronds in clean white paper and waiting a week or so for them to dry and shed their load. Sterile conditions are necessary for spore germination. A 10 cm/4 in wide shallow pot is sterilized in boiling water. The pot is half-filled with standard potting mix, boiling water is poured over this, then a glass cover is placed on top of the pot. As soon as the mix is cool, the spores are sown thinly (see p. 47) and the pot is covered immediately with the sheet of clean glass again. The pot is kept in a warm room out of direct sun. Several months may elapse before the prothalli form, and at least a year passes before the young plants are large enough to be set permanently in containers. Most of the species mentioned here can be multiplied by division as well as by spores.

Adiantum Maidenhair fern
ZONES 3–9   Easy
HEIGHT 15–40 cm/6–16 in
SPREAD 25–45 cm/10–18 in
Clump-forming or spreading habit, depending on species. Leaves dissected, the leaflets rounded to obliquely triangular with lobed or toothed margins.
CONTAINER SIZE 25–40 cm/10–16 in wide by 20 cm/8 in or more deep.
PLANTING In spring; singly, or in groups of three at 30 cm/12 in apart in the larger containers. Stands heavy shade and moderately drafty sites.
PROPAGATION By division in spring, or by spores.
CARE Water regularly, particularly in warm weather, but avoid over-wet soil. Apply liquid feed monthly from late spring to early fall.
SPECIES *A. pedatum*: clump-forming, 30–40 cm/12–16 in tall, light green, deciduous, fronds rounded in outline, the main divisions radiating out like spokes from the tops of the stalks, leaflets oblong to fan-shaped. *A. venustum* (zones 8–9): colonizing habit, 15–20 cm/6–8 in tall, mid-green, evergreen, fronds triangular in outline, composed of numerous small rounded leaflets; fronds killed in hard winters but remain a pleasing russet-brown until the new pinkish-bronze spring growth appears.

Asplenium (Phyllitis) scolopendrium Hart's tongue fern
ZONES 5–9   Easy
HEIGHT 30–60 cm/12–24 in
SPREAD 30–60 cm/12–24 in
Clump-forming habit. Evergreen, straight or curved, bright green, leathery and glossy, entire, strap-shaped fronds, with a heart-shaped base and wavy margin.
CONTAINER SIZE 25–40 cm/10–16 in wide by 20–25 cm/8–10 in deep.
PLANTING During early spring; singly, or in groups of three at 30 cm/12 in apart in the larger containers. Will tolerate full shade and can stand drafty sites.
PROPAGATION By division in spring, or by spores (except *A.s.* 'Crispum').
CARE Water regularly in warm weather, avoiding over-wet soil, less at other times. Benefits from occasional applications of liquid feed during the growing season.
CULTIVARS *A.s.* 'Crispum': sterile variety with elaborately waved and crimped leaves; 'Undulatum': similar appearance to 'Crispum' but leaves less boldly waved and crimped.

Athyrium filix-femina Lady fern
ZONES 3–9   Easy
HEIGHT 30–90 cm/12–36 in
SPREAD 40–60 cm/16–24 in
Clump-forming habit. Deciduous, finely dissected, arching fronds, bright green, densely borne.
CONTAINER SIZE 30–40 cm/12–16 in wide by 25–30 cm/10–12 in deep.
PLANTING In spring or fall; singly, in full or partial shade. Will tolerate moderately drafty sites.
PROPAGATION By division in fall or spring.
CARE Water freely in warm weather, less at other times. Apply liquid feed monthly during the growing season.
CULTIVARS *A.f-f.* 'Cristatum': tips and edges of fronds with fanlike crests; 'Fieldii': narrow fronds to 90 cm/36 in long; 'Victoriae': narrow fronds, the slender segments crossing over each other at right angles and tipped with elegant tassels.

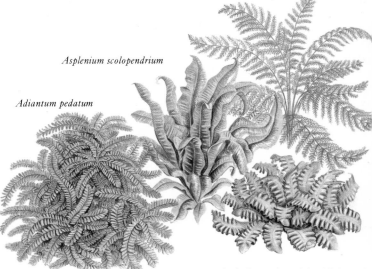

Athyrium felix-femina

Asplenium scolopendrium

Adiantum pedatum

Asplenium scolopendrium 'Crispum'

Blechnum

ZONES 4–9   Easy
HEIGHT 15–30cm/6–12in
SPREAD 30–60cm/12–24in
Colony-forming habit. Evergreen fronds simply pinnate, of two types: sterile, low arching 'normal leaves', with broad lobes, and fertile, erect leaves, with narrow, totally spore-bearing lobes.
CONTAINER SIZE 25–40cm/10–16in wide by 20cm/8in or more deep.
PLANTING In spring; singly, or in groups of two to four at 20–30cm/8–12in apart in the larger containers, in partial shade or sun. *B. penna-marina* makes a useful ground-cover plant around trees and shrubs.
PROPAGATION By division in spring.
CARE Water regularly, especially in warm weather. Benefits from occasional applications of liquid feed during the growing season. *B. spicant* must have acid soil, an all-peat rhododendron mix being ideal. Blechnum is not suitable for areas that are hot and dry in summer. Will tolerate drafty sites.
SPECIES *B. penna-marina* (zones 8–9): mat-forming, sterile fronds 7.5–15cm/3–6in long, coppery when young, fertile fronds 20–30cm/8–12in tall, dark brown. *B. spicant* Hard fern (zones 4–8): tufted and spreading to mat-forming, sterile fronds 20–45cm/8–18in long, deep glossy green, fertile fronds somewhat longer, brown.

Dryopteris

ZONES 3–9   Easy
HEIGHT 40–90cm/16–36in
SPREAD 40–90cm/16–36in
Clump-forming habit, the fronds in shuttlecock-shaped rosettes. Fronds semievergreen, deeply divided (bipinnate), rich green.
CONTAINER SIZE 30–60cm/16–24in wide by 30cm/12in deep.
PLANTING In spring or fall; singly or in groups of up to four at 35–45cm/14–18in apart in the larger containers, in partial shade.
PROPAGATION By division, fall or spring, or by spores.
CARE Water regularly, particularly in warm weather. Apply liquid feed monthly during the growing season. Will tolerate poor growing conditions.
SPECIES *D. filix-mas* Male fern: semievergreen only in mild winters or very sheltered sites, usually 45–75cm/18–30in tall, slender-pointed fronds, oval in outline, stalk a quarter the frond length, covered with rust-colored scales. *D. pseudo-mas* (*borreri*): much like *filix-mas*, but glossier green, narrower fronds, much more coarsely cut, stalk one-third length of frond and more densely scaly.

Matteuccia struthiopteris

Ostrich-feather fern
ZONES 2–9   Easy
HEIGHT 60–120cm/24–48in
SPREAD 60–120cm/24–48in
Clump-forming and colonizing. Deciduous, deeply cut, bright green leaves, forming vase-shaped rosettes.
CONTAINER SIZE 40–60cm/16–24in wide by at least 30cm/12in deep.
PLANTING From spring to fall; singly, or in groups of three at 45cm/18in apart in the larger containers, in partial shade.
PROPAGATION By division in spring.
CARE The soil must be kept moist at all times. In dry areas it is best to stand the container in a tray of water. Apply liquid feed monthly during the growing season.

Osmunda regalis Royal fern

ZONES 2–9   Easy
HEIGHT 90–150cm/36–60in

SPREAD 60–120cm/24–48in
Clump-forming, the base building up a tight mound of black roots. Deciduous, long-stalked, light green fronds, coarsely but deeply cut (bipinnate). On mature plants the frond tips bear plumes of tiny spore capsules.
CONTAINER SIZE 40–60cm/16–24in wide by at least 30cm/12in deep.
PLANTING In spring or fall; singly, in partial shade or sun.
PROPAGATION By spores.
CARE Soil must be kept moist at all times and containers should be stood in trays of water. Apply liquid feed monthly during the growing season.

Polystichum setiferum

Soft shield fern
ZONES 7–9   Easy
HEIGHT 30–45cm/12–18in
SPREAD 45–60cm/16–24in or more
Clump-forming habit. Evergreen, low arching fronds, deeply cut (bipinnate), rich green.
CONTAINER SIZE 30–40cm/12–16in wide by 25–30cm/10–12in deep.
PLANTING In spring or fall; singly, in full to partial shade.
PROPAGATION By division in spring, or by spores; the fronds of *P.s.* 'Acutilobum' can easily be layered (see p. 48).
CARE Water freely in warm weather, less at other times, avoiding overwet soil. Apply liquid feed monthly during the growing season.
CULTIVAR *P.s.* 'Acutilobum' ('Proliferum'): fronds narrower and more finely dissected, with small plantlets forming along the midrib.

Matteuccia struthiopteris

Dryopteris pseudo-mas

Osmunda regalis

Blechnum spicant

Polystichum setiferum

Blechnum penna-marina

Herbs

Certain culinary herbs have long been grown in pots on window ledges, and all the important ones respond well to container culture. Many are aromatic and some have attractive flowers, so they need not be purely utilitarian. Any approved potting mix is suitable: unless otherwise stated, water regularly but avoid over-wet soil. Most herbs need a sunny site to thrive. Some herbs are annuals and need sowing each year, others are perennials or low shrubs. Both sorts can be combined with purely ornamental plants but it is generally best to keep herbs together. Invasive plants such as mint must be grown separately. The remainder can be grouped very pleasingly in large containers by choosing a perennial such as fennel or a shrub such as sage, and planting annuals around, for example, basil, borage, or summer savory. A range of herbs, or a good quantity of one or two species, can be grown in a small space using a tall container with holes in the sides (see p. 30), known as a parsley pot or a herb pot.

Allium schoenoprasum Chives

ZONES 3–9   Easy
HEIGHT 15–25 cm/6–10 in
SPREAD 15–20 cm/6–8 in
Perennial; clump-forming habit. Grassy, hollow leaves, flavoured and smelling of onions. Starry, rose-pink, 2½ cm/1 in wide flowers in dense globular heads. Leaves used for salads, soups, egg and cheese dishes.
CONTAINER SIZE 15–30 cm/6–12 in wide by 15–25 cm/6–10 in deep.
PLANTING Singly, or in groups of up to five at 15 cm/6 in apart in the larger containers, in sun or partial shade.
PROPAGATION By division or seeds, in spring.
CARE Divide every two years. Apply liquid feed monthly throughout the spring and summer growing season.

Angelica archangelica Angelica

ZONES 4–9   Easy
HEIGHT 90–150 cm/36–60 in
SPREAD 60–90 cm/24–36 in
Biennial; erect habit. Large leaves, divided into many toothed leaflets. Tiny, green-white flowers, in spherical terminal heads. Flower stems and leafstalks used as candied cake and pudding decoration.
CONTAINER SIZE 30–40 cm/12–16 in wide by at least 30 cm/12 in deep.
PLANTING Singly, in sun or light shade.
PROPAGATION By seeds sown in spring. Sow a small group of seeds in the growing container and thin to the strongest seedling.
CARE Apply liquid feed every two weeks from midsummer to fall and again the following late spring until gathered for use.

Anthriscus cerefolium Chervil

ZONES 3–9   Easy
HEIGHT 30–45 cm/12–18 in
SPREAD 20–30 cm/8–12 in
Annual; erect habit. Fernlike, aromatic leaves 30 cm/12 in or more long. Tiny, white flowers, in flattened heads. Leaves used in salads, soups, sauces.
CONTAINER SIZE 30–40 cm/12–16 in wide by 20–30 cm/8–12 in deep.
PLANTING In groups of three to five at 10–20 cm/4–8 in apart, in sun or partial shade.
PROPAGATION By seeds sown in situ in spring.
CARE Unless flowers and seeds are required, pinch out flowering stems as soon as they are visible. If young leaves only are required, use small, shallow containers and only a few seeds sown at monthly to six-weekly intervals, from spring to fall.

Artemisia dracunculus Tarragon

ZONES 5–9   Easy
HEIGHT 90 cm/36 in or more
SPREAD 45 cm/18 in
Perennial; clump-forming and colonizing. Erect, branched stems. Narrow, 5–7.5 cm/2–3 in long leaves, grayish-green, aromatic. Tiny, greenish flowers, in loose terminal sprays. Leaves used in wide range of dishes.
CONTAINER SIZE 30–40 cm/12–16 in wide by 30 cm/12 in deep.
PLANTING Singly, in sun or partial shade.
PROPAGATION By division in spring.
CARE Divide and replant every three years in spring. Apply liquid feed monthly during the growing season. Remove tops of flowering stems to promote more young leaves.

Borago officinalis Borage

ZONES 3–10   Easy
HEIGHT 30–60 cm/12–24 in
SPREAD 25–40 cm/10–16 in
Annual; erect habit. Oval to lance-shaped, 10–20 cm/4–8 in long leaves, dark green, bristly, smelling of cucumber. Five-petaled, starry, bright blue, nodding flowers, about 2.5 cm/1 in wide. Young leaves and flowers used in salads, fruit cups.

CONTAINER SIZE 30–40 cm/12–16 in wide by 30 cm/12 in deep.
PLANTING In groups of four or five at 15–20 cm/6–8 in apart, in sun.
PROPAGATION By seeds sown in situ in spring. In zones 8–10 can also be sown in late summer or fall.
CARE Thin seedlings as soon as the seed leaves are fully expanded. Apply liquid feed every two weeks once flower buds show.

Carum carvi Caraway

ZONES 3–10   Easy
HEIGHT 50–75 cm/20–30 in
SPREAD 15 cm/6 in
Annual or biennial; erect habit. Finely dissected, fernlike leaves, 20 cm/8 in or more long, triangular in outline. Tiny, white flowers, in flattened heads. Aromatic seeds about 3 mm/⅛ in long, late summer. Seeds used in bread, cakes, salads, cheeses.
CONTAINER SIZE 30–40 cm/12–16 in wide by 20–30 cm/8–12 in deep.
PLANTING In groups at 10–15 cm/4–6 in apart as an annual, 25 cm/10 in apart as a biennial, in sun.
PROPAGATION By seeds sown in situ in spring as an annual, mid- to late summer as a biennial (zones 8–10).
CARE Thin seedlings as soon as they are large enough to handle. Apply liquid feed every two weeks when flowering stems are visible, ceasing when flowers fade.

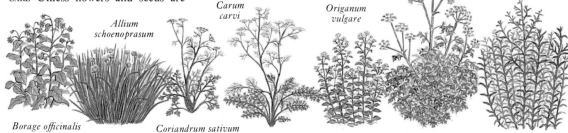

Angelica archangelica

Artemisia dracunculus

Carum carvi

Origanum vulgare

Allium schoenoprasum

Borage officinalis

Coriandrum sativum

Coriandrum sativum Coriander
ZONES 4–10   Easy
HEIGHT 30–50 cm/12–20 in
SPREAD 15–20 cm/6–8 in
Annual; slender, erect habit. Coarsely dissected basal leaves, finely dissected upper leaves. Tiny, white or purplish flowers, in terminal clusters. Rounded, 5 mm/$\frac{1}{5}$ in long seeds, pungently aromatic, in fall. Seeds used in sweet and savory dishes.
CONTAINER SIZE 20–30 cm/8–12 in wide by at least 15 cm/6 in deep.
PLANTING In groups of three to eight at 7.5–10 cm/3–4 in apart, in sun.
PROPAGATION By seeds sown in spring.
CARE Thin seedlings as soon as they are large enough to handle. Apply liquid feed every two weeks once the flowering stem is half grown to when the flowers fade. Cease watering when seeds start to turn yellow.

Foeniculum vulgare Fennel
ZONES 5–10   Easy
HEIGHT 90–150 cm/36–60 in
SPREAD 45–60 cm/18–24 in
Perennial; clump-forming. Erect stems, resistant to wind. Aromatic leaves, elaborately dissected into threadlike segments, to 90 cm/36 in tall. Tiny, yellow flowers, in flattened heads. Leaves used for seasoning fish, cheese, meat dishes.

Laurus nobilis

Foeniculum vulgare

CONTAINER SIZE 25–40 cm/10–16 in wide by 30 cm/12 in deep.
PLANTING Singly, in sun.
PROPAGATION By division or seeds, in spring.
CARE If only the leaves are required, the short, separate flowering stems are best removed when young; the plants then seldom grow above 30–45 cm/12–18 in tall. Apply liquid feed monthly from late spring to late summer. Can be grown as an annual in the smaller containers.

Laurus nobilis Bay laurel
ZONES 8–10   Easy
HEIGHT 1.8 m/6 ft or more
SPREAD 90 cm/36 in or more
Evergreen shrub; erect habit. Lance-shaped, 8 cm/3 in long, leathery leaves, dark green, aromatic when bruised. Small, greenish flowers, in clusters from upper leaf axils. Leaves used in wide range of dishes.
CONTAINER SIZE 45–90 cm/18–36 in wide and at least 30 cm/12 in deep.
PLANTING Singly, in sun or partial shade.
PROPAGATION By cuttings in late summer.
CARE Water freely in hot weather, less at other times. Apply liquid feed monthly from late spring to late summer. Can be trimmed to shape in spring or summer. Protect from severe frost in colder parts of zone 8.
CULTIVARS 'Angustifolia' ('Salicifolia'): very narrow, hardier leaves; 'Aurea': bright golden-green leaves.

Mentha spicata

Melissa officinalis Lemon balm
ZONES 4–9   Easy
HEIGHT 40–60 cm/16–24 in
SPREAD 30 cm/12 in or more
Perennial; clump-forming, slowly colonizing habit. Erect stems. Oval, toothed, strongly lemon-scented leaves, 5 cm/2 in long. Small, tubular, white flowers, from upper leaf axils. Leaves used in salads and fruit cups.
CONTAINER SIZE 25 cm/10 in or more wide by 25–30 cm/10–12 in deep.
PLANTING Singly, in sun or partial shade.
PROPAGATION By division in spring.
CARE Divide every two years. Apply liquid feed every two weeks from midsummer to fall.

Mentha Mint
ZONES 3–9   Easy
HEIGHT 45 cm/18 in or more
SPREAD 30–60 cm/12–24 in
Perennial; colony-forming habit, invasive. Robust, erect stems. Lance-shaped to broadly oval leaves. Tiny, pinkish or pale purple flowers, in terminal spikes. Leaves used in sauces, vegetable dishes, tea.
CONTAINER SIZE 30–40 cm/12–16 in wide by 20–30 cm/8–12 in deep.
PLANTING Singly, or in groups of three to five at 20 cm/8 in apart, in sun or shade.
PROPAGATION By division, in fall to spring.
CARE Divide and replant every three years, retaining only the thicker, white 'roots' (rhizomes). Apply liquid feed every two weeks in the growing season. For a long supply of fresh

Melissa officinalis

Ocimum basilicum

Anthriscus cerefolium

young leaves, remove tops of flowering stems in early summer. To provide out-of-season leaves, pot spare rhizomes and bring them into the home at intervals during the winter.
SPECIES *M. suaveolens* (*M. rotundifolia*) Apple, round-leaved or woolly mint: broadly oval to rounded, 4.5 cm/1$\frac{3}{4}$ in long leaves, hairy, smelling of mint and apples. *M. × villosa alopecuroides* Bowles mint: much like apple mint but more robust and smelling only of mint. *M. spicata* Common or spearmint: lance-shaped, almost hairless, 5–9 cm/2–3$\frac{1}{2}$ in long leaves, smelling of spearmint.

Ocimum basilicum
Basil (sweet basil)
ZONES 3–10   Easy
HEIGHT 30–45 cm/12–18 in
SPREAD 15–30 cm/6–12 in
Annual; erect, branched habit. Aromatic, oval to oblong-elliptic leaves, 6–10 cm/2$\frac{1}{2}$–4 in long. Small, two-lipped, white flowers, in terminal spikes. Leaves used in soups, salads, egg and fish dishes.
CONTAINER SIZE 30–40 cm/12–16 in wide by 30 cm/12 in deep.
PLANTING In groups of three to five at 15–20 cm/6–8 in apart, in sun.
PROPAGATION By seeds sown in warmth in spring.
CARE Set out young plants, but in zones 3–8 only when danger of frost is passed. Once the plants have been established for a month to six weeks, apply liquid feed every two weeks.

Origanum Marjoram
ZONES 3–10   Easy
HEIGHT 30–60 cm/12–24 in
SPREAD 20–40 cm/8–16 in
Perennial, though some species grown as annuals. Clump-forming and shrubby habits. Small, oval, aromatic leaves. Tiny, tubular, white or pinkish flowers, in dense terminal

clusters. Leaves and flowers used in salads, egg and meat dishes.

CONTAINER SIZE 20–30 cm/8–12 in wide by at least 20 cm/8 in deep.

PLANTING Singly, in sun. If grown as annuals can be planted in groups of three or four at 15–20 cm/6–8 in apart.

PROPAGATION *O. majorana* and *O. onites* by seeds in warmth in spring, or by cuttings in spring or summer. *O. vulgare* by division in spring.

CARE In the colder zones (3–8) *O. majorana* and *O. onites* must be protected from frost, or grown only as annuals. Apply liquid feed monthly during the growing season.

SPECIES *O. majorana* Sweet or knotted marjoram (zones 9–10): shrubby, with slender stems, about 2.5 cm/1 in long leaves, white, mauve or pink flowers, in hoplike clusters. *O. onites* Pot marjoram (zones 9–10): shrubby, leaves $\frac{1}{2}$–2 cm/$\frac{1}{5}$–$\frac{3}{4}$ in long, white flowers, in short spikes. *O. vulgare* Common marjoram (zones 3–9): clump-forming, leaves 1–4 cm/$\frac{1}{2}$–$1\frac{1}{2}$ in long, pinkish flowers, surrounded by purple-tinted bracts, in rounded clusters. *O.v.* 'Aureum': young leaves yellow, ornamental.

Petroselinum crispum Parsley
ZONES 4–9   Easy
HEIGHT 15–20 cm/6–8 in
SPREAD 20–30 cm/8–12 in
Biennial or annual; rosette-forming habit. Erect, branched stem. Deeply cut and crested, aromatic leaves. Tiny, yellowish flowers, in flat heads. Leaves used in sauces, stuffings, salads, meat dishes.

CONTAINER SIZE 20–40 cm/8–16 in wide by 20–30 cm/8–12 in deep.

PLANTING Singly, or in groups of three to five at 15 cm/6 in apart in the larger containers, or in parsley pots (see p. 30), in sun or partial shade.

PROPAGATION By seeds sown in warmth in early spring, or *in situ* in late spring.

CARE Unless seeds are required, remove flowering stems to promote further young basal leaves. Apply liquid feed every two weeks once the young plants are established.

Rosmarinus officinalis Rosemary
ZONES 7–10   Easy
HEIGHT 90 cm/36 in or more
SPREAD 45–60 cm/18–24 in
Evergreen shrub; erect to spreading habit. Very narrow, 2–5 cm/$\frac{3}{4}$–2 in long, deep green leaves, white-felted beneath, sweetly aromatic. Tubular, two-lipped, 2 cm/$\frac{3}{4}$ in long flowers, pale violet-blue, in small clusters. Leaves used in marinades, stews.

CONTAINER SIZE 30–45 cm/12–18 in wide by 30–40 cm/12–16 in deep.

PLANTING Singly, in sun.

PROPAGATION By cuttings in late summer or fall.

CARE In colder parts of zone 7, winter protection is advisable. Apply liquid feed monthly during the growing season.

CULTIVARS 'Miss Jessop's Variety': stiff, erect habit; 'Prostratus': dwarf, arching habit, blue flowers; 'Tuscan

Blue': like 'Prostratus' but smaller growing, broader leaves, brighter flowers.

Salvia officinalis Sage
ZONES 6–9   Easy
HEIGHT 40–60 cm/16–24 in
SPREAD 40–60 cm/16–24 in
Evergreen shrub; bushy to spreading habit. Oblong, 2.5–6 cm/1–$2\frac{1}{2}$ in long leaves, gray-green, finely wrinkled, pungently aromatic. Small, tubular, violet-blue flowers, in terminal spikes. Leaves used in stuffings, cheeses, some meat dishes.

CONTAINER SIZE 30–40 cm/12–16 in wide by 30 cm/12 in deep.

PLANTING Singly, in sun or partial shade.

PROPAGATION By cuttings in late summer or the fall, or by seeds in spring.

CARE In the colder parts of zones 6–7, winter protection is advisable. Apply liquid feed monthly throughout the growing season.

Satureja Savory
ZONES 5–10   Easy
HEIGHT 15–30 cm/6–12 in
SPREAD 15–30 cm/6–12 in
Annual and dwarf shrub; erect to spreading habit. Small, very narrow, aromatic leaves. Small, tubular, two-lipped flowers, white to pale purple, in leafy spikes. Leaves used in wide range of dishes.

CONTAINER SIZE 20–30 cm/8–12 in wide by at least 15 cm/6 in deep.

PLANTING Summer savory in groups of up to five at 10–15 cm/4–6 in apart, Winter savory singly or in threes at 20 cm/8 in apart; both in sun.

PROPAGATION Summer savory by seeds sown *in situ* in spring, Winter savory by cuttings in late summer, by layering, or by seeds in spring.

CARE Thin seedlings as soon as they are large enough to handle. Remove old flowering stems of Winter savory in early spring.

SPECIES *S. hortensis* Summer savory: annual, slender, more or less erect, leaves 13–16 mm/$\frac{1}{2}$–$\frac{5}{8}$ in long, palest purple to white flowers. *S. montana* Winter savory: spreading, wiry shrublet, leaves 1–3 cm/$\frac{1}{2}$–$1\frac{1}{4}$ in long, pale purple flowers.

Thymus Thyme
ZONES 5–9   Easy
HEIGHT 20–30 cm/8–12 in
SPREAD 20–30 cm/8–12 in
Small, wiry-stemmed shrubs; spreading habit. Narrow, 3–8 mm/$\frac{1}{8}$–$\frac{3}{8}$ in long leaves. Small, tubular, two-lipped, whitish to pale purple flowers, in short terminal spikes. Leaves used in stuffings, meat and fish dishes.

CONTAINER SIZE 20–30 cm/8–12 in wide by at least 15 cm/6 in deep.

PLANTING Singly, or in groups of three or four at 20 cm/8 in apart in the larger containers, in sun.

PROPAGATION By division in spring or cuttings in late summer.

CARE Every spring, remove old flowering stems and tips of previous season's growth. Apply liquid feed monthly from spring to summer.

SPECIES *T. vulgaris* Common thyme: gray-green leaves with inrolled margins, strongly aromatic. *T.* × *citriodorus* Lemon thyme: broad, mid- to bright green, lemon-scented leaves. *T.* × *c.* 'Argenteus': white-variegated leaves; 'Aureus': yellow leaves; both particularly ornamental.

Petroselinum crispum   *Satureja hortensis*   *Rosmarinus officinalis*   *Salvia officinalis*   *Thymus vulgaris*

Vegetables

Most vegetable plants are annuals and even those that are not are treated as such when grown in containers: from sowing or planting to harvesting may be three weeks to five months. The plants listed below can be grown in almost any kind of container, although a minimum depth of 20–23 cm/8–9 in is essential. The container sizes given below are usually for single plants. With most vegetables, you will need to grow several plants to obtain a reasonable crop.

As a growing medium specially prepared potting mix is best. Good garden topsoil, if available, can be used but may introduce problems of additional pests and diseases, such as the club root fungus. (If soil is used, cover it with a layer of sterile potting mix to inhibit weeds and prevent hardening of the surface due to frequent watering.) The soil or mix can be re-used once, but preferably to grow a different type of vegetable or for growing bulbs, annual flowering plants or hardy perennials. Plants that produce slower-growing vegetables will provide the best yield when given a liquid feed as their crops are maturing. Never allow the growing medium to dry out completely and ensure that excess water can drain away freely.

Most vegetables do best kept in a sunny position, particularly in the early part of the growing season. Later on in summer, quicker-growing vegetables, such as spinach, benefit from some shade, particularly during the hotter part of the day. Avoid placing containers in excessively windy, exposed sites: stems of vegetable plants are not resistant to wind. Climbing and trailing plants must be provided with supports.

It is easy, and most economical, to raise vegetable plants from seed. However, cucumber and tomato especially can be purchased as young plants in spring. It is important to sow or plant vegetables at the correct times. Some, such as lettuce and radish, may be grown *in situ* as soon as spring temperatures start to rise sufficiently for good seed germination. Others, among them tomato and *Capsicum*, can be grown indoors and the seedlings transplanted to small pots; then, when weather conditions permit, the young plants should be moved into larger containers outdoors. Vegetables such as summer/autumn radish, lettuce, beet and carrot may be sown periodically from early or midspring to midsummer or later to provide successional crops. It is best to buy fresh seeds each spring.

In the following plant descriptions, detailed information is given about stems, leaves and flowers only where these are particularly relevant to the growth and harvesting of the vegetables.

Allium cepa Onion
ZONES 2–10   Easy
HEIGHT 23–30 cm/9–12 in
SPREAD to 25 cm/10 in
Grown for its edible bulbs. Thin, cylindrical, light green leaves, arising from flattened or globe-shaped bulbs with a white or light brown outer skin. There are three main types: bulbing, bunching and pickling.
CONTAINER SIZE 30 cm/12 in or more wide by 30 cm/12 in deep.
PLANTING Sow seeds 1–2 cm/$\frac{1}{2}$–$\frac{3}{4}$ in deep, those of bulbing types at 7.5 cm/3 in apart and those of bunching and pickling types at 2 cm/$\frac{3}{4}$ in, in sun, in midspring. Thin seedlings of bulbing onions to leave three plants 30 cm/12 in apart. Use thinnings for salads. To raise bulbing onions from immature bulbs, or sets, plant sets to leave only their tips showing, at 30 cm/12 in apart, in sun, toward the end of late spring.
CARE Water frequently in warm weather, less at other times. Never permit onion plants to get dry at the roots as bulbs may split if dryness is followed by heavy watering. Do not store split bulbs. Remove any weed seedlings as soon as they appear.

The main pest, maggots of the onion fly, eats roots, causing plant foliage to yellow and die. Prevent infestation by thinning onion seedlings carefully so that no foliage is broken; the female flies are attracted to the odor of bruised leaves and lay eggs on them from which the maggots emerge.
HARVESTING Lift bunching onions when of usable size, usually 12–14 weeks after sowing. Dig up pickling onions for immediate use when foliage yellows and starts to shrivel. Bulbing onions may be harvested when they are sufficiently large, but are best left until foliage is brown, brittle and dry, usually 18–20 weeks from sowing. Then, dig up bulbs, hang them in bunches in a sunny position to dry off completely, and store in a cool, dry position. In wet weather, harvest bulbing and pickling onions when foliage has toppled onto the ground but is still green.
CULTIVARS Bulbing types: 'Ebenezer', 'Southport Red Globe', 'Southport Yellow Globe', 'White Sweet Spanish'. Bunching types: 'Evergreen Long'. Pickling types: 'Italian Red', 'Paris Silverskin'.

Allium sativum Garlic
ZONES 2–10   Easy
HEIGHT 30 cm/12 in
SPREAD 13 cm/5 in
Grown for its bulbs, which are split into segments, or cloves, for use as a culinary flavoring. Light green, straplike leaves arise from a grayish bulb to 5 cm/2 in across.

CONTAINER SIZE 30 cm/12 in wide by 20 cm/8 in deep.
PLANTING Plant cloves 5 cm/2 in deep, at 13 cm/5 in apart, in sun, in early spring. In zones 8–10, cloves can also be planted in late fall for a crop the next spring.
CARE Water frequently in warm weather, less at other times. Reduce watering to a minimum as soon as foliage begins to turn yellow. Keep the cloves weeded at all times.
HARVESTING Lift bulbs when foliage starts to shrivel and turn brown in late summer, usually 22–24 weeks from sowing. Tie plants in small bunches and hang to dry in a sunny position outdoors. Rub off dry roots and foliage and store indoors in a cool, airy place.

Allium cepa

Allium sativum

Beta vulgaris Beet
ZONES 2–10 Easy
HEIGHT 30 cm/12 in
SPREAD 25 cm/10 in
Grown for its edible swollen root, the beet. Large, oval, reddish or green crimped leaves, on long, erect stalks, in basal rosette on short stem. There are three main types based on the shape of the root: globe, long and tapering, and intermediate. Only plants producing globe-shaped roots are suitable for growing in containers. The flesh color of these roots is usually crimson but yellow and white forms are available.
CONTAINER SIZE 30 cm/12 in wide by 20 cm/8 in deep.
PLANTING Sow seeds thinly, 2 cm/$\frac{3}{4}$ in deep, in sun, at monthly intervals from midspring to midsummer. Thin seedlings to leave plants at 13 cm/5 in apart.
CARE Water frequently in warm weather, less at other times. Keep plants weeded at all times.

Black bean aphid may attack foliage. To control, spray leaves with a suitable pesticide (see p. 55). Slugs, which can cause damage to both seedlings and established plants, should, if necessary, be prevented using slug bait.
HARVESTING For immediate use, harvest plants when roots are of appreciable size, usually 20–24 weeks from sowing. For a supply of beets all year round, allow roots to attain maximum size and harvest only when foliage starts to change from reddish-green to yellow. Then twist off foliage to 2 cm/$\frac{3}{4}$ in from top of beets and store the vegetables in moist peat or sand in containers kept in a cool, frost-free position. Take beets for use as required.
CULTIVARS 'Boltardy', 'Burpees Golden', 'Cylindra', 'Detroit Dark Red', 'Early Wonder'.

Brassica cernua (B. chinensis pekinensis) Chinese cabbage
ZONES 2–10 Moderately easy
HEIGHT 30–35 cm/12–14 in
SPREAD 25 cm/10 in
Grown for its edible foliage. White-green leaves in globular head or heart which has the appearance of a cos lettuce (see p. 147).
CONTAINER SIZE 25 cm/10 in or more wide by 20 cm/8 in deep.
PLANTING Sow four seeds 1–2 cm/$\frac{1}{2}$–$\frac{3}{4}$ in deep, at 7.5 cm/3 in apart, near the center of containers, in sun, in midsummer. Thin seedlings when they have two or three true leaves – these form above the first two, round, seed leaves – to leave the strongest plant in each container. Alternatively, sow several groups of four seeds at 25 cm/10 in apart, in the larger containers, thinning seedlings to leave only the strongest of each group.
CARE Water plants regularly in warm weather, less at other times. Lack of moisture and sowing at the incorrect time are likely causes of 'bolting', in which the plants grow upward and produce unwanted flowering stems. Keep plants weeded at all times.

Slugs can devour seedlings and damage foliage of larger plants. Use slug bait if necessary. Foliage is also attacked by caterpillars of cabbage white butterflies. Search for these regularly and remove. Turnip flea beetles may attack seedlings. For treatment see Turnip; below.
HARVESTING Dig up cabbages for use when they are full size and the hearts are tightly packed, usually 10–12 weeks from sowing. Always harvest plants before the first autumn frost. Cabbages not wanted for immediate use may be blanched (as with endives, p. 145) and dried, then stored in a freezer.
CULTIVARS 'Burpee Hybrid', 'Mandarin', 'Michihli Jade Pagoda Hybrid'.

Brassica oleracea 'Capitata' Cabbage
ZONES 2–10 Easy
HEIGHT 30 cm/12 in
SPREAD 30 cm/12 in
Grown for its edible foliage. Short, stout stem, bearing round or conical dense head of dark green, light green, pink, purple-red or creamy-white crimped, wavy-margined leaves. Quick-growing varieties are best for raising in containers.
CONTAINER SIZE 25 cm/10 in wide by 25 cm/10 in deep.
PLANTING Sow seeds 1 cm/$\frac{1}{2}$ in deep, at 2 cm/$\frac{3}{4}$ in apart, in shallow pots or seed flats, in sun, in midspring for a late summer-early fall crop. In mild winter areas only, seeds can be sown in late summer for a crop the following late spring. For a summer crop seeds can also be sown in late winter indoors in containers kept in a sunny position. When seedlings have from three to five 'true' leaves – these form above the initial rounded, seed leaves – transplant young cabbages singly to their growing containers. 'Modern Dwarf' may be planted in groups of four or five at 15–18 cm/6–7 in apart if small cabbages are desired. Plant firmly so that the lowest true leaf is just above the surface of the potting mix.
CARE Water regularly in warm weather, less at other times. Slugs, which can devour seedlings and damage plants, should be controlled using slug bait. Caterpillars of the cabbage white butterfly and cabbage moth should be searched for regularly and destroyed.
HARVESTING Cut cabbages for use when they are fully grown and firm, usually 5–6 months after sowing.
CULTIVARS 'Darkri', 'Earliana', 'Early Jersey Wakefield', 'Emerald Cross Hybrid', 'Golden Acre', 'Modern Dwarf', 'Red Head Hybrid'.

Brassica oleracea gongyloides Kohlrabi
ZONES 2–10 Easy
HEIGHT 20 cm/8 in
SPREAD 25 cm/10 in
Grown for its edible, swollen, spherical stem. Elliptic, mid-green, long-stalked leaves, arranged in whorls on stem 5–7.5 cm/2–3 in in diameter. The skin color of the stem may be white, green or purple, the flesh is creamy-white.
CONTAINER SIZE 30 cm/12 in wide by 25–30 cm/10–12 in deep.
PLANTING Sow seeds thinly, 2 cm/$\frac{3}{4}$ in deep, in sun, at monthly intervals from midspring to midsummer. Thin seedlings to leave plants at 13 cm/5 in apart.
CARE Water regularly in warm weather, less at other times.

If necessary, take precautions against slugs (see p. 55). Turnip flea beetle should not attack if a properly prepared seed or potting mix is used; if it does, control by applying a flea beetle dust to the foliage.
HARVESTING Dig up plants for use when stems are of appreciable size, usually 8–10 cm/3–4 in in diameter. This is about 10–12 weeks from sowing. Do not allow kohlrabi to become old as the vegetable is then less palatable.
CULTIVARS 'Early White Vienna', 'Grand Duke Hybrid'.

Brassica rapa Turnip
ZONES 2–10 Easy
HEIGHT 30 cm/12 in
SPREAD 20 cm/8 in
Grown for its edible swollen root, although its tender leaves and young shoots, when blanched, are also used as vegetables. Several stems arising from crown of a swollen, fleshy, usually white root. Elliptic, lobed, green leaves. There are three main types: globular, flattened and long-

rooted. Varieties with globular roots are best for growing in containers.
CONTAINER SIZE 30 cm/12 in wide by 25–30 cm/10–12 in deep.
PLANTING Sow seeds thinly, 2 cm/$\frac{3}{4}$ in deep, in sun, at monthly intervals from midspring to midsummer. Thin seedlings to leave plants at 20–23 cm/8–9 in apart.
CARE Water frequently in warm weather, less at other times. Always keep plants weeded.

Turnip flea beetle may attack the foliage, particularly of seedlings, if a poorly prepared potting mix is used; control by spraying plants with a flea beetle insecticide. If necessary, take precautions against slugs (see p. 55).
HARVESTING Dig up plants for use when turnips are young and tender, to 7.5 cm/3 in across, usually 8 weeks from sowing.
CULTIVARS 'Golden Ball', 'Imperial Green Globe', 'Purple Top Milan', 'Seven Top', 'Tokyo Cross'.

Capsicum annuum
Sweet pepper
ZONES 9–10 Easy
HEIGHT 45 cm/18 in
SPREAD 25 cm/10 in
Grown for its edible fruits. Erect, shrubby habit, stems to 38 cm/15 in tall. Mid-green, oblong to oval leaves. White flowers, singly in upper leaf axils, midsummer. Fleshy, bell- or apple-shaped fruits with furrowed sides, yellow or red when mature, late summer/early fall.
CONTAINER SIZE 20–23 cm/8–9 in wide by 20–23 cm/8–9 in deep.
PLANTING Sow two or three seeds 1 cm/$\frac{1}{2}$ in deep at the center of containers, in sun, in early/midspring. Thin seedlings to leave only one plant in each container. In zones lower than 8, seeds can be sown in containers indoors on a sunny window ledge, moving containers out-

doors as soon as temperatures rise.
CARE Water frequently in warm weather, less at other times. The flowers set fruits readily. As soon as fruits start to swell, apply liquid feed weekly. When bearing fruits, plants may become top-heavy. To prevent stems toppling over, tie them loosely to short lengths of bamboo cane.

Slugs can damage seedlings, stems, leaves and fruits. Search for slugs regularly and use bait if necessary.
HARVESTING Remove fruits when they are fully grown and green, or allow them to ripen to red or yellow before picking.
CULTIVARS 'Bell Boy', 'California Wonder', 'New Ace', 'World-beater', 'Yolo Wonder'.

Cichorium endivia Endive
ZONES 2–10 Easy
HEIGHT 25 cm/10 in
SPREAD 30 cm/12 in
Grown for its edible leaves. Often used as fall lettuce substitute. Resembles lettuce in habit, with pale-green, crisp leaves, in a globular head. There are two types: Staghorns, with curled leaves, and Batavians, with broader, plain leaves.
CONTAINER SIZE 45 cm/18 in wide by 25 cm/10 in deep.
PLANTING Sow two or three seeds 1 cm/$\frac{1}{2}$ in deep in the center of containers, in sun. Thin seedlings to the strongest one when two true leaves show above the seed leaves. Seeds of curled leaf types are best sown in early summer, those of plain leaf types 6–8 weeks later.
CARE Water frequently in warm weather, less at other times. Apply liquid feed monthly. Keep plants weeded at all times.

Protect seedlings from birds with strands of black thread suspended over containers. Search for slugs and trap them with bait if necessary.

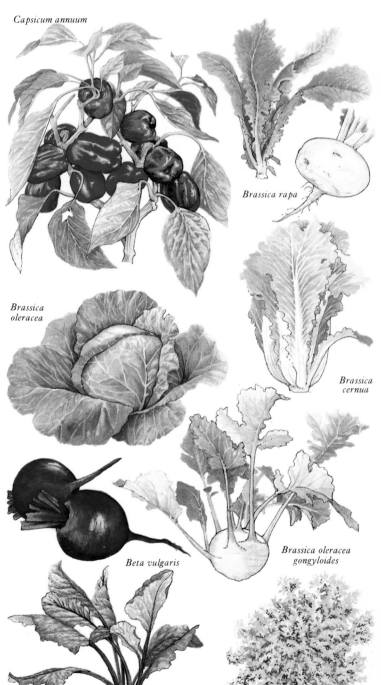

Capsicum annuum

Brassica rapa

Brassica oleracea

Brassica cernua

Beta vulgaris

Brassica oleracea gongyloides

Cichorium endivia

Cucumis sativus

Cucurbita pepo

Daucus carota

BLANCHING AND HARVESTING Before use, to remove their bitter flavor leaves should be blanched by being shaded from sunlight. (The extent of blanching can be varied as desired: shade leaves completely for the least bitter flavor.) When plants are fully grown and resembling unhearted lettuces, usually 20–24 weeks from sowing, cover each one with an inverted flower pot. To exclude light totally, cover the drainage holes in the pots with stones or black polythene sheeting held in position with a heavy object. Complete blanching will take 10–20 days. Should only partial blanching be required, tie the leaves of each plant together fairly loosely with raffia. The leaves at the center of the plant will start to blanch and turn creamy-yellow within ten days. Lift plants for use before the blanched foliage shows deterioration from fungal infections.

CULTIVARS Curled leaf types: 'Giant Green Curled', 'Salad King', 'Ruffec', 'White Curled'. Plain leaf types: 'Batavian Green', 'Winter Lettuce-leaved'.

Cucumis sativus Cucumber

ZONES 2–10 Easy
HEIGHT 18 cm/7 in (as trailing plant)
SPREAD 1 m/3 ft (as trailing plant)
Grown for its edible fruits. Trailing habit. Triangular, green leaves with tendrils. Yellow flowers, in clusters on main stem, in summer. Globular, oblong, or short and cylindrical fruits, with green skins and white flesh, in late summer to early fall. There are two main types: frame cucumbers, which need to be grown in warmth in a greenhouse, and ridge cucumbers, which are ideal for growing outdoors in the ground or in containers.
CONTAINER SIZE 30 cm/12 in wide by 20 cm/8 in deep.
PLANTING Sow two or three seeds 1 cm/½ in deep near the center of containers, in sun, in early spring when danger of frost is passed. Thin seedlings to leave only the strongest one. In cool areas it is preferable to buy young plants in late spring and to set them in containers when tem-

peratures begin to rise noticeably.
CARE Water frequently in warm weather, less at other times. Plants will benefit from an occasional application of liquid feed once cucumbers begin to swell. To keep plants tidy and attractive and to ensure a good crop, train stems on bamboo canes. Allow three canes for each plant, linking the canes with string to produce a 1 m/3 ft high tepeelike open structure. Pinch off the growing point of plants as soon as they reach the top of supports and tie the main stem and all side shoots to supports.

As a precaution against slugs, place slug bait around and beneath containers. Mosaic virus infection leads to yellow mottling of foliage and fruits and stunting of plants (see p. 55). Destroy affected plants immediately.
HARVESTING Pick cucumbers when fully grown but before they ripen, usually 22–24 weeks from sowing. Regular picking of tender cucumbers induces plants to set more fruit.
CULTIVARS 'Burpee Hybrid', 'Bush Whopper', 'Lemon', 'Patio Pik Hybrid', 'Space Master'.

Cucurbita pepo, C. maxima

Zucchini/summer squash, winter squash
ZONES 2–10 Easy
HEIGHT 30 cm/12 in (as trailing plant), 60 cm/24 in (as bush plant)
SPREAD 1–2 m/3–6½ ft (trailing plant) to 1 m/3 ft (bush plant)
Grown for its edible fruits. Compact bush, or trailing, vining habit. Large, triangular, lobed, green leaves. Yellow, tubular flowers, in summer. Summer squash fruits are of three types: green, yellow or striped cylindrical zucchini; pear-shaped, yellow crookneck; and round flute-edged scallops. All produce abundantly from midsummer through early fall.

Winter squash has a similar form and culture to summer squash but requires a longer season and more heat.
CONTAINER SIZE 35 cm/14 in wide by 30 cm/12 in deep.
PLANTING Sow two or three seeds 2 cm/¾ in deep near the center of containers, in sun, in late spring. Thin seedlings to leave only the strongest one.
CARE Water regularly in warm weather, less at other times. Bush-type plants need neither supports nor pruning. Trailing plants are best trained on supports in the manner suggested for cucumbers (see above), but using stronger canes 2 m/6½ ft long. Pinch out growing points when stems reach the top of supports. Tie main stem and side shoots loosely to the supports. Keep plants weeded at all times. Apply liquid feed every two weeks when fruits start to swell. You may need to pollinate the female flowers by hand in order to assist fertilization (see p. 44).

Slugs can destroy seedlings and damage the swelling fruits. Use slug bait if necessary. Mosaic virus causes mottling of leaves and distortion of fruits. Pull up and burn affected plants.
HARVESTING For summer squash, cut fruits when they are 13–15 cm/5–6 in long. Regular harvesting of plants will promote fruiting to provide squash all summer. Winter squash should be harvested when the fruit stem has become dry and hard. Store fruits in a dry, cool, but frost-free place indoors.
CULTIVARS Summer squash – bush types: 'Burpee Golden Zucchini', 'Dixie Hybrid', 'Scallopini Hybrid', 'Zucchini'; Summer squash – trailing types: 'Early Golden Summer Crookneck', 'Richgreen Hybrid Zucchini', 'Scallop Peter Pan'; Winter squash – trailing types: 'Early Butternut'.

Daucus carota Carrot

ZONES 2–10   Easy
HEIGHT 18–25 cm/7–10 in
SPREAD 20 cm/8 in

Grown for its edible root. Rosette of short, light green, erect stems arising from top of root. Leaves dark green, feathery, triangular in outline. Root may be long, cylindrical with a blunt end, short and conical, or barrel-shaped, and yellowish-orange to orange. Short and conical or barrel-shaped carrots are best for growing in containers.

CONTAINER SIZE to 30 cm/12 in wide by 25 cm/10 in deep.

PLANTING Sow seeds very thinly, about 1 cm/½ in deep, at 2 cm/¾ in apart, in sun, at monthly intervals from midspring to midsummer. Thin seedlings to leave plants at 7.5–10 cm/3–4 in apart.

CARE Water regularly in warm weather, less at other times.

The main pest, maggots of the carrot fly, may damage roots of late sowings. Egg-laying female flies are attracted to carrot seedlings by the odor of bruised leaves. If thinning of seedlings is necessary, ensure that foliage of plants is not broken and that none of the thinnings are left in the containers. Slugs can devour seedlings and established plants. If they do appear, lay slug bait around containers.

HARVESTING Dig up carrots for use once they have reached the desired size. Any left to attain full size – usually 16–18 weeks from sowing – and which are not wanted for immediate consumption may be stored in the fall. Before storing cut back foliage to leave 2.5/1 in long stems. Store roots in moist peat or sand in containers kept in a cool, dry place. Store for no more than 4–6 weeks.

CULTIVARS 'Amstel', 'Danvers Half Long', 'Goldinhart', 'Little Finger'.

Lactuca sativa Lettuce

ZONES 3–9   Easy
HEIGHT to 30 cm/12 in
SPREAD to 30 cm/12 in

Grown for its edible leaves. Low-growing, leaves in various shades of green, in some varieties tinged red, purple or bronze, in loose or dense heads. There are three main types: cabbage, with smooth, curled or crimped leaves in a tight, globular head; cos, with oblong, crisp leaves in a loose head; loose-leaf, with crisp, curled leaves in a loose bunch.

CONTAINER SIZE 45 cm/18 in or more wide by 20 cm/8 in deep. L.s. 'Tom Thumb' can be grown in containers 15 cm/6 in wide by 15 cm/6 in deep.

PLANTING Sow seeds thinly, 1 cm/½ in deep, in sun, at three-week intervals from midspring to early fall. Thin seedlings to leave plants at 20–25 cm/8–10 in apart, except L.s. 'Tom Thumb', at 15 cm/6 in apart. If there is danger of frost in spring or winter, sow in shallow containers or seed-flats indoors and transfer young plants to containers outdoors when temperatures rise.

CARE Water regularly in warm weather, less at other times.

HARVESTING Dig up whole plants for use when well-hearted, usually 12–14 weeks from sowing, although individual leaves of loose-leaf types can be picked as required.

CULTIVARS Cabbage types – crisp heading: 'Burpee's Iceberg', 'Great-lakes', 'Minetto'; Cabbage types – butterhead: 'Augusta', 'Bibb', 'Buttercrunch', 'Butter King', 'Dark Green Boston', 'Fordhook', 'Tom Thumb'. Cos types: 'Barcarolle', 'Paris White Cos', 'Valmaine Cos'. Loose-leaf types: 'Black Seeded Simpson', 'Crispy Sweet', 'Grand Rapids', 'Green Ice', 'Red Salad Bowl'. Heat-resistant varieties: 'Hot Weather', 'Slo Bolt'.

Lycopersicon lycopersicum
Tomato

ZONES 3–10   Easy
HEIGHT 30–180 cm/12–72 in
SPREAD 30 cm/12 in or more

Grown for fruit. Tall-growing and bush varieties. Yellow flowers in clusters, in midsummer. Fruits 5–10 cm/2–4 in diameter, red, orange or yellow, globular, pear- or plum-shaped, in late summer.

CONTAINER SIZE 20–25 cm/8–10 in wide by at least 20 cm/8 in deep.

PLANTING Young plants singly, in midspring after danger of frost is past, in sun. Sow seeds 1 cm/½ in deep, at 2 cm/¾ in apart, in warmth, in early spring. Transplant seedlings to 7.5 cm/3 in diameter pots when seed leaves are fully open. As plants outgrow pots, move them onto larger containers or growing bags, outdoors when weather conditions permit.

CARE Water regularly in warm weather, less at other times. Apply liquid feed weekly once fruits have set or use special tomato fertilizer, following manufacturer's instructions. With tall-growing plants support stem and remove side-shoots (see p. 44) and pinch out stem tip once four flower clusters have set fruitlets.

To protect against blight, which attacks stems, leaves and fruits, apply an appropriate fungicide, such as copper spray, in late summer. Straw or matting around the plant will help to prevent attack by slugs and snails (see p. 56).

HARVESTING Pick fruits when ripe and still firm, usually 22–24 weeks from sowing.

CULTIVARS Tall-growing varieties: 'Early Girl'. Dwarf-growing varieties: 'Bitsy VF Hybrid', 'Goldie', 'Minibel', 'Patio F'. Bush varieties: 'City Best VF Hybrid', 'Patio Prize', Pixie Hybrid', 'Tiny Tim'.

Phaseolus coccineus

Lactuca sativa

Lycopersicon lycopersicum

Phaseolus coccineus Runner bean

ZONES 4–9   Moderately easy
HEIGHT to 1.8 m/6 ft
SPREAD 30 cm/12 in

Grown for its edible seed pods. Climbing, twining habit. Red, white or red and white flowers in small clusters, in summer. Light green

Phaseolus vulgaris

Pisum sativum

Raphanus sativus

pods, 30 cm/12 in or more long, in late summer.
CONTAINER SIZE 20–45 cm/8–18 in or more wide by 25 cm/10 in deep.
PLANTING Sow seeds 5 cm/2 in deep at 10–13 cm/4–5 in apart, in sun, in early/midsummer. Late spring sowings can be made in containers in-

doors in a sunny site, moving containers outdoors in summer.
CARE Water frequently in warm weather, less at other times. Provide tall supports for stems, but pinch out growing points when plants reach top of supports.

The main pest, black bean aphid, can be controlled by spraying with a suitable pesticide (see p. 56).
HARVESTING Remove pods regularly while they are still young.
CULTIVARS Heavy cropping varieties include 'Desirée', 'Enorma', 'Painted Lady', 'Prizewinner', 'Streamline'.

Phaseolus vulgaris French, dwarf or kidney bean
ZONES 4–9   Moderately easy
HEIGHT dwarf types 30–35 cm/12–14 in, climbing types to 1.5 m/5 ft
SPREAD 20 cm/8 in
Grown for its edible pods, although the dried seeds are also eaten, either unripe (flageolets) or ripe (haricots). Dwarf bush or climbing habit. White, cream, pink or purple flowers, in summer. Pods in various shades of green and purple, to 13 cm/5 in long, late summer to mid fall.
CONTAINER SIZE 15–30 cm/6–12 in or more wide by 25 cm/10 in deep.
PLANTING Sow seeds as for runner bean (above), but in late spring.
CARE For watering and pests see runner bean (above). Support dwarf plants by tying stems to short bamboo canes, and climbing types using canes to 1.8 m/6 ft long.
HARVESTING If only the pods are required, harvest plants when pods are still tender. For flageolets, pick pods when seeds are soft and green, and for haricots, when seeds have ripened to white or light brown.
CULTIVARS Dwarf types: 'Bluecrop', 'Pencil Pod Black Wax', 'Tendercrop'. Climbing types: 'Blue Lake White Seeded', 'Earliest of All'.

Pisum sativum Pea
ZONES 2–10   Easy
HEIGHT 45–60 cm/18–24 in
SPREAD 10 cm/4 in
Grown for its edible seeds and pods. Includes green pea, petit pois and sugar pea (mangetout). Climbing habit, stem with tendrils. White flowers, solitary or in small clusters, in summer. Pods to 10 cm/4 in long, in shades of green, seeds rounded or wrinkled, green, in fall.
CONTAINER SIZE 30 cm/12 in or more wide by 20 cm/8 in deep.
PLANTING Sow seeds 2.5 cm/1 in deep, at 5–6 cm/2–2½ in apart, in sun, in spring or early summer. Seeds can also be sown in warmth in late winter to early spring, moving containers outdoors when temperatures rise.
CARE Water regularly in dry weather, less at other times. Provide supports and keep plants netted at all times.

Pea moth caterpillars attack peas in pods: control by spraying with suitable insecticide at flowering time.
HARVESTING Gather sugar peas when pods fully grown, tender and before peas swell. Pick pods of other types when filled with swollen peas.
CULTIVARS Standard vines: 'Alaska', 'Green Arrow', 'Laxton's Progress'. Dwarf vines: 'Knight', 'Mighty Midget', 'Novelle'. Sugar pea (mangetout): pod and seeds edible, e.g. 'Snowbird', 'Sugar Snap'.

Raphanus sativus Radish
ZONES 4–10   Easy
HEIGHT 13–30 cm/5–12 in
SPREAD 5–20 cm/2–8 in
Grown for its edible roots. Quick-growing plant of which there are two types: summer and early fall harvesting, with small, round, or long cylindrical roots with white, red, or red and white skins, and fall and winter harvesting, with large round roots with red, white or,

in some cases, dark brown skins.
CONTAINER SIZE 15–30 cm/6–12 in wide by 20 cm/8 in deep; large fall/winter types are best grown in the larger-sized containers.
PLANTING Sow seeds of summer/fall types 1 cm/½ in deep, at 2 cm/¾ in apart, in sun, at two-week intervals from early to late spring. In zones lower than 6, early sowings are best made in containers indoors on a sunny window ledge, moving containers outdoors when temperatures rise. Seeds of fall/winter types should be sown 2 cm/¾ in deep, at 4 cm/1½ in apart, in sun, in late summer. Thin all seedlings to leave the strongest ones at 20 cm/8 in apart.
CARE Water regularly in warm weather, less at other times. Protect from slugs using standard bait.
HARVESTING Pull up summer/fall radishes for use when they are young and succulent; crops should be ready 4–6 weeks after sowing. Dig up fall/winter radishes in late fall; they can be stored as for beet (see p. 144).
CULTIVARS Summer/autumn types: 'Cherry Belle', 'Long White Icicle'. Autumn/winter types: 'Black Spanish Round', 'White Chinese'.

Rorippa nasturtium-aquaticum Watercress
ZONES 2–10   Easy
HEIGHT 15 cm/6 in
SPREAD 30 cm/12 in
Grown for its young shoots. Aquatic plant with low, mat-forming habit. Short, erect, pale green stems, bearing tiny, dark green or bronze-green leaves.
CONTAINER SIZE 30 cm/12 in wide by 25–30 cm/10–12 in deep.
PLANTING Sow seeds thinly, no more than 1 cm/½ in deep, in light shade, in early spring (zones 6–10) or mid-spring (zones 2–6). Thin seedlings

to 10–15 cm/4–6 in apart.

CARE Keep roots moist at all times by standing containers in saucers or trays filled with water or in a small pool. Keep plants weeded and cut off flowering stems as soon as they are noticed to encourage production of more foliage.

Usually pest-free, but leaves may be eaten by caterpillars of the cabbage white butterfly. Search for and remove caterpillars regularly.

HARVESTING Pick shoots when plants are in full growth, usually about 2–3 weeks after sowing.

Solanum tuberosum Potato

ZONES 3–9 Easy
HEIGHT 75 cm/30 in or more
SPREAD 75 cm/30 in or more

Grown for its edible tubers. Shrubby habit. Branched stem, at first upright but topples over when about 60 cm/24 in tall. Long, dark green leaves. Mauve or creamy-white flowers, in summer, which may be followed by inedible green fruits. Tubers round, kidney-shaped or oval, with yellow-brown, brown, pink or red skins, white or pale yellow flesh. There are three main types: first early, second early and maincrop. First early varieties are best for growing in small containers.

CONTAINER SIZE at least 30 cm/12 in wide and deep.

PLANTING Start tubers into growth in trays placed outdoors in a light, frost-proof site. When sprouts are 1 cm/½ in long, plant tubers singly, 10 cm/4 in deep, sprouts uppermost, in the growing containers, in sun. (For growing in a potato barrel, see p. 31.) Plant tubers of first early varieties in early spring, second early varieties 4 weeks later, and maincrop varieties a further 4 weeks later. Set early varieties at 25 cm/10 in apart, maincrop at 45 cm/15 in apart.

CARE Water regularly in dry weather, less at other times. As they start to swell, cover tubers further with a 4 cm/1½ in thick layer of potting mix. This will prevent light reaching the tubers, causing them to turn green and become inedible.

The main pest is potato blight. As a precautionary measure apply a suitable fungicide when plants are fully grown.

HARVESTING Dig up early potatoes as soon as they are large enough, first early varieties usually in early summer, late early varieties from midsummer to early fall. Harvest maincrop varieties in mid fall: those not required for immediate use should be allowed to dry then stored in boxes in a dark, cool but frost-free position.

CULTIVARS First early: 'Chippewa', 'Duke of York', 'Early Gem', 'Red McClure', 'White Cobbler'. Second early: 'Maris Peer', 'Red Pontiac'. Maincrop: 'Russet Burbank'.

Spinacea oleracea Spinach

ZONES 3–8 Easy
HEIGHT to 20 cm/8 in
SPREAD 15–20 cm/6–8 in

Grown for its edible leaves. Clump-forming habit. There are two main types: spring or summer varieties, and winter hardy varieties, both having dark green, oval to triangular, crimped, upright leaves to 20 cm/8 in long. Perpetual spinach, a form of *Beta vulgaris*, has lighter green, more broadly oval-shaped leaves.

CONTAINER SIZE 20–45 cm/8–18 in wide by at least 30 cm/12 in deep.

PLANTING Sow seeds of spring spinach at monthly intervals from midspring to midsummer, and of winter spinach at monthly intervals from late summer to mid fall. Seeds of perpetual spinach can be sown at monthly intervals through-

out spring, summer and the fall. Sow all seeds 1 cm/½ in deep, at 4 cm/1½ in apart, in light shade. Thin seedlings to leave them at 15–20 cm/6–8 in apart.

CARE Water regularly in warm weather, less at other times. Keep containers out of direct sun, which will cause plants to 'bolt' (make unwanted flowering stems). Winter spinach is not suitable for growing in zones 3–6. Perpetual spinach may be overwintered outdoors. With successional sowing of seeds, a continuous supply of leaves is possible.

HARVESTING Just pick the larger leaves as they are ready.

CULTIVARS Spring/summer types: 'America', 'Avon Hybrid', 'Bloomsdale Longstanding', 'Early Smooth No. 424 Hybrid', 'Melody Hybrid', 'No. 8 Hybrid'. Winter hardy types: 'Winter Bloomsdale'.

Valerianella locusta Corn salad Lamb's lettuce

ZONES 2–9 Easy
HEIGHT 10 cm/4 in
SPREAD to 15 cm/6 in

Grown for its edible leaves. Low, clump-forming habit. Mid-green, oblong-oval leaves to 7.5 cm/3 in long.

CONTAINER SIZE 25 cm/10 in wide by 20 cm/8 in deep.

PLANTING Sow seeds thinly, no more than 1 cm/½ in deep, in sun, at three-week intervals from early spring to early summer and again from early fall to mid fall. Thins seedlings to leave the strongest at 10 cm/4 in apart.

CARE Water regularly in warm weather, less at other times. Remove any weed seedlings from containers as soon as they appear. In cold winter areas, overwinter plants in containers kept indoors in a sunny position. As a precaution against slugs, place slug bait around and

Solanum tuberosum

Rorippa nasturtium-aquaticum

Spinacea oleracea

Valerianella locusta

beneath all containers (see p. 56).

HARVESTING Pick leaves for use when they are young and tender, removing two or three at a time. Alternatively pull plants whole and use all the fresh leaves.

CULTIVARS 'Broad-leaved English', 'Cavallo', 'Large-leaved English'.

Fruit

Most fruit-producing plants are trees or shrubs. They may be grown in containers for many years. There are two main types: trees and shrubs producing 'top-fruit', which includes cherry, plum, apple and pear, and bush and cane plants, such as raspberry. The exceptions include strawberry, which is a herbacious perennial, and grape, which produces climbing stems known as vines.

In general, fruit plants should be watered regularly in spring, summer and early fall and only sufficient to prevent the potting mix from drying out completely during winter. Liquid feed should be given when fruits are swelling. A loam-based potting mix is best, but a fertile garden soil, when available, can be used. Containers for fruit trees should be at least 30 cm/12 in wide by 25 cm/10 in deep. Bush and cane fruits and grapes can be grown in 25 cm/10 in wide pots and strawberry plants in containers only 15–20 cm/6–8 in wide. Most plants will need repotting annually. Where repotting is not practicable, remove the top 5–7.5 cm/2–3 in of the growing medium and replace with fresh. Containers should be kept in sun at all times. Where winter conditions are severe, some plants will need to be moved to a frost-free site indoors.

Top-fruit plants are purchased as either pot-grown or open-ground raised specimens, and bush, cane, grape and strawberry plants (except alpine varieties) as young, rooted specimens. Planting and initial pruning is different for each type. Winter pruning of trees and shrubs is most important and comprises removing weak or crossing shoots and dead or diseased stems. (See individual entries for specific details.) Support of stems and fruit-laden branches is an important consideration. Canes

and grape vines should be tied loosely to bamboo supports inserted in the potting mix. Trees and shrubs will need stronger supports. (See pp. 38–44 and p. 97 for details of supporting and pruning fruit plants.)

With most fruit plants, the crop is produced over a period of several weeks and the time for harvesting is best determined by regularly picking and tasting a sample or two. For this reason, specific harvest times have not been given.

Keep plants netted to prevent birds eating the ripening fruits. For details of diseases and pests, see individual entries and pp. 54–57.

Ficus carica Fig
ZONES 2–10 Easy
HEIGHT to 1 m/3 ft
SPREAD 60 cm/24 in
Grown for its rounded to pear-shaped, green, brown or purplish, fleshy edible fruit, in summer to early fall. Small bush tree with deciduous, thick, three- to five-lobed leaves and insignificant flowers.
CONTAINER SIZE 30 cm/12 in wide by 25 cm/10 in deep.
PLANTING Pot-grown specimens at any time of year, those raised in open ground in late fall to early spring, in sun.
CARE Water frequently in spring and summer, less at other times. Apply liquid feed weekly when fruits are swelling. In zones 2–5, stand containers in a sheltered, sunny site. Where frost is a normal winter hazard, keep containers in a frost-free, preferably sunny position during the dormant period. In early summer, prune strong, young stems to leave four to six leaves, providing these stems are not bearing fruits. Fruit will form in leaf axils on new shoots. In zones 8–10, plants can produce two or three crops annually.

Elsewhere, only one crop is produced from figlets that developed the previous summer. In these cases, should second-crop figlets appear just beyond ripening figs, remove these in mid fall. When fruits are ripe and ready for picking, fruit stalks soften and bend down. In addition to a light winter pruning, cut away any inward-growing branches in late spring.

Gray mold may attack young shoots, causing them to die back. If necessary, apply an appropriate fungicide (see p. 56).
CULTIVARS Most named varieties suitable for growing in containers set fruits without fertilization of flowers, e.g. 'Adriatic', 'Black Mission', 'Brown Turkey', 'Calmyrna', 'Negronne', 'Neverella'.

Fragaria × ananassa Strawberry
ZONES 2–10 Easy
HEIGHT 20 cm/8 in or more
SPREAD 18 cm/7 in or more
Grown for its juicy, red, edible fruit, usually in early summer. Low-growing, with leaves divided into three toothed leaflets and white or reddish flowers, in clusters, usually in late spring. There are three types: early summer fruiting, late summer-early fall fruiting, and alpines, which fruit from midsummer to early fall. Early summer fruiting and alpine types are best for growing in containers.
CONTAINER SIZE 20 cm/8 in wide by 15 cm/6 in deep. Plants can be grown in pots, growing bags or special strawberry pots or barrels (see p. 30).
PLANTING Sow seeds of alpine sorts thinly, 1 cm/½ in deep, in seed-flats, indoors in a sunny position, in the fall. Set small, well-rooted plants of other types singly, in containers outdoors, in sun, in late summer or early spring.

CARE Keep alpine seedlings just moist and when large enough to handle in spring, transfer them to larger containers outdoors, spacing plants 15 cm/6 in apart. They will fruit the following year. In zones 2–8, keep containers of other types indoors in a sunny position in winter. Water all plants regularly in spring, summer and early autumn, less at other times. Apply liquid feed every two weeks while fruits swell. Pick berries when fully ripe but still firm. Alpine strawberries are small and lack juice. Stocks of summer and fall fruiting types may be increased from runners produced from mid summer onward (see p. 50).

Stunting of plants may be due to a virus infection. Dig up and burn infected plants.
CULTIVARS Alpines: 'Alexandria', 'Baron Solemacher'. Early to mid-summer fruiting: 'Blakemore', 'Darrow', 'Earlidawn', 'Guardian', 'Pocochontas', 'Sequoia', 'Solana', 'Surecrop', 'Tioga'.

Malus domestica Apple
ZONES 2–10 Easy
HEIGHT to 1.5 m/5 ft
SPREAD 1 m/3 ft
Grown for its round, green-, yellow-green or red-skinned, fleshy, edible fruit, in summer to early fall. Small tree, with shiny, deep green, deciduous leaves and white to pink flowers, in clusters, in early summer.
CONTAINER SIZE 30 cm/12 in or more wide by 25 cm/10 in deep.
PLANTING Pot-grown specimens at any time of year, those raised in open ground in late fall to early spring, in sun. When buying plants for growing in containers, choose specimens with a dwarfing rootstock.
CARE Water regularly in spring and summer, less at other times. Apply liquid feed every two weeks while

fruits swell. In zones 2–8, keep containers in a frost-free, preferably sunny position in winter. Repot plants annually or every two years in early winter. If necessary, prune plants at the same time. Trees bought as pot-grown plants may flower in the first spring; of any fruitlets that form, let only two or three mature. As the plants age, more fruits can be left to mature each season. Stems laden with fruits may need support (see p. 38). With all apple trees, the tips of leading shoots on branches may be pruned back in summer to keep plants tidy. When pruning plants during the dormant period, be sure to remove the thin, somewhat pointed leaf buds, not the thick, rounded buds that will bear flowers and fruits.

There are several major fungal diseases. Brown rot produces circular, brown patches on fruit. Pick off and burn affected fruits and cut off and burn appropriate branches in early fall. As a precaution against mildew, which attacks young shoots, spray plants with an appropriate fungicide in winter and summer, and against scab, which produces large black patches on fruits, spray plants during flowering (see p. 56).

CULTIVARS Cooking apples: 'Astrachan', 'Newton Pippin', 'Rome Beauty', 'Transparent'. Dessert apples: 'Garden Delicious', 'Granny Smith', 'Gravenstein', 'Jonathan', 'McIntosh', 'Red Delicious', 'Yellow Delicious'.

Prunus avium, P. cerasus
Sweet cherry, sour cherry
ZONES 2–10 Easy
HEIGHT to 1.5 m/5 ft
SPREAD to 1 m/3 ft
Grown for their juicy, single-stone fruits, in late summer. Bushy trees with dark green, elliptic, tooth-edged, deciduous leaves and small clusters of flowers, in early summer.

CONTAINER SIZE 30 cm/12 in wide by 25 cm/10 in deep.

PLANTING Pot-grown specimens at any time of year, those grown in open ground in late fall to late winter, in sun.

CARE Water regularly during spring and summer, less at other times. Apply liquid feed weekly when fruits start to swell. Where possible, purchase trees on a semidwarfing stock. Apart from an initial pruning following planting, prune plants only when they need repotting. Sweet cherries are self-sterile and to produce fruit need to be grown in groups of two or more pollinating varieties. Sour cherries are self-fertile and can be grown individually.

Branches bearing leaves affected by silver leaf fungus, which causes a metallic sheen on foliage and staining of wood, should be cut back to 'clean' wood. Caterpillars of the Lackey moth, which eat leaves, usually in midspring, should be picked off.

CULTIVARS Sweet cherries: white flowers, round or oblong, bright or dark red fruits to 2.5 cm/1 in diameter, e.g. 'Bing', 'Garden Bing Sweet', 'North Star'. Sour cherries: white to pink flowers, round, deep red to black fruits to 2 cm/¾ in diameter, e.g. 'Morello'.

Prunus domestica Plum
ZONES 2–10 Easy
HEIGHT to 1.5 m/5 ft
SPREAD to 1 m/3 ft
Grown for its oval, 4–7.5 cm/1½–3 in long, yellow-, red- or purple-skinned edible fruit, with flesh in varying shades of yellow, and a single, flattened stone, in mid- to late summer. Small tree, with oval, dull green, deciduous leaves and small white flowers, solitary or in small clusters, in early summer.

Malus domestica

Prunus avium

'Granny Smith'

'Red Delicious'

Ficus carica

Prunus domestica

Fragaria × ananassa

CONTAINER SIZE 30 cm/12 in or more wide by 25 cm/10 in deep.

PLANTING Pot-grown specimens at any time of year, those grown in open ground in late fall to early spring, in sun. Be sure to buy plants grafted onto rootstocks suited for growing trees in containers.

CARE Water regularly in spring and summer, less at other times. Apply liquid feed every two weeks while fruits swell and color. In zones 2–8, keep containers in a frost-free, preferably sunny position in winter. To fit easily in containers, open-ground grown trees may need their

Prunus persica

Pyrus communis

Vitis vinifera

Rubus idaeus

Rubus fruticosus

roots shortened. Any major pruning required should be carried out in summer. Some plum trees are self-fertile; those that are not must be grown near a suitable pollinating plum variety. Staking of trees is advisable (see p. 38). In the first few years after being planted in a container, a plum tree should not be allowed to bear a heavy crop. Remove all excess fruitlets.

Silver leaf disease and Lackey moth caterpillars sometimes cause serious damage. For treatment see cherries, see p. 151.

CULTIVARS Self-fertile varieties: 'Beauty', 'Damson', 'Italian Prune', 'Santa Rosa', 'Stanley', 'Yellow Egg'. Self-sterile varieties: 'Burbank', 'Eldorado', 'Formosa', 'Greengage', 'Mariposa', 'Satsuma', 'Wickson'.

Prunus persica Peach, nectarine
ZONES 2–10 Easy
HEIGHT to 1.5 m/5 ft
SPREAD to 1 m/3 ft
Grown for its large, round, yellow- to yellow-flushed crimson-skinned, edible fruit, in summer to early fall. Peaches have downy skins, nectarines smooth skins. In both, the large seed is a brown, wrinkled stone, and flesh color is white to yellow, or yellowish-green. Bushy tree, with slender, finely toothed leaves, and pale pink flowers, solitary or in pairs, in early summer.
CONTAINER SIZE 30 cm/12 in wide by 25 cm/10 in deep.
PLANTING Pot-grown specimens at any time of year, those grown in open ground in late fall to late winter, in sun. If available, purchase specially grafted dwarf trees.
CARE Water regularly in spring and summer, less at other times. Apply liquid feed every two weeks while fruits swell and ripen. Nectarine trees should be stood in a sunny

position against a southfacing wall. Both peach and nectarine trees are often fan-trained against a wall or fence (see p. 43). In zones 2–8, keep containers in a frost-free, preferably sunny position in winter. All pruning – apart from any initial cutting back of open-ground grown trees following planting – should be carried out in spring or summer. Fruits are borne on wood that has ripened the previous summer; on established, productive trees pinch out surplus young shoots to encourage fruiting. Trees are self-fertile, but to ensure pollination, transfer pollen from flower to flower with a fine paint brush (see p. 44). When fruits have set, thin to leave them 18–20 cm/7–8 in apart, removing unwanted fruitlets when the size of a pea.

Dieback, a symptom of various disorders, shows in spring; prune diseased shoots back to live wood bearing green leaves. Foliage affected by leaf curl should be picked off and burned (see p. 56): spray with a suitable copper-based preventive preparation in winter. If aphids appear on foliage in spring or summer, spray with a suitable insecticide.
CULTIVARS 'Belle of Georgia' (peach; white flesh), 'Boston' (peach; yellow), 'Elberton' (peach; yellow), 'Golden Prolific' (nectarine; yellow flesh, freestone), 'Hale Haven' (peach, yellow blushed red).

Pyrus communis Pear
ZONES 2–10 Easy
HEIGHT to 1.5 m/5 ft
SPREAD to 1 m/3 ft
Grown for its large, green-, yellow- or reddish-skinned, white- or yellowish-fleshed edible fruits, in late summer to early fall. Bushy tree, with leathery, short-pointed leaves and small white flowers, in clusters, in mid- to late spring.

CONTAINER SIZE 30 cm/12 in wide by 25 cm/10 in deep.

PLANTING Pot-grown specimens at any time of year, those grown in open ground in late fall to late winter, in sun. Buy plants grafted onto rootstocks suitable for growing in pots or other types of containers.

CARE Water regularly from late spring to early fall, less at other times. Apply liquid feed every two weeks while fruits ripen. Trees dug from open ground may need their roots trimmed to fit into containers as well as some initial pruning. In zones 2–8, keep containers in a cool but frost-free sunny position in winter. Pear trees are self-sterile. Grow together varieties which will pollinate each other. It is advisable to hand-pollinate flowers (see Pach, above). Established pear trees grown in containers may need some staking.

Brown rot and scab are serious diseases: for treatment see *Malus domestica*, Apple. Regularly search for and remove Lackey moth caterpillars. Pear blister mite, which causes yellow blistering of leaves, if prevalent, should be controlled by spraying trees with a suitable pesticide in late spring.

CULTIVARS 'Anjou', 'Bartlett', 'Beurre Hardy', 'Bosc', 'Doyenne du Comice', 'Kieffer', 'Packham's Triumph', 'Winter Nellis'.

Rubus fruticosus Blackberry and hybrid brambles
ZONES 2–9   Easy
HEIGHT 2 m/6½ ft
SPREAD 30–45 cm/12–18 in per cane
Grown for its black, edible fruit or berries, in midsummer to early autumn. Shrub with deciduous, pinnate leaves and white, pinkish or rose flowers, in clusters, in early summer. Garden blackberry is a hardy, woody shrub with spreading, spiny stems.

Hybrid brambles include Loganberry (dull claret-red fruits) and Boysenberry (purplish-black fruits). Spine-free varieties of all are best for containers.

CONTAINER SIZE 25–30 cm/10–12 in wide by 25–30 cm/10–12 in deep.

PLANTING Plant young rooted canes singly in containers, in sun, in late fall to early spring.

CARE Water regularly in spring and summer, less at other times. Apply an organically-based manure mulch in spring and liquid feed every two weeks while fruits develop. In zones 2–8, keep containers in a frost-free, preferably sunny position in winter.

After planting prune back the young bramble to a height of 25 cm/10 in. In spring, provide long, bamboo supports, linking these with string and tying them together securely at their tops (see p. 39). Tie new, brittle canes to supports or train them along horizontal wires (see p. 43). Pinch off the growing point of canes when they reach the top of supports. Flowers and fruit appear on growths produced the previous summer. Over a period of a few weeks harvest all berries when fully ripe. Afterward, cut off old fruiting canes at their bases.

After harvesting berries, inspect them for small, white maggots of the raspberry beetle. If the beetle is rife in your area, spray plants with a suitable pesticide in early summer.

CULTIVARS 'Darrow', 'Oregon Thornless', 'Thornfree' (blackberries), 'Thornless Boysenberry', 'Thornless Loganberry'.

Rubus idaeus Raspberry
ZONES 2–9   Easy
HEIGHT 1.5 m/5 ft
SPREAD 30 cm/12 in per cane
Grown for its thimble-shaped, red, yellow, purple or black edible fruit, in midsummer or early fall. Erect canes with deciduous leaves divided into three or five leaflets and small white flowers, in small groups, in early summer.

CONTAINER SIZE 30 cm/12 in wide by 30 cm/12 in deep.

PLANTING As for Blackberry, above.

CARE General cultivation requirements and protection against pests and diseases are as for Blackberry, above. Summer-fruiting plants produce berries on the previous summer's shoots. They should be pruned immediately the last of the crop has been picked. Cut back all fruiting canes at their bases and remove any short weak canes to leave six to eight strong canes. Fall-fruiting plants produce berries on shoots grown the same season. With these, cut away fruiting canes in the fall and in the following spring prune back all canes made the previous summer. Shoots of more new canes will already be showing. These will bear fruit a few months later.

CULTIVARS Summer-fruiting, red berries: 'Allen', 'Brandywine', 'Bristol', 'Latham'. Fall-fruiting, red berries: 'Heritage', 'Indian Summer', 'September'; yellow berries: 'Fallgold'.

Vitis vinifera Grape
ZONES 2–10   Easy
HEIGHT 2 m/6½ ft
SPREAD 30 cm/12 in per rod
Grown for its round, pale yellow or blue-black skinned, green fleshed, usually seeded fruit, in late summer to early fall. Climbing shrub, canes with mid- to deep green, lobed, deciduous leaves, tendrils that cling to supports, and greenish flowers, in clusters, in early summer.

CONTAINER SIZE 25 cm/10 in wide by 25 cm/10 in deep.

PLANTING Singly, in sun, in late fall or early spring.

Because local climatic conditions play an important part in vine culture, consult a specialist nurseryman as to which varieties or hybrids to purchase. When planting, do not disturb the roots of pot-grown vines; the roots of open-ground raised plants should be spread out to span the width of containers.

CARE Water regularly in warm weather, less at other times. Apply liquid feed every two weeks while fruits swell. In zones 2–6, keep containers in a frost-free, preferably sunny position in winter. Pot-grown vines invariably do not need an initial pruning apart from the cutting back of any thin canes at the top of the vine. Prune back open-ground raised vines to leave only two or three buds, from which shoots will develop. In summer, pinch off the two weaker young canes and tie the remaining cane to a support, such as a 2 m/6½ ft bamboo cane. Pot-grown vines may flower and set fruits in the first summer after planting. Do not let such plants overcrop. Pinch off all surplus fruitlets, leaving only two or three bunches of fruits to swell. On established vines, in summer, pinch back all side-shoots not bearing fruit to leave only two leaves on each. Shoots bearing fruit should be pinched back to leave two leaves beyond the swelling grapes. Harvest plants when the grapes are sweet and firm. In late fall, between harvesting and leaf-fall, prune back all side-shoots to leave one or two buds only and cut off any weak growth at the top of the vine. Always keep the main cane or vine tied to the support.

If *Phylloxera* aphids and mildew are prevalent in your area, buy vines grafted on to resistant rootstocks.

CULTIVARS 'Black Monukka', 'Concord', 'Golden Muscat', 'Niagara', 'Red Flame', 'Ribier', 'Tokay'.

Choosing the right plants for your site

In the wild, plants have become adapted to all sorts of environments and there are few places where some plants, at least, will not grow. Since man-made habitats often have similar conditions to natural ones, you should have no difficulty in choosing suitable plants for practically any site. For example, the shaded basement area is similar to the floor of a forest, balconies to cliff ledges, and roofs to cliff- or hilltops. But do bear in mind the following points when making your selection. Which way does your container garden face? If due south, there will be plenty of winter light and summer warmth. East- and westfacing sites will be shaded in the afternoon and morning respectively, but should otherwise be light enough for most plants. North-facing areas or walls will be fully shaded for much of the year and can be colder in winter. However, a southfacing wall might be shaded by a taller building, or a cold, exposed northfacing wall be sheltered by a taller structure.

Wind can be a problem almost everywhere. In towns, the force is usually much reduced, but minor eddies swirling between buildings can cause damage. Where buildings are high, up-drafts are a regular feature even on fairly still, warm days. Temperature is another important factor and you must know the average winter minimum temperature for your area. The city dweller has the advantage that the warmth given off by heated buildings materially reduces the winter minima.

Summer temperatures must also be considered; some plants are unhappy if temperatures stay high for a time.

The accompanying map is divided into zones showing minimum temperatures, and should be consulted when deciding what to grow. However, although information of this sort is important, ancillary factors must be taken into consideration. The effect of absolute low temperature varies both with its duration and with wind conditions (whether conditions are still or windy). Steadily

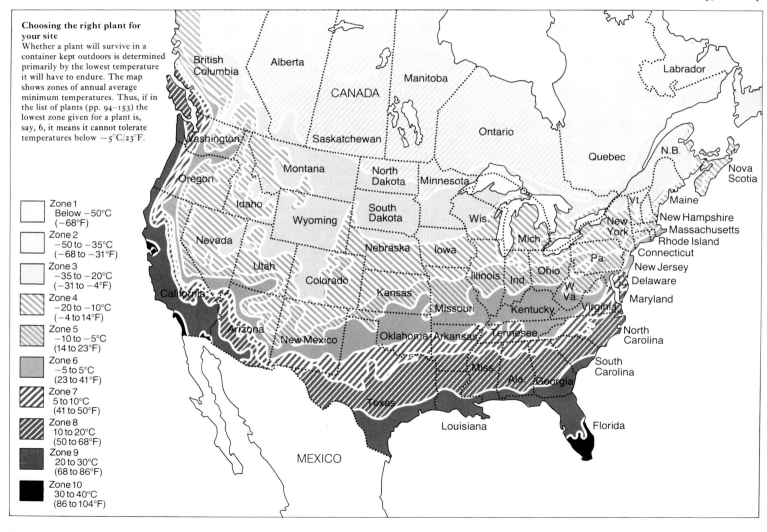

Choosing the right plant for your site
Whether a plant will survive in a container kept outdoors is determined primarily by the lowest temperature it will have to endure. The map shows zones of annual average minimum temperatures. Thus, if in the list of plants (pp. 94–153) the lowest zone given for a plant is, say, 6, it means it cannot tolerate temperatures below −5°C/23°F.

Zone 1
Below −50°C
(−68°F)

Zone 2
−50 to −35°C
(−68 to −31°F)

Zone 3
−35 to −20°C
(−31 to −4°F)

Zone 4
−20 to −10°C
(−4 to 14°F)

Zone 5
−10 to −5°C
(14 to 23°F)

Zone 6
−5 to 5°C
(23 to 41°F)

Zone 7
5 to 10°C
(41 to 50°F)

Zone 8
10 to 20°C
(50 to 68°F)

Zone 9
20 to 30°C
(68 to 86°F)

Zone 10
30 to 40°C
(86 to 104°F)

falling temperatures over a period of several weeks or months allow plants a certain amount of acclimatization, whereas sudden cold spells early in the winter do the most damage. Plants thoroughly ripened by plenty of sun and warmth in the previous fall are more resistant to cold, while growth made in cool, sunless summers is soft and prone to frost.

The following is a selected list of plants recommended for container growing. The sun and shade categories refer to the site in summer. Those plants followed by (W) are also wind and draft tolerant. 'Full shade' means that the plants need little or no sunlight. 'Partial shade' means that more or less half a day of sunlight is needed each day. 'Sun' means that sunlight is needed most of the day. For cultivation details, see plant lists pp. 94–153.

CONIFERS
Full shade:
Taxus baccata (W) and cultivars
Partial shade:
All conifers (W) listed on pp. 95–96, except *Juniperus*
Sun:
All conifers (W) listed on pp. 95–96, especially *Juniperus*
BROAD-LEAVED TREES AND SHRUBS – EVERGREEN
Full shade:
Buxus sempervirens (W)
Euonymus fortunei (W)
× *Fatshedera lizei* (W)
Fatsia japonica
Ilex aquifolium (W)
Partial shade:
Camellia japonica
Euonymus japonicus (W)
Ilex × *altaclarensis* (W)
Ligustrum japonicum
Pieris formosa, *P. japonica*
Prunus laurocerasus, *P. lusitanica*
Rhododendron (all)
Skimmia japonica
Viburnum davidii, *V. tinus* (W)
Sun:
Cordyline australis (W)

Erica (all) (W)
Hebe (all) (W)
Lavandula angustifolia (W)
Myrtus communis (W)
Pittosporum (W)
Santolina chamaecyparissus (W)
Senecio × 'Sunshine' (W)
BROAD-LEAVED TREES AND SHRUBS – DECIDUOUS
Full shade:
Kerria japonica
Partial shade:
Acer negundo, *A. palmatum*
Amelanchier canadensis (W)
Deutzia (all) (W)
Forsythia suspensa, *F.* × *intermedia*
Hydrangea macrophylla (W)
Hypericum patulum (W),
  H. × 'Hidcote'
Philadelphus (all) (W)
Prunus cerasifera, *P. incisa*,
  P. subhirtella
Spiraea (all) (W)
Viburnum opulus (W)
Sun:
Buddleia davidii (W)
Fuchsia magellanica (W)
Gleditsia triacanthos 'Sunburst'
Hibiscus syriacus
Prunus triloba
Syringa microphylla, *S. vulgaris* (W)
Viburnum × *bodnantense*, *V. plicatum tomentosum*
Weigela florida (W)
ROSES (W)
Full shade:
Climbers – *Rosa* 'Danse de Feu',
'New Dawn'
Ramblers – *R.* 'Albéric Barbier',
'Dorothy Perkins'
No other groups in full shade
Partial shade and sun:
All rose cultivars and species
CLIMBING PLANTS
Full shade:
Hedera helix (all) (W)
Lonicera periclymenum (W)
Parthenocissus quinquefolia (W),
  P. tricuspidata (W)
Partial shade:
Akebia quinata (W)
Aristolochia macrophylla
Jasminum officinale (W)
Lapageria rosea
Lonicera sempervirens

Sun:
Actinidia chinensis, *A. kolomikta*
Clematis (all) (W)
Cobaea scandens
Eccremocarpus scaber (W)
Ipomoea (all)
Lathyrus latifolius (W), *L. odoratus*
Mandevilla suaveolens
Passiflora caerulea (W)
ANNUALS AND BIENNIALS
Full shade:
Impatiens wallerana
Lobelia erinus
Myosotis sylvatica (W)
Viola × *wittrockiana* (W)
Partial shade:
Ageratum houstonianum
Bellis perennis (W)
Browallia speciosa
Catharanthus roseus
Lavatera trimestris
Nicotiana affinis
Salvia splendens (W)
Tropaeolum majus
Sun:
Amaranthus (all)
Antirrhinum majus (all)
Arctotis stoechadifolia (W)
Calendula officinalis
Callistephus chinensis
Cheiranthus cheiri
Chrysanthemum (all)
Clarkia (*Godetia*) (all) (W)
Coleus blumei
Cosmos bipinnatus
Dorotheanthus bellidifolius (W)
Gazania (all) (W)
Gomphrena globosa
Heliotropium × *hybridum*
Iberis amara (W)
Kochia scoparia tricophylla (W)
Lobularia maritima
Matthiola incana
Nemesia strumosa
Pelargonium × *hortorum*
Petunia × *hybrida*
Phlox drummondii
Reseda odorata
Salpiglossis sinuata
Tagetes (all)
Verbena × *hybrida*
PERENNIALS
Full shade:
Bergenia (all) (W)
Helleborus (all)

Heuchera × *brizoides* (W)
Pulmonaria (all)
Partial shade:
Aquilegia × *hybrida* (W)
Astilbe × *arendsii* (W)
Doronicum (all)
Geranium endressii, *G. pratense* (W)
Geum chiloense
Hosta (all)
Lamium maculatum (W)
Monarda (all)
Nepeta × *faassenii* (W)
Primula (all)
Rudbeckia fulgida
Sun:
Acanthus spinosus (W)
Agapanthus × 'Headbourne
  Hybrids' (W)
Fritillaria (all)
Gaillardia aristata, *G. pulchella*
Galtonia candicans
Hemerocallis (all) (W)
Heuchera (all)
Iris (all)
Lupinus polyphyllus
Lychnis chalcedonica
Oenothera tetragona (all)
Penstemon × *gloxinioides*
Phormium tenax
Potentilla argyrophylla (W)
Pyrethrum roseum
Salvia argentea
Stachys byzantina
BULBS, CORMS AND TUBERS
Full shade:
Endymion hispanicus (W),
  E. nonscriptus (W)
Eranthis hyemalis
Galanthus nivalis (W)
Narcissus pseudonarcissus (W)
Partial shade:
Begonia × *tuberhybrida*
Cyclamen neapolitanum (W)
Hycinthus orientalis (W)
Lilium (all)
Scilla sibirica (W)
Sun:
Chionodoxa (all) (W)
Crocosmia masonorum,
  C. × *crocosmiiflora* (W)
Crocus (all) (W)
Gladiolus (all)
Iris (all)
Muscari (all)
Tulipa (all)

SUCCULENTS (W)
Full shade:
None
Partial shade:
Haworthia attenuata, H. fasciata
Sedum (all)
Sempervivum (all)
Sun:
Agave americana
Aloe variegata
Echeveria glauca, E. harmsii
Opuntia (all)
WATER-GARDEN PLANTS
Full shade:
None
Partial shade:
Acorus calamus (W)
Ceratophyllum demersum
Elodea (all)
Iris kaempferi
Nymphaea × marliacea
Orontium aquaticum
Potamogeton crispus, P. densus
Sun:
Aponogeton distachyos
Eichhornia crassipes
Menyanthes trifoliata
Myriophyllum aquaticum
Nelumbo nucifera
Pontederia cordata (W)
ALPINE AND ROCK-GARDEN PLANTS (W)
Full shade:
Campanula muralis
Saxifraga moschata
Partial shade:
Campanula cochlearifolia,
  C. carpatica
Erinus alpinus
Geranium (all)
Primula auricula
Sun:
Aethionema × 'Warley Rose'
Alyssum saxatile
Armeria maritima
Aubrieta deltoidea
Dianthus (all)
Helianthemum nummularium
Hypericum polyphyllum
Leontopodium alpinum
Morisia hypogaea
Oenothera missouriensis
Penstemon (all)
Phlox subulata
Saxifraga × apiculata

Thymus drucei
FERNS
Full shade:
Adiantum (all)
Asplenium scolopendrium (W)
Athyrium filix-femina
Dryopteris (all)
Polystichum setiferum
Partial shade:
All ferns
Sun:
Blechnum
Osmunda regalis
HERBS (W)
Full shade:
Mentha
Partial shade:
Allium schoenoprasum
Angelica archangelica
Anthriscus cerefolium
Artemisia dracunculus
Laurus nobilis
Melissa officinalis
Petroselinum crispum
Salvia officinalis
Satureja (all)
Thymus
Sun:
Borage officinalis
Carum carvi
Coriandrum sativum
Foeniculum vulgare
Ocimum basilicum
Origanum
Rosmarinus officinalis
All are best in sun
VEGETABLES
Full shade:
None
Partial shade:
Brassica rapa
Cucumis sativus
Rorippa nasturtium-aquaticum
Sun:
All vegetables listed on pp. 143–149
FRUIT
Full shade:
None
Partial shade:
Fragaria (all)
Rubus fruticosus (blackberry)
Rubus idaeus (raspberry)
Sun:
All fruits listed on pp. 150–53

Drought-tolerant plants

Plants, like all living things, require attention if they are to prosper. A primary requirement is regular watering. In the open ground a plant's roots can wander in search of moisture, and drought conditions need to be prolonged before they cause damage. However, in containers the roots are captive, and if watering is neglected the period between permanent wilting and death can be fairly short. Much depends on the individual plant and its origins. Plants from naturally dry areas, or where summer droughts are a regular feature, are adapted to short water rations. Rocky and sandy, dry soil areas also tend to be inhabited by plants resistant to drying out.

Container gardeners who have to be away from home a lot, especially in the summer growing season, would be wise to choose plants that will not suffer too badly if watering is neglected now and then. The plants listed below can all stand shortish spells of irregular watering or drought. If watering is likely to be very occasional, then succulent plants, which have their own built-in water supply, are the only ones worth considering.

CONIFERS
Juniperus (all)
Taxus (all)
BROAD-LEAVED TREES AND SHRUBS –
EVERGREEN
Buxus sempervirens
Cordyline australis
Erica (all)
Euonymus fortunei
× Fatshedera lizei
Hebe cupressoides
Helichrysum italicum
Lavandula angustifolia
Myrtus communis
Pittosporum crassifolium
Santolina chamaecyparissus
BROAD-LEAVED TREES AND SHRUBS –
DECIDUOUS
Buddleia davidii
Hibiscus syriacus

CLIMBING PLANTS
Hedera helix (all)
Lapageria rosea
ANNUALS AND BIENNIALS
Ageratum houstonianum
Amaranthus tricolor
Antirrhinum majus
Arctotis venusta
Calendula officinalis
Catharanthus roseus
Cheiranthus cheiri
Dorotheanthus bellidiformis
Gazania (all)
Gomphrena globosa
Iberis amara, I. umbellata
Lobularia maritima
Matthiola incana
Pelargonium × hortorum
Tagetes erecta, T. patula
Tropaeolum majus
PERENNIALS
Agapanthus campanulatus,
  A. × 'Headbourne Hybrids'
Bergenia crassifolia
Gaillardia aristata
Nepeta × faassenii
BULBS, CORMS AND TUBERS
Begonia × tuberhybrida
SUCCULENTS
All succulents will stand long periods of drought
ALPINE AND ROCK-GARDEN PLANTS
Alyssum saxatile
Armeria juniperifolia, A. maritima
Aubrieta deltoidea
Campanula (all)
Dianthus (all)
Erinus alpinus
Helianthemum nummularium
Phlox subulata
Saxifraga longifolia, S. paniculata
FERNS
Asplenium scolopendrium
Blechnum penna-marina, B. spicant
HERBS
Allium schoenoprasum
Foeniculum vulgare
Laurus nobilis
Origanum (all)
Rosmarinus officinalis
Salvia officinalis
Satureja hortensis, S. montana
Thymus (all)

The time factor

Minimum-care plants

A number of shrubs, perennials, bulbs and annuals are suitable for use in a minimum-care (long-term, non-time-consuming) container garden. However, if time for maintenance is very limited, then certain points must be borne in mind. Annuals and quick and easy bulbs need replacing every year for a first-rate display. Most perennials benefit from being lifted and divided every third year, although some are best left much longer. All perennial climbers and some rock, alpine and succulent plants also are happy left undisturbed for years. Most of the stronger-growing trees and shrubs are more easily kept at a small size by repotting annually or every second year. Less vigorous sorts can be left for several years with no more than an annual topdressing and/or a regular application of liquid feed in summer. The following list contains some of the best minimum-care plants. For cultivation details, see plant lists pp. 94–153.

CONIFERS
All

BROAD-LEAVED TREES AND SHRUBS – EVERGREEN
All, but especially –
Camellia japonica
Erica carnea
Skimmia japonica

BROAD-LEAVED TREES AND SHRUBS – DECIDUOUS
Acer negundo
Buddleia davidii
Fuchsia magellanica
Spiraea japonica
Viburnum × bodnantense

ROSES
Shrub (modern)
Floribunda
Hybrid tea
Species: *R. rubrifolia*

CLIMBING PLANTS
Clematis × jackmanii
Eccremocarpus scaber

Hedera helix
Parthenocissus (all)
Passiflora caerulea

ANNUALS AND BIENNIALS
Antirrhinum majus
Calendula officinalis
Coleus blumei
Heliotropium × hybridum
Lavatera trimestris
Matthiola incana
Nicotiana affinis
Reseda odorata
Salvia (all)
Tagetes (all)
Tropaeolum majus
Viola × wittrockiana

PERENNIALS
Acanthus spinosus
Geranium (all)
Helleborus (all)
Lamium maculatum
Nepeta × faassenii
Primula × tommasinii
Salvia (all)

BULBS, CORMS AND TUBERS
Cyclamen neapolitanum
Gladiolus (all)
Lilium (all)

SUCCULENTS
All

WATER-GARDEN PLANTS
Aponogeton distachyos
Myriophyllum aquaticum
Nymphaea × marliacea

ALPINE AND ROCK-GARDEN PLANTS
Alyssum saxatile
Armeria maritima
Campanula muralis
Geranium cinereum
Hypericum polyphyllum
Phlox subulata
Saxifraga paniculata

FERNS
All, but especially –
Asplenium scolopendrium
Dryopteris
Polystichum setiferum

HERBS
Allium schoenoprasum

Foeniculum vulgare
Mentha (all)
Origanum (all)
Petroselinum crispum
Rosmarinus officinalis
Salvia officinalis
Satureja montana
Thymus (all)

FRUIT
Ficus carica
Malus domestica
Prunus avium, P. cerasus
Prunus domestica
Prunus persica
Pyrus communis
Rubus fruticosus (blackberry)
Rubus idaeus (raspberry)
Vitis vinifera

Fast-growing plants

Having decided on a container garden, you will be understandably impatient to see it mature as soon as possible. It may well be that you want to create a screen to hide a wall or to provide shelter, to produce a 'kitchen garden', or that you do not intend to live in your present house or apartment for too long, so the quicker the display grows the sooner it can be fully enjoyed. By choosing fast-growing species and/or cultivars, and attending regularly to watering and feeding, this can easily be achieved. The following plants are all quick-growing.

CONIFERS
Chamaecyparis lawsoniana
Pinus sylvestris

BROAD-LEAVED TREES AND SHRUBS – EVERGREEN
Ligustrum ovalifolium
Pittosporum tenuifolium
Prunus laurocerasus
Senecio × 'Sunshine'

BROAD-LEAVED TREES AND SHRUBS – DECIDUOUS
Acer negundo
Buddleia davidii
Deutzia scabra

Forsythia × intermedia, F. suspensa
Fuchsia magellanica
Hydrangea macrophylla
Kerria japonica
Prunus triloba
Spiraea × arguta, S. japonica
Viburnum × bodnantense, V. opulus
Weigela florida

ROSES
All

CLIMBING PLANTS
All except *Lapageria rosea* and the small ivies (*Hedera*)

ANNUALS AND BIENNIALS
All

PERENNIALS
Aquilegia × hybrida
Astilbe × arendsii
Doronicum (all)
Geranium (all)
Hemerocallis (all)
Iris germanica, I. sibirica
Lamium maculatum
Lupinus polyphyllus
Nepeta × faassenii
Primula denticulata, P. × tommasinii
Pulmonaria (all)
Pyrethrum roseum
Rudbeckia fulgida

BULBS, CORMS AND TUBERS
All

WATER-GARDEN PLANTS
All

ALPINE AND ROCK-GARDEN PLANTS
Alyssum saxatile
Armeria maritima
Aubrieta deltoidea
Campanula muralis
Helianthemum nummularium
Hypericum polyphyllum
Phlox subulata
Saxifraga moschata

HERBS
All

VEGETABLES
All

Calendar of work

Early to midwinter

Whether growing plants in containers or in a garden, there is work to be done at all times of the year. However, firstly, on the basis that least need be done in early to midwinter, our calendar starts here. Secondly, since growing periods and frosty weather begin and end in different months of the year depending on geographical location, the calendar is arranged by seasons rather than by calendar months.

This is the time of year when the less than fully hardy plants are at greatest risk from frost damage. Make sure that insulation is securely in place or is ready to use as soon as a cold spell starts. If plants are housed on a closed balcony or in a cool room during frosty weather, make sure a space is reserved for immediate use.

If the weather is mild, and protected plants are screened from rain, make sure that evergreens do not get too dry. During any mild spells that follow cold ones, check that young, small plants set out in fall have not been loosened or heaved up by successive frosts.

Late winter

Continue to protect plants as in midwinter.

BROAD-LEAVED TREES AND SHRUBS – DECIDUOUS Any that need pruning can be attended to during mild spells. Planting can continue during mild weather.

CLIMBING PLANTS *Clematis × jackmanii* and *C. viticella* should be pruned before the end of the period. Planting can continue. Sow seeds of sweet peas in warmth.

ANNUALS AND BIENNIALS If a minimum temperature of about 16°C/60°F can be maintained, an early sowing of *Antirrhinums* is worthwhile. You will need a sunny window once the seedlings appear.

PERENNIALS This is a good time of year to take root cuttings of *Acanthus*.

BULBS, CORMS AND TUBERS Lilies can still be planted if soil conditions are suitable.

WATER-GARDEN PLANTS Check that roots of *Nelumbo* overwintered in a frost-free place have not dried out.

HERBS An early sowing of parsley can be made indoors towards the end of the period. Bring indoors a batch of potted mint rhizomes to continue the supply of young leaves.

VEGETABLES Sow, in warmth, seeds of cabbage.

FRUIT Sow, in warmth, seeds of alpine strawberries.

Early spring

CONIFERS AND BROAD-LEAVED EVERGREENS Topdress all established specimens. Planting can be carried out if the soil is not wet or frozen.

BROAD-LEAVED TREES AND SHRUBS – DECIDUOUS Pruning can still be carried out, especially the hard cutting back of *Buddleia davidii*. Planting can continue. Topdressing should be carried out.

ROSES Spring pruning can now be attended to but not during spells of frosty weather. Topdress all established plants.

CLIMBING PLANTS *Clematis* can still be pruned but care must be taken of the brittle young growth that will be present in mild areas. *Jasminum officinalis* benefits from thinning and light pruning. Planting can continue. Topdressing should be carried out. Woody-stemmed species, notably *Clematis*, *Lonicera* and *Parthenocissus*, can now be propagated by layering. Sow seeds of *Cobaea* and *Eccremocarpus* in warmth.

ANNUALS AND BIENNIALS Halfhardy annuals can be sown indoors and hardy ones *in situ*. Sow thinly to avoid wastage when thinning out and the possibility of damping-off disease (see pp. 56–57).

PERENNIALS Take cuttings of *Chrysanthemum* and *Lupinus polyphyllus*. Now is a good time for propagation by division, and root cuttings can still be taken. Watch out for bird damage on *Primula × tommasinii* (Polyanthus) and other species. A few strands of black thread are still the best deterrent. Topdress all plants that have been in containers for a year or more.

BULBS, CORMS AND TUBERS Watch for bird damage on crocuses and other early flowerers. Again use a few strands of black thread as a deterrent. In mild areas *Gladiolus* (large-flowered and Nanus sorts) can now be planted. Snowdrop clumps can be split up and replanted immediately after flowering.

SUCCULENTS Apply a light dressing of granulated slow-release general fertilizer.

ALPINE AND ROCK-GARDEN PLANTS Apply a light dressing of granulated slow-release fertilizer, preferably just before rain is expected. This is a good time for planting. Sow seeds of *Alyssum*, *Aubrieta*, *Dianthus*, *Erinus* and *Oenothera*, the latter ideally *in situ*. Take root cuttings of *Morisia*.

FERNS Topdress all established plants. Plants of three years or more, which have formed good clumps or colonies, may be propagated by division.

HERBS If not already done, parsley can be sown now, preferably indoors but also outside in sheltered areas. Seeds of basil can be sown in warmth and seeds of borage and chervil outside *in situ*. Mint rhizomes can still be brought indoors for an early crop of young leaves.

VEGETABLES Plant garlic cloves, and potato tubers and pea seeds for early crops. Early in the period sow seeds of radish, repeating at two-week intervals to late spring, of corn salad, repeating at three-week intervals to early summer. In milder areas sow watercress seeds. Now is the time to sow, in warmth, seeds of the following: pepper, zucchini, cucumber, lettuce, squash and tomato.

FRUIT Pot seedlings of alpine strawberries.

Mid spring

CONIFERS AND BROAD-LEAVED EVER-GREENS Topdressing should be completed as soon as possible. Planting can continue; this is the best time in the colder zones (3–7).

BROAD-LEAVED TREES AND SHRUBS – DECIDUOUS All pruning and topdressing should be completed as soon as possible.

ROSES Complete topdressing and pruning as soon as possible. Make sure the climbing and rambling sorts are firmly secured to their supports.

CLIMBING PLANTS Make sure the fast-growing young shoots of *Clematis* are clinging firmly to their supports and tie in if necessary. Sow seeds of sweet peas *in situ* if plants have not been raised indoors. Seeds of *Cobaea* and *Eccremocarpus* can still be sown but do this as soon as possible or the subsequent plants will not have time to grow and flower properly. Harden off sweet peas raised indoors and plant out ten to fourteen days later.

ANNUALS AND BIENNIALS Halfhardy annuals can still be sown in warmth and all hardy ones *in situ*. Seedlings resulting from an early spring sowing should be thinned as soon as possible.

PERENNIALS Complete topdressing and propagation by division of broad-leaved plants as soon as possible. New Zealand flax (*Phormium*) is best divided after young growth has started and now or late spring is the best period. Plants known to need supporting should have the canes or sticks inserted now.

BULBS, CORMS AND TUBERS In cold areas *Gladiolus* (large-flowered and Nanus) can now be planted. Start tuberous begonia (*B. × tuberhybrida*) corms in pots indoors. Apply liquid feed to all bulbs with vigorous leaf growth.

SUCCULENTS If not done earlier, apply a light dressing of slow-release general fertilizer. Congested plants of *Sedum* and *Sempervivum* can be divided in this period.

WATER-GARDEN PLANTS From now onward, all water plants can be planted or placed in the water.

ALPINE AND ROCK-GARDEN PLANTS If not carried out earlier, a light dressing of slow-release fertilizer should be applied to all established plants. Planting can still be done.

FERNS Complete topdressing and propagation by division as soon as possible.

HERBS Apply a dressing of general slow-release fertilizer to all established perennial species, or begin liquid feeding. Seeds of parsley, basil, chervil, angelica, caraway, coriander, borage, fennel, marjoram and summer savory can all be sown.

VEGETABLES Plant potato tubers for the main crop. Cabbage and lettuce seeds can now be sown outside, the latter sown again at three-week intervals until early fall. Sow onion seeds and those of beetroot, kohlrabi, carrot, turnip and spinach, repeating at monthly intervals to midsummer. Continue sowing seeds of radish and corn salad.

Late spring

CONIFERS AND BROAD-LEAVED EVER-GREENS Complete all planting. Make a first application of liquid feed.

BROAD-LEAVED TREES AND SHRUBS – DECIDUOUS Apply first liquid feed to those plants that were not repotted last fall. Cut back flowered stems of *Prunus triloba* and *Forsythia*.

ROSES It is now important that the plants do not lack water. Deal promptly with any infestation of aphids on shoot tips. (See pp. 54–57.)

CLIMBING PLANTS Apply first liquid feed to established perennial climbers. Plant out *Cobaea* and *Eccremocarpus*.

ANNUALS AND BIENNIALS As soon as frost is past, plant out half-hardy species. Sow seeds of *Bellis perennis* cultivars (grown as biennials), *Campanula medium* and *Myosotis sylvestris*.

PERENNIALS Begin liquid feeding of all well-established plants.

BULBS, CORMS AND TUBERS Make a late planting of *Gladiolus* to prolong the flowering season. Once the risk of frost has passed, plant out tuberous-rooted begonias started indoors.

SUCCULENTS Species overwintered indoors can now be put outside if the risk of late frost is over.

WATER-GARDEN PLANTS Planting can continue. Apply pelleted fertilizer to established aquatics, particularly water-lilies and *Aponogeton*. Lotus and *Eichhornia crassipes* overwintered in a frost-proof place can now be put outside.

ALPINE AND ROCK-GARDEN PLANTS To maintain neat plants of *Aubrieta*, cut back once last flowers have faded.

FERNS Water regularly and apply liquid feed to well-established plants.

HERBS Thin out seedlings of annual herbs. Apply liquid feed to established perennials.

VEGETABLES Continue seed-sowing programs initiated in early or mid-spring. Plant onion sets, squash and cucumber seedlings. Sow pea seeds for main crop, and seeds of runner and French beans.

Early summer

CONIFERS AND BROAD-LEAVED EVER-GREENS Remove deadheads of lilac (*Syringa vulgaris*). If not already done, cut back flowered stems of *Prunus triloba* and *Forsythia*. Apply liquid feed.

ROSES Watch out for pests and diseases and deal with them promptly (see pp. 54–57). Give liquid feed as required.

CLIMBING PLANTS To avoid wind damage, tie in any fast-growing stems that fail to secure themselves naturally. Apply liquid feed.

ANNUALS AND BIENNIALS Sow *Bellis*, *Myosotis*, and *Campanula* for a display next spring. Apply liquid feed to those species that benefit most – see information under each plant description (pp. 113–21).

PERENNIALS Remove spent flower stems of *Doronicum* and other early-flowering species. Water regularly and apply liquid feed as required.

BULBS, CORMS AND TUBERS Dormant tuberous begonias can be planted *in situ* as soon as possible.

SUCCULENTS Growth can be rapid at this time so make sure the plants are watered regularly. They will benefit from an application of liquid feed.

WATER-GARDEN PLANTS Planting should be completed as soon as possible but can go on until midsummer.

ALPINE AND ROCK-GARDEN PLANTS Watch out that weeds do not smother small choice plants.

FERNS As for late spring.

HERBS Remove flowering stems from *Angelica* for candying and to prolong the life of the plant. Although grown as a biennial, it will live for several years if prevented from blooming. Pinch out the tops of mint stems to promote further young foliage.

VEGETABLES Continue sowing seeds of beetroot, kohlrabi, lettuce and watercress.

FRUIT Peg down new strawberry runners produced by summer-fruiting parent plants. Apply liquid feed to all plants as fruits start to swell.

Mid- to late summer

During this time, good maintenance is the primary occupation, i.e. watering, feeding, deadheading of plants such as roses and supporting where needed. Other necessary tasks are as follows:

BROAD-LEAVED TREES AND SHRUBS – EVERGREEN AND DECIDUOUS These can now be propagated by cuttings, preferably with a heel and in a propagating case with bottom heat (see pp. 46–50).

CLIMBING PLANTS Most of the woody-stemmed species, e.g. *Actinidia, Akebia, Clematis, Hedera, Jasminum,* can be propagated by cuttings.

BULBS, CORMS AND TUBERS Fall-flowering crocuses are usually obtainable by the end of the summer and should be planted as soon as possible.

SUCCULENTS Propagation by cuttings is easy during these warm months.

ALPINE AND ROCK-GARDEN PLANTS Those species of tufted or mat-forming habit, e.g. *Aethionema, Aubrieta, Dianthus, Helianthemum, Phlox,* can be propagated by cuttings in an unheated propagating case.

HERBS Rosemary, sage, winter savory and thyme can now be propagated by cuttings.

VEGETABLES Continue sowing seeds of lettuce. At the beginning of the period sow seeds of Chinese cabbage and endive. At the end of the period, plant watercress and, in sheltered areas, sow seeds of corn salad, repeating at three-week intervals to mid fall, of winter spinach, repeating at monthly intervals to mid fall, of fall/winter radishes and sow seeds of cabbage for plants to overwinter and mature in late spring.

FRUIT Pot-on young strawberry plants. Harvest, then summer prune, all top-fruit plants (fig, apple, cherry, plum, peach and pear).

Early fall

CONIFERS AND BROAD-LEAVED EVERGREENS Propagation by cuttings can continue to about mid fall. In zones 7–9 early to mid fall is a good time for planting.

BROAD-LEAVED TREES AND SHRUBS – DECIDUOUS Several shrubs can still be propagated by cuttings.

ROSES Continue the headheading and feeding of Floribunda and Hybrid tea cultivars to ensure flowers right through the fall. Carry out fall pruning of roses.

CLIMBING PLANTS Most of the woody-stemmed species can still be propagated by cuttings. It is a good idea to root a few *Passiflora* cuttings and to overwinter the young plants indoors in case the parent plant is killed during the winter. In mild areas sow sweet peas to overwinter as young plants.

ANNUALS AND BIENNIALS Continue to deadhead and feed to maintain a colorful display into mid fall. Fully hardy species (in your area) can be sown now to overwinter as young plants.

PERENNIALS Continue to deadhead where necessary and make a last application of liquid feed.

BULBS, CORMS AND TUBERS New plantings of winter- and spring-flowering sorts can be started now.

SUCCULENTS Ease up on the watering of *Agave, Aloe, Echeveria, Haworthia* and *Opuntia.*

Mid fall

With the exception of propagation, reminders for this period are much the same as for early fall. All feeding should cease early on and all unreliably hardy plants be brought indoors or placed in sheltered sites.

BROAD-LEAVED TREES AND SHRUBS – EVERGREEN AND DECIDUOUS Evergreens can still be planted, and deciduous species can be planted from now onward. Propagation from hardwood cuttings can be carried out throughout this period.

CLIMBING PLANTS From now onward is a good time to plant all border groups. Hardwood cuttings can be taken.

BULBS, CORMS AND TUBERS This is the bulb-planting period, though tulips are best left until early winter.

WATER-GARDEN PLANTS Once the leaves of *Nelumbo* get frosted, drain most of the water from the potting mix and store in a frost-free place.

VEGETABLES Harvest plants that are ready.

FRUIT Remove old fruiting stems of raspberry and blackberry.

WATER-GARDEN PLANTS Drastically but carefully thin out over-exuberant growth of aquatics.

ALPINE AND ROCK-GARDEN PLANTS Planting can be carried out.

FERNS Give a last liquid feed. mid fall.

HERBS Shrubby species can still be propagated by cuttings. As soon as the seeds of caraway and coriander start to ripen, the plants should be gathered, tied in bunches and hung in an airy room to complete ripening.

VEGETABLES Continue sowing second batch of corn salad seeds. Harvest plants that are ready.

FRUIT Harvest remaining plants.

Late fall

CONIFERS AND BROAD-LEAVED EVERGREENS In all zones under 8, lag containers against prolonged hard frost.

BROAD-LEAVED TREES AND SHRUBS – DECIDUOUS Protect from frost, as above. Pruning can be carried out during mild weather.

ROSES In all zones below 8, insulate containers against prolonged hard frost. In zones 6 and below, all Hybrid tea and Floribunda cultivars of rose are best stored in a cellar or similar frost-free, but cool, place.

CLIMBING PLANTS If *Cobaea* and *Eccremocarpus* are to be overwintered successfully, protect whole plants from frost. Insulate roots of hardy plants.

ANNUALS AND BIENNIALS In zones below 8, protect seedlings being overwintered from the worst frost.

PERENNIALS All dead flowering stems can be removed and the plants tidied up. Planting can continue during mild spells in zones 8 and 9.

BULBS, CORMS AND TUBERS Complete planting of tulip bulbs by early winter. Lilies can be planted during mild spells.

SUCCULENTS Protect halfhardy types from frost and keep them dry.

WATER-GARDEN PLANTS Species that are not hardy in your area will need protection from severe frost. The smaller, submerged and floating aquatics can be kept in an aquarium in a cool room (about $7°C/45°F$) for the winter.

ALPINE AND ROCK-GARDEN PLANTS Make sure windblown leaves from nearby trees do not blanket these small plants, especially during wet weather.

FERNS Tidy up deciduous species.

HERBS Species that are not hardy in your area will need protection from severe frost. Rooted cuttings or divisions can be kept in quite small pots in a cool room until spring.

VEGETABLES Harvest remaining plants.

FRUIT Plant or repot all species and give grape and top-fruit plants their winter pruning.

Glossary of terms

Acid (soil) Deficient in lime; most peaty and some very sandy soils come into this category. Simple soil-testing kits can be used to ascertain the degree of acidity, the result being registered on a pH scale. The latter is numbered from 1–14 with a corresponding color gradation from red (acid) to blue (alkaline); pH 7 is the neutral point, everything below being progressively more acid.

Alkaline (soil) Having a high lime content. See also **Acid**.

Annual Plant that grows from seed and completes its life cycle in less than 12 months.

Axil (axillary) Angle between a leaf stalk and its parent stem, at which point buds and new stems arise.

Bedding plant Plant used for short-term display then promptly removed, e.g. wall-flowers in spring.

Bicolored Used when two contrasting colors or shades are juxtaposed in the same flower or variegated leaf.

Biennial Plant whose life cycle spans two years. The seed germinates and grows into a leafy tuft or rosette the first year, elongates, flowers, seeds and dies in the following one.

Bipinnate Twice pinnate (q.v.), i.e., a primary leaflet divided into secondary leaflets.

Bleeding Exudation of sap after pruning or damage to stems. Excessive bleeding can be weakening to the plant.

Bolt To produce flowers and seeds prematurely, usually as the result of poor cultivation conditions.

Boss (flower) Dense, often rounded, prominent cluster of stamens in the center of a flower.

Bract Modified leaf, sometimes small and scalelike and either green or brown, or large and brightly colored. In the latter case it takes over the job of attracting pollinating insects and helps to shelter the insignificant flowers.

Bulb/bulblet Storage organ, usually underground, composed of short, thick, fleshy white leaves or leaf bases (scales) which store food reserves. A bulblet is a small bulb formed at the base of, or on the stem above, a mature bulb. See also **Corm** and **Tuber**.

Bulbil Tiny immature bulb borne on the stems of lilies and some other plants.

Calyx Outer, usually green cap, cup, or ring of tiny leaves that protects the flower while it is in the bud stage.

Channeled Usually descriptive of long narrow leaves that are partially folded upward along the midrib.

Colonizing Plants with vigorous rhizomes or suckering roots that spread sideways and soon invade adjacent plants or territory.

Conifer Class of primitive plants, mainly trees, that bear woody seed clusters known as cones, e.g. pine, fir, spruce.

Corm/cormlet Storage organ, usually underground, formed of a short, thick, fleshy, often rounded stem covered with a fibrous sheath. A cormlet is a small corm arising at the base or on top of a mature corm.

Crown (1) Top of the root system of a herbaceous perennial plant. Situated at or just below ground level, it gives rise annually to the stems, leaves and flowers. (2) Head and branches of a tree above the trunk or main stem.

Cultivar Short for cultivated variety and referring to a distinct variant of a species (q.v.) maintained in cultivation. Such a variety may be purposefully bred by man, or arise as a mutation (sport) in the garden or the wild, e.g. a plant with double flowers or variegated leaves. Such a plant does not usually come true from seed and is maintained only by vegetative propagation (cuttings, division, layering, or grafting).

Cushion-forming Mainly of rock or alpine plants formed of numerous crowded small shoots and leaves.

Cutting Severed piece of stem, leaf or root used for propagation.

Deadheading Removing spent blossom to prevent seed formation, prolong the flowering season, or to improve the appearance of a plant.

Deciduous Used mainly of trees and shrubs that are leafless for part of each year, usually from fall to spring.

Dormant period Resting stage in the annual cycle of a plant's growth, e.g. leafless trees and shrubs in winter, rootless and leafless bulbs in summer.

Double Flowers with extra petals derived from stamens and sometimes also from pistils (q.v.).

Dwarf/semidwarf Used mainly of small or condensed versions (mutants) of normal-sized plants.

Evergreen Plants that retain their leaves for at least one whole year.

Eye (flower) Center of a flower, usually when it is darker or contrastingly colored from the rest of the petals.

F_1 hybrids Plants grown from seeds created by the controlled crossing of carefully selected parents. F_1 hybrid plants have greater vigor and uniformity than ordinary seed raised cultivars. Seeds saved from F_1 hybrids do not come true to type. F_1 hybrids have to be recreated each time by crossing the same parents or parent stocks.

Fibrous Roots that are very thin, wiry and much branched.

Floret Very small flowers borne in large or dense clusters, e.g. the so-called flower of a daisy is composed of many tiny florets. These are of two kinds, the central tubular disk sort, and the strap-petaled ray florets.

Formal Neat and regular, as though designed by a geometrician.

Frond Alternative term for leaf used for ferns and palms.

Genus (plural **genera**) Category of plant classification in which are placed all species with characters in common. See also **Species**.

Grafting Method of propagation used for plants that either do not come true from seed or are difficult to root or establish from cuttings. A piece (scion) of the plant to be increased is severed and united to a vigorously rooted plant raised from seed or a cutting (the rootstock).

Growing-on Used particularly of biennials, perennials and shrubs raised from seed or cuttings that have to be grown for a period indoors or in a greenhouse before they are ready for their flowering quarters.

Habit Overall shape and structure of a plant.

Half-standard Standard (q.v.) with a short main stem less than half the total height of the whole plant.

Harden-off Gradual acclimatization to the open air of plants grown in heated greenhouses, frames or indoors.

Hardwood Fully mature stem at the end of its first growing season; a propagation term used when taking cuttings.

Hardy/halfhardy In the temperate zone, used of plants that live outside from year to year without any kind of protection. Halfhardy plants can survive only limited cold and need either a sheltered or protected site or removal to a more or less frost-free place for the winter.

Herbaceous Used of perennial plants that die back to ground level at the end of the growing season.

Hoary Lightly gray-hairy.

Hummock-forming Of plants with a very dense, low growth habit that takes the form of a partial hemisphere. Such plants are typical of exposed mountain slopes and coastal sites.

Humus In a garden sense, well-decayed manure, garden compost, peat and similar providers of organic matter. Technically, humus is the dark, colloidal substance clinging to the particles of organic matter. Humus is a soil conditioner, enabling it to hold more water and dissolved mineral salts.

Hybrid Plant resulting from crossing two distinct parents. There are three main levels of hybridity: members of two distinct genera (bigeneric hybrids), species within a genus, and forms or varieties within a species. To denote hybrid origin a multiplication sign is used. Before the Latin name means it is a bigeneric, e.g. × *Fatshedera*. Before the species name denotes that two species were crossed, e.g. *Abelia × grandiflora*. Hybrids between distinct forms or varieties of a species are not designated in this way, but the word hybrid may be used in the name, e.g. *Tropaeolum majus* 'Gleam Hybrids'.

Insulation Protection given to a plant to ward off the worst of winter cold, e.g. a wrapping of sacking, burlap, etc.

Lateral Buds, shoots or stems that arise on the side of an existing stem.

Leaching Used of soluble fertilizers and such substances as lime that are washed deep into the soil out of the reach of roots or out of the bottom of containers by rain or continual watering.

Lime/lime hater Vernacular name for various compounds of calcium, an essential element for all plant life. Certain plants, e.g. rhododendrons and heather, require minute amounts, and an excess brings about leaf yellowing and ultimately death.

Loam Ideal soil type, blending particles of clay or silt with sand and organic matter (humus).

Mat-forming Of plants with a dense, prostrate, spreading habit.

Microclimate Climate of a localized area, e.g. of a garden or part of a garden, or even the immediate vicinity of a plant.

Mulching Application of a layer of material that feeds the plant, conditions the soil, or conserves moisture, or does all three things. In the latter category is decayed manure, garden compost, or a fresh potting mix.

Node Point of a stem at which a leaf arises. See also **Axil**.

Offset In the strict sense, plantlets borne at the tip of short, usually horizontal stems. Also used for the small bulbs that form at the base of larger ones. Offsets can be removed for propagation purposes.

Peat Dead plant-remains in a state of arrested decay that form, due to a lack of oxygen, in the waterlogged condition of bogs and fens. Peat is a valuable supplier of humus to soil and, with mineral additives, makes an excellent potting mix for container plants.

Pendent Hanging down; mainly used of stems or branches and flowers.

Perennial Non-woody plant that lives for several years, often called a border or herbaceous (q.v.) perennial.

Petals Usually colored, leaflike bodies that surround and protect the vital organs of a flower. Their color also acts as an attractant to pollinating insects. See also **Stamen** and **Stigma**.

Pinching out See **Stopping**.

Pinnate Compound or dissected leaves or bracts that are cut into several opposite pairs of smaller leaflets with or without a solitary terminal leaflet.

Pistil Female organ of a flower. It consists of an ovary containing ovules (immature seeds) topped by a stalk or style upon which the stigma (q.v.) sits.

Pollarding Regular cutting back of trees or vigorous shrubs to a given point above ground level. The result is a standard (q.v.) with a head of limited size composed of young stems. Pollarding is carried out on plants with colorful winter stems and is usually done annually or every two to three years.

Pollen Dustlike male sex cells formed within the heads (anthers) of the stamens. Pollination is the landing or placing of pollen on the stigma (q.v.) where it grows down into the ovary and fertilizes the ovules to form seeds.

Pollination See **Pollen**.

Potting Placing of a plant in a flower pot or similar rooting container with a suitable potting mix. Potting on is the moving of an established pot-grown plant into a larger container. Repotting involves taking a well-rooted or pot-bound plant out of its container, removing some of the mix and outer roots, and returning it to the same (cleaned) pot or another of the same size with some fresh potting mix.

Potting mix or **soil mix** Rooting medium containing minerals essential for growth, formulated for growing plants in pots and other containers. Loam-based mixes have always been popular, but nowadays moss peat with or without sand or grit, plus fertilizer, is more common.

Prostrate Having stems that lie flat on the soil.

Quilled Used of petals that are rolled into tubes or slender cones, or partially so.

Raceme Type of flower cluster (inflorescence) composed of a usually erect stem bearing stalked flowers at intervals. See also **Spike**.

Rhizome Below or partially below ground, usually horizontal stem that bears erect aerial shoots.

Robust Of plants with a strong, sturdy growth habit.

Rootstock See **Grafting**.

Rosette Leaves that arise in a tight circular or spiral formation from the crown of a plant or a stem tip.

Runner Long, more or less prostrate slender stem, each leaf node rooting quickly and forming a new plant, e.g. strawberry.

Scales White, fleshy leaflike bodies that make up a lily bulb. Also the minute leaves of some conifers.

Self-fertile Of plants that do not need to be cross-pollinated to produce fruits and seeds.

Self-sterile Of fruit trees producing flowers with sterile stamens. They must be cross-pollinated to form fruit, e.g. pears and sweet cherries.

Semihardwood Partially mature stem a bit more than halfway through its first growing season, distinguished by its firm woody base and soft, sometimes still growing tip; a propagation term used when taking cuttings.

Shrub Plant formed of woody persistent stems, usually with most of the main branches arising near to or below ground level, and not much above 4 m/13 ft tall.

Single Opposite of double (q.v.); used in plant groups such as roses where most cultivars have double flowers. It then refers to the wild species or one of similar form having a normal complement of petals, stamens and pistils.

Softwood Soft, sappy, actively growing stem near the start of its first season's growth; a propagation term used when taking cuttings.

Species Plant type within a genus with distinct characteristics which breed true from seeds or spores.

Spur (1) Hollow projection of a sepal or petal containing glands secreting nectar (nectaries), e.g. violet, nasturtium, columbine. (2) Short, slow-growing stem or branchlet often concerned with flower production, e.g. apple, pear.

Spurring-back Cutting lateral stems back to a stub to form a spur (q.v.).

Standard Tree or shrub with an erect unbranched stem topped by a head of branches, the main stem usually occupying at least half of the total height.

Stamen Male organ of a flower, composed of a stalk or filament and two, usually fused heads (anther sacs) which contain the pollen.

Stem 'Scaffolding' of a plant, upon which are carried the leaves, flowers and fruits. In trees and shrubs the stems become woody and increase in girth annually, then also being known as trunks and branches.

Stigma Pollen-catching part of the pistil (q.v.) of a flower. Stigmas adapted to insect pollination are often sticky, those pollinated by wind-borne pollen, long and feathery.

Stopping/pinching out Removal of the tip of a stem to encourage the growth of lateral stems and a bushy habit.

Sucker Stem arising from below ground level, mainly from the base of a tree or shrub, or from its roots nearby, e.g. roses. See also **Offset**.

Temperate Climate zone roughly halfway between the arctic or antarctic and tropical latitudes.

Tender Used in the temperate zone of tropical plants that can be grown outside during the summer only, or must be kept indoors all the time.

Topdressing Like mulching (q.v.), but the surface layer of soil or mix around the plant is first removed, then replaced with fresh material.

Topiary Ancient practice or art of clipping plants into shapes, either geometrical or birds, animals and other objects. Small-leaved, freely branching plants should be chosen, e.g. box, yew, privet.

Trailer Plant with lax, usually slender stems that run along the ground or hang down.

Truss Vernacular name for a flower cluster, botanically, an inflorescence.

Tuber Enlarged root or stem, which functions as a storage organ and is usually, but not invariably, underground. Potato provides the best known example of a stem tuber, bearing buds (eyes) on its surface.

Variegated Mainly used of leaves that are variously patterned, spotted or blotched with white, cream or yellow, sometimes also with pink, red or purple. This is due to mutation, virus infection or a mineral food deficiency and in each case results from localized non-formation of the green coloring matter chlorophyll that is concerned with photosynthesis.

Variety Distinct form of a species that occurs as a true breeding entity in the wild. See also **Cultivar**.

Wintergreen Of a plant that loses its leaves during the year other than in winter.

General Index

Bold type denotes illustrations

Acknowledgments

The publishers would like to thank the following individuals and horticultural organizations for their help in putting this book together.

The Royal Horticultural Society for their advice and the facilities of their library; the Royal National Rose Society for help and information on roses; Fleuroselect of Holland, and Julia Voskuil, for advice on plants for European conditions, and Pamela J. Harper for advising on plants in the United States; the John Innes Horticultural Research Institute of Great Britain for information on mixes.

The following nurseries in London, England, were extremely helpful in supplying tools and equipment for photography or reference: Jack Beanstalk of Chelsea, Clifton Nurseries of Maida Vale and Barralet's of Ealing, who kindly provided materials on an extended loan basis. Special thanks are due to Mr. E. G. Peisner of Hyron's Nursery, St. Alban's, and again to Barralet's for providing facilities for photography and to Lucy Murray for demonstrating techniques for the camera so ably. Geest Horticultural Ltd., Spalding, kindly arranged and supplied a beautiful selection of spring-flowering bulbs for photography. Marion Furner very kindly made her uncle's horticultural transparencies available to us, and Bill Heritage, of Wild Woods Garden Center, gave advice on, and pictures of, water gardens. Neil Holmes deserves thanks and admiration for his extreme patience while photographing in dire weather conditions. Jonathan Hearn helped with additional reference photography. Mr. A. J. Walker, carpenter, expertly constructed the window box.

Thanks are also extended to Jenny MacMichael for acting as horticultural consultant for the American edition and to Joanna Chisholm for editing it; to Susan Berry for her editorial work; to Anne Hardy who compiled the index.

The publishers would also like to give special thanks to artists Paul Wrigley and Jane Cradock-Watson for establishing and maintaining the book's illustrative styles.

Photographs
(l) left, (r) right, (t) top, (b) bottom, (c) centre
Ardea: 82(tl)
B. & B. Photographs/Stefan Buczacki: 57 (1, 2, 6, 11, 13, 15, 19, 22, 23, 24, 26, 29, 30, 31, 32, 33, 34, 35)
Steve Bicknell: 87(t), 90
Pat Brindley: 62(tl), 88(tl)
John Brookes: 70(tr)
Ron & Christine Foord: 57 (3, 4, 5, 7, 8, 9, 10, 12, 14, 16, 17, 18, 21, 25, 27, 28)
Brian Furner: 77(tl), 77(bl)
Bob Gibbons: 88(b)
Tim Gravestock: 76(tr)
Halcyon/H. Hunt: 64(br)
Robert Harding Picture Library: 76(br)
Neil Holmes: 7, 61(t), 70(bl), 83(br)
Alan Hutchison Library: 83(tl)
Leslie Johns: 62(tr)
Frank Lane Agency/Neil Elkins: 66
Bildarchiv Mauritius: 78, 82(br)
Dr. Giuseppe Mazza: 59(bl)

Naturfoto/Inge Esper-Hansen: 63(t), 64(bl), 65, 71, 82(tr), 82(bl), 92(t)
Michael Nicolson: 75(b)
Sally Smallwood: 81(tc), 83(tr)
Duncan Smith: 57 (20)
Harry Smith Collection: 59(tl, tr, br), 63(bl, cr), 64(tr), 76(tl, bl), 77(r), 83(bl), 88(tr), 92(t), 93
Pamla Toler: 61(b), 62(b), 70(tl), 81(br), 89(tr), 89(b)
Michael Warren: 57 (36)
Elizabeth Whiting Associates: 70(br), 81(tr, bl), 87(b), 91

Illustrations
Jane Cradock-Watson: 10–15, 17, 18, 20–37
Sue Hillier: 67–9, 72–4, 79, 80, 85, 86, 122–32
Carole Johnson: 106–12, 133, 135–42
Jim Robins: 38–50
David Worth: 154
Paul Wrigley: 95–105, 113, 115, 117–21, 143, 145–9, 151, 152

PENGUIN HANDBOOKS

The Contained Garden

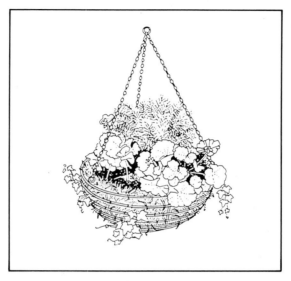

Kenneth A. Beckett trained at Wisley, the Royal Horticultural Society's garden, and has since worked at various botanic gardens, in England and the United States.

David Carr is a freelance gardening consultant. He studied horticulture and has worked in the commercial field and written extensively for the gardening press.

David Stevens is a landscape architect in private practice. He has won five awards for gardens he has designed at the Chelsea Flower Show in London, including a Gold Medal in 1982.